A History of

Criminal Justice

in England and Wales

A **History of Criminal Justice** in England and Wales
John Hostettler

Published 2009 by
Waterside Press
Sherfield Gables
Sherfield on Loddon
Hook
Hampshire
United Kingdon RG27 0JG

Telephone +44(0)1256 882250 Low cost UK landline calls 0845 2300 733
E-mail enquiries@watersidepress.co.uk
Online catalogue www.WatersidePress.co.uk

ISBN 9781904380 511 (Paperback)

Cataloguing-In-Publication Data A catalogue record for this book can be obtained from the British Library.

Cover design © 2009 Waterside Press.

North American distributor International Specialised Book Services (ISBS), 920 NE 58th Ave, Suite 300, Portland, Oregon, 97213-3786, USA
Tel: 1 800 944 6190 Fax 1 503 280 8832 orders@isbs.com www.isbs.com

e-book *A History of Criminal Justice in England and Wales* is available electronically at leading i-libraries and e-suppliers (e-book ISBN 9781906534790)

Printed in Great Britain by the MPG Books Group, Bodmin and King's Lynn

A History of

Criminal Justice

in England and Wales

John Hostettler

☰ WATERSIDE PRESS

Dedication and acknowledgements

I dedicate this book to Dr Richard Vogler, Senior Lecturer in Law at Sussex University and a good friend, who has been an inspiration to me during the last decade. Richard suggested this title, which has not been attempted before, read the manuscript and made a number of valuable suggestions for which I am deeply in his debt. Needless, to say, any errors that exist are my responsibility alone.

Once again I wish to thank my publisher, Bryan Gibson, for his support and encouragement in the production of the book. His dedication to initiating and communicating ideas and knowledge about criminal justice is as unequalled as his friendly interest and knowledge of the law and legal history are outstanding.

I should also like to thank the staff at the London Library for their courtesy and help when needed.

John Hostettler
January 2009

A **History of Criminal Justice** in England and Wales

CONTENTS

Preface

I cannot say that I know much about the law, having been far more interested in justice.

William Temple, Archbishop of Canterbury, at the Inns of Court.[1]

Criminal justice is the complex system, with many aims and agencies, which is used in the main by government to maintain social control, curtail crime, enforce laws and administer justice. It also allows the State to interfere in people's lives and even coerce them. In doing so it is crucial that the rights of both victims and accused persons are balanced and related to each other and the community. Further, the government should adhere strictly to the Rule of Law and protect individual human rights. The importance of the principle of the Rule of Law cannot be overemphasised. It was defined by Dicey as stating that:

> No man is punishable or can be lawfully made to suffer in body or goods except for a distinct breach of law established in the ordinary legal manner before the ordinary courts of the land. In this sense the Rule of Law is contrasted with every system of government based on the exercise by persons in authority of wide, arbitrary, or discretionary powers of constraint ... No man is above the law, but ... whatever be his rank or condition, is subject to the ordinary law of the realm and amenable to the jurisdiction of the ordinary tribunals ... the general principles of the constitution (as for example the right to personal liberty, or the right of public meeting) are with us the result of judicial decisions determining the rights of private persons in particular cases brought before the courts.[2]

To the last point should now be added the human rights protected by legislation.

It will be considered how far government is keeping to this principle which runs through much of English criminal justice. The modern system has evolved since ancient times with different forms of policing, courts, procedures and punishments along the way. It is not surprising that at different stages of history these have reflected changes in the country's culture, customs, laws, political theories and power, and economic circumstances.

In the past some eminent legal historians have underestimated the significance of the criminal law in English society and considered it to have no intellectual pedigree. For instance, in 1969, Professor S F C Milsom claimed that:

> [t]he miserable history of crime in England can be shortly told. Nothing worth-while was created ... Centuries of civilization have passed the subject by .... The criminal law had by the eighteenth century reached an incoherence which seemed to defy even the modest order of the alphabet.[3]

---

1. Sir Alfred Denning. (1955) *The Road to Justice.* London, Stevens & Sons Limited. p.1.
2. A V Dicey. (9th edn. 1950) *Introduction to the Study of the Law of the Constitution.* London, Macmillan & Co. Limited, pp. 188-95.
3. S F C Milsom. (1969) *Historical Foundations of the Common Law.* London, Butterworths. pp. 353, 365.

Modern research has shown that such a view is no longer tenable and it is to be hoped that what follows will reveal just how much of what we treasure in our Criminal Justice System owes to the past and to the struggles of the peoples of this country to effect successive improvements. In particular, this applies to the jury system and the lay magistracy in which large numbers of men (and latterly, women) have participated directly in the administration of justice.

The history that unfolds in these pages runs from the blood-feud and vengeance of the dwellers in Anglo-Saxon England to the vast cumbersome structure of the Criminal Justice Act of 2003 and onwards to the year 2008. Like a river, although its flow is choppy and uneven at times, it is continuous. We can see the shadow of the gallows, even for minor offences, stretching over centuries and, until modern times, being at the very heart of the Criminal Justice System. The conception of what is involved in offences such as homicide, theft and rape has changed over the centuries but they are always with us, although the punishments for them differ at various times. Redress for the victims of crime was there at the beginning but faded away and was lost, only to re-emerge in recent years with the concept of restorative justice.

Like crime, law and punishment have existed in all human history. Law is an integral part of the fabric of society, and indeed of life itself, and we shall see first how the criminal law underlay the existence of Anglo-Saxon men and women in the harsh days when England was coming into being and striving to gain political cohesion. Community courts played an important role before the kings and churchmen became able to exercise near-total control. Trial was by ordeal but it was tempered in favour of the accused. In time, it was replaced by the presenting jury that developed over the centuries into the jury as we know it today.

Apart from the death penalty, fashions in punishment changed along with shifting morals and lifestyles. After the Norman Conquest the power of monarchs and the Church grew immensely until, in the name of the Common Law, Sir Edward Coke challenged the 'divine right' to rule of the early Stuarts. It was left, however, to the English Civil War and the Glorious Revolution finally to reduce that power which from then onwards had to be shared with the aristocracy and landed gentry. Gradually democratic processes and civil liberties grew and generated substantial changes in the Criminal Justice System which will be examined in the pages which follow. This involves consideration of prisons, policing, how adversary trial arose and helped establish a modern culture of human rights, the position of juveniles, rules of criminal evidence and the vast volume of changes in the twentieth and twenty-first centuries. Indeed, the last ten years have seen an enormous outpouring of legislation to deal with these issues and the new development of restorative justice involving, among other things, the interests of the victims of crime.

In a work of this kind it is not possible to deal with every single substantive crime or, indeed, exhaustively with those I have chosen – treason, homicide, theft and rape. I have written on these topics not only as they are today but also in their historical context as elements in an ever-changing Criminal Justice System. After all, the past has bequeathed to us a legacy that still affects criminal justice in the present.

The book is up-to-date as at the time of writing and includes the fundamental changes that have occurred in criminal justice following the attack on the Twin Towers in New York in September 2001 and the bombings in London in July 2005. Moreover, there have been an astonishing 50 new crime and punishment statutes and 3,000 new criminal offences created in the last decade that cover a very considerable range of actions and behaviour. For me this has been an exciting study and I hope the result will appeal to all those involved in the many aspects of the Criminal Justice System such as lawyers, police and prison officers, probation officers and many others as well as those who are outside the system but whose lives are affected by it.

In just a few places this book contains material I had written earlier. Where this occurs I have been able to expand it and bring it up to date. To have failed to use it would have left blanks in the story of criminal justice in England and Wales that would have resulted in a distorted picture. In addition, the books in which such material appeared are now out of print.

John Hostettler
January 2009

About the author

John Hostettler is a solicitor, legal biographer and historian whose subjects have included Sir James Fitzjames Stephen, Sir Edward Coke, Sir Matthew Hale, Thomas Erskine, Lord Halsbury, a History of the Criminal Jury and the Politics of Punishment. He has written widely for the legal press, including as a regular contributor to the leading UK weekly journal Justice of the Peace. He practised in London as well as undertaking civil liberties cases in Nigeria, Germany and Aden. A former magistrate, he played a leading role in securing the abolition of flogging in British colonial prisons and was a member of a Home Office Committee to consider changes to electoral law in the UK. He has also served as chair of Social Security Appeal Tribunals. He holds the degrees of BA, MA, LLB (Hons), LLM and three PhDs – one from the University of London and two from the University of Sussex. He is a member of the Royal Society of Literature.

Other books by John Hostettler

The Politics of Criminal Law: Reform in the Nineteenth Century (1992), Barry Rose
Thomas Wakely: An Improbable Radical (1993), Barry Rose
The Politics of Punishment (1994), Barry Rose
Politics and Law in the Life of Sir James Fitzjames Stephen (1995), Barry Rose
Thomas Erskine and Trial by Jury (1996), Barry Rose
Sir Edward Carson: A Dream Too Far (1997), Barry Rose
Sir Edward Coke: A Force for Freedom (1997), Barry Rose
At the Mercy of the State: A Study in Judicial Tyranny (1998), Barry Rose
Lord Halsbury (1998), Barry Rose
The Red Gown: The Life and Works of Sir Matthew Hale (2002), Barry Rose
Law and Terror in Stalin's Russia (2003), Barry Rose
The Criminal Jury Old and New: Jury Power from Early Times to the Present Day (2004), Waterside Press
Fighting For Justice: The Origins and History of Adversary Trial (2006), Waterside Press

With **Brian P Block**

Hanging in the Balance: A History of the Abolition of Capital Punishment in Britain (1997), Waterside Press
Voting in Britain: A History of the Parliamentary Franchise (2001), Barry Rose
Famous Cases: Nine Trials that Changed the Law (2002), Waterside Press

CHAPTER 1

Origins of Criminal Justice in Anglo-Saxon England

INTRODUCTION

The purpose of this and the next chapter is to outline the genesis of English criminal justice, showing how and why it arose. The development from bloody self-help and private vengeance in violent times to royal dooms imposing compensation by the Crown is examined alongside the growth and power of the Christian Church. Social status was all-important as were oaths and the ordeal and the role of the hundred and shire communal courts. In *Chapter 2*, in particular, the laws of the Anglo-Saxon kings and their ecclesiastical advisers that have come down to us are considered extensively as the earliest examples of criminal law and justice in England.

THE SOCIAL AND ADMINISTRATIVE SYSTEM

Far back in time, under the iron fist of the legions of Rome, the criminal law in Britain was cruel in its punishments. Torture, including crucifixion, was inflicted across the land, slavery was widespread and gladiatorial combat frequent. Nonetheless, except for the most serious crimes, justice could be tempered with mercy. A man might not be sentenced to death unless he confessed, or the witnesses all agreed on his crime. One witness alone was not sufficient. An accusation had to be made in writing and the trial take place within a month. On the other hand, much would depend on the governor sent from Rome and how far he considered it necessary to enforce order by draconian measures.[1]

All this soon disappeared when the Romans finally left Britain shortly after 400 A.D. By the year 603 invading tribes had replaced the remnants of Roman civilisation and there was no continuous tradition of law inherited from it. The new invaders from Europe knew nothing of Roman law and brought with them their own embryonic laws and courts. The Jutes now ruled Kent, the Saxons controlled Wessex and the Angles governed Mercia and Northumbria to the north. Originally, there were seven Anglo-Saxon kingdoms but by the end of the sixth century these had merged into four confederations which exhibited substantial differences in set-up and were significant powers with their own Teutonic religious customs and ideas

---

1. Peter Salway. (1985) *Roman Britain.* Oxford, The Clarendon Press.

of law. Such as they were, their legal systems already existed and in England, 'the Christian influence to which the law was exposed from the end of the sixth century caused some alteration, especially in relation to family law, but it left the structure unchanged.'[2] And, although they came and conquered as soldiers they, and their descendants, gradually began to settle into their new homelands as arable farmers.

Unlike the earlier Roman forms of society the new communities could boast little literacy, few officials and no central administration. But, with exploitation of the agricultural fertility of the land, gradations of wealth and great landowners began to emerge and, led by them, each village community commenced to enforce, so far as it was able, its own peace and customs. No lawyers or developed law as we know them today existed but a system of self-protection evolved based upon the vengeance of kin and neighbours against wrongdoers, usually accused of homicide or forcible breach of land tenures and boundaries.

When Anglo-Saxon law first began to emerge in England it was primitive and harsh, reflecting contemporary life. The community was based on agriculture with the majority of people living in villages and on farms. In addition to flooding, famine and other natural disasters many lived in fear of being robbed or slain. Murder and cattle-rustling were the most common outrages and they were dealt with in turn by private vengeance and constant blood-feuds.[3] Initially, self-help was the primary law.

Before long, however, the whole country had become divided into shires which were political units each with its separate assembly which exercised judicial and administrative powers. The shires were subdivided into hundreds which also had their own assemblies with judicial and administrative powers but they dealt with less important crimes and administration than the shires. The 'hundred' was the equivalent of a hundred hides which was the amount of land considered to support a family. Clearly this would vary from region to region according to the richness of the soil but roughly a dozen or so hundreds made up the average shire.[4]

In every part of England except Kent the primitive unit of land division was a holding which supported a *ceorl* (originally a husband, but by extension head of a peasant household and a freeman) and his household. Such a holding was called a 'hide' and formed the basis of social organization.[5] By contrast, in Kent land division was based upon a unit of cultivation known as 'ploughland'. This meant the amount of land which could be kept in cultivation by a single plough-team of eight oxen and it was far larger than a hide. In both cases, however, the arable holding was the centre of a complex of properties and rights.[6]

---

2. Dorothy Whitelock. (1974) *The Beginnings of English Society*. London, The Pelican History of England. vol. ii. p. 134.
3. Dorothy Whitelock. *The Beginnings of English Society. Op. cit.* p. 47.
4. A. Harding. (1973) *The Law Courts of Medieval England*. London, George Allen & Unwin Ltd., p. 17.
5. Sir F. Stenton. (1971) *Anglo-Saxon England*. Oxford, The Clarendon Press. p.279.
6. Ibid. pp. 281-2.

GENESIS OF ANGLO-SAXON LAW

At first, few could write or keep records and there were no courts and no public officers to pursue or inquire into crime. Injuries inflicted were punished by private vendetta on the part of those who suffered from them or their relatives, and the vengeance was savage. Gradually, however, the rulers of the four kingdoms, whose powers were increasing and who began to exercise direct personal control over their small populations, started to intervene against lawlessness and to compose laws, known as dooms. These were written in the English language derived from Wessex, instead of Latin as used on the continent.

Another motive for the enactment of dooms was the introduction of a new feature in the imposition of fines payable to the king. Our knowledge of the dooms remains fragmentary. We do know, however, that they were created from existing customs, with additions as society grew more complex, and, after the reception of Christianity, were often directed not only against crime but also at securing obedience to the Church and augmenting its wealth. In return, the Church underpinned the rule of the king and invested him with a religious aura. Nevertheless, the early kings had virtually no professional servants in the localities and had to rely upon the great landowners to whom they granted wide powers of peace- keeping.[7] 'There cannot have been much need of courts ... to stand between the wrong-doing and retribution: the peace keeper compelled the payment of the set compensation or cut down the outlaw and the thief caught in the act.'[8]

CHRISTIANITY

Christianity expanded rapidly in England after 597,[9] the year in which Augustine arrived in Kent to fulfil the mission of conversion entrusted to him by Pope Gregory the Great. Æthelbert, (c. 560-616) the king of Kent and southern England at that time, was already familiar with religious practices since his wife, Bertha, a Frankish princess and daughter of Charibert of Paris, was a Christian and had been permitted to hold services in a church at Canterbury with a bishop she brought over to England as her chaplain.[10] Perhaps not surprisingly, therefore, Æthelbert's conversion was completed within a year and Augustine was rewarded with the Canterbury

---

7. A. Harding. *The Law Courts of Medieval England. Op. cit.* p.15.
8. *Ibid.*
9. The Christian faith was not unknown earlier since in 313 AD a certain Restitus attended the council of Arles in his capacity as bishop of London. Peter Ackroyd. (2000) *London: The Biography.* London, Vintage. p. 29.
10. C. W. Previté-Orton. (1971) *The Shorter Cambridge Medieval History.* Cambridge, Cambridge University Press. vol. i, p. 174.

church where he was consecrated a bishop and later appointed archbishop.[11]

At Canterbury, Augustine was able to rely upon royal support and protection which was not available in London, then part of Wessex and still heathen. Here, his 40 monks were given land and a dwelling place just outside the town from whence they could travel to preach their religion and disseminate the code of ecclesiastical law. Gregory had thoughtfully sent over the code with instructions to Augustine to keep his teachings flexible and to respect local customs. Later, Paulinus, who was consecrated a bishop at Canterbury in 625, succeeded in converting Edwin the powerful king of Northumbria who had married Ethelburga, a daughter of Æthelbert, who fortunately for the Church was another Christian wife. Wessex was finally brought into the fold under King Cynegils in 635, although there was to be some backsliding among succeeding kings and pagan rites would continue to persist throughout the country for some time to come.

FROM VENGEANCE TO COMPENSATION

Not a great deal is known about Anglo-Saxon law and even less about how its courts operated in practice. However, a number of early dooms have come down to us and the earliest Anglo-Saxon laws that have been preserved are a series of three from Kent. First, are those of King Æthelbert from about the year 603, followed by those of Hlothháere who reigned from 673 to 685 and Eadric who defeated him in battle and succeeded him for a year-and-a-half. The third was the code of Wihtráed, the brother of Eadric, which was issued in 695 in 695. In the period after Æthelbert had embraced Christianity in Kent he promulgated his laws which are the earliest document we have written in English. No other Germanic language possesses original records of equal antiquity, apart from short inscriptions.[12]

Early Anglo-Saxon law was more concerned to compensate the victims of crimes than to punish offenders. Another motive for the enactment of Æthelbert's laws was the need to provide penalties for offences against God and the Church.[13] After consultation with the clergy and nobility, the king advanced a code of amendments to tribal customs and as Christianity spread he was widely imitated. This meant there was now a royal law-giving power in the land.[14] By 689 Ine (688-726), a strong ruler who reigned as king of Wessex for 37 years, was also issuing an elaborate digest of west Saxon laws which comprised both ancient customs and new rules of conduct

---

11. P. H. Blair. (1965) *Roman Britain and Early England. 55 B.C.-A.D. 871.* London, Thomas Nelson & Sons Limited. p. 225.
12. F. L. Attenborough. (editor and translator) (1922) *The Laws of the Earliest English Kings.* Cambridge, Cambridge University Press. p. 3.
13. Sir F. Stenton. *Anglo-Saxon England. Op cit.* p.60.
14. C. W. Previté-Orton, *The Shorter Cambridge Medieval History. Op. cit.* p. 179.

and punishments. He too consulted his bishops, ealdormen and chief councillors[15] and his code covers 'a wide range of human relationships.'[16] It is a serious attempt to blend ancient custom and new enactment in an elaborate body of law.[17] Private vengeance by blood-feud was still countenanced, indeed it could hardly be stopped. But it was beginning to be seen as an interference with public peace and, in what was a break with the past, Ine endeavoured to curtail it.

Feuding parties were told to cease seeking blood and instead agree to a sum to be paid in compensation for an injury. To cover cases where the parties could not agree on an amount in restitution the king set a tariff fixed according to the social status of the injured party. This included *wergild*—a man's value, although it varied in amount from one kingdom to another.[18] Nothing to do with the offender was taken into account. Intent was not inquired into, so an accidental injury was not excused, nor could any other extenuating circumstances be pleaded. They were just not conceived to be relevant. The punishment was simply a penalty for an evil done and a deterrent from lawbreaking in the future. It took the form first of a civil indemnity, a *bot*—usually the *wergild*—then, in many cases, a further indemnity, a *wite*—to the king. This payment to the king was another innovation and, with later additions, was to feed the wealth, and the growth, of royal power for centuries to come. It represented the beginning of the encroachment of political considerations into the arena of criminal justice with the crown exerting more and more control.

SOCIAL STATUS

As *wergild* was to persist for several centuries it may be useful to consider some features of social status in Anglo-Saxon times. A noble by birth was called an *eorl*. Such a nobleman, and particularly his lord, the king, would have powerful household officers known as *thegns* who formed the landed gentry. Below them in rank were the *ceorls*, free peasant landholders who cultivated their holdings in person. In fact, a man was free precisely because of his ownership of land and in Æthelbert's time he was not subject to any lord but the king. Local lords with power only began to appear on the scene when the kings started rewarding members of their households with grants of estates in land and as a consequence large numbers of *ceorls* were reduced by hardship to villeinage. This was part of the process by which a great many free men, acknowledging no lord below the king,[19] gradually lost economic and personal independence.[20] Things were made worse for *ceorls* by crippling taxes

15. P. H. Blair. *Roman Britain and Early England. 55 B.C.—A.D. 871. Op. cit.* p. 244.
16. F. Stenton. *Anglo-Saxon England. Op. cit.* p. 71.
17. *Ibid.* p. 72.
18. *Ibid.* p. 278.
19. F. Stenton. *Anglo-Saxon England. Op. cit.* p. 277.
20. *Ibid.* p. 470.

for wars and Church dues and many of them found no alternative but to become a subject of the lord on whose estates they became bound to weekly labour. In return they obtained some security but it was a high price to pay.

Such villeinage was close to slavery but there was also a large unfree class of actual slaves. Initially they had included Britons who were criminals guilty of lesser crimes who were not put to death but their numbers were augmented by prisoners captured in wars. Anathema though it is today, slavery was fully recognised in Anglo-Saxon England with slaves being sold and bought openly, even by peasant farmers, and with a slave trade busy through the English ports. Indeed, being sold abroad is found in the laws of Kent as an alternative to capital punishment. Women and children could be reduced to slavery as a punishment (for example, for a false oath) or sold into slavery because of famine or poverty. In some counties of Anglo-Saxon England the proportion of slaves could be 40 per cent of the population, working mainly as ploughmen.[21]

It should also be noticed on the point of status that the higher clergy were granted privileges and played an important role in government and enforcing the will of kings across the country. They were close advisers to the kings and exercised considerable influence in the framing of laws which they helped to enforce as leading members of the shire courts.[22] Fundamental to the Anglo-Saxon legal system was the opposition between privilege and folkright. Folkright was the aggregation of rules which expressed the juridical consciousness of the people or their communities. Its formulation and application were at first in the shire moots. The law was declared and applied by the people themselves in their communities and through the 12 eldest thanes or a similar quorum. Later, it was declared by the councillors of the realm sitting as the Witan. But folkright could be broken or modified by a special law or grant from the monarch, often to the Church, which was a privilege of royal power. In time such royal grants of privilege exceeded folkright and became the starting point of the feudal legal system.[23]

THE KING'S PEACE

It is likely that in small communities the blood-feuds were sometimes successful in preventing criminal activity since it would be known that to commit a crime would produce instant reprisals. Equally, however, they could become self-feeding and lead to warfare and anarchy. And the alternative scales of fixed compensation in the codes of the kings which were meant to prevent such consequences often failed, as succeeding kings often lamented when introducing new sets of laws. And again

21. J. Lindsay. (1977) *The Normans and their World.* Abingdon, Oxon. Purnell Book Services Limited. p. 163.
22. For shire courts see post, pp.16.17.
23. *Encyclopedia Britannica.* (1964 edn.) London, William Benton. vol. i. pp.938-9.

status was important, since with both the blood-feud and the tariff men were not treated equally. For instance, if one *thegn* was killed by a *ceorl* his kin would demand the death of six *ceorls*. It will readily be perceived that such extensive blood-letting was a dangerous threat to the maintenance of law and order on which royal power rested.

At first, compensation was believed to be the only possible alternative punishment to private vengeance. Hence, Ine was not the only king to attempt to suppress this menacing feuding with a tariff. Alfred also tried, even in the midst of ferocious fighting to preserve his kingdom from the Danes. Later, Edmund II (1016) went further and gave killers 12 months in which to pay their *wergild* with a proviso that if they failed to pay within this extended time the feud was still not to proceed against their kindred unless they had harboured them.

Enforcing the king's laws was proving so difficult that it began to be considered that the Crown should intervene on a wider scale to punish those who committed crimes. This led to the gradual emergence of the concept of a breach of the king's peace for which the wrongdoer was deemed to be *botless*. This meant that he could not redeem himself with compensation at all but was entirely at the mercy of the king. For serious offences, including treason to the king or a man's lord, homicide and theft, the penalty for most offenders was death.

Henceforth lawful Anglo-Saxon punishments were both plentiful and barbaric. They included death by hanging, beheading, burning and drowning; branding; the loss of hands, feet and tongue; eyes being plucked out; nose, ears and upper lip cut off; the scalp torn away, the body flayed alive; castration; and sale into slavery. In other words, frightful torments inflicted by the state. For minor offences, such as being a scold, a ducking stool fixed over a pond would be used, and the pillory and stocks were also known. These too sometimes resulted in death.

And, yet again, we witness the social class distinction. A nobleman could commit murder and still redeem himself with one fine to the Church and another to be divided between the kin of the slain and the king. On the other hand, for a slave, a free man of low estate and a woman, the penalty was one of the awesome deaths mentioned above.

COMMUNAL COURTS

At this point something should be said of the Anglo-Saxon courts and how they arbitrarily determined guilt or innocence. Always bearing in mind, as with crimes and punishments, that society and law were not static but were evolving, albeit slowly, throughout this 500-year period.

From early times England was divided into shires, most of which are still with us, and each shire was divided into hundreds. From the tenth century these territorial divisions formed the basis of the organization of public justice and the administration of public finance throughout England south of the Thames, and in English Mercia, East Anglia and the southern Danelaw. Previously there were less structured public assemblies known as folk-moots. As we have seen, the size of a hundred was basically 100 hides but it might vary and might range from fewer than 20 to more than 150 hides.[24] Within each hundred there would be a number of village communities which lived by agriculture and stock farming and would require a wide variety of buildings for use as barns, stables, byres and storehouses. In addition there were the specialised trades of smith, carpenter, weaver and potter.[25] There would be few roads. Even a palace of the king was no more than a long wooden hall with a large number of outhouses.

Each hundred had a court which administered customary law and endeavoured to moderate the fiscal demands of the king's financial officers. It was a local popular assembly, quasi-democratic in nature, meeting in the open air a regular intervals of four weeks. Its judgments were given by peasants who might be guided, but not controlled, by the king's reeve who presided.[26] The origin of the court is still unknown but some of its functions are described in royal ordinances.[27] King Edward the Elder (901-25) refers to meetings held every four weeks by a king's reeve for the administration of customary law[28] and Edmund (939-46) describes it as an established institution.[29] With similar functions to the hundred courts were divisions known as *wapentakes* in the areas conquered by the Danes in Lincoln, Nottingham, Derby, Leicester and the North and West Ridings of Yorkshire.[30] They too met every four weeks, again in the open air.

The shires held county courts under the presidency of an *eorl* and a bishop to administer both the secular and the ecclesiastical law.[31] Like the hundred courts they met at first in public, meeting twice a year for one day until the law expanded and they too met monthly. Proceedings were oral, no records were kept, and initially they sat out of doors until later moving into a castle or shire hall. Their remit was to deal with cases of murder, theft, affray and wounding.

Nonetheless, important as these community courts were they were not generally held in awe by criminals and had few means of compelling obedience apart from their power to punish if an offender were apprehended. Very few lawbreakers were caught in fact and, as a consequence, if a *ceorl* left his home without explanation he

---

24. F. Stenton. *Anglo-Saxon England. Op. cit.* p. 298.

25. P. H. Blair. *Roman Britain and Early England 55 B.C.—A.D. 871. Op. cit.* p. 259.

26. F. Stenton. *Anglo-Saxon England. Op. cit.* p.299.

27. A. J. Robertson. (editor and translator) (1925) *The Laws of the Kings of England from Edmund to Henry I.* Cambridge, Cambridge University Press. pp. 16-19.

28. F. L. Attenborough. *Laws of the Earliest English Kings. Op. cit.* p. 121.

29. A. J. Robertson. . *The Laws of the Kings of England from Edmund to Henry I. Op. cit.* p. 13.

30. F. Stenton. *Anglo-Saxon England. Op. cit.* p. 504.

31. A. Harding. *The Law Courts of Medieval England. Op. cit.* p.20.

would be assumed to be guilty of an offence and could be summarily hanged. In what was a rough age, crime and violence were regarded as normal. As we have seen, the most common crimes were homicide, wounding and cattle-theft. So frequent was the last of these that many laws were promulgated to ensure that the sale and purchase of cattle, and sometimes other chattels, did not take place without the presence of responsible witnesses.[32] And, if a man set out on a journey to make such a purchase he was also obliged to inform his neighbours in advance of his intent and on his return reveal his purchase to them if he had been successful.

When a thief was detected in the act of carrying away what he had stolen there would be no trial but an immediate fine or, if he was poor, immediate death. If a thief or a murderer escaped, a 'hue and cry' would be raised, with much shouting and banging of utensils, and if he were sighted he could be killed on the spot. Were the hue and cry not to succeed in tracking down the offender he would be declared an outlaw, which automatically sanctioned his being lawfully killed at any time, with impunity and without repercussion, like a wild beast. In the meantime his kin would be fined. An alleged offender who refused to attend court on three occasions would also find himself declared an outlaw.

OATHS AND ORDEALS[33]

Once a person was accused of committing a crime and came before a court there could be no trial on questions of fact—such a process was unknown. He had to seek a verdict from the Almighty by means of oath-helpers or with trial by ordeal. If he could swear on oath that he was guiltless and produce sufficient oath-helpers (known as compurgators) who could vouch for his character on oath, that was deemed conclusive evidence of his innocence. On the other hand, if he were unable to find enough oath-helpers, he had to undergo the ordeal which was also a judgment of God and was administered by the Church.[34] In any event, compurgation, which probably led to widespread perjury, in criminal cases was abolished by the Assize of Clarendon (1166) which instead sent suspects to the ordeal of cold water.[35] Anglo-Saxon men sitting as a court did not even consider that they had the ability to determine questions of guilt and innocence without divine intervention and miraculous guidance. It is clear that the ordeal was not considered to be a punishment but was used to determine the innocence or guilt of people accused of serious crimes

---

32. D. Whitelock. *The Beginnings of English Society, Op. cit.* p. 146.
33. For a detailed examination of the ordeal on which this section is based see J. Hostettler. (2004) *The Criminal Jury Old and New: Jury Power from Early Times to the Present Day.* Winchester, Waterside Press. pp. 19-21.
34. George Fisher. (1997) 'The Jury's Rise as Lie Detector'. New Haven. 107 *Yale Law Journal.* p. 587.
35. J. B. Thayer. (1898) *A Preliminary Treatise on Evidence at the Common Law.* Boston, Little Brown and Company. pp. 36-7.

and it always involved a religious ceremony.[36]

One ritual was known as the ordeal by hot water. For this an iron cauldron was placed over a fire in a church. When the water boiled the accused had to reach down into the vessel and snatch up a stone from the bottom. The hand and arm were then swathed in cloth or linen for three days, after which they would be exposed and if the flesh was uninjured God had pronounced the accused not guilty. If the flesh was badly scalded he was guilty and was sentenced by the court, usually to death.

Another ritual involved the suspect walking barefoot and blindfold over nine red-hot ploughshares. If he completed the walk unharmed the verdict was not guilty. Emma, the mother of Edward the Confessor, is said to have undergone this ordeal when he accused her of adultery with the Bishop of Winchester. She appears to have emerged from it successfully.[37]

The ordeal of cold water, which was normally reserved for persons without rank, involved casting the body of the accused held by a rope into a pond near the church, after he had been given holy water to drink. Priests were paid five shillings for preparing the pool and 20 shillings for blessing it. If the accused floated he was held to be guilty, as it was believed that consecrated water would not receive a wicked body. If he sank he was innocent, which would not help him unless he was hauled out in time.[38]

For a cleric the ordeal meant swallowing an ounce of consecrated barley bread, or an ounce of cheese, impregnated with a feather. If the suspect choked that was held to be proof from God of guilt. Sometimes this ordeal was prescribed for non-clerics. Godwin, the Earl of Kent and father of King Harold, was subjected to it when accused of murdering his brother. 'May this bread choke me if I am guilty!' he cried, and promptly fell down dead.[39]

Those who failed an ordeal were mutilated or executed, their goods forfeited to the king and their land to the lord from whom they held it. If they came through the ordeal successfully, and many did, by Chapter 14 of the Assize of Clarendon of 1166,[40] they had to leave the country within eight days as outlaws if they were believed to be bad characters. This suggests that the ordeals were not entirely trusted by Henry II and were too frequently successful for his liking. Indeed, in the reign of Rufus, of 50 men sent to the ordeal of iron all escaped, to the annoyance of the king who railed at God's judgement which he complained could be swayed by men's prayers. According to Pollock and Maitland, 'this certainly looks as if some bishop or clerk had

36. Pollock & Maitland. (1895) *The History of English Law before the Time of Edward I.* Cambridge, Cambridge University Press. vol. i. p. 138.
37. Dick Hamilton. (1979) *Foul Bills and Dagger Money: 800 Years of Lawyers and Lawbreakers.* London, Book Club Associates. pp. 3-4. However, Robert Bartlett claims the account is fictional. Bartlett. (1986) *Trials by Fire and Water: The Medieval Judicial Ordeal.* Oxford, Clarendon Press. p. 17.
38. George Fisher. 'The Jury's Rise as Lie Detector'. *Op. cit.* p. 585.
39. William Forsyth. (1852) *History of Trial by Jury.* London, John Parker. p. 81.
40. 12 Hen. II c. 1.

preferred his own judgment to the judgment of God, and the king did well to be angry.'[41] As a pipe roll (a royal record of trials) reveals that an officiant might allow the iron to cool[42] it seems quite possible that the priest arranged the acquittals.

PROOFS

What has to be remembered is that all these ordeals were inflicted not as punishments—no final verdict had yet been reached when the accused was sent to the ordeal—but as proofs. Moreover, the clergy had entire control over their conduct. This included deciding on the quality of the bandage in the ordeals of hot water and iron, the timing of the attempt to rescue the innocent in the ordeal by cold water and the size of the feather inside the bread or cheese. It is a matter of conjecture whether they endeavoured to mitigate the terrors of the various ordeals in order to improve 'group harmony' in the community. It has been suggested that the ordeal gave a defendant considered guilty by the community a last opportunity of escaping punishment. That they 'were engineered to ensure a high rate of success'[43] certainly appears likely. Indeed, whilst men were generally subjected to the ordeal of cold water, women were suffered to endure the hot iron since, because of higher body fat, 'a woman was much less likely than a man to pass the ordeal of cold water.'[44]

MERCY AND LINKS WITH THE COMMON LAW

Although to modern eyes such modes of proof were savage, most of those who suffered them probably experienced only less severe forms and appear to have survived. A body thrown into a pond with a rope attached might well start to sink initially but be quickly pulled out. It is highly significant that between 1201 and 1219 Maitland found only one case in which the ordeal did not acquit the accused[45] and it has been said that the ordeal was not merely an appeal to the Deity as a 'supra-fact finder' but in practice, if not in theory, it provided a guilty man with a way to purge his wrong and therefore to be adjudged innocent.'[46] Further, a thief caught in the act could be killed on the spot but a man convicted of theft by the ordeal alone faced death only if he was a man frequently accused.[47] All this is a far cry from the belief widely held

---

41. Pollock & Maitland. *The History of English Law Before the Time of Edward I. Op. cit.* vol. ii. p. 599.
42. Pipe Roll. (1897) 21 Henry II. Pipe Roll Society, London, vol. 22, p. 131.
43. Margaret Kerr & Others. (1992) *Cold Water and Hot Iron: Trial by Ordeal in England* .22J. Interdisc Hist. p. 582.
44. *Ibid.*
45. F. W. Maitland. (1888) *Select Pleas of the Crown.* London, Selden Society. p. 75.
46. Trisha Olson. (2000) 'Of Enchantment: The Passing of the Ordeals and the Rise of the Trial Jury'. New York, *Syracuse Law Review.* p. 113.
47. D. Whitelock. *The Beginnings of English Society. Op. cit.* Middlesex, Penguin Books. p. 143.

that most people sent to the ordeal were tortured to death by it.

Fisher links the ordeal to jury trial and claims that, 'the institutional brilliance of the ordeal was that it so neatly merged the appearance of divine judgment with the reality of a great measure of human control' which continued when the ordeal was abolished. He extends this to the petty jury by adding that, 'in the trial jury, the English justice system managed to produce this very useful combination of traits.' He concludes that, 'it may be impossible to understand even the later history of the criminal trial jury without a theory about why the ordeal worked so well and about what its demise left lacking.' It worked, he says, by relying upon the divine sanction when judgment would take the defendant's life or limb and ensuring 'discreet human control under cover of divine judgment.' [48] As Paul R. Hyams has also written, the functioning and demise of the old proofs actually shaped the classical Common Law in multifarious ways. Particularly, since in people's minds crime continued as time passed, to be linked with sin, evil and moral weakness. [49]

MONARCHY AND CHURCH

Once Christianity had become the dominant religion in England by the year 663 there was no serious conflict between secular and ecclesiastical authority. The prime duty of the Christian king was to be the 'moral leader and defender of his kingdom or *Christendom,*' not only in the war against the heathen but also by issuing just laws. 'The Church was therefore concerned with all the laws that were made.' [50] As we have seen bishops and *eorls* presided over the shire courts and the former had a large say in secular justice and lawmaking. Furthermore, ecclesiastical pleas were heard in the hundred courts. However, the king essentially controlled the Church by appointment to its higher offices. And his laws secured substantial income not only for the crown but also for the Church. This was by means of plough-alms, tithes, and church-scot which was a payment in kind, usually grain or livestock, levied on freemen in proportion to the size of their holdings.

An income derived from voluntary payments by primitive farmers was highly unstable so it was supplemented by these compulsory contributions required under the kings' codes. Plough-alms consisted of a penny, paid within a fortnight after Easter, in respect of each plough team working in a parish. The equally compulsory church-scot was a heavier burden and was paid at Martinmas (11 November). Default in payment resulted in a fine of 60 shillings as well as payment of 12 times the sum originally due. [51] The Kentish shilling was an ounce of silver and four times the

48. George Fisher. 'The Jury's Rise as Lie Detector' *Op. cit.* p. 601.
49. Cynthia B. Herrup. (1987) *The Common Peace: Participation and the Criminal Law in Seventeenth- Century England.* Cambridge, Cambridge University Press. p. 3.
50. A. Harding. *The Law Courts of Medieval England. Op. cit.* p. 20.
51. F. Stenton. *Anglo-Saxon England. Op. cit.* pp. 152-3.

value of the West Saxon shilling. In return for these privileges the Church continued to confirm that royal power was conferred by God. Once again we see the Church and crown working in harness to maintain social control and the continuing flow of their ample revenues.

Generally speaking, the power of the kings increased throughout the Anglo-Saxon period, but they were not autocrats and they were not sufficiently powerful to be able to forgo the support of the Church. Formally, they combined heredity with election, taking advice on all important issues from the *ad hoc* Great Council of the Realm, known as the *Witenagemot* or 'Assembly of the Wise', which was originally semi-democratic with every freeman having the right to attend. By the time of Alfred the Great, however, it was normally composed of *eorls*, bishops and the wealthy landowners who together chose the kings' successors.

All the dooms and laws that have come down to us are the enactments of the kings backed by the Witan, as their preambles often confirm. They did not attempt to replace ancient customs. What they normally did was to restate parts of the customary law in order to reinforce it and add new ordinances to meet changing conditions. In their preambles they also enunciated broad legal principles and objectives and religious precepts in the often vain hope that they would be widely observed. The dooms of the Anglo-Saxon kings that are available to us are dealt with in the next chapter.

CHAPTER 2

Saxon Dooms—Our Early Laws

WRITTEN LAW

It was the influence of the Church that caused the early Anglo-Saxon laws to be written down. After all, churchmen and theologians were the Anglo-Saxon scholars and provisions relating to the Church and its income had to be added to existing laws and sent around the country. In consequence, it is noteworthy that, '[t]he record of legislation in England is one of the oldest in Europe.'[1] The first written laws (in Old English) that have come down to us are those of Æthelbert (560-616), King of Kent, a shire where the basis of society was the free peasant landholder. They contain 90 decrees in all.[2] Not surprisingly after Æthelbert's conversion to Christianity, the Church took pride of place with the first doom providing that thefts of the property of God and the Church were to be compensated twelve-fold, those of a bishop elevenfold and of a priest ninefold.

No doubt this was considered to be necessary to protect the newly-arrived missionaries from Rome but it set an example that was followed for a long time to come. Another doom provided that if a freeman stole from the king he had to repay ninefold, the same as for robbing a priest, and less than theft from a bishop. This tariff for men of the cloth being equal to or above that for the king is remarkable, but it should be remembered that the king also exacted a fine known as a *wite*.

Of great importance is that an extensive fixed tariff of compensation to victims or their kin was also clearly set out in an attempt to replace the blood feud. It was decreed that if a man slew a freeman he should pay to the slain man's kin his *wergild* of 100 gold shillings and a fine of 50 shillings to the king. Similar sums had to be paid if a man killed a smith or messenger employed by the king. The burden of the *wergild* was extremely harsh since the huge sum of 100 gold shillings was equal in value to the 100 oxen the freeman was deemed to be worth. Twenty of the shillings had to be paid 'before the grave was closed' and the remaining 80 shillings within 40 days. If the slayer absconded his relatives were liable for half the *wergild*. It is not easy to compare these values with those of today but, as a guide, at the time a shilling would buy a sheep and six shillings an ox. And, by the twelfth century a silver penny was the daily wage for a manual worker, with 12 pennies being equal to one shilling. Harsh though the penalty of *wergild* was, however, it was usually payable

---

1. H. G. Richardson and G.O. Sayles. (1966) *Law and Legislation from Æthelbert to Magna Carta.* Edinburgh, Edinburgh University Press. p. 1.
2. For these dooms, and those which follow of succeeding kings to the reign of Alfred, see F. Attenborough. (editor and translator) (1922) *Laws of the Earliest English Kings.* Cambridge, Cambridge University Press.

for homicide, although not exclusively, and was undoubtedly an improvement as a punishment on widespread revenge killing.

If a freeman robbed another freeman, usually of cattle, he had to pay threefold compensation and the king took all his goods as a fine. So that, already in this early stage, we see the king using the law to enhance his own wealth by a supplement to taxation. A further decree provided that if a freeman lay with the wife of another freeman the husband was not to kill him. Instead, the adulterer had to pay the husband his *wergild* of 100 shillings and then procure a second wife with his own money and deliver her to the husband's house. What happened to the first wife is not mentioned but these decrees were often somewhat ambiguous and in this case it may have been directed at a wife who went to live with the adulterer. We are also not told if the husband had any say in the choice of his second wife. If not, the procedure would have been open to intriguing abuse. Equally unclear is the reason for the lack of the influence of the Church on such laws which suggests that Christianity was only beginning to take hold and custom was still a power in the land. Another example is if a man lay with a servant of the king he had to pay a fine of 50 shillings and if with the servant of an *eorl* a fine of 12 shillings.

For bodily injuries the compensation varied according to their seriousness. For instance, a damaged bone was valued at four shillings, an eye knocked out at 50 shillings, a broken nose at nine shillings and destruction of the generative organ at 300 shillings. If a great toe was cut off the compensation was put at ten shillings, for other toes five shillings and for a foot 50 shillings. A broken rib was worth three shillings and a thigh 12 shillings. But if a broken thigh resulted in the victim becoming lame it was provided that his friends must arbitrate. Even seizing a man by the hair resulted in compensation of 50 *sceattas* having to be paid. The *sceatt* was the predecessor of the penny and was meant to be of the same value.

When a man purchased a maiden in order to marry her the arrangement stood if there was no dishonesty. Nonetheless, to some extent women's rights were taken into account. On marriage a man was required to give his wife a 'morning-gift' of money and land. When a married man died, if there was a child or children, his widow was entitled to half his property as she was also if she left him with her children during his lifetime. Here we see rare examples of property rights for women which were lost after the Norman Conquest. These then give a flavour of Æthelbert's laws, which were rather extraordinary for the time, and the social climate in which they were enacted.

POWERS OF CROWN AND CHURCH

Of Æthelbert's successors as Kings of Kent, Hlothháere and Eadric (673-686), who may have ruled together, issued dooms which in the main followed the lines of those of Æthelbert whilst developing legal procedure. Interestingly, they provided that the men dealing with pleas in popular assemblies were not ministers of the king but 'the judges of the Kentish people.'

By the laws, if a man's servant slew a nobleman, whose *wergild* was 300 shillings, his owner had to surrender the homicide and pay the value of three men in addition. This would not be three *wergilds*, however, but the value of three slaves—a much lower sum.[3] If the slain man were a freeman, the payment would be the value of one slave. If a man died leaving a wife and child, it was decreed that the child should remain with its mother but one of its father's relatives, if willing, should act as its guardian and take care of its property until it was ten years old. And, if a man of Kent wished to buy property in London he was required to have two or three trustworthy men, or the king's reeve in London, as witnesses.

In the year 684 an army from Sussex invaded Kent at the instigation of Eadric and in February 685 Hlothháere died of wounds received in battle. On Eadric's death in the following year the kingdom 'fell apart between a number of obscure Kings.'[4]

The next code which has come down to us was issued by King Wihtráed (d. 725) in an assembly of the Kentish nobles and clergy held at Bearsted near Maidstone late in 695. These dooms gave more powers to the Church and declared it to be free from taxation. Further, it was to receive the same compensation as the king for violence done to dependants. The word of a bishop, like that of a king was declared to be incontrovertible even though unsupported by the sacred oath. More evidence, no doubt, that the Witan contained a good many clerics. Otherwise, the dooms provided penalties for unlawful marriages, heathen practices and the neglect of fasts and holy days.

Despite the fact that recent research shows there is no certainty that all the Anglo-Saxon kings were devout in their professed Christianity they saw the necessity of sharing power to underpin the stability of both their crown and the Church. 'Within 90 years the Church which Æthelbert had taken under his protection had become a power all but co-ordinate with the king himself in the Kentish state.'[5] By this time in Kent the king was largely dependent on the assistance of literate clerical officers to ensure that taxation was regarded as fair and was efficiently collected. Only by mutual help could the ascendancy of both the temporal and ecclesiastical rulers be maintained and the political legitimacy of their control over the lives of the people be demonstrated.

Whatever Wihtráed's faith, his dooms dealt almost exclusively with religious issues and, as mentioned, he formally enacted that the Church should enjoy immunity from taxation, which must have dented the desired perception of fairness. No doubt the power of the Church left him with little alternative. He also pioneered

---

3. F. L. Attenborough. *Ibid.* p. 179.
4. F. Stenton. (1971) *Anglo-Saxon England.* Oxford, The Clarendon Press. p. 61.
5. *Ibid.* p. 62.

Sunday Observance laws. If a servant, contrary to his lord's command, did servile work between sunset on Saturday and sunset on Sunday it was decreed that he must pay 80 sceattas to his lord. If he made a journey on his own on horseback on a Sunday, he had to pay six shillings compensation to his lord or, if he did not have the means to pay, suffer the lash. If a freeman worked on a Sunday he forfeited 20 shillings, of which half went to the informer who was also rewarded with the wage or profit from the freeman's labour.

A husband and wife who made an offering to the devil had to pay a fine of 40 shillings or lose all their goods. If a man gave meat to his household during a religious fast he forfeited 20 shillings, and if a slave ate of his own free will at such a time he paid six shillings or suffered the lash. Already, in the early seventh century the role of the lord in controlling economic and social life was becoming more apparent and with it the weakening of the kin bond. For example, an accused *ceorl* had to clear himself, with the help not of his kinsmen, but of three oath-helpers of his own status. A century later the laws of Ine required, in the case of a man charged with homicide, the inclusion of his lord among those who testified for him.[6]

Twenty sceattas, later 20 silver pennies, equalled one Kentish shilling. The shilling could be a silver or gold coin, the value of which varied from kingdom to kingdom. Payments of all kinds were often made by the weight of silver or gold, and the pound, shilling and penny were originally weights which survived until recently. Indeed, the pound and penny coins are still in circulation for the time being. Only towards the end of the Anglo-Saxon period, however, was a single currency achieved, although Offa's penny held its value until the reign of Henry III—some 500 years later.

INE OF WESSEX AND ALFRED THE GREAT

Let us leave Kent now and consider some of the laws of Wessex promulgated by Kings Ine and Alfred. Ine, whose laws are the earliest we have of Wessex, reigned from 688 to 725 when he abdicated and undertook a pilgrimage to Rome where he founded a hospice for poor English pilgrims and where he remained until his death. In return for monetary compensation he had made peace with Kent in 694 when Wihtráed was king. He too had to cope with a Witan that resembled a synod of bishops but his laws had the effect of centralising his kingdom. Nonetheless, although he is noted for his code of laws there are fewer criminal laws in his dooms than in those of Æthelbert. By his dooms all children were to be baptised within 30 days of their birth, failing which their guardians had to pay a fine of 30 shillings. If a child died before baptism its guardian lost all he possessed. If a slave worked on a

---

6. J. Lindsay. (1977) *The Normans and their World.* Abingdon, Oxon. Purnell Book Services Ltd. p. 169.

Sunday by his lord's command he automatically became a free man and the lord not only lost a slave but also forfeited 30 shillings. By contrast, a freeman who worked on a Sunday was reduced to slavery if he could not pay a fine of 60 shillings, unless he had been obliged to work by his lord.

Anyone failing to pay his church dues not only forfeited 60 shillings but also had to pay the dues 12-fold. There can be no doubt that church dues often impoverished peasant households in difficult years and, as with economic distress and the ravages of war, led many freemen to seek the security of servile status under a lord. On the secular side, any person who killed a reputed thief was allowed to declare on oath that the suspect was guilty, whilst the family and friends of the slain man were not permitted an oath. Other decrees, of which there were 76 in all, were similar to those of the kings of Kent. For instance, in both it was held that a stranger who moved away from a road and did not shout or blow his horn, was to be assumed a thief and either slain or redeemed.

The next set of laws in Wessex are those of Alfred the Great who, from the age of 21, reigned from 871 to 899. His reign was a turning point in English history. After some defeats, in a series of striking victories he stemmed the tide of the pagan Danish invaders and showed that the Vikings could not only be defeated but also baptised. His chief Viking enemy, King Guthrum, was converted to Christianity with Alfred as godfather. He recaptured London from the Danes, built a navy on new lines and saved Wessex. At the time of his death he had confined the Danes to an area in the north and east of England known as Danelaw. With unsurpassed energy the hero king also managed to encourage learning and literature and it is no exaggeration to say that he secured the beginning of English civilisation. And in achieving all this he laid the ground for the concept of one united kingdom of England.[7]

It is for his valiant defence of the kingdom of Wessex against a stronger enemy, for securing peace with the Vikings and for his reconstruction of southern England that Alfred—alone among English monarchs—is known as 'the Great'.[8]

During the early Danish invasions the machinery and enforcement of law had virtually broken down. It was one of the chief tasks of Alfred and his successors to revive them. They faced the challenge so squarely that royal justice emerged stronger than ever before.[9] He incorporated into his book of laws the best of the dooms of Kent, Mercia and Wessex, blended with Christian principles. His laws, extended by his successors, grew into the body of customary law which was administered as a kind of 'Common Law' in the shire and hundred courts.[10]

It was still true, however, that there were no comprehensive codes in the modern sense. There were no professional lawyers, no juries and the judges were kings,

7. C. Brooke. (1965) *From Alfred to Henry III: 871-1272*. London, Thomas Nelson & Sons Ltd. p. 33.
8. Online. www.royal.gov.uk/output/Page25.asp
9. *Ibid*. p. 67.
10. F. N. Lee. (2006) *King Alfred the Great and our Common Law*. Bexley Publications.

ealdormen, bishops, lesser officials and lords or their representatives.[11] In this context Alfred promulgated the first dooms after a century and a half of Danish invasions. In all, he enacted some 77 decrees with numerous sub-clauses, and he succeeded in integrating the English and Danish legal systems with an agreed scale of *wergilds*. The preamble to Alfred's laws contained a translation of the ten commandments into English, numerous passages from the book of Exodus, as well as a brief account of apostolic history. Many of the laws of Æthelbert, Ine and Offa (Offa's laws have been otherwise lost to us) were openly approved and restated with new additions. His councillors, Alfred declared, had approved of all that he had chosen. Wihtráed's religious laws were not referred to.

Alfred proudly proclaimed to all the Wessex hundreds that there was not to be one law for the rich and another for the poor. As with Ine's laws, it was made unlawful to commence a blood-feud before an attempt had been made to obtain compensation. And every man was required to abide by his oath and pledge. If he failed to carry out his pledge he had to give up his weapon and his goods to friends and serve a prison term of 40 days in a royal castle. Anyone plotting the death of the king or a lord was to lose his own life and property. A man carrying off a nun from a minster, without the leave of the king or bishop (when would such leave be given?) had to pay 60 shillings to the king and 60 shillings to the bishop and the 'lord who owns the nun.' A man committing public slander was to have his tongue cut out unless he could pay his *wergild* by way of compensation.

If a man killed another unintentionally by allowing a tree to fall on him whilst they were engaged on a common task of tree cutting, the tree was regarded as the guilty object. It was the slayer, known to the law as a deodand. This must have been a fairly frequent occurrence to have been dealt with by law but, of course, much of the land was covered with forests which farmers would wish to cut back in order to make more arable land available as well as requiring wood for buildings and fires. Permitting a fugitive from justice to seek sanctuary in a monastery was another ancient custom incorporated into Alfred's laws. Although the period of grace was only three days, he was not to be harmed or wounded in any way during that time and, if he were, the perpetrator had to pay *wergild* and a fine of 120 shillings to the monks. Similar sanctuary applied to churches where the period of grace was seven days unless the fugitive gave up his weapon, when he could stay for 30 days. If a person stole from a church he had to pay a fine and have a hand cut off unless clemency were granted. If a man fought in the king's hall or drew his weapon it was in the king's discretion whether he be allowed to live or be executed. If he escaped and was recaptured he had to pay his *wergild* and a fine.

Alfred also provided for compensation of six shillings for the first bite of a dog, 12 shillings for a second bite and 30 shillings for a third. Clearly the modern theory

---

11. Online www.royalgov.uk p.68.

that a dog should be allowed a first bite without penalty does not have the blessing of Alfred, although some writers have fathered the concept on him. There was to be no vendetta or blood-feud against a man fighting another if he had found him in bed or within closed doors with his wife, mother or daughter. This was another example, by making a specific case, of how the general laws against feuding had not proved entirely successful.

Anyone causing injuries to another had to pay compensation. The injuries concerned were similar to those mentioned in the laws of Æthelbert but the amounts of compensation awarded were considerably higher in many cases. In Wessex at this time a pound was made up of 49 shillings of five pennies each. The pound of 20 shillings of 12 pence each, which survived until the twentieth century, was not to come until William the Conqueror.

In Alfred's time law suits were brought in a public assembly known as a folk-moot. There is no suggestion in his laws of any higher court than this, and an appeal from it was made direct to the king. There is evidence that the folk-moot met under the king's reeve every four weeks and it was not until the tenth century that the hundred courts (and, in the Danish counties in the north, the *wapentakes*) came into existence, meeting every four weeks. Above them were the shire courts which met twice a year and to which an appeal from the lower courts could be taken.[12] Some lay and ecclesiastical landowners were also granted the right to hold private courts, although serious offences were reserved for the public courts.

Alfred died in the year 899, aged 50, and was buried in Winchester, the burial place of the West Saxon royal family.

LAWS OF KING EDWARD THE ELDER (901-924)

Two series of laws issued by Edward the Elder, the son of Alfred, have survived. They do not replace the laws of earlier kings but they have a more coherent and logical form. In the first of his ordinances the king commanded his reeves to apply community law without fear or favour and to apply folkright. To avoid delay in justice every case was to have a date by which it was to be determined. Apart from this there were only three laws primarily to ensure that dealings in property, particularly livestock, took place before witnesses.

The second series of laws was enacted in a meeting with Edward's Witan at Exeter. Here, he complained that his peace was being indifferently observed and exhorted the Witan to see that his commands were carried out. Each reeve was to hold a court every four weeks and apply community law. A reeve who failed to do so or collect fines imposed by law was himself to pay a fine of 120 shillings for in-

---

12. D. Whitelock. (1974) *The Beginnings of English Society*. Middlesex, The Pelican History of England. vol. ii. p. 137.

subordination to the king. Any person wrongfully denying the right of another to land was to be liable to a fine of 30 shillings payable to the king. A similar fine had to be paid for a second offence and 120 shillings for a third offence. Committing perjury was to result in the perjurer being sent to the ordeal. Members of the Witan were told that they should see that their peace was better observed than before with fines for those committing minor offences. Men accused of theft were required to produce sureties until judgment was obtained. It was also made an offence to protect a convicted offender. At the same time a significantly new penal system was evolving and in the codes of Edward lists of fines for criminal offences are less prominent than before and were slowly giving way to outlawry, confiscation and capital and corporal punishment.[13]

Edward died leading an army against a Mercian rebellion on 17 July 924 and was buried at Winchester.

ENGLISH AND DANISH CO-OPERATION

It was during the reigns of Alfred and Edward the Elder that accommodations were first made with the Danes in the parts of middle and northern England the invaders had conquered, with provisions that all people should acknowledge one God only and 'zealously renounce' every kind of heathendom. Both parties also agreed that as not everyone was willing to submit to divine laws they would therefore enforce their control by secular dooms. Primarily, the peace of the king and the peace of the Church were to be inviolate. Violating Christianity or reverencing heathenism resulted, in the south, in the person involved paying his *wergild* and, in the north, a fine appropriate to the offence. If a priest misdirected the people about a festival or fast, he had to pay 30 shillings among the English and among the Danes three half-marks. Non-payment to the Church of tithes, light-scot or plough arms resulted in a fine in both kingdoms and killing a man caused the killer to be deemed an outlaw who could himself be killed at will.

Ordeals and oaths were forbidden on festival and fast days with a breach resulting in a fine. No one was to be executed on a Sunday festival but was to be securely held until the festival was over. Witches and perjurers, or 'foul, defiled notorious adulteresses' (but not adulterers) found anywhere in the land were to be driven from the country and 'the people cleansed'. Alternatively, the offenders could be executed unless they desisted and paid a fine.

---

13. *Encyclopedia Britannica*. (1964 edn.) London, William Benton. vol. i. p. 938.

KING ATHELSTAN'S LAWS (924-939)

As a result of Alfred's military prowess and political wisdom the supremacy of Wessex over much of southern England was assured by the year 930. Around this time King Athelstan, a distinguished and audacious soldier who was victorious in bloody battles with the Danes, taking York from them and subduing Scotland, enacted six new series of laws. These strengthened royal control over his large kingdom. However, again, they did not replace earlier laws and customs which were often repeated. He did, however, with Archbishop Wulfhelm and the bishops, declare that all taxes and tithes were to be paid to him and the Church at the appropriate times under threat of severe confiscations for failure to do so.

Athelstan introduced the first social legislation in England, providing for the relief of the poor. If a king's reeve failed to provide, from the rents of the royal demesne, for the poor in the manner prescribed he had to find 30 shillings to be distributed among the poor under the bishop's supervision.

Athelstan also promulgated a doom providing that no thief caught in the act was to be spared if he were over 12 years of age and the value of the stolen property was more than eight pence. Later, the age limit was raised to 15. Anyone sparing such a thief had to pay the thief's *wergild* which might be a severe penalty. Furthermore, witchcraft, sorcery and issuing deadly spells which were believed to result in death were made capital crimes. And a mere allegation might be fatal when the only mode of proof was the ordeal. People failing to attend court on three occasions were to pay a fine to the king for contempt.

Innovative also was a law which established the *tithing*, whereby in every hundred men were grouped into units of ten with each such unit being held responsible for acts of wrongdoing by any member of it. If the other nine failed to bring the offender to justice they were to pay compensation personally for any damage the offender had caused. Unless exempted by wealth and high rank, every man had to enrol in a *tithing*. Presumably, such a law was required because large numbers of offenders were not apprehended. Later, this institution was to be used by William the Conqueror when a Norman was killed by someone unknown but presumed to be English.

If any person was due to face the ordeal he had to go to the priest on each of three days beforehand and feed himself with bread, water, salt and herbs until the ordeal was held. He had to attend mass on each of the three days and on the day of the ordeal swear an oath that he was, according to the community law, guiltless of the charge. The number of witnesses of the ordeal was not to exceed 12 and if more than that number accompanied the accused the ordeal was void unless an appropriate number withdrew. In the ordeal of hot water the witnesses were to test the heat of the water and they had to fast and remain apart from their wives on the night preceding the ordeal. They also had to have holy water sprinkled over them and to taste the holy water as well as kiss the image of Christ's rood. If this law were broken the ordeal was void and the prisoner had to pay a fine of 120 shillings to the king. The same amount had to be paid by anyone aiding a thief so that penal sums were now payable to the king even though the offence was not directed at him.

Currency was regulated to control the weight of silver and punish fraud and trade was largely confined to the towns, such as they were. Athelstan died at the height of his powers and was buried at Malmesbury. A church charter of 934 described him as 'king of the English, elevated by the right hand of the Almighty ... to the Throne of the whole Kingdom of Britain.'

THE LAWS OF KING EDMUND I (939-946)[14]

Edmund was born in the year 921, the son of the third wife of Edward the Elder and half-brother to his predecessor, Athelstan. Following a decisive battle at Leicester he secured all southern Mercia and the five Danish boroughs and freed them from the fear of raids from Northumbria.

Religious laws and ferocious punishments continued to loom large in the ordinances of kings who reigned after Athelstan. There are three series of laws issued by King Edmund, the first promulgated by a council which met in London and the third at Colyton in Devonshire. Edmund convened a great synod in London during Easter, possibly in the year 942, with Archbishops Oda and Wulfstan and many other bishops to meditate on the condition of their souls and of those who were subject to them. In the preamble to his laws Edmund declared that their purpose was to promote Christianity and bring to an end the manifold illegal deeds of violence which so distressed him. Anglo-Saxon kings constantly bewailed their inability to control crime, not surprisingly failing to foresee, like Canute and the waves, that the task of abolishing crime was to defeat all governments in known history.

In Edmund's laws church tithes, Peter's Pence and plough-alms were to continue to be compulsory tributes to the Church. Failure to pay resulted in excommunication. Ecclesiastics had to remain chaste and failure to do so resulted in the forfeiture of their worldly goods and a consecrated burial place. The number of cases in which property was forfeit to the king was increased and was to include breaches of the King's Peace, attacks on dwellinghouses and harbouring the kinsmen of those who had killed others. Where a number of slaves committed theft the leader was to be captured and slain without delay and each of the others scoured three times, have his scalp removed, and one little finger mutilated as a visible sign of his guilt.

On 26 May 946 Edmund's brief reign came to an untimely end when he was stabbed to death at the royal villa of Pucklechurch in Gloucestershire by an exiled robber

---

14. For these laws and those of Edgar, Ethelred, Canute and Henry I, see A.J. Robertson. (editor and translator). (1925) *The Laws of the Kings of England from Edmund to Henry I*. Cambridge, Cambridge University Press.

whose return to the court was not known by the king and his officials. Described at the time as 'Edmund the Magnificent', he was buried at Glastonbury Abbey.

THE LAWS OF EDGAR (959-975)

Edgar, known as 'the Peaceable', was the younger son of Edmund I. He was acclaimed king north of the Thames by Mercian nobles in 958 and actually succeeded to the throne a year later. He consolidated the Anglo-Saxon kingdom and the service at his coronation forms the basis of the British coronation ceremony of today. Yet after his death, on three occasions England suffered conquest, two Danish and one Norman.

The origins of the Danelaw lie in the Viking invasions of England in the ninth century. It held sway in the Kingdoms of Northumbria and East Anglia and the five boroughs of Leicester, Nottingham, Derby, Stamford and Lincoln. When the English kings brought back under their rule the areas of the country using Danelaw they did little to interfere with its legal customs. King Edgar stated expressly,

> It is my will that among the Danes such good laws shall be valid as they best appoint; and I always conceded this to them and will concede it as long as my life lasts, on account of your loyalty, which you have always shown to me.[15]

This king reinforced custom by an ordinance which provided that men belonging to the hundred should assemble every four weeks without fail, 'and every man shall do justice to his fellow.' Heavy fines were to be payable for failing to respond immediately to a 'hue and cry' and, as theft was frequently of livestock, articles of assistance in pursuit of a thief, such as a cow's bell, a dog's collar and a blast-horn were each given a value of one shilling by law and reckoned to be an informer.

Another ordinance issued by Edgar, which he conceded was an attempt to enhance royal legitimacy, proclaimed that every man, rich or poor, was to enjoy the benefit of public law and be awarded just decisions. To that end, if a judge gave a false judgment he was to pay 120 shillings to the king as a penalty. As with all Anglo-Saxon laws we have little information as to how this could be successfully enforced and whether it caused the king to experience difficulty in finding sufficient judges for the fairly new borough courts[16] which met three times a year. The shire and hundred courts had no judges, as we have seen. In any event, a false accusation before any court would result in the loss of the tongue or other severe punishment.

And the religious influence surfaced again with an ecclesiastical code. At one time during Edgar's reign a plague was raging. This, declared one of his decrees, was the consequence of sin. If tenants obstinately refused to pay their rents their lord

---

15. D. Whitelock. *The Beginnings of English Society. Op. cit.* vol. ii. p. 136.
16. A. Harding. (1973) *The Law Courts of Medieval England.* London, George Allen & Unwin Ltd., p. 19.

was permitted to seize their property and their lives were forfeit. Likewise, Church dues had to be paid or God would act again in a similar manner. In fact, archbishops often framed the Anglo-Saxon dooms, copies of which were sent to the more important ecclesiastics and as was stated at the end of one of Edgar's codes,

> Many copies of this are to be written and sent both to the Ealdorman Ælfhere (of Mercia) and Ealdorman Æthelwine (of East Anglia), and they are to send them in all directions, so that this measure be known both to the poor and the rich.[17]

Copies were also sent to bishops and it is to the Church that we owe the preservation of Anglo-Saxon laws where official records and law books have not survived. As Dorothy Whitelock has written, 'Anglo-Saxon law would be poor indeed but for the preservation of the archives of the cathedrals of Rochester, London and Worcester.'[18]

Edgar died suddenly, while still a young man, on 8 July 975 at Winchester, and like his father he was buried at Glastonbury Abbey.

ETHELRED'S LAWS (978-1016)

Edgar was succeeded by his son, Edward the Martyr, who, after reigning for three years, was brutally assassinated by the retainers of his brother Ethelred at his stepmother's castle at Corfe in Dorset. He was succeeded by Ethelred who, as far as is known, was not directly implicated in the murder but who nevertheless bore the stigma of guilt that rocked the Crown. Ethelred proved to be a weak king, known to history as 'the Unready'—which meant indecisive. Certainly, he was incompetent. At his accession to the throne in 978 he was still a boy,[19] but most of his reign was taking up with defence against large Viking invading forces. On St Brice's Day (13 November) 1002 he ordered the massacre of the Danes living in England and prompted a series of Viking campaigns to conquer England which succeeded in 1013. Ethelred fled into exile in Normandy but returned the following year. He died on 23 April 1016 in London and was buried at St. Paul's. He was succeeded by his son Edmund II who shared the kingship of England with Canute.

Ten series of laws (two of them only short fragments) issued by Ethelred are known, four of them dealing with secular affairs and six almost entirely ecclesiastical. Ethelred's first laws were enacted at Wantage in Berkshire, then a royal manor and birthplace of Alfred the Great. They constitute an important document in the history of criminal justice in England since they introduced the sworn jury to provide evidence from their own knowledge. They provided that a moot was to be held

---

17. D. Whitelock. *The Beginnings of English Society. Op. cit.* p. 137.
18. *Ibid.*
19. C. Brooke. *From Alfred to Henry III: 871-1272. Op. cit.* p. 58.

in every wapentake, with the 12 eldest thegns to go out with the reeve and swear upon the relic that he put into their hands that they would accuse no innocent man and conceal no guilty man. Naomi Hurnard has argued that this was the first presenting jury in English history[20] but this was not the view of Pollock and Maitland who believed that Ethelred's jury was found only in areas subject to Danelaw.[21] Others share this view, but Hurnard wrote after Pollock and Maitland and, in any event, it must be seen as a development of the greatest significance at the time, even if confined in jurisdiction.

Ethelred's dooms also established that a breach of the peace could not be atoned for by compensation if the breach was confirmed by the king himself. This did not apply, however, in the Danish military centres known as the 'Five Boroughs' namely, Derby, Leicester, Lincoln, Nottingham and Stamford, where 1,200 silver coins was the accepted fine for such a breach. In London, by now an important trading town, Ethelred's laws provided that the gates at Aldersgate and Cripplegate should be protected by guards and that ships calling at Billingsgate should pay tolls.

Death, with burial in an unconsecrated grave, was the penalty countrywide for serious crimes such as homicide, or assault on the king's highway. For trivial offences, on the other hand, Christians were not to be condemned to death but were to have 'merciful' punishment which involved a payment of compensation to the injured party and a fine to the king. The Church did not favour the death penalty preferring that a criminal should be able to expiate and save his soul. Thus in laws composed for Ethelred by Archbishop Wulfstan it was said that, 'Christian men shall not be condemned to death for all too little; but one shall determine lenient punishments for the benefit of the people, and not destroy for a little matter God's own handiwork.'[22]

At all costs to be avoided, proclaimed the laws, were

untrue weights; false measures; horrible perjuries; devilish deeds such as murders, thefts and robberies; greed; gluttony and intemperance; frauds; breaches of law; violations of holy orders and of marriage; breaches of festivals and fasts; and misdeeds of many kinds.

Wizards, sorcerers, magicians and prostitutes were to be driven from the land or executed, and the nation purified. From this extensive catalogue of crimes, misdemeanours and punishments it appears that at least Ethelred was not so unready when it came to extending the sweep of the criminal law as he may have been in resisting renewed Viking invasions.

At the time of one such invasion the king decreed that, as a national penance,

20. N. Hurnard (1941) 'The Jury of Presentment and the Assize of Clarendon'. 56 *The English Historical Review* .London, Longmans, Green & Co. pp. 374-410.
21. Pollock & Maitland. (1968 edn) *The History of English Law Before the Time of Edward I.* Cambridge, Cambridge University Press. vol. i. p. 142.
22. D. Whitelock. *The Beginnings of English Society. Op. cit.* p. 143.

'the whole people shall fast on bread and herbs and water for three days, namely, on the Monday, Tuesday and Wednesday before Michaelmas.' Furthermore, 'everyone shall come barefoot to church without gold or ornaments and shall go to confession' and pay a penny as dues with a penalty for non-payment of a fine of 30 pence for a householder, 30 shillings for a *thegn,* while a slave was to undergo the lash.

Another aspect of these laws of Ethelred was the determination that so far as punishments were concerned not all persons were to be treated alike. This was a critical advance on the earlier position that personal considerations, other than status, could not be taken into account when determining penalties. Perhaps the desire of the Church to save souls was having an influence on secular law. At all events, the courts were now to bear in mind when fixing punishments the variables of age and youth, wealth and poverty, and health and sickness as well as rank. In a startling breakthrough there was to be clemency for involuntary misdeeds and discrimination in judging every wrongdoing. Clearly new concepts of what the law should be were filtering into the Anglo-Saxon mind.

THE LAWS OF CANUTE (1016-1035)

Finally, before the Norman Conquest brought to an end 500 years of Anglo-Saxon rule we should briefly consider the laws of Canute,—'King of all England and the Danes' at the age of 22 years (1016-1035). One long code of laws was issued at Winchester one Christmas, probably about the year 1027. Canute was the first king to compile a list of Pleas of the Crown—a concept which was to have far-reaching consequences in the future with the sovereign claiming to be injured by, and compensated for, every breach of public rights.

Declaring that he had a special interest in such cases, Canute had them brought directly before him or his sheriffs. He nourished a strong desire for extra sources of property and money, and forfeitures extended his estates whilst considerable numbers of fines went straight into the royal coffers. The result was that by this time criminal justice and criminals had become an important source of crown revenues—a process commenced by Ine but now expanded to a new level.

Canute reiterated that all men, rich and poor alike, should enjoy the benefit of the law and that punishments were to be justifiable in the sight of God and acceptable in the eyes of men. They were to be merciful with no death for trivial offences. But apparently not too merciful for although, as we have seen, the Church did not like the death penalty it approved of mutilation, and a woman who committed adultery was to lose her nose and her ears. Nothing was said, however, of the man involved. In the main, Canute's Code (although usually so described, it was a code in name only and not in the technical sense of including all laws) was based on the earlier decrees of different kings and, as usual, included a great many customs.

Canute established elaborate legal procedures to regulate the manner in which an injured person brought his opponent to court and how the court dealt with the dispute. At the same time the king claimed that certain cases were his alone to adjudicate. These included breach of the king's peace, fighting at the king's court, obstructing his officials, ambush, corrupting the processes of law and neglecting military service.[23] These constituted the king's pleas and were the forerunner of the Common Law. There was a reluctance to execute criminals, which left them no opportunity for repentance, and a sliding scale of mutilation was provided ranging according to whether it was a first or subsequent offence.[24]

Canute was king by violent conquest from Denmark. Nevertheless, he was anxious to establish his own legitimacy as the monarch of England with its flourishing agriculture, established towns and trade, and relatively advanced system of law. As a consequence, he became a classic example of poacher turned gamekeeper. This involved accepting and observing Anglo-Saxon laws and customs, and his code remains the supreme relic of his reign from which it is clear that the ideal of the political unity of the whole of England had become familiar before the Norman Conquest.

CONCLUSION

The Anglo-Saxon laws that have come down to us, as preserved in the archives of the Church, range over a period of nearly 500 years from the reign of Æthelbert to the Norman Conquest. Indeed, in essence they continued in use for some time after 1066. Over such a period and several kingdoms there were, of course, numerous changes although they evolved, or were imposed, slowly. However, three main features emerge.

The first is the power of the Church. Once Æthelbert, and subsequently other kings, were converted to Christianity the Church looms large in all the dooms that were enacted. Considerable sums were payable to it by way of taxation and fines and, at times, it was itself made exempt from taxation imposed by the crown. As not all the Anglo-Saxon kings were steadfast in their religion there must have been strong pressure on them to assist the Church as a means of ensuring both stability in their nations and their own legitimacy.

The second important feature is the attempt to replace the blood-feud with the payment of compensation for murder, violence causing injuries, cattle-rustling and other crimes. Revenge was to be compounded by a payment in kind instead of blood. And, as the power of the kings grew they too, in addition to the Church, saw a means of increasing their wealth by imposing fines in addition to compensation to the victim or his kin. Private wrongs continued to be settled between the parties but

---

23. A. Harding. *The Law Courts of Medieval England. Op. cit.* p. 22.
24. *English Historical Documents.* (ed. D. Whitelock) (1955) London, Eyre & Spottiswoode. vol. i. p. 423.

public wrongs, or crimes, were to be punished by the state. In the later Anglo-Saxon period there were some offences for which compensation was deemed not sufficient. For instance, by the laws of Canute these royal rights, as they were called, included breaches of the king's peace, housebreaking, ambush and sheltering outlaws. Again to aid royal finances, such crimes were punishable by death or mutilation and forfeiture of the offender's property to the king.

The third feature is the concept of communal responsibility for the preservation of order which involved the beginnings of legal procedure and criminal justice. This was exemplified by the hundred and shire courts which were composed largely of freemen under the king's reeve or a nobleman. These courts settled disputes between individuals and also helped secure the dominance of the king and the Church but their significance lies in the idea of communal involvement. As we have seen both Kings Edward the Elder and Edgar decreed that the hundred courts were to be held throughout the country every four weeks with each man doing justice to another. Similarly, the shire courts, which dealt with more serious matters, met twice or three times a year and in both cases they were in the nature of public meetings which transacted public business including the judging of cases. In doing so from local knowledge they were unwittingly laying the basis for the future of trial by a community jury of laymen as well as the adversarial system of trial which was to become a principle feature of English law.

CHAPTER 3

The Norman Influence and the Angevin Legacy

WILLIAM THE CONQUEROR

With his autocratic rule William I laid the foundations for strong centralised government and a Common Law. Yet, Normandy had little to offer by way of law or custom, in respect of both of which English law was superior. As Richardson and Sayles put it, 'The Normans were without learning, without literature, without written law.'[1] Partly because of this, and also because he pleaded direct descent from the Anglo-Saxon line of kings by way of gift from Edward the Confessor and election by the Witan, William enacted few new laws but confirmed those of Edward the Confessor.

In only three areas of law did he make any substantial changes. Of first importance was his ordinance which separated lay and ecclesiastical jurisdictions.[2] In future no bishop or archdeacon was to hear spiritual pleas in the hundred court and no cause relating to the government of souls was to be heard in any lay court. From then onwards an accused cleric had to make amends before a bishop in accordance with canon law until, with royal sanction, Archbishop Lanfranc established church courts in 1077. Their jurisdiction was not confined to clerical misdeeds, however, but included matrimonial disputes, adultery, usury, perjury and defamation—a jurisdiction they were to retain for centuries.

Overall control of the Church was to remain with the king. Church legislation had to be ratified by him and no bishop was permitted to excommunicate a baron or minister of the Crown without his sanction. This breach with Anglo-Saxon traditions was in accordance with Norman practice and it sowed the seeds of violent conflict to come between the Crown and the Church of a kind unknown in earlier times.

William also introduced from Normandy trial by battle to replace the ordeal in certain circumstances.[3] Having an awareness of the complex origins of men's deeds, and believing that only God, and not they, could resolve a dispute, the Normans made trial a ritual non-rational physical combat.[4] An Englishman who accused a Frenchman of theft or homicide could choose trial by battle but if he declined to do so the Frenchman could clear himself by an oath supported by his compurgators. If a Frenchman accused an Englishman, trial was by combat unless the Englishman

---

1. H. G. Richardson and G.O. Sayles. (1966) *Law and Legislation from Æthelbert to Magna Carta.* Edinburgh, Edinburgh University Press. p. 30.
2. A. J. Robertson. (editor and translator) (1925) *The Laws of the Kings of England from Edmund to Henry I.* Cambridge, Cambridge University Press. p. 235.
3. *Ibid.* p. 233.
4. A. Harding. (1973) *The Law Courts of Medieval England.* London, George Allen & Unwin Ltd. p. 25.

chose the ordeal by hot iron.

In practice, for most criminal charges, including outlawry, the Normans chose trial by battle whilst Englishmen continued with the ordeal, and battle was not imposed on them. Nevertheless, as we have observed earlier, there was a special protection for the lives of Frenchmen since when one was killed by an unknown person a heavy fine, known as a *murdrum,* was imposed on the hundred where the murder took place on the legal presumption that the killer was English.

William retained the Witan but converted it into a royal council which he consulted on important questions of state. However, he also established a royal court with which he was more intimate and which, as the *Curia Regis,* was destined to replace the Witan and effect vast changes in the English constitution. This was composed of archbishops, bishops, abbots, earls, thegns and knights, thus maintaining the political rule of the secular authority and the Church in partnership but at this stage it was mainly concerned with the collection of revenue. Shires now became counties and earls as well as bishops ceased to sit in the county courts where the sheriff became an executive officer responsible only to the king. The procedure of the shire and hundred courts, however, remained largely unchanged. William also extended the Anglo-Saxon system of fines payable to the king to such an extent that Stubbs wrote,

> So intimate is the connection of judicature with finance under the Norman Kings, that we scarcely need the comment of the historian to guide us to the conclusion that it was mainly for the sake of the profits that justice was administered at all.[5]

The *tithing,* introduced in the reign of King Athelstan, gave rise to *frankpledge* which was a compulsory fine fixed for individuals in each hundred prior to any arrests but in anticipation of them. It was probably introduced to protect Frenchmen living in a hostile land. After all, a murdered Norman might have no kin in England to bring the murderer to court and a communal responsibility for crime was seen as the answer. With some exceptions males over 12 years of age had to belong to the *tithing* and if an offender, accused of any serious crime was not brought to justice— which was frequently the case—the *frankpledge* had to be paid by the members of his *tithing* or village. In keeping with William's character, this was operated with more vigour than the Anglo-Saxon *tithing* and to ensure that the system was working efficiently the sheriff would preside over the hundred court twice a year to 'view the *frankpledge.*' In particular, he would ensure that no one was living in the village or hamlet outside a tithing. If there were such persons the village was fined.

Here also, at what became known as the sheriff's tourn, leading freemen from each village acted as presenting juries as in the earlier wapentakes. Juries of 12 'hundredmen' considered any accusations made and if they accepted them the suspects

---

5. W. Stubbs. (1875) *Constitutional History.* Oxford, The Clarendon Press. vol. i. p. 438.

were arrested to face trial by ordeal. These presenting juries were the origin of the grand jury which developed into a body of 23 men who, meeting in secret, were to decide by a majority not if an accused was guilty but whether there was sufficient evidence to justify trial. Later, as will be seen, it was from the grand jury that members of the petty jury were selected to create the form of trial that replaced the ordeal.

William also abolished capital punishment. This was not out of humanitarian concern about the death penalty, however, since he replaced it with blinding, castration and other mutilations to the face and body in the belief that people who were thus maimed being seen at large would serve as a more lasting warning to potential criminals than death. Whether mutilation was the reason or not the incidence of serious crime was reduced by the time of William's own demise.

WILLIAM'S HEIRS

Following the death of the Conqueror outside Rouen on 9 September 1087 the succeeding reign of misrule by his son Rufus was one of cold comfort politically and was barren of new law. It was left to his younger son, Henry I (1100-1135), in his Coronation Charter to reaffirm English law by restoring the laws of Edward the Confessor together with, 'all the reforms which my father introduced with the consent of his barons.' What these laws and reforms were is not known despite this 'renewal'. But, significantly, the king's council was taking on flesh and, at the same time, was in the process of becoming a court of law. Henry was the first king to send judges through the counties to hear pleas of the Crown whilst the powerful in the land brought their disputes to him at Westminster. However, a treatise on the criminal law of the time, *Leges Henrici,* dealt with the administration of local courts and did not address in any detail the growth of royal justice. Henry also gave London its charter of freedom with its many privileges, an act which was followed for other cities and towns later.

The death penalty was restored and the king decreed that all thieves caught in the act should be hanged. According to the *Anglo-Saxon Chronicle* in Leicestershire on one day alone in the year 1124 Ralph Bassett, Henry's chief judge, sentenced 44 thieves to death by hanging, whilst six others lost their eyes and testicles.[6] Theft to the value of 12 pence or more also became a capital offence and remained so until 1827, despite the fall in the value of money during the intervening centuries.

---

6. *Anglo-Saxon Chronicle.* (1975 edn.) London, J.M. Dent & Sons Ltd. p. 254.

LAWLESSNESS

When Henry died the council set on the throne William's grandson, Stephen but his reign dragged into a struggle for power between him and the supporters of Henry's daughter Maud. The *Chronicle* also tells us that in Stephen's reign of civil war and anarchy (1135-54) a new low was reached in the use of torture. According to an English monk named Laud, of the monastery of Peterborough, the barons, unrestrained by the king, enhanced their wealth by wanton savagery against the unhappy people of the country. Innocent men and women were flung into the prisons of the barons where they were put to 'unspeakable tortures' in order to lay hands on their gold and silver. He continues:

> They hung them up by the feet and smoked them with foul smoke. They strung them up by the thumbs, or by the head, and hung coats of mail on their feet. They tied knotted cords round their heads and twisted it until it entered the brain. They put them in dungeons wherein were adders and snakes and toads and so destroyed them. Some they put into a short, narrow, shallow chest into which they put sharp stones; and they crushed the man in it until they had broken every bone in his body ... They plundered and burned villages. It lasted throughout the 19 years that Stephen was king, and always grew worse and worse.[7]

When the 'nineteen long winters of discontent', when men said 'Christ and his saints slept', was approaching its end in 1153, Archbishop Theobald managed to bring together the supporters of both Stephen and Maud and it was agreed that Stephen should be king for the rest of his life, but that Maud's son, Henry should succeed him. Stephen died the following year.

KING HENRY II (1154-1189)

Henry II and his successors are commonly known as the Angevin kings because they were descended from Geoffrey, Count of Anjou, who was Henry's father. It was fortunate for England that Stephen was succeeded by such a supreme legislator and administrator, so strong a king, as Henry II. Not that Henry consciously set out to change the face of English justice, but that is what he achieved with the form and content of both civil and criminal law. We are not here concerned with the momentous revolution he effected in the land law or its consequences but Henry made an equally significant impact on the administration of the criminal law. The truth is that the medieval political and economic conflicts were fought out on legal terrain and they are closely tied in with criminal justice which was then beginning to emerge in a more professional form as Henry centralised royal power.

---

7. *Ibid.* p. 263.

THOMAS À BECKETT

As a consequence of the Conqueror embracing the idea of separate ecclesiastical courts, under Henry II the king and the Church came into bitter conflict for the first time since the seventh century. Unlike the Anglo-Saxon kings, Henry was strong enough to challenge the power of the Church which saw itself as at least equal to the monarchy. The trouble really commenced, when Henry was still a young man and he called the Great Council of the Realm to meet at the royal palace of Clarendon in the New Forest in 1164. There the king demanded that the bishops agree to respect the customs of the land, which recently they had declined to accept, calling in aid their overriding duty to Rome or, as they put it, to God. Now they were required by the king to set their seals to a document containing 16 such customs—henceforth known as the Constitutions of Clarendon—which Henry claimed were only a restatement of the customs of his grandfather's time by which the Church had always abided in the past.

At this stage, to everyone's surprise Becket capitulated but only later to renege on his pledge. Among other things, the Constitutions laid down that if a cleric had confessed to a crime or been convicted, a church court or bishop would unfrock him and he would then be punished in a lay court. Henry was upholding royal custom and Becket the law of the Church, claiming that Henry's demand meant that a man would be punished twice for the same offence. This was a crucial issue on two counts. First, it is estimated that one in six of the population at the time was a cleric if the lower orders are included, and that many clerics were guilty of murder and rape. Secondly, if a cleric committed a serious crime it was only the secular courts that could impose an appropriate punishment, the penalties of the ecclesiastical courts being confined to suspension from office or banishment from the altar.

BENEFIT OF CLERGY

At the time the Church acted as a 'kingdom within a kingdom' with its own courts and, within its jurisdiction, answerable to the Pope and not English law. Henry argued that once a cleric had been defrocked he was no longer a clerk in holy orders and should be sent to a lay court for a punishment to fit the crime, and this was not being punished twice for the same offence. The subsequent murder of Becket in Canterbury Cathedral ensured his apparent triumph on the issue. That was undermined, however, because it caused Henry to accept the bizarre 'benefit if clergy' which, since it was used as an arbitrary measure of mercy which meant that criminals would go free, was to bedevil the penal law for centuries to come. As late as the nineteenth century Sir James Fitzjames Stephen, an eminent authority on the criminal law, was to claim that the benefit of clergy had for centuries reduced the administration of justice to a farce.[8] 'It fixed upon our criminal law', he wrote, 'a classification which for centuries made it impossible to reach a satisfactory analysis of offences or of penalties.'[9]

At all events, the clergy were now free of the jurisdiction of the lay courts. Instead, a 'criminous clerk', as he was called, would go before a bishop or his deputy where he could state on oath that he was innocent. In a reversion to early Anglo-Saxon law, if 12 compurgators supported him he was acquitted. If not, he was merely degraded or put to penance, even if he was guilty of murder. The definition of a cleric was already wide when later, in 1352, in the reign of Edward III, it was enacted by the statute *pro clero* that, 'all manner of clerks, as well secular as religious ... shall freely have and enjoy the privileges of the holy church.'[10] This meant that assistants to clerks, such as doorkeepers, exorcists and sub-deacons were henceforth to be treated as clergy.

For some reason the judges went even further and extended the meaning of the legislation to cover everyone who could read. Moreover, the only test made of literacy was an ability to read the first verse of the 51st psalm—appropriately known as the 'neck verse'—even if recited from memory by an illiterate person.[11] The verse reads:

Have mercy on me, O God, according to thy loving kindness; according to the multitude of thy tender mercies, blot out my transgressions.

It was even known for judges to send a prisoner who had been found guilty back to the cells to learn the verse before returning to the court to be set free.[12] A serjeant-at-law named Daniel apparently saved a convict's life by lending him his spectacles so that he might read the neck verse.[13] And on one occasion a Kent justice of the peace called out, as a prisoner claimed benefit of clergy, 'He will read as well as my horse!'[14]

It is apparent that this privilege would have startling consequences, as will be seen later. Thinking of it as a merciful mitigation of harsh punishments, which to some extent it was, Blackstone wrote that the law, 'in the course of a long and laborious process, extracted by noble alchemy rich medicines out of poisonous ingredients.'[15] Blackstone generally wore rose-tinted spectacles in regard to English criminal law,

8. J. F. Stephen. (1883) *A History of the Criminal Law of England.* London, Routledge/Thoemmes Press. vol. i. p. 463.

9. T. F. T. Plucknett. (1960) *Edward I and Criminal Law.* Cambridge, Cambridge University Press. p. 79.

10. 25 Edw. 3. st. 3, c.4.

11. A. K. R. Kiralfy. (1958) *Potter's Historical Introduction to English Law and its Institutions.* (4th edn.) London, Sweet & Maxwell. p. 362.

12. Sir Matthew Hale. (1736) *The History of the Pleas of the Crown.* London, E. & R. Nutt and Others. vol. ii. p. 379.

13. J. S. Cockburn. (1972) *A History of English Assizes, 1558-1714.* Cambridge, Cambridge University Press. p. 126.

14. J. A. Sharpe. (1985) 'Last Dying Speeches': Religion, Ideology, and Public Execution in Seventeenth-Century England.' 107 *Past and Present.* London, Past and Present Publishers. p. 167.

15. Sir William Blackstone. (1830) *The Commentaries on the Laws of England.* London, Thomas Tegg. vol. 4, p. 364.

however. In reality, large numbers of criminals escaped punishment, and the 'merciful mitigation' blunted any desire there might be to reform the otherwise harsh criminal law where death was the penalty for all felonies. Benefit could not be claimed by women, except nuns, until 1693[16] and, since it commuted hanging, it did not apply to treason, where the penalty was more severe, or to misdemeanours, where it was more lenient.

PLEAS OF THE CROWN

In regard to Henry's laws it is necessary to bear in mind that the kingdom was troubled by extreme violence and he was concerned to protect men's property and their lives. The Crusades were at their height and kept many noble landowners away from their lands for years at a time; as a consequence local authority was undermined. Crime was both brutal and rife following the civil war between King Stephen and Empress Maud and after Stephen's misrule, Henry was determined to tackle it.

Minor crimes could still be dealt with in the hundred courts and more serious crimes in the county courts. But with a great advance in criminal justice, Pleas of the Crown committed, 'against the peace of our lord the King, his Crown and dignity' were dealt with only by the king's judges on circuit or at Westminster. The more serious crimes, such as murder, were now prosecuted by the king and, in the lower courts, fines payable to the Crown took the place of the Anglo-Saxon system of compensation. The *Curia Regis,* convened in the *Aula Regis* of the king's palace, had gradually become a law court and was constantly enlarging its jurisdiction at the expense of the lower courts.

Whilst on the continent of Europe criminal trials continued to be held in secret and with torture widely used to extract confessions, Henry, the 'lawyer king', was transforming the criminal law of England from a divinely ordained system to a system based on evidence. He was unifying customary law and royal codes into the Common Law[17] by establishing a permanent body of professional judges, by increasing the number of circuits of itinerant judges and, with the Assize of Clarendon (1166)[18], introducing the seeds of the new mode of trial by jury. There was a strong shift away from Anglo-Saxon feuds and *wergild* to Angevin public prosecution, and from 'predominantly private resolution through monetary compensation to predominantly capital punishment at the hands of the Crown.'[19] From this time on a crime was seen not merely as a wrong against the victim but against the Crown,

16. 3 & 4 Will. and Mary. c. 9.
17. W. I. Warren. ((1973) *Henry II.* London, Eyre Methuen. p. 360-61.
18. 12 Hen. 2. c.1.
19. T. A. Green. (1988) 'A Retrospective on the Criminal Trial Jury, 1200-1800.' In J. S. Cockburn and T. A. Green (eds.) *Twelve Good Men and True: The Criminal Trial Jury in England, 1200-1800.* New Jersey. Princeton University Press. p. 359.

with the king as the symbolic victim who had to be revenged. It is also at this time that the old crimes of 'theft' and 'man-slaying' got the 'newer and more hateful name of *felony*.[20] This was soon extended to include other crimes but at the time the only felonies were rape, larceny, homicide, robbery, burglary and arson.

Apart from increasing Crown revenues, the reason for the change to revenge for the king appears to have been that if the government wanted criminals to be prosecuted it had to do so itself. As Theodore Plucknett put it:

> It was useless to depend upon injured parties or their kin to maintain the difficult procedure of bringing a criminal to justice. The chances were at least even that such proceedings would be used as a means of oppression by the powerful instead of a means of prosecution and redress by the victims of crime. As for the expectation that injured parties would bring 'appeals' and engage in judicial combat with murderers, thieves, highwaymen and such like, all experience showed that there was nothing to be expected from that quarter.[21]

Nevertheless, the Angevin monarchs would not have been exempt from the dubious motives attributed here to the 'powerful.' In any event, appeals of felony, where the accuser instigated the action himself and the Crown was not involved still remained. With this the person charged had the right to trial by battle either in person or with a champion to fight for him. As we have seen this was a Norman innovation and was not popular in England with the growing stress on the king's pleas of the Crown and presenting juries.

THE PRESENTING JURY

The first reference to the jury in criminal cases is in the Constitutions of Clarendon in 1164 where, in the case of a layman so rich and powerful that no individual dared appear against him, it was provided that, 'the sheriff shall cause 12 loyal men of the neighbourhood, or of the *vill*, to take an oath in the presence of the bishop that they will declare the truth about it.'[22]

This was followed two years later by the Assize of Clarendon as part of a royal campaign against crime and in an effort to unify the criminal law. Trial by compurgation was abolished and the private appeal of felony was supplemented by a new public process of trial in the name of the king for heinous crimes including murder, theft, robbery, arson and forgery. For these serious crimes mutilation was prescribed but it was only one of the punishments that were common at the time. For instance, in 1166 the sheriffs of London and Middlesex asked the exchequer to repay the cost

---

20. T. F. T. Plucknett. *Edward I and Criminal Law. Op. cit.* p. 48.
21. *Ibid.* p. 66.
22. W. Forsyth. (1852) *History of Trial by Jury.* London, John Parker. p. 195.

of 34 ordeals, 14 mutilations, 14 hangings and five duels.[23]

The Assize also provided that from each hundred 12 men of good repute and without criminal records, and four lawful men of every *vill*, were to report persons in the locality accused or notoriously suspected of serious crimes. If there were any, they were to be arrested and charged before the sheriff in the shire court or held until they could be brought before visiting royal justices. In either case they faced being sent to proof by the ordeal of cold water.[24]

The presenting jury exercised significant discretion in determining who would undergo the ordeal and, in doing so, broadly reflected, 'communal attitudes about the sorts of persons who ought to suffer capital punishment or the types of offences for which persons ought to suffer such punishment.'[25] They therefore gave medial verdicts. At no time did they act in the judicial capacity of a trial jury but even at this early stage they exercised a screening role in that they could decide not to proceed if an offence was insufficiently serious or the accused was of good fame. Even when they presented an accused, if they subsequently stated that he was 'not suspected', he would not be sent to the ordeal. In other words, they reported all those alleged to be criminals and then designated which of them they themselves suspected.[26]

But to be suspected by hundred jurors alone, i.e. without the four *vills*, there had to be supporting evidence of some kind beyond the mere suspicion of the presenter. For example:

> Andrew of Burwarton is suspected by the jurors of the death of a certain Hervey because he concealed himself on account of that death, and therefore let him purge himself by the judgment of water.[27]

In other words, by the 1190s a simple assertion of guilt by a presenting jury, even if based on local reputation, had become insufficient and the accused could be sent to the ordeal only if the hundred jury produced inculpatory evidence and confirmed that the accused was truly suspected, or if it and the townships joined in an assertion of suspicion based upon reputation.[28] This involvement of the local community thus pre-dated the trial jury, 'the adoption of which ought to be understood as a continuation and enhancement of traditional practices, not as a revolutionary step.'[29] Indeed, Susan Reynolds has shown that community decision-making had a

---

23. *Pipe Roll.* 12 Hen. 2, p. 131.

24. 12 Hen. 2 c.1.

25. T. A. Green. 'A Retrospective on the Criminal Trial Jury: 1200-1800.' *Op. cit.* p. 359.

26. R. D. Groot (1988) 'The Early-Thirteenth-Century Criminal Jury.' In Cockburn & Green. *Twelve Good Men and True. Op. cit.* pp. 5-6.

27. G. Wrottesley. (ed.) (1882) *Staffordshire Suits: Collections for a History of Staffordshire.* 3; 94. Cited by Groot *Ibid.* p. 6.

28. R. D. Groot. 'The Early-Thirteenth-Century Criminal Jury.' *Op. cit.* p. 16-17.

29. T. A. Green. 'A Retrospective on the Criminal Trial Jury. 1200-1800.' *Op. cit.* p. 363.

long history in England.[30] For instance, the councils of the Church were attended by representatives from each diocese; spokesmen for the town gave evidence before the Domesday commissioners; representatives of the hundreds and townships sat in the shire courts and on early presenting juries; they attended the justices in eyre; and other itinerant judges were assisted by knights elected by the counties under article 18 of *Magna Carta*. Nevertheless, whilst an appeal of felony—a private action—was still possible, suspected felons presented by the jury could be dealt with only by a royal appointed judge who had the power to send them to the ordeal.

THE KING'S JUSTICE

Henry I had encouraged the local communal courts and was, 'intent on strengthening shire justice rather then replacing it with royal' justice.[31] Henry II took a different approach and wanted justice centralised in the king's name, dealing with serious crimes as pronounced by the Assize of Clarendon. The punishments for these crimes were sanctioned by the state and any person indicted for them could be tried only by the judges of the king who claimed for him all the forfeitures and fines which they imposed. To cope with the increased business the Assize also provided that public gaols and prisoners' cages were to be built in all districts for those awaiting trial. These were not meant for permanent imprisonment since it was the duty of the judges to empty the gaols by awarding other punishments including death. In the absence of sufficient judges, however, the Assize of Clarendon was not rigorously enforced although it laid the basis for subsequent statutes.

Henry built up a new team of justices based on the *Curia Regis*[32] and known as 'justices in eyre'. Difficult cases would be adjourned from the county courts to be decided by the king and his justices and some were remitted to Westminster.

As we have seen, the presenting jury also 'presented' lists of people suspected of serious crimes who were to be imprisoned to await trial before the justices when they came to the shires. By the time of the Assize of Northampton (1176) there was a larger central judiciary to enforce the revised Assize of Clarendon. If an accused were properly presented he was sent to the ordeal of water and if he failed he lost a foot and his right hand and was banished from the realm. If he came through the ordeal safely he had to abjure the realm within 40 days[33] presumably because he was of ill-fame. This Assize also put the *Curia Regis* and the itinerant judges' circuits on a permanent footing and prepared the way for the criminal jurisdiction of the justices

30. S. Reynolds. (1997) *Kingdoms and Communities in Western Europe, 900–1300.* Oxford, Clarendon Press.
31. A. Harding. *The Law Courts of Medieval England. Op. cit.* p. 52.
32. M. Stenton. (1964) *English Justice Between the Norman Conquest and the Great Charter, 1066–1215.* Philadelphia, American Philosophical Society. pp. 73ff.
33. D. Douglas and G.W. Greenaway. (1953) *English Historical Documents.* London, Eyre and Spottiswoode (Publishers) Ltd. vol. ii, pp. 411–13.

in eyre. The elaborate Anglo-Saxon tariffs of compensation now 'disappeared with marvellous suddenness.'[34]

EYRES

In 1166, when Henry was endeavouring to strengthen the criminal law with the Assize of Clarendon, he sent two senior judges on a tour of the whole country to ensure that the provisions of the Assize were carried into effect and to co-ordinate six trial circuits which were to have over 20 judges. By 1180 the judges were known as justices in eyre and this led to the General Eyre which, as law court and itinerant government, over a period of years, visited each county in the realm to the dismay of law-abiding citizens as well as criminals. The higher clergy were present, the important men of the county attended and every local community was represented. Presenting juries were chosen. Local courts were suspended, all suits in the common pleas were brought before the justices, county administration was inquired into and the eyre dealt with all the outstanding criminal cases, which at the Eyre of Gloucester in 1221, for example, included 300 acts of homicide and 100 orders for outlawry. The latter figure illustrates the extent to which criminals were able to evade capture for their crimes when policing was almost non-existent.

Some examples of the matters dealt with at eyres can be gleaned from the record of Pleas of the Crown at the Bedfordshire Eyre held in 1202.[35] In the Hundred of Flitt, 'Stanard of Eye' was in mercy for not raising the hue and cry when his son was found dead and slain. In one case there is an early example of benefit of clergy. Henry Bussel appealed (prosecuted) Gilbert of Flitton for the murder of his brother John, to which he claimed Gilbert had confessed. Robert, the Dean of Bedford, craved 'court Christian' since Gilbert was a clerk and a subdeacon. In the Hundred of Rebornstoke, William of Morton and Simon Carpenter were outlawed for the death of Walter of Leigh, it being considered that they murdered him. In the same Hundred, Aubrey, the wife of Peter Crawe, appealed Oliver and Roland, brothers of the parson of Cranfield, for wounding her husband. She had not proceeded with the appeal and because her husband had died the jury were asked if he died of those wounds. They said he did not and the two men were set free.

In the borough of Bedford, Maud, wife of Hugh, was taken selling beer by a false gallon. Since she could not defend this she was fined two marks. In the hundred of Clifton, Robert of Sutton appealed Bonefand of Bedford for mutilating Robert's nephew Richard who died of his wounds. Bonefand attended the hearing, defended himself, and offered the king a mark to hold an inquest to determine whether he

---

34. Pollock & Maitland. (1898) *The History of English Law before the Time of Edward I.* Cambridge, Cambridge University Press. vol. ii. pp. 458ff.
35. F. W. Maitland. (ed.) (1888) *Select Pleas of the Crown. 1200-1225.* London, Bernard Quaritch.

was guilty or not. The jury decided he was not guilty and Bonefand was freed and Richard was arrested for his false appeal.

These are interesting cases taken from contemporary records but they do not reveal the full scope and power of the eyres. Apart from delivering the gaols, i.e. trying those who had earlier been arrested on suspicion of committing crimes in the area, an eyre also dealt with any misconduct brought to its notice including negligence by officials. These justices with their 'roll of secrets' and their 'book of death'[36] struck terror into the countryside, and technical errors in legal and administrative procedure, and slight inaccuracies in matters of detail, were made the excuse for fines on entire villages or even counties. Whole areas could be reduced to poverty and, in 1233 the men of Cornwall fled to the woods to avoid the forthcoming eyre.[37] However, the eyres were not only unpopular, they eventually became unnecessary as the powers of the judges of Assizes increased, and they ceased to be used in the first half of the fourteenth century.[38]

COMMON LAW

Henry II had, of course, been attempting to enforce a system of law and order but, like the Anglo-Saxon kings, he also saw the profitability of criminal justice in delivering revenues to the Crown. Hence, justice had to be paid for by those seeking it as well as by those breaking its rules. Henry's fees, forfeitures and fines were what replaced the old tariffs of compensation and fines. The king's judges became an established sight on their circuits and also at Westminster where the central court, the *Curia Regis,* was busy consolidating a criminal law common to the whole country. The criminal jurisdiction of the king with the Pleas of the Crown had taken hold nationwide. The *Curia* supervised other courts and was responsible for the consolidation of the Common Law. By 1178, or a little later, the Courts of King's Bench and Common Pleas, dealing with actions between subjects, had been established.

It was not usual, however, for ordinary criminal trials to be held before the *Curia* itself. They were dealt with by royal judges in eyre or sitting under special commissions known as 'oyez and terminer' and 'gaol delivery' which were issued at least twice a year for most counties. Under the first the commissioners had authority to hear and determine all treasons, felonies and misdemeanours which the grand jury presented to them. With gaol delivery they could try all prisoners who were in the county gaol when they arrived. The Commissioners had to include at least one Common Law judge or a serjeant and eminent laymen could also be included.[39]

---

36. *Ibid.*
37. Pollock & Maitland. *The History of English Law before the Time of Edward I. Op. cit.* vol. i, p. 202.
38. W. Holdsworth. (1956) *A History of English Law.* London, Methuen & Co. and Sweet & Maxwell. vol. i. p. 272.
39. Radcliffe and Cross. (1964) *The English Legal System.* London, Butterworths. p. 194.

At this time there was no legal distinction between murder and manslaughter. All homicides were murder except killing in self-defence or by accident, and even they needed a pardon from the king before the accused could be set free. But it was a step in the right direction when later, by c.9 of the Statute of Gloucester (1278), juries were required to state whether a homicide was murder or a killing by misadventure. If a slaying was in self-defence, the prisoner was generally pardoned but it was not necessarily a full pardon and he might have to wait in prison for it. As for punishments, murder still attracted the death penalty, a rapist would suffer castration and blinding and for arson the penalty was death by burning alive, as it was for a woman found guilty of any serious crime.

Hanging was the general mode of execution for murder, burglary, robbery and theft to the value of 12 pence or more, known as grand larceny. In the next century hanging was gradually extended to all felonies (which meant nearly all crimes). But status and gender also counted. Decapitation was regarded as a right reserved for the wealthy and burning at the stake was considered to be suitable for women. Felonies were considered somehow to be caused by the poisoned blood of the felon and his family and to merit death, with escheat of lands to the man's lord or the king. Other modes of execution were burial alive at Sandwich, being thrown from the cliffs at Dover, mutilation at Winchester and, at some ports, being tied to a stake below high water and being left to drown.[40] For petty larceny of money or goods worth less than 12 pence the punishments were whipping, the pillory or loss of an ear. For a second offence, if the ear had been taken, the second ear was removed and for a third offence the culprit was hanged. Thus were the two different degrees of theft that were created in 1109 dealt with by different punishments that were to persist for centuries to come.

For treason the punishment for a man was to have his heart, bowels and entrails torn out whilst he was still alive, then to be beheaded and cut into four with the head exhibited in some public place as a deterrent to others. It was said that a traitor should perish in torments that would make hell-fire come as a relief. In addition the lands of the executed man passed to the king. At this time treason could be committed against a man's lord as well as the king and it was never subject to the benefit of clergy.

Actions for adultery, incest and bigamy could not be pursued in the lay courts since they were solely within the jurisdiction of the Church. However, for embracing the Jewish religion, for heresy and for sorcery people were sent to death by burning at the stake. In these cases, which were really ecclesiastical offences, the Church believed itself to be threatened and ironically preferred the lay courts, which could impose condign punishments, to deal with them.

---

40. Pollock & Maitland. *The History of English Law Before the Time of Edward I. Op. cit.* vol. ii. p. 496.

THE EARLY TRIAL JURY

In 1215, after serious theological questioning, the Church at the fourth Lateran Council held in Rome forbade the clergy from participating in what it rather belatedly discovered was a barbaric practice. Although it was not abolished, this spelt the end of the ordeal. P. R. Hyams argues that the ordeal was brought to a slow end by social developments[41] but Robert Bartlett shows that it was flourishing in the eleventh and twelfth centuries.[42] In any event, it was abandoned in England by 1219.[43] This has been described as, 'the most important event in the history of the criminal jury' by necessitating a search for a successor to the most common method of proof in the English criminal process.[44] However, no obvious and suitable replacement was seen immediately. King Henry III was still a boy of nine and, left to themselves, the judges were unclear about what to do.

After some hesitation by the judges at a time when there was serious civil commotion, in January 1219 the king's council addressed a writ to the justices in eyre which told them that nothing had as yet been decided about replacing the ordeal.[45] In the interim, it continued, those suspected of serious crimes should be imprisoned without trial, though not to incur danger of life or limb; those whose crimes were less heinous should be made to abjure the realm, and those accused on minor offences should be released if they could find sureties to keep the peace. 'We have left', the writ concluded, 'to your discretion the observance of this aforesaid order … according to your own discretion and conscience.'

In regard to minor offences this meant that the council believed that there were accused persons who were not suspected and 'thus recognised and assumed the continuation of the older medial jury verdict, which had been the mechanism that distinguished the merely accused from the truly suspected.'[46] In general, however, many prisoners were either freed or temporarily imprisoned without any trial at all.

Such a situation could not last since the judges were faced with crowds of prisoners whom they were unable to try. No further writ followed from the council and, in the event, England turned to trial by jury at the same time as many European countries, where the rules of criminal law and procedure were more precise, adopted

41. P. R. Hyams. (1981) 'Trial by Ordeal: The Key to Proof in the Early Common Law.' In Morris S. Arnold & Others (eds) *On the Laws and Customs of England. Essays in Honour of Samuel E. Thorne.* Chapel Hill, The University of North Carolina Press. pp. 90, 101.

42. Robert Bartlett. (1986) *Trial by Fire and Water: The Medieval Judicial Ordeal.* Oxford, The Clarendon Press. pp. 42-3.

43. J. B. Thayer. (1898) *A Preliminary Thesis on Evidence at the Common Law.* Boston, Little, Brown and Company. p. 37.

44. R. D. Groot. 'The Early-Thirteenth-Century English Jury'. In Cockkburn and Green. *Twelve Good Men and True: The Criminal Trial Jury in England 1200-1800. Op. cit.* p. 3.

45. Patent Rolls. 1216-25, p. 186.

46. R. Groot. 'The Early-Thirteenth-Century Criminal Jury.' *Op. cit.* p. 11.

Roman forms of proof, 'which exalted the probative power of sworn eyewitness testimony and of the accused's confession, often coerced by torture.'[47] By this means, 'the law encouraged and, indeed, often required, the torture of the accused in order to produce a confession, which was considered of particularly high evidentiary value.'[48] According to Olson, the system of, 'roman-canonical proof constituted an evidentiary revolution, shifting the focus of evidencing to accurate fact finding. The same, however, cannot be said of the jury trial. Unlike the roman-canonical proofs, the jury trial, like the ordeal, aimed primarily at resolve. Moreover, it was a resolve that carried a sacerdotal meaning.'[49]

The important point is that although the continental *inquisitio* was available from this time, it was not adopted by English judges who followed Bracton's dictum that the law should go from precedent to precedent. In contrast, western Europe, long closer than England to Rome and its influences, developed the principles of the civil law by means of commentaries upon the text of the books of the celebrated Roman jurist, Justinian.

Since the more independent judges in England would not follow this example and take upon themselves the deciding of fact as well as law in a judicial inquisitorial manner, they began to offer the accused the opportunity of having 12 laymen from the presenting jury determine his guilt or innocence. This startling and momentous innovation meant that by their verdict these 12 men would have to decide the case, as up to a point they had already done when sending an accused before a judge and on to the ordeal. The necessity for torture was by-passed and the decision turned from the judgment of God to the conclusions of mortals. However, they were not required to give reasons for their decisions, their oath being sacrosanct like the ordeal and possibly, in practice, because there might be as many reasons as there were jurors. Equally, their verdict could not be challenged. Not simply because they were men of substance but because initially they were largely self-informing. Their decisions were regarded as 'proofs' like the ordeal, with no detailed inquiry into evidence. And, as with the ordeal, their verdict was inscrutable and remains so today.

Using community-established jurors was a means of legitimising the Angevin kings. As one writer has put it:

> At a time when the Continental sovereigns were looking to the theory of Roman law to strengthen their own pretensions to power, the English rulers had already achieved a high degree of centralisation of power in the hands of the royal government, As a result, English royal judges were able to administer justice all over the country and they soon superseded the

---

47. George Fisher. (1997) 'The Jury's Rise as Lie Detector.' New Haven, 107 *Yale Law Journal.* p. 587.
48. Barbara J. Shapiro. (1983) *Probability and Certainty in Seventeenth-Century England. A Study of the Relationships between Natural Science, Religion, History, Law and Literature.* New Jersey, Princeton University Press. p. 174.
49. Trisha Olson. (2000) 'Of Enchantment: The Passing of the Ordeals and the Rise of the Jury Trials.' New York, 50 *Syracuse Law Review.* p. 112.

local courts. Wherever the royal justice went, they used the jury .... as a means of determining facts. The jury system was therefore an instrument of royal power, and spread as rapidly and widely as the royal courts.[50]

Nevertheless, the defendant was putting himself into the hands of his local community. And at the time, juries exercised a significant degree of discretion based upon morals, justice and mercy. In a sense there was a continuation of community involvement in which, in the king's courts and at local and county level, lay judging was seen as an integral element of justice. It should be remembered, however, that not all members of the community could have been involved, and certainly were not after the Statute of Westminster II of 1285.[51] This introduced a property qualification in providing that jurors must own freeholds to an annual value of 20 shillings within their own county or 40 shillings outside it. These sums were raised to 40 shillings and 100 shillings respectively in 1293.

Standing before the court in the thirteenth century, the accused would be asked in what manner he would be tried. If, fearing the alternative of indefinite imprisonment, he answered, 'by my country' the jury would be assembled and would reach a verdict on the basis of their own knowledge of the circumstances of the case and that of their neighbours. They might act as witnesses providing information but they also had a duty to make inquiries of their neighbours, which as men of good standing they were well placed to do.[52] In what had become a quasi-judicial capacity they were to collect testimony, weigh it and state the net result in a verdict.[53] Clearly, by involving others in their assessments they were more than witnesses. As Holdsworth has written, they represented the sense of the community from which they were drawn.[54] And the finality of the jury's verdict may have arisen in part because the defendant had chosen to put himself in their hands. The consequence that the verdict was not open to challenge meant that jury discretion was an integral element in criminal justice from the beginning.[55]

However, trial by the local community could lead to, 'trial by local prejudice' and it is significant that as early as the middle of the thirteenth century Bracton had said that a defendant might object to the inclusion of false and malicious accusers on the trial jury.[56] Thus began jury challenges. The defendant might also object to jury trial altogether, but that involved certain disadvantages, as will shortly be seen.

---

50. M. Ploscowe. (1935) 'The Development of Present-Day Criminal Procedures in Europe and America.' 48 *Harvard Law Review*. Cambridge, Mass. Review Association. p. 455.

51. 13. Edw. c. 1.

52. Sir W. Holdsworth. *A History of English Law. Op. cit.* vol. i. p. 317.

53. Pollock & Maitland. *The History of English Law before the Reign of Edward I. Op. cit.* vol ii. pp. 624-5.

54. Holdsworth. *A History of English Law. Op. cit.* vol. i. p. 317.

55. T. A. Green. (1985) *Verdict According to Conscience. Perspectives on the English Criminal Trial Jury 1200-1800.* Chicago, University of Chicago Press. pp. 19-20.

56. Leonard W. Levy. (1999) *The Palladium of Justice: Origins of Trial by Jury.* Chicago, Ivan R. Dee. pp. 22, 63.

There was, however, some resistance to the incoming tide of jury trial because there was no presumption of innocence, which was a concept as yet still unknown-.[57] The defendant had to *prove* his innocence, unlike compurgation and the ordeals where he had an opportunity to clear himself without evidence and, as we have seen, was frequently successful. In a trial by jury he was in the hands of people in whose choice he had no voice and who were usually the very men who had presented the charge against him. Nevertheless, we must not be misled into believing the jury was unpopular. It was widely accepted as central to the criminal justice system, there were many acquittals and jury power became a potent, although fluctuating, influence over the centuries up to the present day.

HARD PRISON

As already noticed, when an accused person was in court and about to face trial he would be asked in what manner he would be tried. If he replied, 'by my country' that was the formula for trial by a jury along the lines mentioned above. Initially the jury decided by a majority vote. Only in 1367, in a landmark case,[58] did the courts decide that a majority verdict was void. The jury were now required to reach the same unambiguous judgment as the ordeal had done. As we have seen this had nothing to do with a presumption of innocence and, indeed, the period was devoid of any systematic analysis of legal ideas.[59]

If an accused of 'evil name' declined to be tried by his country, and stood mute when charged, it was provided by the Statute of Westminster I (1275)[60] that he be confined in a hard prison, *prison forte et dure,* until he changed his mind. However, two judges, Pateshull and Bereford, decided that harsher methods were required in order to 'persuade' prisoners to accept jury trial and changed 'hard prison' into 'hard pain', *peine forte et dure*.[61] According to Coke, this judgment of penance, as it was called, meant:

> The man or woman shall be remanded to the prison and laid there in some low and dark house where they shall lie naked on their backs on the bare earth. One arm shall be drawn to one part of the house with a cord and the other to another part. The same shall be done with their legs and there shall be laid upon their bodies iron and stone —as much as they shall bear and more ... The following day they shall have three morsels of barley bread without any drink. The second day they shall drink thrice of the water that is next to the prison (except running water), without any bread, and this shall be their diet until they be dead. So they shall die by weight, famine and cold.[62]

57. Charles L. Wells. (1914) 'Early Opposition to the Petty Jury in Criminal Cases.' 117 *The Law Quarterly Review*. London, Stevens & Son. pp. 97-110.
58. Y. B. Mich. 41. Edw. 3, 31 pl. 36.
59. T. F. T. Plucknett. *Edward I and Criminal Law. Op. cit.* p. 7.
60. 3 Edw. 1, c. 12.
61. A. K. R. Kiralfy. *Potter's Historical Introduction to English Law. Op. cit.* p. 247.
62. Sir Edward Coke. (1797) 2 *Institute*. London, E. & R. Brooke. p. 179.

A person's reason for suffering this frightful, and often prolonged death, was that his or her lands and goods passed to their family, instead of being forfeit to the king if they were tried and found guilty. This punishment applied to women as well as men but not men or women found guilty of the crime of treason for which staying mute meant the even more barbaric executions reserved for that crime.

It is often said that this was the only form of torture known in England prior to the Tudor and Stuart reigns. But mutilation was expressly provided for by the Assizes of Clarendon and Northampton, although this was as a punishment after trial and not to extract a confession as on the continent. At no time did torture in that sense become institutionalised in England.[63]

Nevertheless, if a judge considered a jury verdict to be perverse he could fine or imprison the jurors in an attempt to get them to change their minds. This went some way to ensuring Crown control over juries but was to be seen mostly in state trials for treason whilst in felony trials juries retained a great deal of independence and power. A further check on Crown influence over criminal trials was provided by Bracton's dictum that although the king was below no man he was below God and the law.[64] Henry Bracton was a judge of the *coram rege* court (later the King's Bench) from 1245-1250 and again from 1253-1257. He produced, or edited, the long treatise, *De Legibus Et Consuetudinibus*, (Of the Laws and Customs of England) which described the whole of English law of the time, a task not undertaken again until Blackstone's *Commentaries* in the eighteenth century. It was the most famous medieval law book which Maitland called, 'the crown and flower of English medieval jurisprudence.'[65] Nevertheless, the power of the king remained immense, even though in theory he was subject to Chapters 39 and 40 of *Magna Carta* (1215). These provided that no free man was to be arrested, imprisoned, outlawed or banished except by the lawful judgment of his equals or by law and that the king might not sell or refuse or delay right or justice.[66]

BIRTH OF THE LEGAL PROFESSION

Lawyers of a kind, known as narrators, existed as early as 1230[67] but it was during the long reign of Edward I (1272-1307) that a legal profession became established in England. They were recognised by statute in 1275, when it was decreed by the Statute of Westminster I, that lawyers found guilty of deceit should be punished.[68]

63. J. H. Langbein. (1977) *Torture and the Law of Proof: Europe and England in the Ancien Regime.* Chicago, University of Chicago Press. p. 4.
64. *De Legibus.* Lib. Iii. F. 118, c.1250.
65. Pollock & Maitland. *The History of English Law Before the Time of Edward I. Op. cit.* vol. i. p. 206.
66. Henry Marsh. (1971) *Documents of Liberty.* Newton Abbot, David and Charles (Publishers) Ltd. p. 46.
67. J. H. Baker. (1979) *An Introduction to English Legal History.* London, Butterworths. p. 135.
68. Statute of Westminster I. (1275) c, 29.

But an Ordinance of 1292 conferred full status on them when it instructed the judges to provide a certain number of 'apprentices and attorneys' in the place of clerical practitioners in the courts.[69] and it was about this time that the Inns of Court were founded in London. Edward has been termed the 'English Justinian'. That was not because he followed Justinian in codifying the law or because his laws were based on Roman law but it emphasised the importance and permanence of his legislation.[70]

Courts that originated in Anglo-Saxon times still existed but were declining in influence. As Edward ascended the throne, circuits for assize hearings were emerging and four circuits were securely established 20 years later. In 1299 the statute *De Finibus Levatis* gave assize justices the duty of delivering gaols.[71] Of growing significance were the central courts of royal justice, the King's Bench and the Court of Common Pleas as well as the itinerant justices of their eyres. Statutes were now being enacted more regularly and the need for a legal profession was becoming apparent. Edward wanted to retain ultimate control, however, and gave the task of recruiting the profession to his judges and the serjeants-at-law who were selected by the king on the recommendation of the judges. Furthermore, only the serjeants, who as the leading counsel were known as 'servants-of-the king' could be elevated to the bench. Royal control had to be tight, however, and on the king's return from Gascony in 1289 he was faced with serious accusations against many of the judges whom he was obliged to dismiss.[72]

Nonetheless, the arguments of the serjeants in court and their cases were reported in the Year Books for use as precedents and they thus 'made' the Common Law. According to Fortescue, English lawyers were the wealthiest advocates in the world.[73] The ordinary lawyers were divided between pleaders and attorneys. At this time a pleader stood next to his client in court and spoke for him, whilst an attorney represented his client who might not attend the court but would be bound by what his attorney said or agreed to on his behalf. This was a division later solidified into court operatives (barristers) and office operatives (solicitors). It was from the ranks of the pleaders that serjeants were drawn and, if the king chose, they could be imprisoned for collusive or deceitful practice. In lively courtroom scenes pleaders proved to be vigorous advocates and soon commenced the practice of citing and distinguishing earlier cases. They also played a vital role in teaching students at the four Inns of Court and the ten lesser Inns of Chancery. As part of their education the students frequented court to listen to cases and take notes of likely precedents. They

69. T.T. Daniell. (1976) *The Lawyers: The Inns of Court: The Home of the Common Law.* London, Wildy & Sons Limited. pp. 6-7.

70. W. Stubbs. (1906) (4th edn) *The Constitutional History of England.* Oxford, Oxford, Oxford University Press. vol. ii. p. 109.

71. M. Prestwich. (1988) *Edward I.* London, Guild Publishing. p. 290.

72. *Ibid.* p. 267.

73. J. Fortescue. (1470) *De Laudibus.* c. 124.

also performed their own mock trials known as 'moots' and attended lectures.

The Inns of Court were born when the Court of Common Pleas was settled at Westminster and the lawyers formed themselves into guilds and purchased an area of land north of the Thames between the cities of London and Westminster. This led to the creation of Lincoln's Inn, Gray's Inn, Middle Temple and Inner Temple together with the Inns of Chancery. Each Inn had chambers where the lawyers could reside and the whole system has survived to the present day. Of great significance for the survival, growth and independence of the Common Law in face of the revival and potential penetration of Roman law, was the fact that, unlike students at the universities, the students at the Inns of Court[74] were taught English law, based to an ever-increasing extent on precedents in earlier cases, and not canon law. And, only those called to the bar were allowed by the judges to practise in the courts. However, it should always be remembered that in criminal trials the accused could not have a lawyer to defend him in cases of felony—where the penalty was death.

CRIME AND LAWS UNDER EDWARD I (1239-1307)

Edward came to the throne in 1272. He supported Simon de Montfort in 1259 but later fought against him and for his father, Henry III, at the battle of Lewes (1264). He finally defeated Montfort at Evesham a year later and restored royal power. After the experience with Montfort, and with constant wars with Scotland and France and in Wales that required financing, he called regular Parliaments and used legislation to strengthen royal control over the court system and reformed the feudal land law.

Edward was acutely aware of the importance of maintaining law and order and was distressed at what he saw of its serious breakdown at the end of his reign. It was during his reign that *peine et forte dure* was introduced, crime was perceived as endemic and the Statute of Westminster I (1275) called upon all men to join in the pursuit and arrest of felons. The Statute of Westminster II (1285)[75] was remarkable in that it touched upon almost every aspect of the law. A good many of its 50 chapters dealt with complex issues of land law but dealing with criminal law it provided for imprisonment for a false accusation of homicide or other felony, burning to death for arson and loss of life by hanging for rape. Indeed, as shown earlier, the only felonies at this time were homicide, larceny, robbery, burglary, arson and rape.

In the same year of 1285 the Statute of Winchester was enacted.[76] It was principally concerned with urban crime and, for the first time, stated that statutory penal-

---

74. Coke said of the Inns that they 'altogether do make the most famous universities for profession of law only, or of any human science, that is in the world, and advanceth itself above all others.' (1602) *Reports*. Preface. Dublin, J. Moore.

75. M. Prestwich. *Edward I. Op. cit.* p. 279.

76. 3 Edw. I, c. 1.

ties were more effective than the sanction of an oath. It claimed in its preamble that crime was occurring more frequently than in the past and that juries were failing to indict felons. Local communities were, therefore, to be made responsible for losses arising from robberies. It also reaffirmed the customary laws in regard to 'watch and ward' to give more security in cities and towns. 'Watch' was the duty of constables to apprehend rioters and robbers by night; 'ward' by day. Roads were to be widened with a space of 200 feet to be cleared on each side of every highway, and within the same number of feet, no dykes were to be dug out of fear that criminals would be able to lurk in them. And, of great importance for the future administration of the law, 'keepers of the peace' were introduced. How far these measures were effective is hard to say. As in the present day, court statistics reveal how much crime was prosecuted not how much took place.

In fact, in certain respects Edward's imposition of stiffer penalties did little to deter crime since it made it harder to obtain accusations and convictions.[77] For instance, prior to the Westminster statutes cases of rape were quite common. Once proved there might be a small fine and frequently the parties concerned would agree to marry. In one case of seduction, rather than rape, the accused man was, 'given the choice of death, kissing the girl's backside or marriage' and chose the third option.[78] The changes made in the law with a statutory period of imprisonment for rape made the courts reluctant to convict rapists.

The Westminster statutes also had their effect on juries. Thomas A. Green concludes that the great majority of defendants in felony trials in the thirteenth and fourteenth centuries were acquitted by conscious jury nullification where they often considered the sanction too severe.[79] And another change in the law may have assisted criminals. An ordinance of 1293 introduced a form of action for cases of conspiracy to hinder justice. Hence, when a defendant was acquitted he could allege malice in the plaintiff. This may have made plaintiffs think very seriously before making accusations until the law was changed in 1304.[80]

TRAILBASTON COMMISSIONS

At the beginning of the fourteenth century violent affrays were becoming commonplace. Royal officials were assaulted, men were kidnapped, towns besieged and armed bands, often led by noblemen roamed the countryside pillaging, murdering

---

77. M. Prestwich. *Edward I. Op. cit.* pp. 281-2.
78. J. B. Post. (1978) 'Ravishment of Women and the Statute of Westminster.' In J.H. Baker (ed) .*Legal Records and the Historian.* London, Royal Historical Society. p. 155.
79. T. A. Green. *Verdict According to Conscience. Perspectives on the English Criminal Jury Trial 1200- 1800. Op. cit.* p. 34.
80. M. Prestwich. *Edward I. Op. cit.* p. 284.

and setting houses on fire.[81] Contributing factors were peasant land-hunger and seigniorial oppression which led to a widespread breakdown of manorial discipline at all levels and a serious collapse of public order.[82] The response of government in 1304 was to commence a series of *ad hoc* Trailbaston Commissions, named after the bastons or staves carried by criminal gangs, in Lincoln, London and other areas.[83]

These special commissions were also charged to deal with those who threatened jurors to prevent them telling the truth and those who, 'by reason of their power and state,' protected criminals in return for fees.[84] Such commissions did not survive the fourteenth century but the evidence of the Lincolnshire trailbaston proceedings in 1328 has been studied by McLane and is useful in revealing juror attitudes towards local disorder at that time.[85]

The Lincolnshire commission was composed of a judge of the Court of Common Pleas, a serjeant-at-law and two local magnates. They commenced their sittings at Lincoln on 6 June when juries began to make their presentments.[86] A total of 248 men have been identified as jurors sitting in court during the sessions of June and July 1328. Eighteen served both on presentment and trial juries (an interestingly low number for the time), another 148 only on presentment juries and 82 others only on trial juries.[87] Fifty-three per cent of the offences dealt with were felonies, 27 per cent were trespasses committed by non-officials and 20 per cent trespasses by local and royal officials.[88] The last indicates considerable corruption by those holding power of one kind or another over others.

Apprehending offenders was a serious problem and in Lincolnshire at this time only one-third of the accused were successfully brought before royal justices to answer the charges against them. When they were tried, trespassers found guilty were usually imprisoned for a brief period and then released after being fined, the fine being levied according to the ability of the accused to pay rather than the seriousness of the offence. For instance:

81. *Ibid.* p. 285. and J, Hostettler. (1994) *The Politics of Punishment.* Chichester, Barry Rose Law Publishers. p. 45 .

82. Colin Platt. (1978) *Medieval England.* London, Book Club Associates. p. 108.

83. See, for example, R.B. Pugh. (1975) *Calendar of London Trailbaston Trials under Commissions of 1305 and 1306.* HMSO.

84. B. W. McLane. (1988) 'Juror Attitudes to Local Disorder: The Evidence of the 1328 Lincolnshire Trailbaston Proceedings.' In Cockburn an Green, *Twelve Good Men and True: The Criminal Trial Jury in England 1200-1800.* New Jersey, Princeton University Press. p. 40.

85. *Ibid.*

86. The Public Record Office. File JUST1/516.

87. McLane. 'Juror Attitudes to Local Disorder.' *Op. cit.* p. 41.

88. *Ibid.* p. 43.

Ralph Payknave was accused in six presentments of assault, false imprisonment and extortion, as well as being a 'common malefactor,' while Hugh Tyler was presented only once on a charge of conspiracy. Yet Tyler was fined £10 and Payknave only 40 pence. The reason, no doubt, was that Payknave was of moderate means in the city of Lincoln and Tyler was one of the city's wealthiest citizens.[89]

Felony convictions, on the other hand, were punishable with execution, although only 18 per cent of the alleged felons who were tried were found guilty and few of those were hanged. The remainder were acquitted and released.[90] As an extraordinary 72 per cent of those accused of felony did not appear and were outlawed, it is possible that those who did attend court were innocent or the jury could not decide if they were guilty.[91] Apparently trial jurors, at least in trailbaston cases, were largely no longer self-informing by this time, many of them travelling ten or more miles away from the scene of the alleged crime.[92] Or perhaps they thought the penalty of death was too high for the crime, such as, for example, homicide without malice aforethought. Moreover, Green suggests that, 'from the community's point of view' it was legitimate for a violent attack to be met with a violent response. 'A man whose life was threatened did not have to seek some means of escape; indeed, he need not do so though he was not in danger of losing his life,'[93]

ORIGIN OF JUSTICES OF THE PEACE

Another problem for the king was the power of the sheriffs who had grown over-mighty and corrupt. In order to circumvent them the king created a new commission made up of local gentry who were charged with keeping the peace. At first they only held prisoners in custody until they could bring them before the itinerant royal justices who delivered the gaols. But by 1344 they had acquired the authority to try and punish prisoners and by the Statute of Westminster (1361)[94] they became officially 'Justices of the Peace', as they remain today. The statute provided,

That in every shire of England shall be assigned for the keeping of the peace one lord, and with him three or four of the most worthy in the shire, with some learned in the law; and they shall have power to restrain the offenders, rioters, and all other barrators, and to pursue, take, and chastise them according to their trespass or offence; and to cause them to be imprisoned and duly punished according to the laws and customs of the realm, and according to what shall seem best to them to do by their discretions and good deliberation...

---

89. *Ibid.* p. 54.
90. *Ibid.*
91. *Ibid.* p. 56.
92. *Ibid.*
93. T. A. Green. *Verdict According to Conscience. Op. cit.* p. 38.
94. 34 Edw. 3. c.1.

This led to an end to the jurisdiction of the hundred and county courts, although they were not formally abolished until 1867. As the eyres were replaced, the justices became the administrative, legal and political deputies of the Crown in the counties, under the direct control of the king, who appointed them, and his council. By this time the Trailbaston Commissions were a thing of the past and justices had been given the power to try felonies.

CHAPTER 4

Criminal Law in Medieval and Early Modern England

Substantive law was now being more clearly defined and will be dealt with here and on later occasions when it underwent substantial changes.

TREASON

In general, the crime of treason involves the violation of the allegiance due from the subject to the sovereign as supreme head of state. It might appear that to define this in legal terms would present little difficulty. Indeed, because treason was regarded as the most heinous offence in the calendar of crimes it was one of the first to be defined by statute in the Middle Ages. However, later statutes, and interpretations by the judges, led to 'constructive treasons' and a great many problems.

The kings of England in medieval times saw treason as the most foul offence since it threatened their thrones. The times were dangerous and the Crown was still not powerful enough to prevent continuing blood-feuds, executions and arbitrary punishments among powerful barons at the head of large bodies of armed retainers. They posed a constant threat to the king's peace and sometimes attempted to exercise royal power.

It is often claimed that the Statute of Treasons of 1352[1], passed in the first Parliament to sit after the Black Death, was enacted to preserve the land of the barons from Edward III. Certainly the king's justices were securing widespread forfeitures by multiplying new treasons that held any thing to be treason which directly or indirectly diminished the king's dignity or his prerogative. The forfeitures took the property of traitors that would otherwise have escheated to the mesne lords for felony. However, John Bellamy indicates a clear division between historians on whether the design was legal, to settle the rules about forfeiture in the king's favour, or political, to prevent reckless royal charges and arbitrary punishments which were ruining so many noble families. As an example of the latter, in one case in 1348, in Edward's reign, a knight of Hertfordshire, Sir John Gerberge, was adjudged a traitor for forcibly detaining a man until he paid him £90, this being deemed by the court as an attempt to exercise royal power. 'Perhaps,' Bellamy writes, no English statute of the late Middle Ages has yielded its secrets more reluctantly to the historian than the Treason Act of 1352.'[2]

---

1. 25 Edw. 3. st, 5. c.2.
2. J. G. Bellamy. (1970) *The Law of Treason in England in the Later Middle Ages*. London, Cambridge University Press. pp. 59–60.

Yet, however that may be, this famous statute notably codified and entirely replaced the Common Law of treason, severely narrowed earlier explanations of treason and, significantly, went on to provide that any extensions of its own definition should be made only in Parliament. The statute made treason consist of:

a. compassing or imagining the death of the king, his consort, or his eldest son; violating his consort, or eldest unmarried daughter, or the wife of his eldest son;

b. levying war against the king in his realm, or adhering to his enemies in his realm, giving them aid and comfort in the realm or elsewhere, if proved by open deed;

c. forging the great seal or the coinage, and knowingly importing or uttering false coin; and

d. slaying the treasurer, chancellor or judges while sitting in courts.

Each of these acts involved forfeiture of life, in the brutal manner reserved for treason, as well as land and goods to the Crown. As will be seen later, with the decay of feudalism and the emergence with the Tudors of the nation state headed by an all-powerful monarch, the 'imagining' of article (a) and the 'open deed' of article (b) were to prove a rich source of legal construction. This enabled the statute to be widened in scope and used by the state in succeeding ages as a means of wide-ranging political control. In fact, important treason cases were tried not at gaol delivery but by commissioners of oyer and terminer with jurors carefully chosen and it was very rare for a person accused of treason to be acquitted. Furthermore, over the centuries the Act was closely associated with the laws of sedition and riot in efforts to suppress grassroots political opposition to the government of the day.

To secure the royal title of Henry VIII, Thomas Cromwell, at the instigation of the king, secured a Treason Act in 1534 that contained the first definition of treason since the statute of Edward I. Although the Act was short it set out three new treasons. Attempting the death of the king or queen by an overt act was enlarged to include a desire or attempt to cause them bodily harm even if maliciously expressed in words instead of writing. Secondly, it became treason slanderously to call the king, in writing or spoken words, a heretic, tyrant or usurper of the Crown. Thirdly, detention of royal castles, ships and munitions was included in the meaning of 'levying war'. The Act silenced criticism of Henry's adoption of spiritual power and enabled the government to enforce the Oath of Succession on penalty of death.

Under the Act Henry Marpurley, a gentleman of London, was indicted in October 1537 for saying. ' I set not a pudding by the king's broad seal, and all his charters be not worth a rush.' And, Harry Weston of Hanham in Gloucestershire, was indicted in May 1538 for getting a priest to tell the people to disregard all preaching of new fashions, 'for the old fashion will come again.' Both men had their indictments quashed in the King's Bench but only on technicalities.[3] That spoken words alone could constitute treason remained on the statute book. The Act was repealed in 1547 but treason by speech remained the law, as will be seen.

As a consequence of Henry VIII's enlargement of the scope of the law of treason, and the increased severity of the criminal law, some 72,000 persons were executed during his reign, according to John Stow in his *Survey of London,* published in 1601. The most prominent of these was Sir Thomas Moore, former lord chancellor and famous Renaissance figure, described by the humanist, Erasmus, as a 'holy and righteous judge.' Moore had doubts about the royal supremacy over the Church and, although he would not deny the supremacy directly, he was found guilty of high treason and beheaded.

When Henry's successor, the young Protestant King Edward VI, died in the Summer of 1553 efforts were made by the Duke of Northumberland to secure the throne for his daughter-in-law Lady Jane Grey in place of Edward's Roman Catholic sister Mary Tudor. However, with the active assistance of Sir Nicholas Throckmorton, Mary was spirited away to Catholic friends in Norfolk where she at once declared herself queen. The people rallied to her cause, Northumberland's army deserted him and he was taken prisoner and executed.

Later, Mary announced her intention of marrying Philip of Spain which would mean absolute submission to the Pope and an end to the Reformation in England. As a consequence, Sir Thomas Wyat led a rising in Kent and proceeded to London. However, when he arrived the gates were closed against him and he was arrested and taken to the Tower of London. There he was tortured for evidence against Princess Elizabeth who, knowing of the rebellion in advance but probably not supporting it, was also incarcerated in the Tower for a short period. Wyat was executed for treason on 11 April 1554 declaring that Elizabeth and Throckmorton had no part in his treason. Mary married Philip on 20 July and in the next three years sent to the stake some 300 Protestant martyrs including Archbishop Cranmer, although not for treason.

Six days after the execution of Wyat, Throckmorton, as an alleged supporter of Wyat, was also tried on a charge of high treason for imagining the death of the queen, levying war in the realm and adhering to the queen's enemies. The case was heard at the Guildhall before Sir Thomas Bromley, the Lord Chief Justice, Sir Thomas White, the Lord Mayor of London, an assortment of earls and knights and a jury. Despite his plea of innocence, the defendant was not permitted to call witnesses in his defence and one, John Fitzwilliams, who had the temerity to present himself anyway was peremptorily sent away by the judges. At the time defence witnesses in state trials were not allowed to give evidence as it was held that to do so would be to

---

3. G. R. Elton. (1972) *Policy and Police: The Enforcement of the Reformation in the Age of Thomas Cromwell.* Cambridge, Cambridge University Press. pp. 286-7.

testify against the monarch in whose name the proceedings were brought. Throckmorton pointed out to the judges that Queen Mary herself had enjoined that:

> Notwithstanding the old error amongst you which did not admit any witness to speak or other matter to be heard in the favour of the adversary, her majesty being party, her highness's pleasure was that whatsoever could be brought in favour of the subject should be admitted to be heard.

Bromley replied that Throckmorton had no reason for complaint since he had been allowed to say as much as he wanted.[4]

Only one witness appeared for the prosecution, a Cuthbert Vaughan who was under sentence of death for his part in Wyat's rebellion. Throckmorton protested that, by a statute of Edward VI, the law of treason required that at least two witnesses be brought face to face with the prisoner.[5] Here, he said, we have but one and he a condemned man whose testimony was worthless as he meant to save his own life. But to no avail. Faced with this unanswerable legal objection the court simply ignored it. However, to the surprise and chagrin of the judges, the jury returned a verdict of, not guilty. For this they were committed to prison charged with arriving at a 'perverse verdict'.[6] Four of them then accepted that they had offended and were released. Regardless of the effect on their families, the remaining eight had their homes sealed up and were kept in prison for six months. At the end of that time they were taken to the Star Chamber. There, the foreman and two others were ordered to pay the astronomical sum of £2,000 each within a fortnight and the other five 1,000 marks each.[7] In the event, six weeks later five jurors were discharged on paying £220 each and nine days later the rest on paying £60 each. Still huge sums at the time. The effect on potential jurors must have been considerable and Throckmorton was one of only two Tudor subjects acquitted on charges of treason. He went on to become a favourite of Queen Elizabeth who sent him to be her ambassador, first to Paris and afterwards to Scotland

MURDER

By the time of Coke's *Institutes,* the criminal law of the early sixteenth century comprised eleven Common Law offences enumerated by Bracton and about 30 statutory felonies and as many misdemeanours. Still a very small corpus of law by later standards, but developing fast and already a lot of crimes compared with the days of Henry III when the criminal law consisted of only Bracton's eleven offences, almost

---

4. *State Trials.* i. pp. 887-8.
5. A requirement not dispensed with until the Treason Act, 1945.
6. *State Trials. Op. cit.*
7. An English mark was worth 13/4d. (66.8p).

all of which were capital. [8]

After treason the most serious crime was murder, one of the categories of the generic term 'homicide'. Homicide is the killing of one human being by another. It has always held a particular fascination for society, but it is difficult to define for penal purposes owing to the great variety of circumstances and intentions by which death can be caused. In fact, Stephen listed seven forms of homicide of which only three were punishable as crimes in England.[9] However, in Anglo-Saxon times killing either wilfully or accidentally had the same consequences, at first the blood feud and later the payment of *wergild*. Later, in medieval England every homicide was a crime and a plea of the Crown to be dealt with in the royal courts. Even by the sixteenth century every person charged with murder was considered to have acted with malice. Only gradually was it accepted that a killing could be the result of an accident, self-defence or provocation.

The general source of confusion on whether homicide is culpable or excusable is revealed by the age-old debate on the topic which constantly fluctuates with changes in society. Differences in ideas of morality, changing fashions, weapons, and economic developments, such as the growth of urban crime and traffic, have all played a part. Even what constitutes the crime of murder, which might be considered simple to define, has undergone considerable variation over the course of time and has not been finally settled to this day. Although section 6 of the Offences Against the Person Act of 1861 actually defined murder, it was repealed by the Indictments Act of 1915.

The first true treatise of English law, was *Tractabus de legibus consuetudininibus regeni Angliae*. Meaning 'treatise on the laws and customs of the realm of England' it is popularly known as *Glanvill* after the warrior, statesman and lawyer who was Chief Justiciar to Henry II, although it was probably written by his nephew and secretary, Hubert Walter.[10] Glanvill's date of birth is unknown but he died at the siege of Acra, Palestine in 1190. His treatise indicated that in the late twelfth century murder was defined as killing by secrecy or stealth where there were no witnesses and the identity of the killer was unknown. Other killings were collected together as simple homicide (*simplex homicidium*). In Bracton's time (c.1210-1268) murder still meant the same thing. Homicide was not defined separately. According to Pollock and Maitland, 'As the prosecutor for a *murdrum* only a near kinsman of the slain may appear, while any one connected with the slain by blood, homage or lordship may take action if there has been open homicide.' They continue that the point of distinction seemed to be that, 'normally an appellor must declare that he

---

8. J. Hostettler. (1992) *The Politics of Criminal Law; Reform in the Nineteenth Century.* Chichester, Barry Rose Law Publishers. p. 18.

9. J. F. Stephen. (1883) *A History of the Criminal Law of England.* London, Macmillan. vol. iii. p. 19.

10. Glanvill. (c. 1187) *The Treatise on the Laws and Customs of the Realm of England.* See George E. Woodbine (ed) (1932) *Glanvill: De Legibus.* New Haven, Yale Historical Publications.

saw the crime committed, but that, this being impossible in the case of a *murdrum*, very close kinsmen are allowed to take action without protesting that they were eye-witnesses of the deed.'[11]

Murder was one of the crimes mentioned in both the Assize of Clarendon of 1166 and the Assize of Northampton in 1176 and thereafter the word was not used officially for over a century. However, it was used by both Glanvill and Bracton and to them it meant a secret killing by intention and not by accident. By the early thirteenth century it seems that juries could take note of misadventure and self-defence provided there was no malice. But in the fourteenth century murder and homicide appeared as crimes to be dealt with by commissions of oyez and terminer and trail-bastons. And, in 1347 the House of Commons complained of the too frequent issue of pardons that had much encouraged murderers, homicides and other felonies.[12] This was followed, in 1390, by a statute which defined murder as killing by *malice prépensé* and endeavoured to make it unpardonable.[13] By inference other forms of culpable homicide could not be called murder and, later, they acquired the name manslaughter. Finally, by statute in 1547, Parliament turned an administrative difference into one of substance by withdrawing benefit of clergy from murder.[14] By this time it was accepted that not all culpable killings should be treated as murder.

The modes of killing described by Coke included poison, any weapon whether sharp or blunt or a gun or crossbow, smothering, suffocating, strangling, drowning, burning and leaving a sick man in the cold.[15] Poison was considered so odious (and, perhaps, relatively easy to administer) that by statute its use to kill was made high treason and subject to a more lingering death than at Common Law, namely boiling to death in hot water.[16] According to Coke, a young woman named Margaret Davy was done to death for the 'poisoning of her mistris' and some others were also boiled to death in Smithfield. However, the Act was too severe to last long and was repealed by Elizabeth I.

For Coke, 'There is no difference between Murder and Manslaughter, but that the one is upon malice forethought, and the other upon a sudden occasion.'[17] Malice forethought, he said, was, 'compassing to kill, wound, or beat another and doing so *sedato animo.*' Malice was also to be implied in three cases. First, in regard to the manner of the deed, i.e. without provocation, or by poisoning, including by the 'powder of spiders.' Secondly, in regard to the person slain as, for example, a magis-

11. Pollock & Maitland. (1968) *The History of English Law Before the Time of Edward I.* Cambridge, Cambridge University Press. vol. ii. p. 486.
12. J. M. Kaye. (1967) 'The Early History of Murder and Manslaughter' 83 *The Law Quarterly Review.* London, Stevens and Sons Limited. p. 378.
13. 13. Ric. II. St. 2, c.1.
14. J. M. Kaye. 'The Early History of Murder and Manslaughter'. *Op. cit.* p. 368.
15. Sir. E. Coke. (16664) 3 *Institute.* London, E. & R. Brooke. p. 47.
16. 22 Hen. 8. c. 9.
17. Coke. 3 *Institute. Op. cit.* pp. 55–6.

trate or any officer endeavouring to serve a warrant. Thirdly, in regard to the person killing as, for instance, if a person killed in the course of robbery.

Most subsequent problems arising on malice aforethought seem to stem from Coke's definition of implied malice. It had inherent contradictions which should have made later writers and judges more wary of accepting it uncritically than was to be the case. The first example of implied malice given by Coke was killing without provocation or by poisoning. No malice at all could exist if a killing was by accident without provocation, and in the examples he gave there was intent so the malice must have been express. Similarly, Coke's second and third examples of malice implied by law could also be included in his definition of express malice. The problem arose because Coke's definition of express malice was based upon mere ill-will which refers to the motive and not the intention of the person who feels it.

MANSLAUGHTER

Homicide was said by Coke to comprise petit treason (a servant killing his master or a wife her husband[18]), murder and manslaughter. Some manslaughters, he said, were voluntary and might be a felony or might not as with self-defence or upon some sudden falling out. Others were involuntary, as by misadventure which arose when a man did an act which was not unlawful and which, without any evil intent, led to death. This was qualified, however, by the felony/murder rule which Coke attributed to Bracton, although that was giving seventeenth-century authority to a medieval law of harsher times. In any event, Stephen claimed that Bracton did not support Coke, and that the three passages quoted by Coke from the *Year Books* either had nothing to do with the matter, or were a long way from the propositions for which he cited them.[19] Baker thinks Stephen was probably wrong in thinking that Coke extended the doctrine.[20] On the contrary, however, he seems to have originated it,

However that may be, Coke explained that by the rule if the involuntary act was unlawful then it ceased to be misadventure and became murder. Thus, if A meaning to steal a deer in the park of B, shot at the deer, and by the glance of his arrow killed a boy hidden in a bush, that was murder as the act was unlawful, even though A had had no intent to hurt the boy and had not even known of him. Yet, if B, the owner of the park, had shot at his own deer and, without any ill intent, had killed the boy that would have been homicide by misadventure and no felony.

So far as ill intent was concerned, said Coke, it need not be aimed at killing a particular person. Consequently, if a man knowing that many people would come into the street from a sermon, threw a stone over a wall intending only to frighten

18. Not, however, a husband killing his wife.
19. *Ibid.* p. 57.
20. J. H. Baker. (1977) 'Introduction to Spelman's Reports'. London, *Selden Society.* vol. 94. p. 310. ff. 1.

them or give them a slight injury and happened to kill one, it was murder, for he had an ill intent even though it did not extend to death and he did no know the person slain.

The turning point with manslaughter came in 1578 when *Saunders' Case* was decided at Warwick Assizes.[21] John Saunders, wishing to kill his wife, impregnated an apple with poison and handed it to her in the presence of the couple's daughter, a child aged three. His wife, after eating a small portion, handed the apple to the child, who ate it and died. Saunders took no steps to prevent the child being poisoned. The question was whether Saunders was guilty merely of manslaughter since, although having the *mens rea* to kill his wife the child was killed by mischance. No, said the court, Saunders was guilty of murder. In other words, a person who deliberately performed an act of violence must take the consequences of any mistake or misapplication of force.[22]

Later, Hale also gave detailed consideration to what malice aforethought implied. He defined malice in fact as a deliberate intention of doing any bodily harm to another, not authorised by law. Although this involved an intention inside the person's mind, Hale believed it could be evidenced from external circumstances such as lying in wait, earlier menaces, former grudges and the like but designing to do bodily harm was an essential ingredient. Implied malice, on the other hand, arose by presumption of law on the three criteria mentioned by Coke. The first of these presumed malice which could be rebutted by provocation. But the provocation always had to be sufficient. Thus if A distorted his mouth and laughed at B who thereupon killed him, B was guilty.[23]

In the legal theory of homicide, Hale brought out the importance of provocation far more fully and clearly than Coke. For example, he gave six practical illustrations of what did and what did not amount to provocation whereas Coke dealt with the matter in a much more cursory manner. The difference was not merely one of style between the two men, but reflected the changes in national manners and social life that were taking place.

Although, said Hale, many were of the opinion that bare words could not of themselves be sufficient provocation to reduce a crime from murder to manslaughter, where A spoke indecent language to B and B struck A who hit back and was then killed by B, that was manslaughter for the second strike made a new provocation and thus produced a sudden falling out. But this does not seem to prove the point. Hale also expanded on the question of when force might be used for the defence of the property or person of the one using force. Thus homicide was justifiable if a man shot another who had come to burn his house, or if a woman killed in the course of

21. Plowd. *Comm.* ff. 473-76.
22. J. M. Kaye. *The Early History of Murder and Manslaughter. Op. cit.* p. 588-9.
23. *Brain's Case.* M. 42, 43.

resisting a rape. But he made clear that any excess of force made the killing unlawful and manslaughter.

Nevertheless, the legal punishment of death was the same for murder and manslaughter. However, it was easier to obtain a royal pardon for manslaughter and jury nullification was more likely. Nullification has been defined as the power 'to acquit the defendant on the basis of conscience even when he is technically guilty in light of the judge's instructions defining the law and the jury's finding of the facts.'[24] It was quite widespread in the thirteenth and fourteenth centuries with Green concluding that the great majority of defendants in felony trials were acquitted by 'conscious jury nullification.'[25] Consequently, trial rolls reveal juries acquitting the great majority of those charged with simple homicide and sending murderers to the gallows about 50 per cent of the time.[26]

Manslaughter soon came to include culpable recklessness and the death penalty was modified since it was always permitted benefit of clergy, although only for a first offence. Hence the penalty for that offence was imprisonment not exceeding one year, and branding with the letter 'M' on the brawn of the left thumb to ensure that there was no subsequent pleading of clergy. Indeed, by the reign of Henry VII a statute[27] lamented how persons relying on the benefit had become bold in committing murder, rape, robbery and theft and enacted that all those not in holy orders who had pleaded clergy once should not be permitted to do so again. Murderers were to be branded with an 'M' and other felons with a 'T' until benefit was denied to murderers by statute in 1512.[28] By 1576 the handing of a 'cleric' over to the Church was abandoned and instead he would be imprisoned for up to a year at the discretion of the court and then released. The benefit was finally abolished by the Criminal Law Act 1827.[29]

By the early sixteenth century the division of culpable homicide into murder and chance-medley or loss of control (manslaughter) had begun to appear, with the distinction based on whether the killing was deliberate or accidental. Premeditation was not an essential factor.[30] Both murder and chance-medley were capital crimes but were distinguished because their indictments differed, because murder was not included when there was a general pardon for all other felonies and because murder was made non-clergyable by statute.

---

24. Alan Scheflin and Jon Van Dyke. (1980) 'Jury Nullification: The Contours of the Controversy.' 43 *J.L. and Contemporary Problems*. Durham, North Carolina, Duke University, p. 56.

25. T. A. Green. (1985) *Verdict According to Conscience: Perspectives on the English Criminal Trial Jury in England 1200-1800*. Chicago, Chicago University Press. p. 34.

26. *Ibid.* pp. 22, 34 and 52.

27. 4 Hen. 7. c. 13.

28. 4 Hen. 8. c. 2.

29. 7 & 8 Geo. 4. c. 28.

30. Generally, on the early history of homicide see, Kaye. 'The Early History of Murder and Manslaughter'. *Op. cit.* pp. 365 and 369.

By a strange irony, statutes in turn caused the Common Law judges to respond by redefining murder and chance-medley to make the distinction depend precisely on the presence or absence of premeditation, with chance-medley becoming a killing with 'heated blood' in a sudden fight where there was no malice aforethought. Another cause of the distinction was the growth of the affray type of murder in the new social conditions of the sixteenth century.

THEFT

In early Anglo-Saxon times the theft of goods could result in the offender having to pay compensation to their owner rather than facing trial. By the reign of Canute, however, trial was required if the thief was caught with the stolen goods. However, a thief had to be convicted several times before he could be executed. Even then the gallows might be avoided if his kinsmen paid his wergild and stood surety for his behaviour. If a thief confessed or was convicted his kinsmen had to pay a fine of 120 shillings if the goods were worth 60 shillings or more. If he was executed the value of the stolen goods was taken from his possessions.[31] Even in Anglo-Saxon times the distinction between simple (or petty) larceny and grand larceny existed. The first was the theft of goods valued at less than 12 pence and was not a capital crime. Punishment would involve the loss of a hand or a foot.

With grand larceny the goods were valued at 12 pence or more and the crime was capital.[32] However although grand larceny was a felony, in later medieval England it was often treated as a trespass with only about one-third of those tried being convicted. [33] According to Groot juries were reluctant to convict and often declared that stolen goods were of little value to avoid the death penalty being imposed. As a consequence the Statute of Westminster I (1275)[34] did not create the difference between grand and petty larceny but simply recognised the existing practice of juries since 1220 when it provided that a person indicted for 'Petty Larceny that amounteth not [above the Value] of 12 pence' should be bailable. [35] That distinction lasted until 1827.

By the thirteenth century the legal writers were seeking to reach a definition of theft and the concept of intent to deprive another of his property emerged even if the owner had entrusted his goods to another person. Chattels real could not be the subject of larceny and this included a box of deeds that concerned land. Similarly

31. F. L. Attenborough. (editor and translator) (1922) *The Laws of the Earliest English Kings*. Cambridge, Cambridge University Press. pp. 70, 157-9.
32. *Ibid.* pp. 49, 127, 157, 169.
33. T. A. Green. *Verdict According to Conscience: Perspectives on the English Trial Jury 1200–1800. Op. cit.* . p. 61.
34. E Edw. 1. c. 15.
35. R. D. Groot. (2002) 'Petit Larceny, Jury Lenity and Parliament.' In Cairns and McLeod. (2002) *The Dearest Birthright of the People of England*. Oxford, Hart Publishing. pp. 47, 58-61.

the theft of lead from a house or church was not larceny unless it were put down and returned for later. According to Baker,[36] in 1533 Spelman reported the case of a man indicted for stealing stones from the turrets of the town walls of Oxford who was discharged on the ground that the stones were part of the freehold. Domestic cattle were not included in the rule but wild animals were. Fruit growing on a tree was subject to the rule but not if it had fallen to the ground from where it was taken.

There had to be an actual taking and a forcible violation of possession so that a delivery was excluded as being a receipt, and one already in possession of an article could not take it by force. If a bale of merchandise or a tun of wine were delivered to a carrier who took the whole for his own use, no felony was committed. However, once he opened it and took any part with intent that was larceny. On the other hand if the carrier carried it to its proper destination and subsequently took the whole bale or tun with intent that also was larceny, for the delivery had been effected and the privity of the bailment determined.

These contrived contortions of the law arose from the celebrated *Carrier's Case*[37] which was debated in both the Star Chamber and the Exchequer Chamber. This attempted to modify a law of theft which was both inflexible and unsuited to the growth of commerce and trade. Although an improvement on the law it altered, changing conditions of commerce made the case equally deficient soon after it was decided. It remained an example of the judges attempting by construction to solve one of society's problems where only legislation was adequate.

By Elizabethan times theft was undoubtedly the most common crime and was commonly committed by poor people against others of their own class.[38] Pick-pockets and cut-purses were to be found everywhere and particularly at public hangings and fairs. Bartholomew Fair in London was notorious and one medical man, 'had his pocket picked of his purse, with nine crowns *du soleil* which, without doubt, was so cleverly taken from him by an Englishman who always kept very close to him, that the doctor did not in the least perceive it.'[39]

ROBBERY

Robbery was an open and violent assault to forcibly take property of any value from the victim provided it put him or her in fear. In other words, theft accompanied by violence. In the laws of Canute in Anglo-Saxon law the injured party was entitled to compensation from the robber of twice the value of the stolen goods, and four times the value in the thirteenth century. Even if the attempt to take property failed

---

36. J. H. Baker. (1977) 'Introduction to Spelman's Reports'. *Selden Society. Op. cit.* vol. 94. p. 317.
37. (1473) Y.B. 13 Edw. 4. f. 9.
38. See J. Samaha. (1975) 'Gleanings from Local Criminal Court Records: Sedition amongst the "Inarticulate" in Elizabethan England.' London, *Journal of Social History.* vol. viii. p.62.
39. P. Hentzner. (1889) *Travels in England during the Reign of Queen Elizabeth.* London, Cassell & Co., p. 37.

the crime was still committed. Hence a man could be hanged even if nothing was actually taken—the use or threat of force was sufficient.

Highway robbery was considered particularly serious because it almost always involved violence to the individual and also because it threatened freedom of travel and commerce. It was removed from the benefit of clergy in 1531 and its perpetrator was unlikely to receive a royal pardon but would be sent to the gallows.

In Tudor times it was said that robbery was usually committed by highwaymen or footpads. The difference between them it was claimed, was that, 'The first sort are called gentlemen robbers, or thieves, and these ride on horses well appointed, and go in show like honest men. The other rob on foot, and have no other help but a pair of light heels and a thick wood.'[40] On 4 December 1575, the Privy Council complained that the queen had been informed of the high number of recent highway robberies and that it was, 'a common thing for the thieves to carry pistols whereby they either murder out of hand before they rob, or else put her subjects in such fear that they dare not resist.'[41] An interesting trial involving two highwaymen, William Spiggot and Thomas Phillips, occurred at the Old Bailey in January 1720 when both the accused refused to plead. As pressing to death was not abolished until two years later they were sent to that torture. Once in the press room Spiggot begged to be taken back to plead and was allowed to do so. Phillips was laid on his back and suffered for half an hour with 350 pounds of weight on his body. When another 50 pounds were added he too asked to be allowed to plead and was taken back to court. Both men were convicted and hanged at Tyburn on 8 February 1720 but only after Phillips, in Newgate Prison, had sworn and sung songs 'while the other prisoners were engaged in acts of devotion.'[42]

BURGLARY

Burglary was breaking into a dwellinghouse with intent to commit a felony or actually doing so. It caused a good deal of fear, particularly as it was sometimes accompanied by physical violence to the occupants. At first, it was not essential to the crime that it be committed at night but by the reign of Edward I the breaking had to be at night and 'night' began when 'the dog slept and the wolf sought his prey'. But by Coke's (1552-1634) time it came when daylight was sufficiently dimmed that 'the countenance of a man could not be discerned'. Since every entrance to a house by a trespass was a breaking in law, for burglary there had to be an actual physical

40. S. Rid. (1930) 'Martin Markall, Beadle of Bridewell'. In A.V. Judges (ed.) *The Elizabethan Underworld.* London, George Routledge, pp. 415-6.
41. Anon. (1888) *Calendar of the Manuscripts of the Marquis of Salisbury at Hatfield House.* Part II, London, HMSO, p. 123.
42. Sir Norman Birkett. (ed.) (1974) *The Newgate Calendar.* London, Folio Press, J.M. Dent & Sons Ltd., pp. 64-6.

breaking and entering. However, the seeds of future difficulty were sown when it was deemed by the courts an entry once the thief's body or any part of it, such as his foot or arm, was within any part of the house. Or, when he put a gun in a window which he had already broken with intent to commit a felony. It was one of the first offences to lose the benefit of clergy in the sixteenth century,

By the time of Hale, in the seventeenth century, 'breaking and entering' as a component of burglary was still causing difficulties. He cited a case which had been before him at Cambridge where the offender had gained entry by climbing down a chimney. He had doubted at first whether this was burglary, but the fact that some bricks had become loose in the descent and had fallen into the room below apparently satisfied him. [43] However, the jury acquitted the man on the facts. In any event, Manwood C. B. had already held that such an entry was burglary, even without the fall of bricks,[44] and Dalton had agreed on the ground that a chimney was as shut as the nature of the thing would admit. Putting a pistol over the threshold, but without a foot or any other part of the body was held by Hale to be a sufficient breaking.[45] In this connection Baker has found, in the Harvard Law School manuscript law Reports written by Arthur Turnour, an interesting case where a man lived in adultery with the wife of A, a neighbour, and they both conspired the death of A. Since their houses adjoined the adulterer made a small hole in the partition wall through which to shoot A. The deed was done at night, but as A was wounded and not killed the adulterer and the wife could not be charged with murder. They were, however, tried before Houghton J. for burglary. Both were found guilty and executed, which James I commended as an excellent piece of justice.[46] Presumably it was shown that the tip of the pistol entered the injured man's room.

Under the Tudors, housebreaking was made capital if carried out in daytime and the occupants were put in fear. By the end of Elizabeth's reign it was a capital offence even if there was no one in the house, provided goods worth more than five shillings in value were stolen. The death penalty applied to burglary, as with robbery, whether any goods were actually stolen or not.

RAPE

The earliest Saxon laws of Æthelbert spoke of a fine for carrying off a maiden by force but did not mention sexual assault. It was not until the reign of Alfred that the legal concept of rape was recognised with mention of assaulting a woman for the purpose of having sexual intercourse. Two other laws of Alfred punished a man who

43. Sir. Matthew Hale.(1736) *The History of the Pleas of the Crown*. London, E. & R. Nutt and R. Gosling. vol. 1. p. 552.
44. *Crompt.* fol. 32. b.
45. Sir Matthew Hale. *The History of the Pleas of the Crown. Op. cit.* p. 553.
46. J. H. Baker. (1973) 'Criminal Justice at Newgate 1616-1627) *The Irish Jurist*. vol. 8. p. 317.

touched a woman's body in a lustful manner and in the codes of Ethelred and Canute there was provision for punishing sexual assaults on widows. The Anglo-Saxon
penalty for rape was death and dismemberment. Such laws show an acute apprecia-
tion of what must have been the need to protect women from male predators when
there was no police force.

William the Conqueror, as we have seen, disapproved of the death penalty and
preferred mutilation. In cases of rape he substituted castration and loss of eyes on
the grounds, according to Bracton, that he should lose the testicles which excited his
lust and his eyes which gave him sight of the maiden's beauty. Then, in the twelfth
century the raped woman could seek an indictment for trial before a jury instead of
by combat. She still had, however, to go to the county court in the manner described
in the next paragraph. However, the procedure 'seldom if ever resulted in conviction
for felony; appeals were normally nonsuited on technicalities or were unprosecuted;
[and] anyone convicted at the Crown's residual suit was merely amerced.' On the
other hand, many defendants compromised with the victim, either by financial
compensation or marriage.[47]

By the time of Glanvill, the first significant lawyer not in holy orders, in the
reign of Henry II, it was provided that the woman raped had to go as soon as possible to the nearest village and show to trustworthy men the injury she had received
including any flow of blood and staining or tearing of clothing.[48] After announcing her claim publicly in the county court she could then bring an appeal of rape
against the offender. This was an ordeal that must have reduced the number of cases
considerably and records of some eyres show quite large numbers of women appellants not turning up in court. Little changed in the next three-quarters of a century
but Bracton made it clear that if the case was made out the offender was to lose his
'life and members.' He also wrote that if the accused denied the claim the woman
had to be physically examined by four trustworthy women.[49] If the man continued
his denial he might claim, in what might be modern terms, that the woman had
consented to intercourse or that she had accused him at the behest of her relatives.
Prior to the court's verdict the woman might consent to marry the man provided
their families agreed. If there was no marriage and the man were found guilty the
punishment was castration, until the end of the thirteenth century when the penalty
became hanging.

The Statutes of Westminster of 1275 and 1285 took matters forward.[50] The first
Act declared it an offence to rape *any woman* against her will and any underage girl

47. J.B. Post. (1980) 'Sir Thomas West and the Statute of Rapes, 1382'. 53 *Bulletin of the Institute of Historical Research*. Reproduced in Jennifer Temkin (ed) (1995) *Rape and the Criminal Justice System*. Aldershot, Dartmouth Publishing Co. Limited. p. 177.
48. Sir Ranulf de Glanvill. (c.1187) *De Legibus Angliae*. *Op. cit.* pp. 175–6.
49. Henry de Bracton. (c.1256) *Tractatus de legibus Angliae*. ii. p. 416.
50. 3 Edw. I. st. I. c. 15 and 13 Edw. I. st. I. c. 34.

with or without her consent. Previously virginity in the raped woman had been an important factor. Moreover, the woman no longer had to proceed at once 'while the deed is newly done' but was given 40 days in which to commence an action. If she failed to do so the king would start proceedings so that like other offences rape had become a crime of public interest to be dealt with by the state. A successful appeal by the complainant was punished by mutilation. If she did not appeal and proceedings were initiated in the name of the king the punishment, on a finding of guilt, was a minimum of two years imprisonment and a fine. Thus the procedure which led to mutilation remained and a new procedure which resulted in imprisonment was added. The term of imprisonment could be low but this may have been intended to encourage juries to present offenders instead of the victim relying on a private appeal. A decade later, the second statute restored the death penalty for all forms of rape regardless of who brought the action. Subsequent consent by the victim would not alter the punishment if the case were by jury presentment.

The purpose of protecting wealthy families, as well as rape victims, is made clear by a statute in October 1382 in the reign of Richard II. This provided that where noble ladies who suffered rape and abduction afterwards gave their consent, which they had frequently been doing to the encouragement of fortune-hunters, then both parties were barred from any inheritance or dower. Even with subsequent consent the next male by blood to the victim could sue the rapist and have him hanged.

Rape was defined by Hale, following Coke, as 'the carnal knowledge of any woman above the age of ten years against her will, and of a woman-child under the age of ten years against her will.'[51] Earlier, it will be recalled, that under the first Statute of Westminster, the consent of an under-age girl was considered irrelevant. In such cases, as defined by Hale in the sixteenth century, it was his opinion that if the victim was too young to take the oath she should nevertheless be allowed to give evidence since what she could say was the most direct testimony. For this reason her evidence was more valuable than that of her mother to whom she had probably confided what had happened and who could give evidence on oath but whose testimony was second-hand. Behind this view was the belief that rape, 'was an accusation easily to be made and hard to be proved, and harder to be defended by the party accused tho' never so innocent.'[52] The victim's story should, therefore, be checked against her character. It was important to know if she had reported the rape without delay and whether she had shown the signs of her injury and the place where the deed occurred. In effect, this was again returning to the position at the time of Bracton and before the first Statute of Westminster.

Men charged with rape in late medieval England had faced little risk of being convicted. For instance, in the Berkshire eyre of 1248 of nine cases of rape only two

51. Sir Matthew Hale. *The History of the Pleas of the Crown. Op. cit.* vol. i. p. 628.
52. *Ibid.* vol. i. pp. 634-5.

men were found guilty. And in the surviving rolls of the Kent keepers of the peace for 1316-17 only one accused out of 15 is known to have been found guilty. A study of the gaol delivery rolls of a number of counties between 1388 and 1409 revealed no convictions in 493 cases where rape was the sole crime charged.[53]

However, the situation changed in the sixteenth century when convictions for rape increased dramatically. This was in line with a rise in convictions for other felonies and may have been influenced by the fact that juries were ceasing to be self-informing and witness testimony was increasingly influencing court verdicts. It is also possible that as society became more sophisticated the crime of rape became more seriously regarded with Hale calling it, 'a most detestable crime that should severely and impartially be punished with death.'[54]

53. J. G. Bellamy. (1998) *The Criminal Trial in Later Medieval England: Felony Before the Courts from Edward I to the Sixteenth Century*, Stroud, Gloucestershire., Sutton Publishing Ltd. p. 179.
54. Sir Matthew Hale. *The History of the Pleas of the Crown. Op. cit.* p. 653.

CHAPTER 5

The Common Law in Danger

ROYAL POWER

Although arbitrary power was exercised by the Tudor monarchs, at all times they sought the legitimacy given by the law and constantly secured the enactment of new statutes. Nevertheless, they established a strong central government and a nation state.[1] 'The royal power created a machinery to make its power effective throughout the land' and 'writ all over the period is the compelling force of the royal sovereignty.'[2] As part of its fostering strong government, the Crown was well disposed towards the continental civil law, with its central role of the judge and the exercise of torture to obtain confessions. As a consequence, in a new departure the Tudors introduced by statutes a number of reductions in the availability of benefit of clergy as well as encouraging widespread torture under cover of the royal prerogative.

As the nation state was coming into existence, Henry VIII's despotism, together with his break with Rome, meant the 1352 Treason Act was not sufficient to quell rebellions of the over-mighty barons.[3] For example, the Act did not include conspiracy to levy war or make it treason to form an intent to depose or incapacitate the king. In an attempt, therefore, to make secure the Reformation Settlement a statute was passed in 1533-4 (the year of the Act of Supremacy) which provided that anyone who maliciously published by words or writing that the king was a heretic or tyrant should be guilty of treason.[4] When Mary became queen, as a Roman Catholic and opposed to the Reformation, she had this and other treason statutes of Henry repealed so that the statute of Edward III became once again the sole treason statute in force. On Elizabeth ascending the throne she introduced new legislation against the Pope and Roman Catholics to protect her own position. For instance, a statute of 1558 made it treason to affirm by writing, printing or overt act that the queen ought not to be queen or that any other person was entitled to the throne. To affirm such by words was made high treason on a second conviction—on a first conviction the offence was held to be misprision of treason which was punished with imprisonment for life and forfeiture of goods.

Nevertheless, by Elizabeth's reign (and into that of James I) treason statutes were less necessary as the judges were prepared to find constructive treason, particularly

---

1. See J. D. Mackie. (1992) *The Earlier Tudors 1485-1558*. Oxford, The Clarendon Press. p. 562.
2. *Ibid.* pp. 562-3.
3. For extensive treatment of the law of treason under the Tudors see John Bellamy. (1970) *The Tudor Law of Treason: An Introduction*. London, Routledge & Kegan Paul.
4. 26 Hen. 8. c. 13.

as a means of political control. Hence, the 'compassing or imagining the king's death' of the 1352 statute was extended by construction with serious consequences. The courts had long held that the 'open deed' of article (b) of the Act applied also to article (a), although this is not apparent from the text. Thus, an intention to kill the monarch had to be proved by an overt act (i.e. 'open deed') which showed that the person doing it had such an intention. 'This compassing, intent or imagination', said Coke, 'though secret is … to be discovered by circumstances precedent, concomitant and subsequent.'[5] However, the judges declined to limit themselves to overt acts pointing to a design to kill the monarch. By construction they began to consider the overt acts of the accused more widely, 'with all endeavour for the safety of the monarch.'[6] As a consequence, they ruled that acts which showed no intention to kill, but to put any kind of restraint upon the monarch, might be good evidence of an intention to kill. The doctrine was recorded in the early part in Coke's *Third Institute* where he approved the process of extension of the Act to include certain assemblies and meetings.[7]

Coke took the matter even further when he himself decided in *R. v. Owen* that it was treason to say that the queen, being excommunicated by the Pope, might lawfully be deposed and killed and that such killing was not murder.[8] Clearly he thought that in the climate of the times such a statement could lead to the death of the queen and that this might easily threaten the Reformation itself. It needed a good deal of ingenuity, however, to construe such words as open deeds. Still, Coke would not go too far and he expressed the opinion that mere scandalous words about the monarch, unless they 'disabled his title', were not an overt act from which a compassing of his death could be inferred, adding, in contradiction of his earlier dictum, 'it is commonly said that bare words may make a heretick, but not a traytor without an overt act.'[9]

All Coke's brother judges agreed with him to this effect in *Pine's Case*,[10] following an exhaustive survey of the earlier precedents. Similarly, in the earlier *Peacham's Case*[11] neither he, nor some of the other judges, were prepared to accept that the writing of treasonable words in a sermon, which had never been preached or published, or intended to be, was treason. Peacham had, however, predicted that James would meet a violent death which caused the king to barricade his room every night with feather beds. It also caused him to send Peacham for trial at Taunton before Chief Baron Tenfold who obediently found him guilty, although he was not ex-

---

5. Sir E. Coke. (1797) 3 *Institute*. London, E. & R. Brooke. p. 6.
6. *Ibid.*
7. *Ibid.* p. 12.
8. (1616) Rolle Reports, 185.
9. Coke. *3 Institute. Op. cit.* p. 14.
10. (1629) Cro. Car. 117.
11. (1615) Cro. Car. 125.

ecuted but died in Taunton gaol after being tortured on the rack.

However, rioting was another matter. Even earlier, according to Coke:

> it was resolved by all the judges of England in the reign of King Henry VIII that an insurrec-
> tion against the Statute of Labourers, for inhancing of salaries and wages, was a levying of war
> against the king, because it was generally against the king's law, and the offenders took upon
> them the reformation thereof, which subjects by gathering of power ought not to do.[12]

As for levying war against the king, although this was declared treason by Edward III's statute it did not include a conspiracy to levy war until extended by construction in the trial of the Earls of Essex and Southampton in 1600.

Hale was not prepared to follow Coke on the question of rioting and claimed it
was the first instance he had seen of, 'this interpretative levying of war.'[13] To Hale
the offence of high treason was a crime directly against the person or government
of the king. Dealing with section 1 of the Statute of Treason he saw, 'compassing
or imagining' as words of great latitude. They referred to a purpose or design of the
mind or will, even if such purpose or design was not effected. It was an internal act
which, without something to manifest it could not possibly be recognised by the
law, only by God. The statute, therefore, required evidence of such an overt act as
might render the compassing or imagining capable of a trial and sentence by human
judges. But, where the king was actually murdered it was the compassing his death
which was the treason not the killing which was only an overt act. That is why compassing was treason even if not effected, but it was still only an 'act of mind' and an
overt act to evidence it was essential.[14]

Accordingly, although Hale sought out the essential principles of Edward's Act
he found that giving effect to them was more difficult than stating them since many
later statutes had muddied the waters. On the question of treason by speech Hale
stated that generally words could not be an overt act unless committed to writing
because they could easily be mistaken, misapplied, misrepeated or misunderstood
by the hearers. And, he noted a harsh judgment in the reign of Edward IV whereby
a certain Walter Walker, living at the sign of the Crown in Cheapside, having told
his young son that if he would be quiet he would make him heir of the Crown, was
executed for high treason.[15]

Hale accepted that an assembly actually formed to levy war against the king,
either to depose or restrain him or force him to do any act or to remove his coun-
sellors or ministers, was an overt act proving the compassing of the death of the
king. 'But what,' he asked, ' if there was a levying of war against the king merely by

---

12. Coke. *3 Institute. Op. cit.* p. 10.
13. Sir Matthew Hale. (1736) *The History of the Pleas of the Crown.* London, E. & R. Nutt and R. Gosling.
    vol. i. p. 132.
14. *Ibid.* p. 108.
15. Sir Matthew Hale. *The History of the Pleas of the Crown. Op. cit.* vol. i. p. 115.

interpretation and construction of the law?' The courts had already held that whilst raising a force to burn a particular enclosure was only a riot, to go from town to town to cast in all enclosures was treason.[16] Hale refused to accept the justice of this, however, in *Messenger's Case*[17] when, as Chief Baron, he stood out against ten of his brother judges led by Kelyng in holding that the particular riot was not treason. He would not agree that the riot was even remotely evidence of an overt act to prove compassing the death of the king. He saw only an unruly group of eight London apprentices among whom a custom of pulling down bawdy houses had long existed. He believed they meant to destroy two or three brothels at most and that, in any event, the statute 1 Mar. c. 12, although discontinued, had made assemblies of this kind felonies, not treason.

Hale had to accept that the law held it was constructive treason to attempt to pull down all enclosures, or to enhance servants' wages or alter the established religion. These cases being settled, he said,

> We must acquiesce in them; but in my opinion, if new cases happen for the future, that have not an express resolution in point, nor are expressly within the words of 25 E. 3, though they may seem to have a parity of reason, it is the safest way, and most agreeable to the wisdom of the great Act of 25 E. 3, first to consult the Parliament and have their declaration and to be very wary of multiplying constructive and interpretative treasons, for we know not where it will end.[18]

Hale seems to have made his point with *Messenger's Case* because seven years later, in September 1675, when he and the other judges were asked to give an opinion on a riot by several hundred weavers in London who had violently broken into homes and destroyed engine-looms valued at several thousand pounds which they considered were taking away their jobs, the judges were divided five against five and induced the prosecution to proceed for riot only. Despite the damage and the death of one man they argued it was a riot and not treason on the ground that it was a domestic dispute.[19] In so deciding, they prevented the statutory law of treason overriding the Common Law.

Also in Tudor times the use of the power of nullification by jurors brought about government distrust of the jury system. This distrust was fortified in some cases by the failure of jurors to present certain offenders, or even to attend court, either because they believed the penalty of death was too high for the crime, or from fear of repercussions in their communities and for their own safety. On occasion jurors may

---

16. *Bradshaw's Case.* (1597) Coke. 3 *Institute*, pp. 9-10.
17. (1708) Sir John Kelyng. *A Report of Diverse Cases in Pleas of the Crown Adjudged and Determined in the Reign of the Late King Charles II With Direction for Justices of the Peace and Others.* London, Isaac Cleave. vol. i. pp. 134-5.
18. Sir Matthew Hale. *The History of the Pleas of the Crown. Op. cit.* vol. i. p. 132.
19. *Ibid.* pp. 143-5.

have been threatened. The original Trailbaston Commission in 1304 had spoken of, 'those who have disturbed jurors on Assizes, that they dare not speak the truth, for if they do so they cause them to be so beaten and ill-treated that many lose their lives, or are maimed for ever more, so that for fear of them the truth cannot be known before the king's justices.'[20] This was repeated in summarised form by the 1328 commission and McLane gives examples of corrupt practices and coercion including cases where the juries simply did not appear or actually fled.[21] Anthony Musson also found that in gaol deliveries in Norfolk at this time jury default occurred frequently with, for example, juries defaulting in Norwich in six out of 14 sessions held from 1324 to 1328.[22] There is no evidence to suggest matters had improved in the next century or two.

SUMMARY PROCEDURE

One consequence was the limited increase in the use of summary procedures. For instance, in the reign of Edward III justices were permitted to act without an indictment although only to a narrow extent in dealing largely with employment law. More significant was a statute of Richard II which permitted wealthy people to be certified to allow them to arrest rioters causing terror without waiting for an indictment,[23] although the Act was soon repealed. Increased powers were given to justices of the peace by another statute of Richard's under which persons arrested for forcible entry could be convicted without a trial on the word of the justices who attended the place where the offence was committed.[24] Similar powers were given to enable justices to deal with a limited number of offences in subsequent reigns including those of the Tudors.

THE COMMON LAW COURTS

The Common Law courts were royal courts and the judges who sat in them were royal justices.[25] In Tudor and Stuart times there were three Common Law courts, the King's Bench, the Common Pleas and the Exchequer. In theory the King's Bench was superior and its chief justice was Chief Justice of England. In addition to its civil side it had a wide criminal jurisdiction with a right to interfere with other

---

20. B. M. McLane. (1988) 'Juror Attitudes to Local Disorder: The Evidence of the 1328 Lincolnshire Trailbaston Proceedings.' In Cockburn and Green. (eds) *Twelve Good Men and True: The Criminal Trial Jury in England 1200-1800*. New Jersey, Princeton University Press. p. 62.

21. *Ibid.*

22. A. Musson. (1997) 'Twelve Good Men and True? The Character of Early Fourteenth-Century Juries.' 15 *Law and History Review*. University of Illinois Press. p. 130.

23. 2 Rich. II st. 1. c. 6.

24. 15 Rich, II. c.2.

25. Sir W. Holdsworth. (1956) *A History of English Law*. London, Methuen & Co. Ltd., Sweet & Maxwell. vol. i. p.194.

courts from which indictments could be removed to the King's Bench by writ of *certiorari*. The court was concerned with the rights of, and crimes against, the king. It determined the ancient pleas of the Crown—breaches of the king's peace, treason, murder and other felonies.

The court of Common Pleas was meant to safeguard the rights of the people by exercising jurisdiction over actions between subject and subject and in the seventeenth century it acquired a general jurisdiction to issue writs of prohibition and *habeas corpus*. As will be seen, it was these writs that Coke used in his struggles to limit the powers of the prerogative courts such as the Star Chamber and the High Commission.

The Court of Exchequer, presided over by a chief baron, originally decided only revenue cases, but in the seventeenth century it also began to deal with some of the civil suits previously dealt with by Common Pleas. It had no criminal jurisdiction.

THE HIGH COURT OF CHANCERY

It is likely that the lord chancellor began to act independently of the king's council in the reign of Richard II. But whatever the actual time, by 1377 the council was overwhelmed with petitions and, on behalf of the king, the chancellor began to act in cases where the Common Law had no remedy or was inflexible.

The Chancery was not in origin a court of law at all but the secretariat of the lord chancellor who was a bishop. It took its name, *cancellaria*, from the latticed screen behind which its many clerks worked. In time the House of Commons became alarmed at the flexibility of the rules fashioned by the chancellor, known as equity, which he considered superior to the law. It petitioned the king to prevent the chancellor, who acted as judge and jury, from going outside the Common Law. This had no real effect, however, and eventually, in the reign of Henry VI, the chancellor finally established that he could always intervene, in accordance with equity and fairness, in cases where he argued there was no remedy at Common Law.[26] In fact, the chancellor gave relief as he thought fit, 'in equity and good conscience', often with little regard to the strict letter or spirit of the Common Law. As a consequence Chancery became known as a 'court of conscience', described in the memorable words of John Selden as 'a roguish thing', governed by the chancellor's conscience, the measure of which was, 'his foot'.[27] Indeed, it was not at the time a judicial court but was used by the Crown to gain power over the Common Law courts in the name of strong government.

Not only did the Court of Chancery encroach upon the Common Law but, like the Star Chamber and the High Commission, it used Roman law and procedure

---

26. J. Hostettler. (1997) *Sir Edward Coke: A Force for Freedom.* Chichester, Barry Rose Law Publishers. p. 199.
27. Sir Frederick Pollock. (ed.) (1927) *Table Talk of John Selden.* London, Selden Society.

and was staffed by civilians learned in the civil and canon laws of Rome. Through the canon law torture also came to England and was used extensively under the Tudors and early Stuarts as part of their claim to absolutism and divine right. The whole process was deplored by Coke and when Lord Chancellor Ellesmere interfered with the Common Law courts by re-opening cases already decided by them his anger was aroused. The King's Bench thereupon decided that where a decision had been reached in a Common Law court Chancery could not intervene. But Ellesmere was a fervent royalist who proclaimed, 'the monarch is the law' and likened him to a Roman emperor. 'Our constitution', he said, 'is to be obeyed and reverenced, not bandied by persons sitting in ordinaries drowned with drink, blown away with a whiff of tobacco.'[28] And Coke failed, despite using *habeas corpus,* to stem the growth of Chancery which was always sitting and not subject to term times like the Common Law courts. Eventually, by the Judicature Act 1873, the Court of Chancery was merged with the Common Law courts and the judges in all the branches of the High Court of Justice were given power to administer both law and equity.

TORTURE

As a punishment torture has always been illegal in English Common Law. Sir Edward Coke, in his *Institutes,* declared that, 'There is no law to warrant tortures in this land nor can they be justified.'[29] Clearly, he did not regard pressing to death, as described earlier, as torture. In fact, torture has featured in our criminal justice system at numerous times particularly with the Star Chamber which made no pretence of practising the Common Law. In the reign of Henry VIII a statute[30] provided that murder by poisoning was high treason and was to be punished by boiling to death. A young woman named Margaret Davy was so executed for the 'poisoning of her mistris' and some others suffered this fate in Smithfield before the Act was repealed by Henry's son. Nevertheless, torture was usually imposed extra-judicially.

THE COURT OF STAR CHAMBER

The Star Chamber was the king's council sitting as a court until 1540 when it acquired a separate existence and the council became the Privy Council. The Star Chamber was situated in a long building across New Palace Court from Westminster Hall and faced the Thames—then the highway of London. Coke wrote that, 'It is called the Star Chamber in respect the roof of the court is garnished with golden

---

28. *Ibid.* p. 85.
29. Sir. E. Coke. (1797 edn.) 3 *Institute. Op. cit.* p. 12.
30. 22. Hen. VIII. c. 9.

stars.'[31] It met twice a week in term time, on Wednesdays and Fridays—'Star-days' as they were called. After the Reformation Henry VIII faced opposition from some powerful barons and used the Star Chamber as ancillary to the Common Law courts for dispensing justice with speed and flexibility, as indeed it did at first. Coke wrote that it, 'is the most honourable court (our Parliament excepted) that is in the Christian world … this court does keep all England in quiet.'[32]

The Star Chamber wielded immense power in attempting to substitute the will of the sovereign for the Common Law. It was composed of the lord chancellor, the chief justices of the King's Bench and the Common Pleas and privy councillors. Its sessions were held *in camera* and there were no witnesses, no indictments and no juries. Evidence was presented in writing. It punished conspiracy, false accusations, riots, forgery, bribery and intimidation, often bringing to book the powerful who were evading the law. But although it came into existence to check abuses, as a prerogative court it gradually became an instrument of arbitrary rule, even evading writs of *habeas corpus* issued by the Common Law courts. This brought no outraged response since the judges were appointed by the king and were subservient to him. The Star Chamber's political role was to deal, usually with brutality, with offenders it considered likely to imperil the authority of the state.

After a time it made itself feared and hated as a ruthless arm of royal power transcending the Common Law. And, although it had no power to impose the death penalty, it could and did use pitiless tortures to secure confessions and persuade prisoners to implicate others. The well-known martyr, Edmund Campion, was only one of the Jesuit priests who was subjected to the most appalling tortures before being executed. Indeed, under Elizabeth alone 187 priests are said to have been put to death after suffering torture. And, invoking the royal prerogative, the queen was usually directly involved in the decision. For instance, in 1571, in authorising the wanton torture of two servants of the Duke of Norfolk, she wrote, 'We warrant you to cause them both, or either of them, to be brought to the rack … and to find the taste thereof.'[33]

The rack was a mechanism for stretching and dislocating the limbs of victims and loosening joints from their sockets. Another form of torture was known as the 'scavenger's daughter', named after Skevington who was Lieutenant of the Tower in the reign of Henry VIII. This painfully squeezed the victim up into a ball with iron hoops and manacles until frequently blood was forced out of the nose and ears and the ribs and breastbone were broken by the pressure. Clause 39 of *Magna Carta* had forbidden torture and on the trial of John Felton, who had assassinated the Duke of Buckingham at Portsmouth in 1628, all the 12 judges sitting at Serjeant's Inn

31. Sir E. Coke. *4 Institute, Op. cit.* p. 65.
32. *Ibid.* pp. 63–5.
33. J. Hostettler. (1994) *The Politics of Punishment.* Chichester, Barry Rose Law Publishers Ltd., p. 63.

declared unanimously that no man should be tortured on the rack since, 'no such punishment is known or allowed at Common Law.' That clearly indicates that the judges knew of the existence of the rack and the use of torture by the royal prerogative, but at least they ruled against it.

David Jardine, a nineteenth century barrister and writer on historical and legal matters, was to expose the vast cover-up of the operations of torture in the Tudor and Stuart reigns with his *Reading on Torture,* delivered at New Inn Hall, in Michaelmas Term in 1836.[34] Jardine's researches into the *Registers of the Proceedings of the Council* and the original torture warrants of the State Papers Office revealed the extensive use of the rack. Letters from successive Tudor and Stuart monarchs were brought to light which instructed the Lieutenant of the Tower of London to use torture. In addition to the mechanisms mentioned above, there were also an iron gauntlet compressed by a screw, a spiked collar known as 'the necklace' and thumb screws. Sometimes a prisoner was put into a rat-infested dungeon. One such was Thomas Sherwood in 1577. Accused of hearing mass he was placed in a Tower dungeon below the high-water mark. Water ebbed in and out with the tides bringing with it rats which tore the flesh from his arms and legs. He was then put to the rack. Despite such cruelty he admitted nothing and was executed for high treason.

Torture in its narrow sense means using violence to extract a confession or evidence against others. But William Prynne, a barrister of Lincoln's Inn, might be forgiven for thinking that his open punishment bore a strong resemblance to torture in a more general sense. As a Puritan he wrote a book in 1633 called *Histriomastix* which contained critical references to stage plays, masques, dancing, bonfires and maypoles. Despite Prynne's sincere motives it was not an uplifting book. Nevertheless, as Queen Henrietta was sometimes a spectator at such events, he was charged with high treason. For thus offending the majesty of Charles I's escort Prynne was fined £500, placed in the pillory, burned on the forehead, had both his ears cut off and was sentenced to imprisonment in the Tower for life. In passing this sentence, the judges, who were beside themselves with rage, added that he should never be set at liberty since he was a mad dog not fit to live in a den with such monsters as wolves and tigers like himself.[35]

Star Chamber torture was not brought to an end until the court was abolished by the Long Parliament in 1641. The important thing is that, despite the prerogative, the use of torture had not been regularised in English criminal procedure.[36] Although the Tudor and Stuart monarchs admired continental practices, they were unable to bring together into a common bond their new activist judges and the

---

34. *A Reading on the Use of Torture in the Criminal Law of England Prior to the Commonwealth.* Printed in the *Edinburgh Review.* vol. 67, (April-July 1838).
35. *State Tryals.* (1735) London, T. Goodwin and Others, p. 273.
36. John H. Langbein. (1977) *Torture and the Law of Proof: Europe and England in the Ancien Regime.* Chicago, University of Chicago Press. pp. 73, 77-8.

practice of torture. Ironically, this was in part due to the use of the prerogative and not the courts to prescribe torture. As a consequence, the Crown had no ability to institutionalise the practice.

The Star Chamber was not demolished until 1806 and its door now hangs in the Westminster School.

THE HIGH COMMISSION

In addition to the Star Chamber the Tudors also established the High Commission which following the Reformation was the supreme court of ecclesiastical discipline. Its original purpose was to enforce the laws of the Reformation Settlement and exercise control over the Church after Henry VIII's breach with Rome. It was controlled by the prerogative of the Crown and had power to fine and imprison. Like the Star Chamber it became hated for its overbearing use of its powers. By its Letters Patent issued by Queen Mary to 22 Commissioners in 1557, its powers included inquiring into 'heresies, heretical opinions, Lollardies, heretical and seditious books, concealments, contempts, conspiracies, and all false rumours, tales and clamorous words or sayings raised against … the quiet governance and rule of our people and subjects … ' Heresies included non-acceptance of the Book of Common Prayer and refusing to attend church services.[37]

Again like the Star Chamber, the High Commission used the self-incrimination *ex officio* oath, first authorised by Mary,[38] although Coke advised the Privy Council that such use was illegal.[39] Coke also urged that since neither the Common Law nor the ecclesiastical law permitted the High Commission to fine or imprison, except for heresy and schism, only statute, and not the Crown, could confer such wider authority and this had not been done.[40] As Chief Justice of the Court of Common Pleas Coke constantly issued writs of prohibition to prevent the High Commission and the Star Chamber hearing cases which would result in imprisonment for adultery and other offences. He ignored the wrath of Archbishop Bancroft and the king that his writs provoked, asserting that they were well warranted by law.[41] Using the writ of *habeas corpus* he also secured the release from prison of persons already incarcerated for adultery. In taking these steps he was not only undermining the prerogative but also proclaiming the subordination of the Church and ecclesiastical law to the Common Law.

---

37. R. G. Usher. (1968 edn) *The Rise and Fall of the High Commission.* Oxford, The Clarendon Press. pp. 23-24.
38. An oath whereby a prisoner, knowing nothing of the case against him, was forced to give evidence incriminating himself. Refusal to take the oath resulted in imprisonment for contempt.
39. R. G. Usher. *The Rise and Fall of the High Commission. Op. cit.* p. 169.
40. *Ibid.*
41. Sir E. Coke. (1797) 2 *Institute. Op. cit.* p. 601.

Fuller's Case[42]

In 1607 a test case was brought in an attempt by Puritans to have the Common Law judges declare the High Commission illegal. A puritan MP and barrister named Nicholas Fuller volunteered to be the means.[43] Two men who refused to take the *ex officio* oath had been imprisoned for contempt by the Commission. Fuller boldly denied it had any right to fine or imprison any subject and he obtained writs of *habeas corpus* for the temporary release of the two men until he could argue before the Court of King's Bench that his clients were detained illegally. When before the court he declared that the commission was 'popish' and was used to suppress true religion, that the oath led to the damnation of the souls of those who took it and the commission had not been created by statute as a permanent body. The court adjourned the case for argument before all the 12 judges. However, before the judges could be assembled Archbishop Bancroft and other commissioners arraigned Fuller before them for scandalous statements, schism and malicious impeachment of the king's authority in ecclesiastical causes. Before the commission Fuller refused to take the *ex officio* oath and immediately obtained from the King's Bench a prohibition against a premature hearing.

Ultimately, he was convicted by the commission of schism, fined £200 and imprisoned for a short time in the Fleet gaol. However, the judges, whilst admitting that the commission could punish for schism, held that it could not punish a barrister for anything said in presenting his client's case. They also forcefully stressed that they themselves could determine the limits of the ecclesiastical jurisdiction and use writs of prohibition where it was exceeded.[44] It was left to Coke to lead a vigorous assault on the commission from the Court of Common Pleas and, as a consequence, the number of prohibitions that now flowed from the Common Law courts sent the commissioners reeling. The Commission was finally abolished, along with the Star Chamber, by the Long Parliament in 1641.[45]

PUNISHMENTS IN TUDOR TIMES

As part of their nation-state building the Tudors increased the severity of the law. In the 150 years from the accession of Edward III to the death of Henry VII only six capital statutes were enacted whilst during the next century and a half a further 30 were passed.[46] Felonies were punishable with the death penalty and forfeiture of

---

42. For a fuller examination of this case see R.G. Usher. *The Rise and Fall of the High Commission. Op. cit* pp. 170-79.

43. Sir E. Coke. (1642) 12 *Reports.* p. 21.

44. *Ibid.*

45. 16 Car. 1, c. 11.

46. L. Radzinowicz. (1948) *A History of English Criminal Law and its Administration from 1750.* London, Stevens & Sons Limited. p. 4.

property. So large was the number of people executed that Coke complained, 'What a lamentable case it is to see so many Christian men and women strangled on that cursed tree of the gallows.[47]

The punishment for treason was merciless. For a man it was to be drawn behind a cart from the prison to the gallows (he being unworthy to tread anymore on Mother Earth), hanged and cut down whilst still alive, disembowelled and castrated (since he was evilly begotten), with his intestines burnt before his eyes and finally decapitated and quartered. Women, on the other hand, were burned at the stake after being tarred, although in many cases the executioner managed to strangle them before they were engulfed by the flames of the fire. A remnant of Norman policy, the burning of women alive was said by Blackstone to be out of, 'the decency due to the sex [which] forbade the exposing and publicly mangling their bodies.'[48]

Hanging was the penalty for felony with the felon, it was said, dying between heaven and earth since he was unworthy of both.[49] Even for minor offences punishments were often cruel and intended to stigmatise and dishonour an offender. The stocks, whereby the victim was seated with his head, ankles and wrists locked in the frame, were used for such offences as petty theft, vagrancy, drunkenness and resisting a constable and by 1406 it had become compulsory for every town and village to have one. For the same minor offences, but also for sedition, libel and forgery the pillory, or stretch-neck, was resorted to in order to expose the victim to public ridicule. For instance, John Mundy, a baker, was put in the pillory in Cornhill for making and selling false bread and Agnes Deynte for selling false butter.[50] The pillory consisted of a platform raised several feet above the ground on which the offender stood and was surmounted by a wooden frame with holes through which his head and hands were thrust. The ears might be nailed to the device and a paper naming the offence attached to his clothing. Sometimes with political offences the person in the pillory might be fêted, as with 'Freeborn' John Lilburne, but on other occasions a crowd would stone a victim, often killing him. Sollom Emlyn wrote of the pillory:

> As to the pillory that is intended to expose the offender to shame and infamy, and to mark him out to the public as a person not fit to be trusted, but to be shunned and avoided by all creditable and honourable men. Never did the law design that he should be exposed to the peltings of a mob, or the assaults and injuries of a furious rabble.[51]

Pillories were erected where large crowds could assemble, often on a market day, and although an offender would generally be there for no more than an hour very

47. Sir E. Coke. 3 *Institute. Op. cit.* London, E. & R. Brooke. Epilogue.
48. W. Blackstone. (1830) *Commentaries on the Law of England.* London, Thomas Tegg. vol. iv. p. 78.
49. E. Leigh. (15 May 1652) *A Philological Commentary.* BL. E 1272 (1), p. 97.
50. Peter Ackroyd. (2000) *London: The Biography.* London, Vintage. p. 65.
51. *State Trials.* (2nd edn. 1730) Preface.

serious injuries were frequently occasioned. As imprisonment became the secondary punishment to the death penalty in the early nineteenth century the need for the pillory disappeared and it was abolished by statute in 1837.[52]

Whipping was a common punishment for the offence of simple larceny. Beattie has shown that, at Assizes in Surrey in the 18 years between 1736 and 1753, 85 per cent of those tried for grand larceny but convicted of petty larceny were whipped.[53] This punishment was also used against vagrants and parents of illegitimate children. The whipping could be carried out privately in a gaol or publicly by a local constable. Some public whippings took place at a 'whipping post' but more often the prisoner was tied to the back of a moving cart, stripped to the waist and whipped 'until his back be bloody.' The cart would pass down a prescribed street and in the City of York the practice is recalled by a narrow street named 'Whip-ma-Whop-ma-Gate' a short distance from the city gaol. This type of corporal punishment was class based. 'Gentlemen (and, it goes without saying, gentlewomen) were not subjected to whippings in public because the loss of honour they would incur would be a greater punishment than the law intended.'[54]

The ducking stool was used for scolds who were ducked over head and ears in what was often muddy or stinking water and this also sometimes resulted in death. Fines were imposed for a whole variety of offences including the use of insulting words, cheating, petty fraud and contempt of officials. The actual fine could range from a few pence for a minor offence to 100 pounds for a serious offence such as insulting words amounting to sedition.

Ecclesiastical courts had no power to imprison but enforced their decisions with penance and excommunication. Penance involved the person found guilty publicly confessing that he deserved punishment and asking for the Almighty's pardon. Excommunication by the Church resulted in severe legal penalties such as denial of the right to sue or to receive a legacy. The rich could commute both penance and excommunication with a money payment which, in the main, left the poor to suffer the punishments.[55] A person could be made to appear before an ecclesiastical court, in private and without any knowledge of who his accuser was, on mere suspicion of immorality or irreligion. Questions would be asked about private affairs including relations between husband and wife or with a person of the opposite sex. An accused had to defend himself by bringing compurgators to swear on oath as to his character—a method of 'defence' abandoned by the Common Law centuries earlier. Stephen wrote that such courts were,

52. 7 Will. and 1 Vict. c. 23.
53. J. M. Beattie. (1977) 'Crime and Courts in Surrey in 1736-1753.' In J.S. Cockburn. (ed.) *Crime in England 1550-1800*. London, Methuen & Co. Ltd. p. 177.
54. J. M. Beattie. (1986) *Crime and the Courts in England 1660-1800*. Oxford, Clarendon Press. p. 463.
55. Donald Veall. (1970) *The Popular Movement for Law Reform: 1640-1660*. Oxford, The Clarendon Press. p. 11.

in name as well as in fact an inquisition, differing from the Spanish Inquisition in the circumstances that it did not ... employ torture, and that the bulk of the business of the courts was of a comparatively unimportant kind.[56]

IMPRISONMENT AND BRIDEWELLS

Generally speaking prisons were not kept for punishing offenders as in modern times. In the main they housed prisoners awaiting trial and debtors, who could be incarcerated indefinitely. Official investigations into the debtors imprisoned in the Fleet and Upper Bench prisons in 1653 revealed that, 'the largest committals were 29 years for a debt of £832 3s. 4d. and 24 years for a debt of £1,150.'[57] They were not purpose-built, generally being part of a castle or dungeons under the courthouse or other public building. It is estimated there were about 200 throughout the country.[58] Conditions in prisons varied in that the wealthy could pay to be properly fed. Generally speaking, however, conditions were appalling. Prison officials would often steal food intended for the prisoners and near starvation was common. Conditions were normally insanitary and gaol fever was endemic. The income of prison officials was drawn from fees paid by prisoners at various stages including a fee payable on release which did not occur until the fee was paid.

A peculiar institution was the bridewell or house of correction. The first of these was presented to London by Edward VI in 1553. Earlier it had been Bridewell Palace, a residence of Henry VIII. It stood on the banks of the Fleet river and was so named as it stood close to a well dedicated to St. Bride. The papal delegation had met here in 1528 to discuss the king's divorce from Catherine of Aragon. It was also used by Cardinal Wolsey but abandoned by the king after Wolsey's fall from grace in 1530.[59] Its purpose, when given by Edward VI, was to set the poor and idle to work instead of imprisoning them.

Nevertheless, the paramount need was seen to be to keep order in the land and an Act of 1572[60] claimed that the country was infested with vagabonds who were daily responsible for horrible murders, thefts and other great outrages. On that premise it provided that all able-bodied vagrants over 14 years of age should be seized, prosecuted, whipped and burned through the right ear. After that they would be immune from further seizure for 40 days but if after that time they were still vagrants they were to be put to death.

56. J. F. Stephen. (1883) *A History of the Criminal Law of England.* London, Routledge/Thoemmes. vol. ii. p. 402.
57. Donald Veall. *The Popular Movement for Law Reform: 1640-60. Op. cit.* p. 13.
58. S. & B. Webb. (1936 edn) *English Prisons under Local Government.* London, Cass. pp. 3-4.
59. Wikipedia online.
60. 14 Eliz. c. 5.

Perhaps in response to such a draconian measure the statute was followed in 1576 with another[61] of Elizabeth requiring justices of the peace (JPs) in Quarter Sessions to set up houses of correction in order to punish vagrants but also to set them to work. The governor was appointed by the justices and was paid a salary rather than fees from the inmates. This was the first serious attempt to use labour as a reformative aspect to punishment and it laid the basis for the later retreat from the ubiquitous death penalty and the rise of the penitentiary. Indeed, under the Gaols Act of 1823 houses of correction were incorporated into the county gaols to become prisons, although still under the control of JPs in Quarter Sessions.

Clearly, under the Tudors there was a substantial increase in the severity of the criminal law and punishments in order to reinforce the coercive power of the Crown after the break with Rome. So far as the Common Law is concerned it has been said that by the sixteenth century it had done, 'no more than systematise barbarity.'[62]

CRIMINAL PROCEDURE

A person accused of felony was imprisoned until his trial. Following the Marian bail and committal legislation of the 1550s,[63] on preliminary hearings he was examined by a magistrate and his answers recorded to form the depositions for his trial. He was assumed to be guilty and the magistrate acted inquisitorially rather than judicially. The statutes established that the magistrate was not a judicial officer but an agent of the king (the prosecutor) who should ensure effective prosecution of the felon. Witnesses for the prosecution were bound over to appear at the trial whilst the accused could not compel the attendance of witnesses and could not know the exact nature of the indictment against him or have access to the depositions of prosecution witnesses.[64] The accused (and his witnesses, if any) were not permitted to give evidence on oath, since following the precedent set by trial by ordeal, the result of a trial by jury was believed to bear a 'divine Imprimatur'[65] and a conflict of oaths between the parties was considered blasphemous and inappropriate. Thus the evidence of prosecution witnesses, given under oath, had greater credibility and impact.

In English criminal law indictments for felony have always been taken in the name of the monarch and, in early times, it was considered *lès majesté* for those indicted to be allowed counsel against the king or queen, except on a point of law so certified by the judge. This was laid down judicially in a landmark case in the reign

---

61. 18 Eliz. c. 3.
62. S. F. C. Milsom. (1969 edn) *Historical Foundations of the Common Law*. London, Butterworths. p. 361.
63. 2 & 3 P. and M. c. 10.
64. J. M. Beattie. (1991) 'Scales of Justice: Defence Counsel and the English Criminal Trial in the Eighteenth and Nineteenth Centuries.' 9 (2) *Law and History Review*. University of Illinois Press. pp. 223-3.
65. George Fisher. (1997) 'The Jury's Rise as Lie Detector'. New Haven, *Yale Law Journal*. p. 602.

of Edward I, for all indictments for treason and felony.[66] By Tudor times jurists such as Coke sought other explanations for the 'no counsel' rule and held that a prisoner could better express the truth in person than through the medium of a lawyer. In addition, the judge would act as his or her counsel.[67] Unfortunately, most prisoners were completely at a loss in court and the Law Reports of the time are full of cases where judges patently failed to assist those brought before them. In one felony case, when the judge addressed the jury he said he could not sum up the evidence fully and concluded his short address to them by saying, ' I am sensible I have omitted many things; but I am a little faint and cannot repeat any more of the evidence.'[68]

In State Trials the defence could call no witnesses at all. In his trial Sir Walter Raleigh was not allowed to call as a witness Lord Cobham whose confession the prosecution had relied upon as evidence against Raleigh. It was said that if Cobham gave evidence he might retract his confession.[69] Similarly, in the trial of Sir Nicholas Throckmorton in 1554 for high treason a defence witness, John Fitzwilliam, was peremptorily removed from the courtroom without being allowed to speak. 'The court have nothing to do with you,' said the judge who revealingly added, 'probably you would not be so ready in a good cause.'[70] Throckmorton reminded the judges that Queen Mary had told the court that defence witnesses should be heard, but it was to no avail. And, when Puritan minister, John Udall, was tried at Croydon Assizes in 1590 for seditious libel his witnesses were not permitted to give evidence 'against the queen's majesty.'[71] He sensibly replied, 'Which seemeth strange to me, for methinks it should be for the queen to hear all things on both sides, especially when the life of any of her subjects is in question.'[72]

There were no criminal rules of evidence as we understand them today to assist prisoners. Hearsay evidence and confessions of accomplices were admissible, originals of documents were not required and a presumption of innocence was unheard of as was cross-examination. In some cases the trial could be a free-for-all with the prisoner, the judge and members of the jury all speaking or asking questions as they wished.

In conclusion, it may be summed up that at the time English criminal law was a monstrous mess of strange technicalities, curious anomalies and barbarous penalties, all lacking any principles of reason or justice. The principal redeeming feature was the presence in trials of the petty jury.

---

66. Year Books 30 and 31. Edw. I. (Rolls Series) pp. 529-30.
67. Sir E. Coke. 3 *Institute. Op. cit.* p. 49.
68. 13 Howells *State Trials.* (1818) col. 1187.
69. 2 *State Trials.* cols. 16-23.
70. 1 *State Trials.* col. 8091271-81.
71. *Ibid* .col. 1271.
72. *Ibid.*

BARRISTERS

These formed the higher echelon of lawyers. The Inns of Court were centres of general education not only for those intending to enter the legal profession but also for many who had no intention of practising law. In the latter half of the sixteenth century they were the intellectual, geographical, and fashion centre of London. Of the 310 members of the Long Parliament who went to an Inn of Court, only 75 practised as barristers afterwards.[73] Seven years studying preceded call to the Bar and recruits were restricted to sons of the wealthy. Coke said somewhat tortuously of the Inns that they, 'altogether do make the most famous universities for profession of law only, or of any human science, that is in the world, and advanceth itself above all others.'[74] At least, the law of the Inns was the Common Law as distinct from the emphasis on civil law in the universities.

Only a barrister could be elevated to become a judge and then only after becoming a serjeant-at-law, a title purchased from the king for £600 in the seventeenth century. On his appointment a serjeant had to present gold rings to all existing serjeants and 'other great persons' and hold a celebratory feast.[75] According to Coke, a serjeant's hood, robes, coif[76] and other significant ornaments were a special mark of dignity by the Crown. Serjeants and judges not only dominated the bar but they formed a wealthy elite at the centre of government.

To give a few examples, David Williams (1537-1613), a judge of the King's Bench, was said to have been enormously rich as a result of his profession and to have invested heavily in landed property.[77] Thomas Coventry (1578-1640), Recorder of London, Solicitor-General, Attorney-General and Lord Keeper, 'raised a great fortune and barony for posterity.'[78] Henry Calthorpe (1586-1637), Attorney of the Court of Wards, 'by his great prudence and eminent practice together with the profits arising out of the Court of Wards in a great measure augmented the ancient inheritance of his ancestors.'[79] John Popham (1531-1607), Solicitor-General, Attorney-General and Chief Justice of the King's Bench who presided at the trials of Essex, Raleigh and the Gunpowder Plotters, was believed to have left a vast estate worth £10,000 a year to his son.[80] Thomas Egerton (1540-1617), Solicitor-General,

---

73. Donald Veall. *The Popular Movement for Law Reform: 1640-60. Op. cit.* p.44.
74. Sir E. Coke. *Reports. Op. cit.* Preface.
75. *Ibid.* pp. 46-7.
76. A coif was a white silk cap worn by serjeants in court. Coke once observed that it was like the helmet of Minerva, the goddess of counsel, and likened its four corners to science, experience, observation and recording.
77. *Dictionary of National Biography.* lxi. p. 389.
78. James Whitelocke.(himself a judge of the King's Bench) (1858) *Liber Famelicus.* London, Camden Society Publications. vol. vxx. p. 94.
79. H. Phillips. (1684) *The Grandeur of the Law: an Exact Collection of the Nobility and Gentry of this Kingdom whose Honours and Estates have been Acquired by the Practice of the Law.* London, A. Jones p. 148.
80. *Aubrey's Brief Lives.*(ed. O.L. Dick) (1972) London, Penguin Books. pp. 407-9.

Attorney-General, Master of the Rolls, Lord Keeper and Lord Chancellor, left an estate at his death worth £8,000 a year.[81]

ATTORNEYS

These were considered to be the junior—and inferior—branch of the legal profession. In the main they were the sons of skilled artisans and farmers and originally acted as agents of their clients in court. They represented suitors who did not appear in court in person, often to avoid the trouble and expense of long journeys to Westminster. As today, by the sixteenth century they had become officers of the court and generally dealt with all the preliminary work leading to trial. As persons accused of felony were not allowed counsel to appear in court the attorneys dealt mainly with civil litigation and, on the criminal side, misdemeanours. For admission as an attorney a man had either to study at one of the Inns or serve five years as a solicitor or clerk to a judge, serjeant, barrister or court clerk. To be a solicitor, on the other hand, no qualifications were necessary and their ranks naturally included unscrupulous persons.

PUBLIC IMAGE

At the time lawyers generally were held in low esteem. A popular rhyme about barristers ran:

> These are the busie days when the Green Bag
> At Westminster about the Hall doth wag;
> The effects whereof (Brethren and Friends) are double,
> The lawyers get the coin, clients the trouble.[82]

It was said by Hale to be a great dishonour that a man was capable, for a little money, to be hired to say or do otherwise than as he thought. But the dishonour did not end there. Clients were often ill-used, as well as fleeced, for their advocate's personal advantage and the courts themselves were frequently misled by unscrupulous lawyers. It is little wonder that during the Commonwealth John Lilburne and the Levellers urged Oliver Cromwell to get rid of the 'vermin and caterpillars', as they called the lawyers of the day.[83]

So far as attorneys are concerned, Hale disparagingly referred to them as, 'Multitudes of Attorneys practising in the Great Courts at Westminster, who are ready at

81. H. Phillips. *The Grandeur of the Law. Op. cit.* p. 148.
82. David Ogg. (1967 edn.) *England in the Reign of Charles II.* Oxford, The Clarendon Press. p. 133.
83. *Agreement of the People.* (1648) In D.M. Wolfe. (1944) *Leveller Manifestoes of the Puritan Revolution.* New York, Thomas Nelson & Sons. p. 303.

every market to gratify the Spleen, Spite or Pride of every plaintiff.'[84] Not untypical was attorney Richard Farr who was stated to have forged title deeds, received stolen goods and engaged in the sale of bottled ale! He was eventually hanged for burglary. According to historian David Ogg, 'As a bird of prey [Farr] had lived, as a bird of plumage he died, dressed in a purple gown and a vermilion waistcoat, having left 20 shillings for a sermon on the text, *Blessed are the dead which die in the Lord,* afterwards amended by the chaplain to the more appropriate, *Except ye repent ye shall all likewise perish.* [85] As for solicitors, Parliament had to pass a law to weed out the many who were dishonest.[86] As one authority, cited by Sir William Holdsworth exclaimed, 'In our age there are stepped up a new sort of people called solicitors, unknown to the records of the law, who, like the grasshoppers of Egypt, devour the whole land.'[87]

Judges were frequently no better and the Bench was often an object of both scorn and fear. Lacking independence under the Tudors and Stuarts they were intimidated and sometimes sacked for not doing as they were told by the monarch. When Coke refused to accept the king's interference in a case he was dismissed as Chief Justice of the King's Bench on 14 November 1616 although James admitted he was in no way corrupt but a good judge. Perhaps, his dismissal was for the best as he played a prominent role in framing and carrying the *Petition of Right* in the Parliament of 1628 against Charles I's attempts at personal rule by the 'divine right of kings'. Altogether, the role of lawyers in bringing to an abrupt end the rule of authoritarian kings who wished to use the law simply to buttress their own power was pre-eminent.

---

84. Sir Matthew Hale. (3rd edn. 1739) *History of the Common Law of England.* London, T. Waller. p. 175.
85. David Ogg. *England in the Reign of Charles II. Op. cit.* p. 133.
86. 3 Jac. I. c. vii.
87. Sir William Holdsworth. (1966) *A History of English Law. Op. cit.* vol. vi. p. 454.

CHAPTER 6

The Commonwealth

EXECUTION OF THE KING

When the Civil War broke out between king and Parliament in 1642 the execution of Charles I was no part of Parliament's purpose. His opponents wanted to change his policies and the style of his rule, not end that rule. But once his armies were defeated this was to change. Particularly since he continued not only to hold to the doctrine of 'divine right' but to intrigue with the Scots in a plot to overthrow his victorious opponents. Although the Presbyterians in Parliament continued to endeavour to reach an agreement with the king the army, led by Oliver Cromwell, decided he should face trial.

Accordingly, on 6 December 1648 Colonel Pride's regiment purged the House of Commons by force, in what became known as 'Pride's Purge', and prevented some 140 members from attending. The resulting Rump Parliament, as it was called, was deeply hostile to the king and, buttressed by the army, set its mind to destroying the monarchy. Even so, on 6 January 1649 only 46 members were present when the Commons decided to appoint a High Court to try the king. The House of Lords refused to participate and the vote in the Commons was a mere 26 to 20.

Despite this apparent reluctance, on 20 January Charles was brought by river in the king's barge to the new *ad hoc* High Court of Justice sitting in the Painted Chamber of Westminster Hall. Here he was charged with high treason in levying war, causing thousands to be slain, exhausting the public treasury and destroying trade. Lawyer John Bradshaw presided over the 135 Commissioners who consented to act as judges although only 58 of them actually sat regularly. In contrast, another lawyer, John Cook, eagerly agreed to act as prosecutor. Charles refused to recognise the court and plead, on the constitutional ground that as the House of Lords had been abolished there was no properly constituted Parliament. Cook argued that if a prisoner stood mute he could be treated as having confessed although in law this did not apply when the charge was treason. The enthusiastic Cook was not to be denied, however, and added that the Commons had already decided that the treason was notorious and the facts 'as clear as crystal and as the sun that shines at noonday.' He then produced witnesses who gave evidence of the king's crimes and without a presenting a defence Charles was found guilty and executed in Whitehall on 30 January 1649.[1]

---

1. For a lively account of the trial and the role of Cook, see Geoffrey Robertson, (2005) *The Tyrannicide Brief*

In historical terms the Civil War was the means by which Parliament and those it represented secured their freedom from absolute monarchy. But, like the sorcerer's apprentice they faced the danger of being overwhelmed by the flood of popular demands the war had generated in the army and radical groups such as the Levellers. In the famous Putney Debates held between the Levellers and the army council in October and November 1647 the Levellers proposed a degree of male suffrage and won a great deal of support from the army representatives. However, saying he feared anarchy, Cromwell successfully insisted that the vote be tied to property and managed to prevent the repercussions going too far and endangering property rights altogether. In effect, he intervened to hold back coercively the progress of the Rebellion. In the course of doing so he succeeded in suppressing the Levellers whose programme of liberty of conscience and reform of the franchise and government had a strong following among the rank and file of the army and among the urban population. Nonetheless, the Protectorate was never popular with the landed gentry, the merchants and the professional classes and, once Cromwell had accomplished his task and they felt secure, they were prepared to compromise with the king's son as a restraining influence provided he would work with Parliament to preserve their interests.

CRIMINAL JUSTICE AGITATION

Prior to the Commonwealth (1649-1653) and the Protectorate (1653-1659) there was considerable and justifiable agitation for reform of criminal justice, although it did not extend to the ranks of the legal profession. The impulse for the agitation was driven by the fact that at the time some judges and lawyers were corrupt and the criminal law deficient in principles of reason or justice. As we have seen, felony, which covered most crimes, attracted the death penalty and an accused was not permitted to testify, have witnesses give evidence on oath or engage counsel except on points of law. Generally penalties were harsh. Juries could be imprisoned merely for reaching a verdict the judge did not want to hear.

The general population had been able to do little about this, until the world was turned upside down when Johann Gutenberg invented the printing press in Germany around 1450. This world-shattering new invention was introduced into England by William Caxton (c.1422-1491) where it soon expanded the scope of literature so that many people, for the first time, could read, argue and discuss the issues that concerned them in their daily lives. So far as criminal justice is concerned, cheap printing produced an absolute avalanche of books, pamphlets and tracts advocating reform for some time before the Civil War and this continued during the Commonwealth and the Protectorate.

The Story of the Man who Sent Charles I to the Scaffold. London, Chatto and Windus.

LANGUAGE OF THE LAW

One of the grievances of the pamphleteers was that the language of the law was a bastardised form of Norman-French. Court documents were written in Latin and were obtuse and verbose. Yet, as early as 1362 a statute in the reign of Edward III had enacted that courts should use the English language and not French. The justification it gave for this was that,

> the laws, customs and statutes of this realm are not commonly known ... for that they be pleaded, shewed and judged in the French tongue, which is much unknown in the said realm, so that the people do implead, or be impleaded in the king's court, and in the courts of others, have no knowledge or understanding of that which is said for them or against them by their serjeants and other pleaders.[2]

It was not only people who appeared in person, therefore, that the statute was concerned about. Those who were represented by lawyers were also at a disadvantage and, perhaps more important, the law and statutes were not generally understood. However, the statute remained a dead letter, largely because legal language had become technical. Even Sir Edward Coke, who wrote his *Institutes* in English, 'to derive from the Conqueror as little as we could'[3] said that, 'So many ancient terms and words drawn from that legal French are grown to be *vocabula artis* ... so apt and significant to express the true sense of the laws, and are so woven in the laws themselves, as it is in a manner impossible to change them, neither ought legal terms to be changed.'[4] And, indeed, no change was to be effected until the Commonwealth—three centuries after the 1362 statute.

OLIVER CROMWELL AND THE LAW

From his words to Parliaments, and elsewhere, it is clear that Cromwell shared the strong belief in the necessity for criminal law reform. In 1650 he told Edmund Ludlow, a staunch republican, that he was determined to reform the clergy and the law. 'But', he said,

> the sons of Zeruiah are yet too strong for us and we cannot mention the reformation of the law but they presently cry out, we design to destroy property; whereas the law as it is now constituted, serves only to maintain the lawyers and to encourage the rich to oppress the poor.[5]

---

2. 36 Edw. III, st. 1c, 15.
3. Sir E. Coke (1797) 3 *Institute*. London, E. & R. Brooke. Preface.
4. Coke on Littleton. (1823 edn) London, Hargrave and Butler. Preface.
5. Edmund Ludlow. (1894) *Memoirs of Edmund Ludlow* (ed. C.H. Firth) Osford, The Clarendon Press. vol. i. p. 246.

Then in a string of speeches he went on to confirm his reforming credentials. In April 1653, in his closing speech to the Rump Parliament before it was dissolved he complained at the inability of its law committee to accomplish any reform of the law. He charged the Parliament with having 'espoused the corrupt interest of Presbytery and the lawyers who were supporters of tyranny and oppression.'[6]

A new Parliament was elected in September 1654 and when he opened it Cromwell told its members of the government's intention to reform the law, make the laws plain, short and inexpensive. He promised that appropriate Bills would be put before them to carry the reforms through.[7] Then, addressing Parliament on 17 September 1656, Cromwell said:

> there is one general grievance in the nation. It is the law ... [t]he truth of it is, there are wicked and abominable laws that will be in your power to alter. To hang a man for six-and-eightpence and I know not what; to hang for a trifle and quit murder—it is in the ministration of the law, through the ill-informing of it. I have known in my experience abominable murderers acquitted. And to see men lose their lives for petty matters! This is a thing God will reckon for.[8]

Again, in April 1657, Cromwell returned to the need for law reform when addressing a parliamentary committee formed to discuss a constitutional settlement. On this occasion he said,

> I hope you will think sincerely, as before God, that the laws must be regulated; I hope you will ... I confess, if any man would ask me 'why, how would you have it done?' I confess I do not know how.[9]

This confession of doubt came, however, near the end of his rule and it is ironic that all his yearning for reform of the law came to naught because each time there was hope he dissolved Parliament.

During Cromwell's rule Matthew Hale reluctantly served as a judge.[10] He told Cromwell that he was not satisfied with the lawfulness of his authority and was averse to accepting any commission under it. He finally accepted the position, however, after Cromwell told him that, 'if they would not permit him to govern by red gowns, he was resolved to govern by red coats.'[11]

Following the Restoration, Hale returned to the question of law reform and

---

6. *Ibid.* p. 352.
7. W. C. Abbott (ed.) (1937-47) *The Writings and Speeches of Oliver Cromwell*.Cambridge, Mass. Harvard University Press. vol. iii. p. 439.
8. *Ibid.* vol. iv. p. 274.
9. *Ibid.* p. 493.
10. John Hostettler. (2002) *The Red Gown: The Life and Works of Sir Matthew Hale.* Chichester, Barry Rose Law Publishers.
11. Sollom Emlyn. (1736) Preface to Matthew Hale. *The History of the Pleas of the Crown.* London, E. and R. Nutt and R. Gosling. vol. i. p. ii.

wrote his, *Of the Alteration, Amendment or Reformation of the Lawes of England.*[12] In it he argued that the reason law reform was so greatly desired, during the Interregnum, by 'those then in power', and why it was resisted by many 'good and knowing men', was that in the absence of any constitutional settlement, men were afraid that if the laws were reformed, their estates would be jeopardised should there be a restoration of the old order.' He believed, he said, that, if there had been a thoroughgoing reformation of the courts and the property laws, a Restoration would have been much more difficult to achieve.[13] Seemingly unaware of the deep conflicts existing in Cromwell's Parliaments, Hale concluded that although there was a deep desire for law reform, MPs felt that Cromwell's rule could not last, the king would return and it would be better to leave the existing law alone for the time being. Yet, this ignores the fervour with which many MPs seized upon the work of the Hale Commission in an endeavour to effect reform which Cromwell inadvertently thwarted.

There were, however, influences other than Cromwell's problems with his Parliaments that stood in the path of reform. The lawyers and the judges, for example, were opposed to law reform. The wealthiest of the lawyers were among the richest men of their day.[14] And, of 31 judges who held office during the Interregnum only Hale was a law reformer. Of 47 barristers called to be serjeants a mere four were reformers. 'In spite of all the political changes of the times, the legal establishment remained remarkably secure; there was no real challenge to the authority of the legal dynasty.'[15]

THE LEVELLERS AND LAW REFORM

Of all the groups of agitators, pamphleteers and libertarian sects of the time the Levellers were the most prominent. The word 'Leveller' was, in fact, a term of abuse, used by their opponents to denigrate them and their beliefs and falsely suggest they wished to abolish property rights. Some of their demands were democratic but they were not democrats and in their struggle for a better franchise they excluded servants, paupers and even wage-earners. Nevertheless, believing that all men were born free and equal and had natural rights as individuals many of their ideas are incorporated in the United States Constitution and Bill of Rights.[16] They argued that the law should protect the poor and the wealthy equally, but they disliked the lawyers with a deep intensity and looked back to a misty concept of a kind of popular Anglo-Saxon justice. Although their picture of Anglo-Saxon law was unreal it nonetheless led them to demanding decentralisation of justice and increased power for the

---

12. *Hargrave Tracts.* (1665) BL. *Add. Mss.* 18,234.
13. (1665) pp. 274-5.
14. See ante. *Chapter 5*, pages 95, 96.
15. Donald Veall. (1970) *The Popular Movement for Law Reform. 1640-1660.* Oxford, Clarendon Press. p. 229.
16. See Leonard W. Levy. (1968) *Origins of the Fifth Amendment.* New York, Oxford University Press.

jury. This last was to ensure that the lower classes participated in the administration of justice. What the Levellers wanted was,

> freedom from arbitrary arrest, no self-incrimination, the right to bail, no crime without a law, equality before the law, separation of law-making from law execution, trial by witnesses, no long imprisonment, no imprisonment for debt, humane treatment of prisoners, limitation of the death penalty ...[17]

Deployed against them were the lawyers and the officers of state.

One pamphleteer, William Cole, wrote *A Rod for the Lawyers*,[18]—a fierce tirade, not only against the lawyers but also the Common Law itself. The criminal law, he wrote, because it was made for the benefit of the king and lords of manors and 'other great officers who were the king's creatures', had no compunction in taking away a man's life and property. If the hanging of thieves was to continue it should be 'the great ones' who were hanged not 'the little ones.' Parliament had been unable to make the nation free due to the large numbers of lawyers in Parliament. It was no good expecting grapes from thorns or figs from thistles. The lawyers, those 'insatiable cannibals whose carcases will never be full gorged with the spoils of the poor and innocent,' had a complete monopoly and exploited it to the full. He denounced the concept of precedent when so many decisions were based on bribery and he advocated local justice without the 'lying sophistry or quibbles' of lawyers.[19]

In 1649, when the Leveller leader John Lilburne, a Lieutenant-Colonel in the republican army, and others, were held in the Tower of London for declaring that Cromwell had betrayed the revolution they smuggled out a manifesto for constitutional reform called the *Agreement of the People*. This set out the Leveller programme and, among other things, called for:

- a reformed franchise;
- equality of all before the law;
- jury trial in all cases where life, liberty or property was threatened;
- a right against self-incrimination;
- abolition of capital punishment in most cases;
- freedom of religion and the press;
- punishments to fit the crime; and
- no imprisonment for debt.

17. Donald Veall. *The Popular Movement for Law Reform 1640-1660. Op. cit.* p. 101.
18. William Cole. (12 July 1659). *A Rod for the Lawyers.* BL. Thomason Tracts. E985 (15)
19. *Ibid.* pp. 319-26.

This amounted to a clarion call for justice. And, not for much longer was it considered politic to allow Lilburne opportunities to express his opinions, and those of his comrades, in public.

TRIALS OF JOHN LILBURNE

Hence, on 24 October 1649 the Lord Mayor of London was one of 40 dignitaries who attended the Guildhall to constitute an extraordinary commission of *oyez and terminer*. They were to try, with a jury, this outspoken Leveller leader. Born a gentleman, Lilburne was a complex character who had a passion for liberty. Held in the Tower, he was charged with high treason for publishing sundry, 'scandalous, poisonous and traitorous books asserting that Cromwell's government was tyrannical, usurped and unlawful.'[20] It is worth considering the case in some detail as it illustrates the ideas behind much of what the Levellers stood for, what they were demanding and how they conceived of criminal justice.

At the commencement of the trial Lilburne told the presiding judge, Mr. Justice Keble,

All the privilege that I shall crave this day at your hands is no more but that which is properly and singly the liberty of every free-born Englishman, namely the benefit of the laws and liberties thereof, which by my birthright and inheritance is due to me and which I have fought for as well as others have done.[21]

Before he would plead, Lilburne asked to see the indictment under which he was charged and for counsel to assist him on points of law. Both requests were refused and after prolonged argument he pleaded not guilty. Holding in his hand a book by Sir Edward Coke—'that great Oracle of the Laws of England'—he argued that his trial by the Special Commission of *oyez and terminer* was contrary to the *Petition of Right* of 1628 and to the Act of 1641 which abolished all such extraordinary tribunals.[22]

JUDGES MERE CIPHERS

Lilburne asked to be allowed to speak to the jury who, he asserted, were judges not only of law but of fact. Keble expressed his fury at the suggestion that juries could decide questions of law, upon which Lilburne burst out, 'You that call yourselves

---

20. 1 *State Tryals*. (1719) London, T. Goodwin and Others. pp. 580-640.
21. Clement Walker. (1649) *The Trial of Lt. Col. John Lilburne … Being as Exactly Penned and Taken in Shorthand, as it was Possible to be Done in such a Crowd and Noise*. London, Theodorus Verax.
22. *State Tryals. Op. cit.* p. 582. Lilburne excluded ordinary commissions of *oyez and terminer*. He was attacking only special commissions.

judges of the law are no more but Norman intruders; and indeed and in truth, if the jury please, are no more but ciphers to pronounce their verdict.'[23] This was a direct appeal from the Levellers' belief that the jury was born in Anglo-Saxon times before the Normans had cast their alien yoke on the country. The concept of what was called the 'Norman Yoke' had a patriotic appeal and was of significance to the Puritans struggling against what they saw as an alien aristocracy.[24] The Levellers subscribed to the myth of a golden age of Anglo-Saxon liberties under which all men were free, held their land freely, met in free popular assemblies, declared the law and judged one another in popular local courts. The theory, which was not all myth, drew disdain from the judges but was calculated to be popular with juries.

Finally, Lilburne addressed the jury in a direct and personal way. He defiantly returned to his theme that the jurors were the judges of both fact and law. He resoundingly declared that they, 'by the law of *England* are the Conservators and sole Judges of my Life, having inherent in them alone the judicial Power of the Law, as well as Fact ... I desire you to know your Power and do your Duty.'[25]

On hearing him say that the jurors had inherent in them alone, 'the judicial Power of the Law as well as Fact,

the spectators who crowded the courtroom cried in a loud voice, 'Amen, Amen,' and gave an extraordinary great hum, which made the judges look something untowardly about them, and caused Major-General Skippon to send for three more fresh companies of foot soldiers.[26]

'PERVERSE VERDICT'

After Lilburne had addressed the jury, Keble instructed them that 'You will clearly find that never was the like treason hatched in England.'[27] Notwithstanding this direction, the jury found the prisoner not guilty of any of the alleged treasons. Whereupon, 'Immediately the whole multitude of people in the hall gave such a loud and unanimous shout as is believed was never heard in Guild Hall, which lasted for about half an hour without intermission.'[28] Amidst wild jubilation bonfires were lit and church bells rung throughout London with the army celebrating with the people in support of the supposed ancient rights of the jury.[29]

After the trial, the jurors themselves were taken to the Old Bailey for individual examination on their 'perverse verdict'—an earlier procedure the Commonwealth had not dispensed with. Several of them told their interrogators that they had only

23. *Ibid.* p. 627.
24. Donald Veall. *The Popular Movement for Law Reform 1640-1660. Op. cit.* p. 105.
25. *State Tryals. Op. cit.* p. 633.
26. *Ibid.*
27. *Ibid.* p. 1402.
28. H. N. Brailsford. (1961) *The Levellers and the English Revolution.* London, The Cresset Press. p. 603.
29. *Ibid.* p. 602.

discharged their consciences and others vowed that despite what the judges had told them they took themselves to be 'Judges of Matters of Law' as well as of fact.[30] Cromwell is reported to have looked upon the acquittal of his former friend as a greater defeat than the loss of a battle[31] and, because the press of the Commonwealth avoided all mention of the trial, the Levellers had the last word. They struck a medal with a portrait of their hero on one side and the names of the jurors on the other. Its inscription reads: 'John Lilburne, saved by the power of the Lord and the integrity of his jury, who are Judges of law as well as fact. October 26, 1649.'[32]

However, the view of the jury put forward by Lilburne and the Levellers was not without its critics. The opinion of the government was well expressed by Henry Parker. In a class-ridden tract attacking Lilburne's stand at his trial, he declared:

> The judges because they understand the law are to be degraded and made servants to the jurors; but the jurors because they understand no law are to be mounted aloft, where they are to administer justice to the whole kingdom. The judges because they are commonly gentlemen by birth and have had honourable education are to be exposed to scorn, but the jurors because they be commonly mechanics bred up illiterately to handicrafts are to be placed at the helm … cobblers must now practise physic instead of doctors; tradesmen must get into pulpits instead of divines and ploughmen must ride to the sessions instead of justices of the peace.[33]

Lilburne continued to dissent and in 1653 he was subjected to a second prosecution by the Commonwealth. This produced an argument about the jury that was to re-appear with embellishments when adopted by the Whigs during the events leading to the Glorious Revolution at the end of 1689. Having, under statute, been banished abroad on pain of death if he returned, Lilburne decided he was free to return when Cromwell dissolved the Rump Parliament. As a consequence he was brought to trial at the Old Bailey on 13 July 1653 for breaching his banishment. At his trial he once again appealed to the jury to decide the law as well as fact and acquit him on the ground that the statute under which he was banished was null and void under the true fundamental law of England.[34] At the end of the trial the jury found him not guilty of any crime worthy of death. Although acquitted for a second time, Lilburne was imprisoned for two years following this trial and died shortly thereafter. He had, however, planted the seeds of the dream of the jury's right to decide the law which was later to dominate Whig literature on the trial jury. It has been said that,

> Trial rights established by Leveller and Quaker activists were, later in the century, triumphantly mobilised by the Whigs in their own power struggle with the Stuart monarchy. Within just a few

---

30. *State Tryals. Op. cit.* pp. 638-40.
31. Brailsford. *The Levellers and the English Revolution, Op. cit.* p. 603.
32. *Ibid.*
33. *Ibid.* p. 490.
34. *Five State Trials.* (1886) col. 444.

decades, demands for free jury trial were to make the significant transition from the manifestos of radical libertarian puritanism to the mainstream ideology of the dominant political class.[35]

THE DIGGERS

Of the wealth of seventeenth century sects the Diggers, or True Levellers as they were sometimes known, alone spoke for agricultural workers. They also had less time for constitutional issues and were more concerned with economic questions and with defending the poor against the rich than the Levellers. They sought far more radical changes in society than the Levellers, but they too believed that a 'Norman Yoke' had been imposed on an idyllic Saxon England by William the Conqueror and his successors. Denouncing the Common Law, their leader Gerard Wynstanley, claimed that the, 'binding and restraining laws that have been made from one age to another since the Conquest were the cords, bands, manacles and yokes that the enslaved English, like Newgate prisoners, wear upon their hands and legs as they walk the streets.'[36]

Unlike the Levellers, the Diggers were hostile to trial by jury altogether since, Wynstanley complained, its composition meant that it was biased in favour of the landowners. As a consequence of that bias, juries had dispossessed them from their settlement at St. George's Hill on Walton Heath in Surrey. They were composed, he said, of 'rich freeholders and such as stood strongly for the Norman power.'[37] In fact, Wynstanley, who described himself as a servant, probably spoke for those whom the Levellers would have disenfranchised namely, servants, labourers, paupers and the economically unfree.[38]

Although believing in the theory of a Norman Yoke he transcended it. 'The best laws that England hath,' he declared, 'are yokes and manacles, tying one sort of people to another … All laws that are not grounded upon equity and reason, not giving a universal freedom to all but respecting persons, ought … to be cut off with the king's head.'[39] Kingly power, clergy, lawyers, and buying and selling were all linked; 'if one truly fall, all must fall.'[40] A sentiment unwittingly echoed by James I in his well-known aphorism, 'No bishop, no king' to show that if the Presbyterians abolished bishops in the Anglican Church he would quickly find himself without a crown.

---

35. Richard Vogler. (2005) *A World View of Criminal Justice*. Aldershot, Ashgate Publishing Limited. p. 204.
36. G. Wynstanley. (April 1649) *The Levellers Standard Advanced*. In G.H. Sabine (ed.) (1941) *The Works of Gerard Wynstanley*. Cornell University Press. p. 259.
37. *Ibid.* p. 327.
38. Christopher Hill. (1972) *The World Turned Upside Down: Radical Ideas During the English Revolution*. London, Temple Smith Ltd., p. 97.
39. G. H. Sabine.(ed.) (1941) *The Works of Gerrard Wynstanley*. Cornell University Press. pp 303, 390.
40. *Ibid.* pp. 381-2.

THE HALE COMMISSION

As we have seen, as part of the new society that both Cromwell and the Rump Parliament were endeavouring to establish they desired to introduce a reformed system of law. After all, there was considerable popular demand for law reform. As one prominent pamphleteer wrote, the nation should no longer be misgoverned by

> a hotch-pot of lawes so numerous as not to be learned or comprehended, some so differing as that they contradict and give the lye to one another, so irrational and absurd, to spare worse words, as that they character us to be one of the most barbarous people in the world.[41]

One consequence was the appointment of what became known as the Hale Commission in January 1652. This was charged by the House of Commons with, 'taking into consideration what inconveniences there are in the law; and how the mischiefs which grow from delays, the chargeableness and irregularities in the proceedings in the law may be prevented, and the speediest way to reform the same, and to present their opinions to such committee as the Parliament shall appoint.'[42] The Commission was named after Sir Matthew Hale who, although he only took the chair on ten occasions and attended 25 of its 59 meetings, had a considerable influence on the Commission and the Bills it produced.

No members of Parliament were allowed to sit on the Commission, which naturally could not legislate but was required to report to the Parliamentary Law Committee. Nevertheless, it could, and did, produce draft Bills. Eight lawyers were found who desired reform of the law and with 13 laymen they were appointed to the Commission which generally sat three times a week from 23 January to 23 July 1652 in the chamber of the abolished House of Lords. Apart from the lawyers its members included landed gentry, merchants and senior army officers. Prominent, in addition to Hale, were Major-General Desborough, an attorney and Cromwell's brother-in-law; Hugh Peters, a dedicated law reformer and scourge of the lawyers; the influential John Rushworth and Sir Anthony Ashley Cooper (afterwards Lord Shaftesbury).[43]

The lawyers proved to be the most active participants with one of their number always in the chair, and they prepared the draft Bills. But the other members had some knowledge of the law, with six of the laymen having been educated at the Inns of Court. The Commission's Minutes show that the debates were well-informed.[44]

---

41. Henry Robinson. (1653) *Certaine Proposals in order to a new Modelling of the Lawes.* Thomason Tracts. BL. E. 616(2). p. 3.
42. *House of Commons Journals.* (1652) vii. p. 58.
43. Charleston in South Carolina is at the confluence of two rivers, the Ashley and the Cooper, named after him for his efforts in establishing the old colonial town.
44. Commission Minutes. Hardwicke Papers. BL. *Add. MSS.* 35863.

They were written during the Commission's sittings and contain many deletions and alterations made as its arguments proceeded. Its meetings were often lengthy and there were sub-committees of three or four members who prepared papers on various subjects as well as drafting Bills.[45] It was a Commission eager to make proposals for comprehensive law reform and for this the lawyers, and Hale in particular, were of crucial importance. There is no evidence in the Minutes to confirm the belief of Sir William Holdsworth that the lawyers had a difficult time with the lay members.[46]

In its short life the Commission produce sixteen Bills. Some of them were read in the House of Commons in the months of March, April and May, while the Commission was sitting, and the remainder were presented to the Parliamentary Law Committee towards the end of July of that year.[47] Both the Law Committee and the Rump Parliament proved to be sympathetic but, despite this and the agitation for law reform in the country, they failed to secure the enactment of a single one of the Bills. Nevertheless, as we shall see, a number of reforms contained in the Bills were later introduced by the House of Commons itself and, indeed, whilst the Commission was being appointed, in a foretaste of what might be in store, the Commons had enacted that the fees and extravagant perquisites paid to judges should be replaced by fixed salaries to prevent abuse.

Humanitarian reform denied

The Commission was clearly not radical in some of its proposed revisions of the law. For instance, for perjury, which had a religious dimension under Puritan influence, the Commission proposed that the penalty should be placing in the pillory, loss of ears, slitting of the nostrils, searing with a hot iron and six months' imprisonment. Not that such punishments were unusual at the time but they did not reflect well on the Commission. What is important, however, is that many of the Commission's recommendations were more enlightened and foresighted and anticipated a great deal of humanitarian reform by more than 150 years.

With the criminal law, for example, it suggested a reduction in the sweeping incidence of the death penalty, around which every other aspect of the penal system turned. 'Wilful murderers' were still to be executed, however, and the abduction of a child under 16 years of age was to be made a capital offence. The Commission also proposed that prisoners should be permitted to engage counsel in all cases where the prosecution was represented and that their witnesses should be able to give evidence on oath. These proposals were not given effect under Cromwell, as will be seen, and had to wait until the eighteenth and nineteenth centuries before they were found to be acceptable.

---

45. Mary Cotterell. (1968) 'Interregnum Law Reform: the Hale Commission of 1652.' London, 83 *English Historical Review*. pp. 689-724.
46. Sir W. Holdsworth. (1966) *A History of English Law*. London, Methuen & Co. and Sweet and Maxwell. vol. vi. p. 423.
47. *Journals of the House of Commons*. (1652) vol. vii. pp. 121, 124, 130-1.

Legal aid for the poor was considered but was undermined by the condition that if a poor prisoner lost his case he was to be whipped and sent to a workhouse for a month. The Commission also proposed that the punishment, or more correctly torture, of *peine forte et dure*, under which an accused person was slowly pressed to death for refusing to plead, should be abolished. In its place they wanted a refusal to plead to be taken as a plea of guilty, rather than not guilty, with conviction following automatically—a strange means of mitigating an inhuman law. However, pressing to death was not done away with and was to continue, with the last case occurring in Cambridge in 1741. It was not until 1772 that statue finally made a refusal to plead equivalent to a plea of guilty in all cases and until 1827 that 'standing mute of malice' as it was called became treated as a plea of not guilty.

In fact, under the Commonwealth the plea of not guilty itself was dispensed with and replaced by 'I abide my lawful trial'[48]—hardly an improvement. It was also proposed that the burning at the stake of women felons should be replaced by hanging—a change not achieved until 1790. Claimed to have been a remnant of Norman policy, the burning of women alive was, as we have seen, accepted by Blackstone in graphic terms.[49] The Commission, against Hale's wishes, called for the abolition of benefit of clergy. Hale accepted 'benefit' because, 'tis in the parent's power to breed his child to read' [50] which entirely failed to address why a guilty person should be able to avoid the consequences of his crime. It was proposed by the Commission that pickpockets should not be executed for a first offence and that those charged with justifiable homicide should be acquitted.

All these proposals, and others dealing with civil cases, were under consideration during the Protectorate. However, most of them were successfully obstructed by lawyers and men of property in Parliament (but not from those lawyers sitting on the Commission who would not have been eligible as members had they been MPs). The Rump Parliament was committed to law reform but was closed down against its will by Cromwell on 19 April 1653. Cromwell still needed a Parliament, however, for reasons of legitimacy if nothing else. Accordingly, on 4 July 1653 a limited assembly of 140 nominated members was brought together and became known as 'Barebones Parliament' after Praise-God Barebone, a London leather salesman and Anabaptist preacher, who was member for the City of London and noted for his long prayers, sermons and harangues which greatly amused the people.[51] In what may have been a mad moment, he had his son, Dr. Nicholas Barbon, baptised, 'If-Jesus-Had-Not-Died-For-Thee-Thou-Hadst-Been-Damned.' In spite of that he was a conscientious and active MP.

---

48. Somers *Tracts*. (1748) BL. vol. vi. p. 234.
49. Sir W. Blackstone. (1809) *Commentaries on the Laws of England*. London, Cadell. vol. iv. p. 78.
50. Hardwicke Papers. BL. *Add, Mss*. 35,863. f. 7.
51. Liza Pickard. (1997) *Restoration London*. London, Phoenix. p. 30.

Although this Parliament had no practising lawyers among its members it commenced with an agenda for law reform. Indeed, when it was summoned its purpose was proclaimed to be, 'to encourage and countenance all God's people, reform the law and administer justice impartially.'[52] Seven of its members had sat on the Hale Commission and all the 16 Bills the Commission had prepared were published in 300 copies as a 'System of the Law' and presented to all members who spent two days reading them.[53] Parliament also appointed a, 'committee for the business of the law' which was charged with codifying the law. One day a week was set aside for debating law reform and it was also resolved unanimously to abolish the dilatory Court of Chancery with a committee asked to prepare the necessary Bill.[54]

With regard to the criminal law this Parliament made it clear that it intended to follow the recommendations of the Hale Commission and reduce the number of crimes that attracted the death penalty, abolish burning at the stake as a punishment for women and generally make punishments more proportionate to the crime. However, the Parliament went much further than attempting to reform the law and it set about abolishing Church tithes and proposing that army officers holding the more senior ranks should serve for a whole year without pay. These proposals inflamed the Church and the army and on their instigation the Parliament was brought to an end by Cromwell. A small groups of radical MPs known as 'the saints' continued to sit and when a colonel came to clear the House he asked what they were doing. 'We are seeking the Lord,' they replied. 'Then you may go elsewhere', he said, 'for to my certain knowledge he has not been here these 12 years'.[55]

DEFEAT OF PENAL LAW REFORM

Law reform lost favour after the Restoration of Charles II when those reforms that were introduced under Cromwell were repealed. These included the use of English in the courts and law books; the replacement of judges fees with a fixed annual salary; the principle of judges holding office during good behaviour, and the abolition of the High Court of Chivalry which punished those who uttered scandalous words against a gentleman. However, there were more general and irreversible changes about which the government of Charles II could do nothing. Above all, the prerogative courts and their criminal inquisitorial procedures were not revived, the torture engaged in by the Tudors and early Stuarts was not re-introduced and the Common Law largely squeezed out ecclesiastical law.

---

52. S. R. Gardiner. (1899) *Constitutional Documents of the Puritan Revolution, 1625–60.* Oxford, Oxford University Press. p. 402.
53. *Journals of the House of Commons.* (1653) vol. vii. p. 250.
54. *Parliamentary History.* vol. iii. col. 1412.
55. Ivan Roots. (1966) *The Great Rebellion, 1642–1660.* London, B.T. Batsford Ltd., p. 169.

It may be observed that Holdsworth claimed that if all the reforms proposed during the Interregnum had been enacted they would have done nothing but harm to the English legal system.[56] He did accept that the abolition of *peine forte et dure* and benefit of clergy would have been beneficial but he believed that if Parliament had gone much further it would have met bitter opposition from the lawyers and the conflict would have been adverse to the orderly development of the law by judicial decisions. Perhaps there lies the point since Holdsworth was a Common Law man at heart who believed deeply that the doctrine of precedent was more important than statute law. Although a formidable jurist, his opinion on this matter is flawed and cannot seriously be supported. As we have seen, by the time of the Interregnum the medieval criminal law lacked any principles of reason or justice and, by the eighteenth century it had descended into what Sir Robert Peel called the 'Bloody Code' with well over 200 offences punishable by death.

It was not until the nineteenth century that by statutes the incidence of the death penalty was severely reduced, that defence counsel were permitted to address the jury, that benefit of clergy was abolished and a Court of Criminal Appeal established in 1907. None of these belated improvements, and those in civil law, were, or could easily have been, brought about by 'the orderly development of the law by judicial decisions'. And they were just as timely in Cromwell's day as the Hale Commission recognised.

Although Cromwell blamed the lawyers for preventing wide scale law reform it has to be recognised that it was he who prematurely dissolved the Parliaments that alone could have secured it. And can it really be believed that if these and other important changes that exercised the minds of MPs and the members of the Hale Commission, which was held in high regard as a moderate body, had been effected under their guidance the fabric of English law would have been torn apart? It is more likely that we would have been honouring such pioneers for their farsighted enhancement of our criminal justice system and the concept of justice.

All in all, however, there can be little doubt that the Republic was doomed to fail because in the temper of the times it had to accept the Common Law and make its claims in legal terms that in the final analysis were based upon a monarchical-type of rule.[57]

56. Sir W. Holdsworth. *A History of English Law. Op. cit.* vol. iv. pp. 428-30.
57. See Alan Cromartie, (1995) *Sir Matthew Hale 1609-1676. Law religion and natural philosophy.* Cambridge, Cambridge University Press. p. 58 and Stuart E. Prall. (1966) *The Agitation for Law Reform during the Puritan Revolution, 1640-1660.* The Hague. Martinus Nijhoff. p. 1.

CHAPTER 7

The Whig Supremacy and Adversary Trial

THE SEVEN BISHOPS' CASE

When James II was on the throne he carried through a number of measures to assist Roman Catholics of whom he was one. Unconcerned about the storm this brewed he endeavoured, in 1688, to force the Anglican clergy to read from the pulpit in every church in the land his second Declaration of Indulgence, giving toleration to Catholics. The Archbishop of Canterbury, William Sancroft, and six other bishops petitioned the king against this, saying it was illegal. Apart from the archbishop, the others were: Ken (Bath and Wells); White (Peterborough); Turner (Ely): Lloyd (St. Asaph); Trelawney (Bristol); and Lake (Chichester). James had them imprisoned in the Tower and charged them with publishing a seditious libel in what became known as the *Seven Bishops' Case*.[1]

At the end of the hearing the judges of the King's Bench were evenly divided and, unlawfully, allowed the jury to find in favour of the bishops. Such was the fear in the country of a Catholic succession that this was seen as having saved the country from a Catholic tyranny and led directly to the Glorious Revolution.

BILL OF RIGHTS

James fled the country at the end of the year and to avoid a Roman Catholic succession to the throne, leaders of both the Whigs and the Tories invited William, Prince of Orange, to replace the king and to enforce both the law and the Protestant religion in England. Already prepared, William landed with his army at the small fishing port of Brixham in Devon in 1688 and secured a revolution without a single shot being fired. A Convention was then called in London which offered the throne to William and his Stuart consort, Mary, in February 1689 on his acknowledging the constitutional supremacy of king-in-Parliament. This was accompanied in both the Commons and the Lords with a *Declaration of Rights* which was later embodied in the *Bill of Rights* that ranks second only to *Magna Carta* as a charter of English liberty. It both preceded and influenced the United States Constitution, the Universal Declaration of Human Rights and the European Convention on Human Rights and is still law in the United Kingdom.

---

1. 12 *State Trials*. cols. 183-522.

The *Bill of Rights* forbade a standing army in peacetime without the consent of Parliament. It provided for Parliament to function free from the interference of the sovereign who was forbidden to set up courts or act as a judge. It further provided for the free election of MPs and their complete freedom of speech in the House of Commons which it settled was to meet frequently, and for jurors to be empanelled fairly. By clause 10 it further provided, 'that excessive bail ought not to be required, nor excessive fines imposed; nor cruel and unusual punishments inflicted.' Then, in 1701, the Act of Settlement[2] completed the process by establishing the independence of the judiciary.

This peaceful 'Glorious Revolution' signalled the partial triumph of the disciplined power of the propertied Whigs over royal despotism and the nobility. At last the Common Law was to be supreme over the prerogative and the Rule of Law began to displace royal discrimination. Although the king was to retain important powers, including the appointment of Ministers, henceforth he was a constitutional monarch subject to the law, as Bracton and Coke had long before maintained he was.

CHANGING ATTITUDES TO PUNISHMENT

At the same time there were subtle changes occurring in public attitudes to the place of the individual in society and towards criminal procedure. For the first time, an accused person was allowed to decline to answer questions in court and was permitted to cross-examine witnesses as well as call sworn witnesses in his own defence. Furthermore, hearsay evidence was coming to be distrusted and jurors, who were now more often drawn from the wealthy groups in society, had entirely ceased to be witnesses and were expected to judge the evidence. By judicial pronouncements, Sir John Holt, who became Chief Justice of the King's Bench after declining William's offer to appoint him lord chancellor, encouraged these processes. He established the rule that evidence of previous convictions against an accused person should not be admitted before the jury's verdict, and also held that prisoners should no longer be kept in irons during their trial.

He invited prisoners in the dock to interrupt him if they thought he was not stating their case fairly in summing up to the jury. And, in a significant decision in the case of *Smith v. Browne*[3] he declared that, 'as soon as a Negro comes into England, he is free,' even if he came in as a slave. It is noteworthy also that he always secured an acquittal in the trials of witches that he presided over. In a remarkable tribute to Holt for the time, Richard Steele wrote in the *Tatler*, 'the prisoner knew … that his

---

2. 12 & 13. Will. 3. c. 2.
3. Holt. K. B. 495.

Judge would wrest no law to destroy him, nor conceal any that could save him.'[4] The cruelty of earlier judges whose tenure of office had been dependent on pleasing the king had been moderated.

RUFFIANS IN ERMINE

The Treason Act of 1352 had provided, *inter alia,* that it was treason to compass or imagine (i.e. plot) the king's death and was still in force at the beginning of the eighteenth century. Indeed, the late seventeenth century saw a number of treason trials, in which the concept of constructive treason was widely used and extended by the judges. The courts had begun to extend the scope of the 1352 Act so that a full defence became difficult and the, 'security of men's lives is wholly overthrown by this artifice of construction of the treason statute.'[5] Lord Justices Scroggs and Jeffreys had been particularly prominent in the trials arising from the Popish Plot during the years 1678 to 1681 and the Rye House Plot in 1683, following both of which Catholics and prominent Whig leaders suffered, often with their lives.

The Popish Plot, manufactured by Titus Oates, a depraved cleric who had earlier been found guilty of indecency and perjury, had alleged a Jesuit plan to murder the king, put the Catholic Duke of York on the throne and bring a French army into England. The resultant public panic enabled the judicial enemies of the Whigs to impeach, execute or send to the Tower a number of their leaders in the course of widespread judicial corruption. They did not quite manage that with Lord Shaftesbury, the leading figure in organising the Whig party and promoting an ideology for its cause, since, hearing that warrants were out for his arrest,[6] he fled to Holland where he died on 21 January 1683.[7]

As far as the Rye House Plot is concerned, the plan was to seize the king on a narrow road near Newmarket but he left the races early and the plan was frustrated. Two leading Whigs, William Lord Russell, and Algernon Sidney, were promptly brought to trial on charges of high treason. They were found guilty on slight evidence and executed for what many believed was merely dissent.[8] As Sir John Rawles, afterwards Solicitor-General in the reign of William III, remarked of the judges in the case, 'the summing up of the evidence against Sidney was barbarous, being invectives and no consequences.'[9] But, of course, the judges—even Jeffreys—were

---

4. *The Tatler.* No. 14. (12 May 1709).
5. Sir R. Atkyns. (1689) *A Defence of the Late lord Russel's Innocency.* London, Timothy Goodwin, p. 10.
6. A. H. Shapiro. (1993) 'Political Theory and the Growth of Defensive Safeguards in Criminal Procedure: The Origins of the Treason Trials Act 1696.' Illinois, 11(2) *Law and History Review.* American Society of Law and History. p. 219.
7. David Ogg. (1967) *England in the Reign of Charles II.* Oxford, Oxford University Press. p. 647.
8. *9 State Trials.* cols. 666-935.
9. *Ibid.* col. 1004.

carrying out the policy of the king and this led, as Alexander Shapiro has put it, to critics being 'disturbed that in a trial system already heavily weighted in favour of the prosecution, the government was abusing its advantage.'[10]

Leslie Stephen, usually a mildly spoken biographer, described Jeffreys as a, 'kind of demoniacal baboon placed on the Bench in robes and wig, in hideous caricature of justice.'[11] And, as seen by Lord Campbell (a future lord chancellor) the Bench of the time, 'was cursed by a succession of ruffians in ermine who, for the sake of court favour, violated the principles of law, the precepts of religion, and the dictates of humanity.'[12]

THE TREASON TRIALS ACT 1696

The actions of Jeffreys and Scroggs, in closely associating the judiciary with royal despotism, proved counter-productive. The judges were demeaned in the eyes of the government and the public and this, together with the result of the *Seven Bishops' Case*,[13] served only to strengthen the Whigs. Smarting at their cruel treatment by the later Stuarts and their judges, the Whigs secured both the independence of the judiciary with the Act of Settlement in 1701,[14] and the enactment of the Treason Trials Act of 1696.[15] This radical statute, transformed the defendant accused of treason from, 'an essentially passive prisoner into an active participant in the trial.'[16] It was a direct parliamentary response to the misconduct of judges in state treason trials in the preceding decades. According to the House of Commons report, the design of the Whigs 'was to prevent those abuses in trials for treason ... by means of which, during the violence of late reigns, they had observed divers had lost their lives.'[17] It is also true that the diminished authority and prestige of the judges, and their partial disempowerment, was by no means unacceptable to the Whig hierarchy.

The statute allowed prisoners in treason trials to have counsel act for them in all respects. Accepting that a defendant might be innocent—a new concept in treason trials—the preamble to the Act declared, 'Nothing is more just and reasonable, than that Persons prosecuted for High Treason ... should not be debarred of all just and equal means for the defence of their Innocencies in such cases.'[18]

By section 1 the Act also gave the treason defendant the right to have the indict-

---

10. A. H. Shapiro. *Political Theory and the Growth of Defensive Safeguards in Criminal Procedure: The Origins of the Treason Trials Act 1696. Op. cit.* p. 222.

11. Leslie Stephen. (1991) *Hours in a Library.* London, The Folio Society. vol. iii. p. 302.

12. Lord Campbell. (1868) *Lives of the Lord Chancellors.* London, John Murray. vol. iv. p. 416.

13. See ante p.113.

14. 12 & 13, Wm. 3. c. 2.

15. 7 & 8, Wm. 3. c. 3.

16. A. H. Shapiro. 'Political Theory and the Growth of Defensive Safeguards in Criminal Procedure; The Origins of the Treason Trials Act of 1696.' *Op. cit.* . p. 219.

17. 5 Cobbett's *Parliamentary History.* p. 693.

18. Preamble to the 1696 Act.

ment against him or her at least five days before the trial, to have the assistance of counsel before the trial and to have counsel act in 'full defence', including address the jury during the trial. For the first time the statute also provided, by section 7, that prisoners should be allowed to subpoena witnesses to appear for them and give evidence on oath.

On 23 March 1696, two days before the Act came into force, the lord chief justice, Sir John Holt, in effect adopted section 7 in the trial for high treason of Sir John Friend.[19] The prisoner asked for a witness he required to call to be brought from the Gatehouse Prison where he was incarcerated. Holt granted the request and issued a writ of *habeas corpus.* He would not, however, allow Friend to instruct counsel to appear for him and when he was asked by the prisoner to act as counsel for him, Holt merely replied that he was, 'obliged to be indifferent between him and the king.'

The first case in which counsel appeared for a defendant after the Act came into force was the trial of Charles Cranburne on a charge of high treason on 21 April 1696.[20] After Holt had ordered the removal of the irons in which the prisoner was tightly held, Sir Bartholomew Shower (and later a Mr Phipps) rose to defend him. They questioned what they said were four defects in the indictment and entered into lengthy legal arguments with the Attorney-General which would undoubt-edly have been beyond the competence of the accused. They failed to secure their points, however, but then proceeded with cross-examination of prosecution wit-nesses throughout the trial, questioning their credibility and, on occasion, arguing with the judges. Nonetheless, the case against the accused was a strong one and he was found guilty. What is important is that defence counsel had created a precedent by vigorously defending an alleged traitor and had set an example which was to be followed by other members of the Bar.

It is significant that these overdue provisions of the Act were not considered by Parliament to be necessary for prisoners facing felony charges who were still not allowed to engage counsel. As will be seen, it was defence barristers who later seized the right to appear for defendants and cross-examine prosecution witnesses although still not allowed to address the jury. This was to prove to be the beginnings of adversary trial in England and Parliament had no part in it.

BIRTH OF ADVERSARY TRIAL

It is commonly believed that something like the same antiquity can be ascribed to adversary trial in our criminal courts as to Parliament and trial by jury. In reality,

19. 13 *State Trials.* col. 1.
20. *Ibid.* col. 222.

however, the opposite is true with adversary trial emerging in England, as indicated above, only in the eighteenth century.[21] Moreover, its origins and existence have tended to go unrecognised by judges, lawyers, jurists and researchers until relatively modern times when conflict has become a key social issue. Even now, there is a major dispute as to how and why adversary trial came about and little connection has been made with its contribution to the genesis of many rules of evidence and procedure and the modern day doctrine of human rights whereby citizens are able to take a stand against the power of the state and vested interests.

The procedural revolution this involved produced, 'the very first sighting of a recognisable human rights culture in western, if not global civilisation.'[22] It was an achievement of English Common Lawyers and, 'was to provide the empirical basis for the great universal codes of the American Bill of Rights and the French *Declaration of the Rights of Man* and to transform the relations between the individual and the state in a way which would lead eventually to a political and legal culture based primarily on rights.'[23]

Three factors are generally put forward to explain the entry of defence lawyers in criminal trials and their introduction of adversary trial. The first is the creation of a rewards culture for bounty hunters.[24] By a series of statutes at the end of the seventeenth century, and into the first half of the nineteenth century, prosecutors and their witnesses could receive substantial sums of money from the state for informing that led to a conviction. Hundreds of thousands of pounds were paid out in this way and not unnaturally this led to a good deal of perjury and accusations against innocent people. The second factor is the conduct of defence campaigns through the criminal courts by political reform movements such as those of John Wilkes in the mid-eighteenth century and anti-slavery campaigners at the end of that century.[25] Such activists would desire, and be able to pay for, defence counsel. The third reason put forward for the entry of defence lawyers into criminal trials is the creation of rules of evidence. However, since it was the presence of defence lawyers in trials that brought about the emergence of such rules that is putting the cart before the horse.

---

21. For the origins and development of adversary trial in England see John H. Langbein. (2003) *The Origins of Adversary Criminal Trial.* Oxford, Oxford University Press (anti-adversary trial) and John Hostettler (2006) *Fighting for Justice: The History and Origins of Adversary Trial.* Winchester, Waterside Press (pro-adversary trial).
22. Richard Vogler. (2005) *A World View of Criminal Justice.* Aldershot, Ashgate Publishing Limited. p. 131.
23. *Ibid.*
24. See L. Radzinowicz. (1956) *A History of English Criminal Law: The Enforcement of the Law.* London, Stevens & Sons Ltd., vol. ii. pp. 57—82.
25. S. Landsman. (1990) 'The Rise of the Contentious Spirit: Adversary Procedure in Eighteenth Century England.' New York, *Cornell Law Review.* p. 583.

A CHANGING WORLD

These three practical explanations for the entry of defence lawyers into criminal trials may or may not be convincing, says Richard Vogler. There has been, he writes, 'a strong tendency in the recent academic literature to see the whole creation of adversariality as merely an *ad hoc* development.'[26] But, he continues, whilst the practical reasons may have been important and go some way to explain the chronology of change, 'it is not unreasonable to link the birth of adversariality with the more profound shifts in contemporary understanding of the world and the political economy which followed from the Glorious Revolution of 1688.'[27] He argues that during the period prior to 1688 the bloody judicial retribution of judges such as Jeffreys and Scroggs brought the rights of criminal defendants to the heart of the Whig political agenda. As a consequence, the Whig ascendancy of Hanovarian England was content with the disempowerment and growing neutrality of the trial judge. But even more important, whereas these explanations may give us some insight into the timing and logistics of change, it is impossible,

> bearing in mind the subsequent spread of adversariality around the globe, to escape the conclusion that it bore some deeper relationship to the social and industrial changes then underway in England. It seems too much of a coincidence that the first industrial nation should also be the first to develop this mode of trial process and at the very same time. As has already been pointed out, the 'lawyerisation' of the trial was in many respects an opening of the feudal court hierarchy to the market and in that sense, just as much a 'commercialisation'. Moreover, the constitution of the defendant as a rights-bearing actor in the process cannot be unconnected with changes in the status of the individual in the new employment market.'[28]

It seems clear that these developments flowed from the Industrial Revolution and the explosive consequences of the European Enlightenment in the epoch of revolutions. A new world was coming into being with marked changes in social conditions, political theories, class relationships and in people's attitudes to life and their fellow citizens. Naked violence and injustice were diminishing. Public disquiet was asserting itself about slavery, prison conditions and the rights and status of the individual.

Adversary trial is usually contrasted with the inquisitorial system operating in countries like France where the *juge d'instruction* controls the proceedings prior to and during the hearing of the case. On the basis of a dossier prepared by the prosecution the judge decides which witnesses to call and examines them in person with lawyers confined to a subsidiary role. There is always a danger that the judge may at an early stage become committed to one side or the other. This system was consid-

---

26. R. Vogler. *A World View of Criminal Justice. Op. cit.* p. 142.
27. *Ibid.* pp. 142-3.
28. *Ibid.* p. 143-4.

ered by the Royal Commission on Criminal Justice (1991-93)[29] which criticised its very lengthy pre-trial detention of many defendants and the close involvement of judges with prosecutors and the police. Adversary trial is, of course, confrontational but the notion of opposing parties is deep-rooted in the Common Law and the English psyche and cross-examination is a proven weapon in exposing lies.

In contrast to the view of the Royal Commission, on 21 March 2006 the then Home Secretary, Charles Clarke, told the House of Commons Home Affairs Committee, 'I think that a supervisory system and investigating magistrates' regime is very superior to the system that we have in this country.' He then added for good measure that he did not think the adversary system had been a particularly effective means of securing justice. Yet, adversary trial is more likely to result in both an acquittal of the innocent and a conviction of the guilty. There is no doubt that in the present climate, with its long-term terrorist threat, government is impatient with many features of both the trial jury system and adversariality. But for those outside government, the jury, lay magistrates and the adversary system of trial ensure that all important decisions are made in public before impartial tribunals and not in secret by a state bureaucracy as with the inquisitorial method.

ADVERSARY TRIAL AND HUMAN RIGHTS

As we have seen, in England prior to the early eighteenth century lawyers were not permitted to appear for prisoners charged with felony even though the latter faced the gallows if found guilty. From the 1730s, however, defence counsel, and in particular Sir William Garrow, by aggressive cross-examination of prosecution witnesses, often bounty hunters, were instrumental in bringing about a revolution in criminal procedure. They gave birth to adversary trial and rules of criminal evidence, such as the presumption of innocence, which led to their capturing the courtroom. In doing so they created a working culture of human rights which later was given constitutional recognition in the United States *Bill of Rights* and the French *Declaration of the Rights of Man*.

Indeed, the English model of criminal justice was adopted in the French Revolution until reversed by Napoleon in 1808 when he re-introduced the secret, authoritarian inquisitorial system which for nearly two centuries has straddled across those parts of the world not influenced by the Common Law. Torture and oppression have formed part of the history and structure of inquisitorial trial. Hence, Stalin's Russia could boast in 1936 of its 'democratic' constitution which, in the absence of due process and adversary trial sank without trace in the Great Terror of the same year in which millions of people lost their lives or were sent to the gulag by administrative measures.

---

29. Cm 2263.

Today the picture is changing. In the last decade 80 per cent of all Latin American states have drawn up new criminal codes based on the adversary system. Russia enacted an adversarial procedure code in 2001 and China is proceeding to a similar goal, as are Georgia and the Ukraine. Similarly, there are moves towards adversary trial in France, Spain, Italy and Germany.[30] The impact of such developments is to create a global shift in criminal procedure and due process that makes human rights meaningful.

What is surprising is that in England, the country that gave the gift of adversary trial to the world, there are trends in the opposite direction. The question arises whether the former Home Secretary, in the remarks cited above, was 'flying a kite' with a view to further changes to undermine lawyers and juries in a move away from the conflict philosophy so ingrained in the English psyche. Recent governments have not been slow to challenge the judiciary and the legal profession and, as juries have become more democratic since 1974 with the use of the electoral register for selecting them instead of a property qualification, there have been numerous moves to diminish their powers.[31] These tendencies should be resisted when so much of the non-Islamic world is moving towards adversary trial and effective human rights.

The suggestion, often made, that only the inquisitorial system seeks the truth is false. As Lord Denning said, in England the role of the judge is not that of a mere umpire, his object above all is to find out the truth.[32] Although it may be that a different kind of truth is being sought. And that is best done by experienced counsel conducting examination and cross-examination before a randomly selected jury rather than by an investigator producing a dossier for use in court. What is important is a fair trial and in the adversarial system the defence is central as are the rules of evidence introduced to assist defendants (although they are now under threat as will be dealt with later).

THE AMERICAN AND FRENCH REVOLUTIONS

The American Revolution quickly introduced its Constitution but a number of states desired a further document to prevent abuses of power and thus, four years later, was born the United States' Bill of Rights as a series of Amendments to the Constitution. Amendment 5 provides that no person was to be twice put in jeopardy of life or limb for the same offence, nor compelled in any criminal case to incriminate himself. It also confirmed the principle of due process. Amendment 6 reads as follows:

---

30. See Richard Vogler. *A World View of Criminal Justice. Op. cit.*
31. See John Hostettler. (2004) *The Criminal Jury Old and New. Jury Power from Early Times to the Present Day.* Winchester, Waterside Press.
32. (1957) *Jones v. National Coal Board.* 2 QB, 55.

In all criminal prosecutions, the accused shall enjoy the right to a speedy and public trial, by an impartial jury of the state and district wherein the crime shall have been committed ... and to be informed of the nature and cause of the accusation; to be confronted with the witnesses against him; to have compulsory process for obtaining witnesses in his favour; and to have the assistance of counsel for his defence.[33]

In large measure the existence of the American Bill of Rights was due to Thomas Jefferson who, ironically, was not even in Philadelphia when it was drawn up. He was in Paris, as Minister to France, when he heard that the Constitutional Convention was unconvinced about the need for a written Bill of Rights. Accordingly, he wrote constantly to the Founding Fathers stressing the urgent need for the rights and liberties to be specified in permanent form. And, he succeeded. His persistence came from two sources. First, in his own state of Virginia hanging, whipping and dismemberment were common punishments and they appalled him. Secondly, he was influenced by the movement for criminal law reform sweeping Europe and England at the time. He had read Beccaria's *Of Crimes and Punishments*,[34] in the original Italian, and copied long passages into his commonplace book. Similarly, he had read Blackstone, Montesquieu, Helvetius and William Eden (later Lord Auckland), a pioneer English penal law reformer.[35] In the event, his influence was decisive in securing for the United States both jury trial and adversary trial.

In the French Revolution, on 26 August 1789 the Constituent Assembly approved the *Declaration of the Rights of Man and of the Citizen*. Article 7 of the Declaration provided that no person should be accused, arrested, or imprisoned except in the cases, and according to the forms, prescribed by law. Article 8 stated that the law should provide only such punishments as were strictly and obviously necessary and were prescribed by law and promulgated before the commission of the offence. Article 9 declared that all persons were innocent until proved guilty.

But the Revolution went further. The reformers of the Assembly in 1789-91

succeeded at first in sweeping away almost all traces of the inquisition process and replacing it with what was effectively a French copy of Anglo-American adversariality, complete with justices of the peace and the grand and petty juries. No such fundamental transformation had ever been attempted in criminal justice in Europe since the 13th century and it was not surprising that the next few years of political turbulence should see the slow re-emergence of the authoritarian *Code Louis*.[36]

By 1808 Napoleon had largely restored the inquisitorial system with, 'a superficial and brief gloss of adversariality and publicity to a procedure which essentially

33. The USA Bill of Rights Institute Online. (www.billofrightsinstitute.org)
34. See post p 193.
35. Merrill D. Peterson. (1970) *Thomas Jefferson and the New Nation: A Biography.* New York, Oxford University Press. p. 124.
36. R. Vogler. *A World View of Criminal Justice. Op. cit.* p. 49-50.

retained all the most authoritarian characteristics of its predecessor, [to make it] a much more effective weapon of repression than the original' Code Louis.[37]

On the other hand, in England the growth and development of adversary trial was to proceed throughout the eighteenth and succeeding centuries by the dynamic of criminal lawyers in the setting of trial by jury.

---

37. *Ibid.* p. 50.

CHAPTER 8

The Jury in the Eighteenth Century

JURY NULLIFICATION

The power of the criminal trial jury reached its zenith in the eighteenth century with its frequent and conscious nullification of the law. As we have seen, jury nullification has been defined as exercising the power 'to acquit the defendant on the basis of conscience even when the defendant is technically guilty in light of the judge's instructions defining the law and the jury's finding of the facts.'[1] Further, as Green adds, historically some cases of nullification 'reflect the jury's view that the act in question is not unlawful, while in other cases the jury does not quarrel with the law but believes that the prescribed sanction is too severe.'[2] This is not to be confused with the jury not believing a witness or failing to understand the directions of the judge. Nullification in order to convict can also exist but seems to be remote in practice except possibly in modern times as an expression of racial prejudice.[3]

The background to jury nullification in the eighteenth century was the extensive use of capital punishment in the period of the 'Bloody Code' when over 200 offences attracted the death penalty. According to one legal historian,

> The long dispute over the death penalty lay near the very eye of political life. The eighteenth-century ruling class—small in number, hungry for property and its attendant power—had to maintain stability and order without the civil police of modern times. Capital punishment formed an ugly apex to a system of social control through legal processes which functioned to a significant degree at the pleasure of the governors.[4]

This undoubtedly had an effect upon jurors who did not want to send offenders to the gallows for minor crimes. In a sense, the government was seeking to use juries for political purposes which may also explain why juries frequently found prisoners guilty of theft for a lower amount than alleged in the charge in order to reduce the penalty. However, there were two pre-conditions for modern jury nullification. The first was essential: namely a jury free from intimidation, which came about after the landmark *Bushell's Case* in November 1670 when John Vaughan, Chief Justice

---

1. Alan Scheflin and Jon Van Dyke. (1980) 'Jury Nullification: The Contours of the Controversy.' 43. *J.L. and Contemporary Problems*. Durham, North Carolina, Duke University. p. 56.
2. T. A. Green. (1985) *Verdict According to Conscience: Perspectives on the English Criminal Jury Trial 1200-1800*. Chicago, University of Chicago Press. p. 19.
3. *Ibid.*
4. W. R. Cornish. (1978) ' Criminal Justice and Punishment. In *Crime and Law in Nineteenth Century Britain*. Dublin, Irish University Press. p. 18

of the Common Pleas, declared that the verdict of a jury on questions of fact was unassailable.[5] The second, which was helpful but not crucial, was the existence of a free Bar with lawyers able to act for the defence in an adversarial confrontation with prosecution witnesses.

INCREASE IN ACQUITTALS

During the eighteenth century the proportion of acquittals increased in Essex and the Home Circuit and this was not untypical of the country as a whole.[6] For example, King found that '[l]ess than half those indicted for major property crimes in south eastern England were found to be guilty as charged.'[7] The extension of the death penalty, along with the removal of benefit of clergy for numerous offences, focused jurors' minds and produced more partial verdicts where the circumstances of the defendants or the offences appeared to justify them.[8]

The unanimity rule for juries was also a factor in the increase in acquittals in the eighteenth century. The jury would want to avoid delay in reaching a verdict which resulted in their being held overnight without food, heat or water, and often without light. Hence, if one or two jurors were holding out against a majority in favour of acquittal it was easier for them to bend towards mercy than to continue with their disagreement. The influential Doctor of Divinity, William Paley, wrote,

> in criminal prosecutions [the unanimity rule] operates considerably in favour of the prisoner; for if a juror find it necessary to surrender to the obstinacy of others, he will much more readily resign his opinion on the side of mercy than condemnation.[9]

Errors in indictments could also help secure acquittals. Indictments were lengthy documents and had to be precise. If a date were incorrect the prosecution could fail. The misspelling of a name would result in the case being thrown out, unless the defendant answered the indictment initially in ignorance of the mistake,[10] which probably explains why, in political cases at least, the prisoner was not allowed to see the indictment until after he had pleaded—certainly not pre-trial. Yet, even before counsel were permitted to appear for the defence, Hale had written that 'more of-

---

5. *Six State Trials.* cols. 999-1026
6. P. J. R. King. 'Illiterate Plebeians, Easily Misled': Jury Composition, Experience, and Behaviour in Essex, 1735-1815.' In Cockburn and Green (eds.) (1988) *Twelve Good* Men *and True, The Criminal Trial Jury in England 1200-1800.* New Jersey, Princeton University Press. pp. 254-5.
7. *Ibid.* p. 255.
8. J. M. Beattie. (1986) *Crime and the Courts in England 1660-1800.* Oxford, The Clarendon Press. p. 420.
9. W. Paley. (1785) *The Principles of Moral and Political Philosophy.* In *The Works of W. Paley.* (1825) vol. vi. Edinburgh, Peter Brown and T. & W. Nelson. p. 130.
10. Sir Matthew Hale. (1736) *The History of the Pleas of the Crown.* London, E. & R. Nutt and Another. vol. ii. p. 175.

fenders escape by the over-easy ear given to exceptions in indictments, than by their own innocence.'[11]

PIOUS PERJURY

The widespread enlargement of the 'umbrella of terror', bringing large numbers under the threat of death[12] for minor as well as serious offences, resulted in juries blatantly exercising their discretion to avoid sending hapless defendants to the gallows. And, they often did so with the blessing of the judges. Age and necessity were factors often taken into account. Indeed, juries frequently reached their verdicts on assessments of the character or disposition of the accused as well as the seriousness of the offence. The Old Bailey Sessions Papers abound with cases where there is no real defence put forward, only the testimony of character witnesses, often successfully. And, from the Surrey Assizes, Beattie cites the case of an Elizabeth Radford of Croydon where it was clearly the favourable testimony of three of her former employers that encouraged the jury to acquit her when the man for whom she worked as a charwoman prosecuted her for stealing a silver spoon from his house and all she could say in her defence was that she had 'found it'.[13]

The Old Bailey Sessions Papers are also full of cases where, in exercise of pious perjury, juries reduced the value of goods stolen, sometimes substantially. Their aim was to circumvent the death penalty when they considered it to be too harsh a punishment and out of proportion to the offence. Here are a few examples. In 1731, a young man named William Booth was tried at the Old Bailey for stealing two shillings and six pence in cash. The jury found him guilty but reduced the vale of the cash to ten pence;[14] in 1784, Elizabeth Jones and Mary Smith were charged with shoplifting goods valued at 14 shillings. There was too much evidence against them for an acquittal but the jury found them guilty of stealing fans worth 4s. 10d.[15] By putting the value of the stolen fans below five shillings the jury in a fine example of pious perjury, avoided the women being sent to the gallows and they were each sentenced to be privately whipped and confined to hard labour for 12 months in a house of correction—a harsh enough punishment in any event by modern standards.

In trials for housebreaking, recorded by Beattie, examples included the theft from a house of 23 guineas, lace valued at more than £100, gold rings and jewel-

---

11. Cited by Peter King. (2000) *Crime, Justice, and Discretion in England, 1740-1820.* Oxford, Oxford University Press. p. 240.

12. J. M. Beattie. (1977) 'Crime and Courts in Surrey 1736-1753.' In J.S. Cockburn (ed.) *Crime in England 1550-1800.* London, Methuen & Co. Ltd., p. 171.

13. *Surrey Assize Proceedings.* August 1742. p. 13.

14. *Gentlemen's Magazine. (1731)* London. F. Jefferies. vol. i. p. 401.

15. OBP Online. (www. oldbaileyonline.org) 15 September 1784 Ref: t17840915-68.

lery valued at more than £300—all of which together the jury found to be worth 39 shillings.[16] Indeed, it has been said that at the time, 'the entire legal fabric, from prosecution to punishment, was shot through with discretion.'[17] Certainly, pious perjury had the effect of making the penal law of the time less harsh than has previously been supposed. And, in some types of serious cases, such as burglary and aggravated larceny (i.e. serious since usually violent), Peter King concludes that a partial verdict, 'effectively limited the range of sanctions available by preventing the judge from passing a capital sentence.' He adds that, 'trial before the petty jury was the principal public moment in the long chain of individual and collective choices and interactions that determined the fate of the accused.'[18]

King finds that around

one-seventh of those indicted for property crimes in the major courts of Essex between 1740 and 1805 had the indictments dismissed as `not found' by the grand jury.' The trial jury acquitted almost a third of the remainder and brought in partial verdicts, reducing the charge and effectively lessening the punishment in a further ten per cent.[19]

These figures are highly significant and, between 1782 and 1787, similar figures were to be found in the counties of Surrey, Hertfordshire, Kent and Sussex.[20] Beattie found that petty juries acquitted in 33.9 per cent of capital cases in which grand juries had indicted in Surrey in the period from 1736 to 1753 and returned partial verdicts in 29.4 per cent of cases.[21] In the Old Bailey, Langbein shows that 171 cases produced 203 defendants, of whom 84 were acquitted. He did not calculate the frequency with which juries down-valued or convicted of lesser offences for the whole of his sample, but in October 1754, of 31 guilty verdicts 14 involved those two types of partial verdicts.[22] He concludes, therefore, in his polemic against Douglas Hay, that in '*Property, Authority and the Criminal Law*'[23] Hay developed a theory of ruling-class conspiracy against the lower orders and, whilst exaggerating the extent of prosecutorial discretion, he 'underemphasised the importance of jury discretion.'[24]

King, who gives little support to Hay's conspiracy theory, asserts that, 'less than half those indicted for major property crimes in south eastern England were found

16. J. M. Beattie. *Crime and the Courts in England, 1660-1800. Op. cit.* p. 424.
17. John Brewer and John Styles. (1980) *An Ungovernable People: The English and their Law in the Seventeenth and Eighteenth Centuries.* London, Hutchinson. p. 18.
18. P. King. "Illiterate Plebeians, Easily Misled" *Op. cit.* p. 254.
19. *Ibid.* p. 254-5.
20. *Ibid.* p. 255.
21. J. M. Beattie. 'Crime and Courts in Surrey, 1736-53.' *Op. cit.* p. 176.
22. John H. Langbein. (1983) 'Albion's Fatal Flaws.' 98 *Past & Present.* Oxford, The Past and Present Society, p. 106.
23. D. Hay. (1975) In *Albion's Fatal Tree* .London, Allen Lane. p. 52.
24. John H. Langbein. 'Albion's Fatal Flaws.' *Op. cit.* p. 105.

to be guilty as charged.'[25] These were principled decisions, he suggests, and juries applied what should be called a strong presumption against capital verdicts. There was also evidence indicating that females, the young and those with families to support were the most likely to be given partial verdicts.[26]

Green gives a different perspective on the process:

> The selection of offenders by Crown, bench and jury for one or another level of punishment became a complex and, at times, an awe-inspiring ritual. Authorities were all the readier to share the power of mitigation with juries in a system in which most of the beneficiaries of mitigation suffered some substantial punishment.

> As the jury's role in this evolving system of mitigation became formalised, and in a sense tamed, that role expanded accordingly; but the jury was now more than ever just one part of the system, and the scope of its role in practice depended increasingly upon surrounding institutions and procedures.[27]

Nevertheless, in capital cases in particular, partial verdicts and the tradition of jury nullification remained important and significant, with pious perjury continually being resorted to by criminal trial juries. On capital theft in particular, the oft-quoted words of Blackstone may be recalled. He wrote that, 'the mercy of juries often made them strain a point, and bring in larceny to be under the value of 12 pence, when it was really of much greater value … a kind of *pious perjury.*'[28] Blackstone believed such under-valuation was largely a response to inflation over the centuries and achieved justice by preventing from being condemned to death a person whom the legislature had not originally had in mind.[29] This led Milsom to suggest that, 'So far as justice was done throughout the centuries, it was done by jurors and in spite of savage laws.'[30]

This does not mean, however, that people facing trial were tried by their peers who might have been sympathetic to their problems. The property qualification made this impossible in most cases and detailed studies of criminal juries in individual counties suggest that they were almost always comprised of the fairly well-to-do who would have very little contact with most of those brought before the courts.[31] The cottager who appeared in court charged with theft, saw 12 men sitting opposite him who were the equals and neigbours of the prosecutor; they were employers, overseers of the poor and propertied men.[32] That makes pious perjury all the more

25. King. "Illiterate Plebeians", *Op. cit.* p. 255.
26. *Ibid.*
27. T. A. Green. *Verdict According to Conscience. Op. cit.* p. 267.
28. Sir William Blackstone. (1809) *Commentaries on the Laws of England.* London, Cadell. vol. iv. p. 248.
29. *Ibid.* p. 239.
30. S. F. C. Milsom. (1981) *Historical Foundations of the Common Law.* London, Butterworths. p. 403.
31. See essays by Post, Powell, Lawson and Cockburn in Cockburn and Green, *Twelve Good Men and True. Op. cit.*
32. Douglas Hay. *Property, Authority and the Criminal Law. Op. cit.* p. 38.

striking. Nevertheless, adds Hay, the point, 'is not that such juries convicted against the evidence, but rather that a more democratic jury might not have convicted at all.'[33] But that is transposing the morality of today to the eighteenth century.

And, as the number of capital offences was increased, the judges themselves began to interpret the penal law in an increasingly narrow manner that sometimes encouraged the jury to leniency.[34] As Hay continues:

> Many prosecutions founded on excellent evidence and conducted at considerable expense failed on minor errors of form in the indictment ... prosecutors resented the waste of their time and money lost on a technicality ... But it seems likely that the mass of Englishmen drew other conclusions from the practice. The punctilious attention to forms, the dispassionate and legalistic exchanges between counsel and the judge, argued that those administering and using the laws submitted to its rules. The law thereby became something more than the creature of the ruling class—it became a power with its own claims, higher than those of prosecutor, lawyers and even the great scarlet-robed assize judge himself.[35]

Partial verdicts did not, however, occur at random across various types of offences. According to King, 'the most important function of partial verdicts [was] to prevent capital sentences in burglary, housebreaking and aggravated larceny cases.'[36] And juries distinguished first, according to the offence and its degree of seriousness, and secondly, according to the conduct and the character of the accused in a particular case. According to Langbein, in his sample of cases at the Old Bailey, partial verdicts were not returned in any cases of livestock theft or highway robbery but in pickpocket cases the jury almost invariably reduced the value of the property stolen to below a shilling to make them non-capital. They would not, however, reduce the value where the evidence indicated that the offenders were professional thieves or gang members.[37]

CLASS IN JURIES

Today some 95 per cent of criminal cases are dealt with by magistrates without a jury. By contrast, in the eighteenth century most criminal prosecutions were dealt with by jury trial. And a grand jury, hearing prosecution evidence *in camera* to decide whether there was a *prima facie* case to go to trial, was required for all prosecutions by indictment. At the trial itself the jury was known as the petty jury. For this latter jury, which could not include women, the occupations of farmer, artisan

---

33. *Ibid.* pp. 39-9.
34. *Ibid.* p. 32.
35. *Ibid.* pp. 32-3.
36. P. King. *Crime, Justice, and Discretion in England, 1740-1820. Op. cit.* p. 233.
37. John H. Langbein. (1983) 'Eighteenth Century Criminal Trial.' Chicago. 50. *University of Chicago Law Review.* pp. 53-4.

and tradesman typified its eighteenth century membership. The jury was, therefore, neither aristocratic nor democratic.[38] Moreover, the 1692 statutory requirement[39] of ownership of freehold land rated £10 per annum still operated as a property qualification for jury membership.[40] The importance of a property qualification in the eyes of the judiciary was shown by the reassurance Lord Chief Justice Pemberton felt it necessary to give Lord Russell, in his trial for high treason in 1683, about a higher one for London jurors:

> I must tell you, you will have as good a jury, and better than you should have had in a county, of £4 or 40 shillings a year freeholders. The reason of the law for freeholds is that no slight persons should be put upon a jury, where the life of a man, or his estate, come in question, but in the city, the persons that are impanelled are men of quality and substance, men that have a great deal to lose.[41]

The names of persons who satisfied the property requirement were compiled annually in each county in a book of freeholders prepared under the supervision of justices of the peace.[42] Later, it was widely suggested that owing to inflation the real value of the qualification was seriously reduced and, as a consequence, many more relatively poor men who were not competent for the duty, and were open to corruption, sat on juries that the authorities desired.[43]

However, Hay argues from his research in the counties of Northampton and Stafford that this was emphatically not the case since, 'inflation ceased to reduce the jury qualification in the eighteenth century.'[44] In 1730 Parliament enacted that land tax returns were to be the test of jurors' qualifications[45] and this remained so in the eighteenth and early nineteenth centuries.[46] But whilst land rentals declined in that period land tax assessments remained fixed at the 1692 level and this meant that the jurors selected were men with higher and higher rental values.[47] As a consequence, Staffordshire in the 1780s and Northamptonshire in the 1770s registered 8.5 and 10.4 jurors per thousand of the population respectively, and by 1823 they had only risen to 9.4 and 10.5 per thousand.[48]

---

38. John H. Langbein. (1987) 'The English Criminal Trial Jury on the Eve of the French Revolution.' In Padoa Schiappa, (ed.) *The Trial Jury in England, France, Germany, 1700-1900*. Berlin, Durcker & Humbolt. p. 25.
39. 4 W. & M. c. 24.
40. Douglas Hay. (1988) 'The Class Composition of the Palladium of Liberty: Trial Jurors in the Eighteenth Century'. In Cockburn and Green. (eds.) *Twelve Good Men and True. Op. cit.* pp. 309-10.
41. Howell. (1818) *Nine State Trials*. col. 594
42. John H. Langbein. *The English Criminal Trial Jury. Op. cit.* p. 25.
43. See James C. Oldham. (1983) 'The Origins of the Special Jury.' Chicago University Press, 50 *The University of Chicago Law Review*. p. 145.
44. Douglas Hay. 'The Class Composition of the Palladium of Liberty.' *Op. cit.* p. 314.
45. 3 Geo. II. c, 25, s,1.
46. Douglas Hay. 'The Class Composition of the Palladium of Liberty. *Op. cit.* p. 314.
47. *Ibid.*
48. *Ibid.* p. 321.

Furthermore, the qualification had a significant effect, as shown by a sample year in Staffordshire (1783), when in theft cases (the most common crime) none of those accused was qualified to sit on a jury whereas one-third of prosecutors in such cases were.[49] In another sample year in Staffordshire a mere two per cent of the accused were men who were qualified to be jurors, whereas 21 per cent of all prosecutors in that year appeared on the lists of freeholders. In theft cases, one third of all prosecutors were qualified and eligible to be jurors.[50] Three-quarters of adult males were too poor, even if their entire wealth were in land, to qualify as jurors.[51] Hay concludes that the jury was a 'site of significant class power in the legal system rather than a neutral institution broadly representative of all English society' and that this followed from a 'deliberate, conscious policy.'[52] Nevertheless, and somewhat undermining the conclusion, farmers constituted almost half the jurors at Assizes and fully three-quarters at Quarter Sessions with tradesmen and artisans making up the balance.[53]

Hay found juries were more sympathetic to the prosecution than King has found in Essex. They were, he says, a class apart from most of the people who appeared before them. That was also true elsewhere, including Essex, where King's jurors of the middling sort, who 'saw their interests as often very separate from those of the gentry'[54] and from the higher reaches of society, were often repelled by harsh penalties.'[55]

Clearly the social status of jurors could be too modest. In the trial of Francis Crossfield in 1796 for high treason in plotting to kill the king, jurors were disqualified who were not householders or freeholders. Moreover, two members of the panel from which the jury were chosen who were excused on this ground were listed as 'gentleman' by occupation—although one of them was an inmate of a Bridewell hospital![56] Apparently, religion was not entirely a disqualification. Although Catholics, Quakers and other dissenters could be excluded even relatively poor Jews served on juries. For example, Jacob Spinoza, a Bishopsgate confectioner sat on a special jury in 1794 that acquitted Susannah Milesent of theft on grounds of insanity.[57] Jurors could be disqualified by deafness, illness and age and, in the Crossfield trial, anyone who had served on the grand jury was ineligible to sit on the trial jury.[58]

---

49. *Ibid.* pp. 350-1.
50. *Ibid.*
51. *Ibid.* p. 315.
52. *Ibid.* p. 311.
53. *Ibid.* p. 330.
54. Peter King. 'Illiterate Plebeians' *Op. cit.* p.304.
55. *Ibid.* p. 255.
56. (2004) *Twelve Good Men and True.* www.headheeb.blogmosis.com/archives/026334.html. p. 1.
57. *Ibid.* pp. 1-2.
58. *Ibid.* p. 2.

INTERFERENCE WITH SELECTION OF JURORS

Corruption in the selection of jurors existed in the eighteenth century and an Act for the Better Regulation of Juries was enacted in 1730 referring to 'many evil practices ... used in corrupting of jurors' and 'many neglects and abuses ... in making up the lists of freeholders , who ought to serve on such trials.'[59]

E. P. Thompson has traced the accounts of Baptist Nunn, the ultra-active gamekeeper at Windsor, who, on several occasions in the 1720s, after the notorious Black Act[60] introduced the death penalty for many new offences, scrutinised and altered jury lists with the connivance of the under-sheriffs responsible for the selection of jurors. For instance, his accounts for 1723 included the following items:[61]

£ s d
July 25. Attended again in London desired pannells of Jury
to be altered with Under Sherriffs 1 16 8
26 and 27. Waited upon Mr Walpole to obteyn Perryman's
Tryal respited. Promised amendment of Jury Spent
With Under Sherriffs. 0 11 9

And in the case of James Barlow, indicted in 1724 for breaking the head of a fishpond and speaking seditious words, it was noted that the King's Counsel involved for the Crown, 'thought it proper to defer the Tryal, the Jury having in some Tryals given Verdicts contrary to Evidence.'[62] On the other hand, when, in 1723, the king took an interest in a case at the Old Bailey and told the Attorney-General to take the case in hand and prosecute, at the trial the jury were untainted and acquitted the defendants.[63]

In December 1748 a Special Commission was set up to try on charges of murder a number of smugglers captured in Sussex. The Duke of Richmond, who was personally concerned in the prosecution, petitioned the lord chancellor that the commission should be held at Chichester, rather than Horsham, since it was only a few miles from his estate at Goodwood and would be, 'more convenient for all of us in this part of the country, where the murders were all committed and all the evidences live, most of the Grand Jury live, and where a sheriff can get a Petty Jury whose probity can be depended upon.[64] On 22 July 1749 the under-sheriff at Lewes

---

59. 3. Geo. II. c. 25.
60. Geo. I., c. 22.
61. E. P. Thompson. (1975) *Whigs and Hunters. The Origin of the Black Act.* London, Allen Lane. p. 78.
62. *Ibid.* p. 79.
63. Old Bailey Sessions Papers. (April 1723) Cited by Langbein. 'The Prosecutorial Origins of Defence Counsel in the Eighteenth Century: The Appearance of Solicitors.' Cambridge, 58 *Cambridge Law Journal.* p. 333.
64. West Sussex Record Office. Goodwood MSS. 155/H42. Cited by Carl Winslow. (1975) 'Sussex Smugglers'. In Douglas Hay. *Albion's Fatal Tree: Crime and Society in Eighteenth Century England.* London,

in East Sussex wrote to the same Duke of Richmond on the coming Assizes:

> I am favoured with your Grace's letter and have sent enclosed a copy of the jury, which I have made out as well I can, and have returned a great part of them out of West Sussex, that your Grace may be easier informed about them, and if they should not be the proper persons, they may be challenged by the Crown at the Assizes.[65]

According to Thompson, most of the important political trials of the late eighteenth century took place in London, where shopkeepers and tradesmen made up the juries. Lists of possible jurymen, he says, are preserved in the Treasury Solicitor's papers and show how the Crown sought to eliminate Jacobin sympathisers from juries:

> On one such list, the names from which the jury was to be drawn were marked G. (good), B. (bad), and D. (doubtful). The many Bs included such tradesmen as a scale-maker, a glass-seller, grocers, a sailmaker, and brewers (one Southwark brewer being marked 'very B').[66]

Juries were not generally trusted to deal with game cases and excise prosecutions,[67] both of which were generally taken before magistrates despite their lower sentencing powers. As one steward complained while preparing to prosecute a poacher for assault, 'There is no answering for a Common Jury (who must Try the Indictment) as they have in general a Strong Byass upon their Minds in favour of Poachers, being professed Enemies to all Penal Laws that relate to the Game.'[68] Thus, according to King,

> By removing the judicial process to their own parlours, the gentry avoided the expense and possible humiliation of a jury trial and made the prosecution of game offenders more convenient, but the price they had to pay was considerable since the summary conviction laws usually allowed only relatively minor punishments of a fine or imprisonment.[69]

Not that a fine or imprisonment would have been minor for the defendant and his family, particularly set against the possibility of an acquittal by a jury.

SEDITIOUS LIBEL

The earliest definition of seditious libel was by the Star Chamber in a 1606 case, *De Libellis Famosis,* as 'criticism of public persons, the government or the king.' How-

Allen Lane. p. 138.
65. Winslow. *Ibid.* p. 165.
66. E. P. Thompson. (1968) *The Making of the English Working Class.* London, Penguin Books. p. 509.
67. Peter King. *Crime, Justice and Discretion in England 1740-1820. Op. cit.* pp. 247-8.
68. Douglas Hay. (1975) 'Poaching and the Game Laws on Cannock Chase.' In *Albion's Fatal Tree. Op. cit.* p. 211.
69. Peter King. *Crime, Justice, and Discretion in England 1740-1820. Op. cit.* p. 248.

ever, in time it changed and, as Green has argued, 'the seditious libel trials of the eighteenth century constitute an important chapter in the history of freedom of the press and the growth of democratic government.'[70] The charge of seditious libel was, indeed, a serious obstacle to the growth of a free press and democratic government. It also had a large impact on the role of the jury in these important trials. The crime was a misdemeanour and not a felony which meant that defendants could instruct counsel in any event. Its essence involved the intentional publication of a writing that it was alleged scandalised, and tended to bring into contempt, the government of the day.[71] Truth was not a defence and once the jury found there had been publication then it followed as a presumption of law that there was a seditious intent.

In the reign of James II, as we have seen, the Archbishop of Canterbury and six bishops petitioned the king against his decision that his second Declaration of Indulgence, giving toleration to Roman Catholics, be read from every pulpit in the land. It was, they said, illegal. James had all seven of them imprisoned in the Tower and charged with publishing a seditious libel. Their trial became known as the *Seven Bishops' Case*.[72] The defendants were well represented by counsel and the judges of the King's Bench were evenly divided and allowed the jury to find in favour of the bishops on the question not only of publication of the petition but also on the legal issue of whether or not it was libellous. The verdict was greeted with tumultuous enthusiasm in London and the bishops offered the jury fees and a dinner, estimated to cost between 150 and 200 guineas, but they declined the offer.[73]

This verdict of the jury was regarded by many as a useful precedent. But in seditious libel cases in the eighteenth century Chief Justice Holt ignored it and followed the practice of the defunct Star Chamber in requiring the jury to find a general verdict of guilty if it found the accused published the writing and it bore the meaning alleged by the prosecution.[74] This was, in effect, taking what was known as a special verdict whereby the judge would ask for an answer by the jury to specific questions, reserving the right to require the jury subsequently to give the general verdict that appeared to follow in law from their answers to the questions of fact.[75] Juries, however, were often unhappy about this, perhaps because it ignored the issue of intention—normally an essential element in crime—which to jurors distinguished 'not only accidents from crimes, but also minor offenders from real criminals.'[76]

70. T. A. Green. *Verdict According to Conscience: Perspectives on the English Trial Jury, 1200-1800. Op. cit.* p. 318.
71. *Ibid.* pp. 318-19.
72. *12 State Trials.* cols. 183-522.
73. George Hilton Jones. (1990) *Convergent Forces: Immediate Causes of the Revolution of 1688 in England.* Iowa State University Press. p. 43.
74. T.A. Green. *Verdict According to Conscience. Op. cit.* pp. 318-19.
75. Glanville Williams. (1963) *The Proof of Guilt: A Study of the English Criminal Trial.* London, Stevens and Sons, pp. 264-5.
76. Cynthia B. Herrup. (1985) 'Law and Morality in Seventeenth-Century England.' 106 *Past & Present.* Oxford, The Past and Present Society. p. 110.

In 1752, William Owen, a bookseller, was indicted for a libel on the House of Commons.[77] He had published a pamphlet in which he argued that an Alexander Murray had been unjustly and oppressively committed to prison by the House for riotous conduct during the Westminster election of that year. The defendant's counsel urged the jury not to convict unless they thought Owen had a guilty intent. Lord Justice Lee directed them to convict if they believed simply that publication had been proved. The jury exercised their power and acquitted the defendant.

The mid-eighteenth century also saw the emergence of John Wilkes as a national figure. On 23 April 1763 he published his famous No. 45 of the *North Briton* paper in which he branded the King's Speech of the Grenville government as dishonest.[78] A general warrant was issued, not against a named person, but for the arrest of all concerned in the production of the *North Briton* and the seizure of their papers. Wilkes appeared in the Court of Common Pleas on May 3-6 1763 and was set free under the privilege of a member of Parliament.[79] When he later sued Under-Secretary Robert Wood for trespass the case was heard before Charles Pratt (afterwards Earl Camden), lord chief justice of the Common Pleas, and a jury. Large crowds invaded Westminster Hall crying, 'Wilkes and Liberty!' and the jury may have been influenced by them. Whether they were or not, they found a general verdict in his favour with surprisingly large damages of £1,000. More importantly, the judge ruled that general warrants, which did not name the person to be arrested, were illegal, as they have remained ever since.[80]

In 1770 John Almon was tried for selling in his shop Junius's celebrated letter to the king about the American colonies.[81] His defence was that the letter had not been sold by him but by his servant in the shop. He was found guilty, however, the law being clear on his vicarious responsibility. In the same year, John Miller and Henry Woodfall were tried for printing and publishing the same alleged libel.[82] In the case of Miller there was no doubt as to publication, for the letter had been reproduced in the *Evening Post* published by him. But, after Lord Mansfield had told the jury they had to determine nothing except the question of publishing and the innuendoes, they found Miller not guilty. In Woodfall's case the jury returned a verdict of 'guilty of publishing only.' These two cases were clear examples of jury nullification in the light of the law as it then was.

---

77. 18 *State Trials*. cols. 1203-1230.
78. 19 *State Trials*. cols. 1075-1138.
79. J. Steven Watson. (1960) *The Reign of George III 1760-1815*. Oxford, The Clarendon Press. p. 99.
80. 19 *State Trials*. cols. 1154-1176. And see Raymond Postgate. ((1956) *That Devil Wilkes*. London, Dennis Dobson. pp. 51-58.
81. 20 *State Trials*. cols. 803-868.
82. *Ibid.* cols. 870-895.

DEAN OF ST. ASAPH

The year 1783 saw the spectacular trial of William Shipley, the Dean of St. Asaph.[83] It has been said by Lord Devlin that this case is the most important in English law not to be discussed in the textbooks.[84] Shipley had published a tract[85] which was alleged to be a seditious libel and he was tried at Shrewsbury. Edward Bearcroft QC, leading counsel for the Crown, described the tract as a libel and argued that this was not a question for the jury since they were bound to convict the defendant simply if he caused it to be published[86]—which was not denied. Thomas Erskine appeared for the dean and insisted that it was the right of the jury to decide whether the tract was or was not a libel. All the prosecution evidence amounted to, he said, was just publishing the *Dialogue* which contained nothing seditious and had the dean's preface which contained a solemn protest against all sedition.

Erskine knew that the judge, Mr. Justice Buller, would take the correct legal position, at the time, that it was for the judge to decide whether or not a writing was libellous and that the jury should decide only if it had been published. In order, therefore, to forestall judicial reproof at what he was proposing to argue to the contrary, he mischievously said to the jury,

> When I reflect upon the danger which has often attended the liberty of the press in former times, from the arbitrary proceedings of abject, unprincipled and dependent judges ... I cannot help congratulate the public that you are to try this indictment with the assistance of the learned judge before you, much too instructed in the laws of this land to mislead you by mistake, and too conscientious to instruct you by design.[87]

Erskine declared that the dean had published, but was not guilty of publishing since that was not in itself a crime. Reminding them of their consciences he told the jury, 'if you say he is guilty then you say he is guilty of seditious libel and seditious intent.' You are asked, he continued,

> To deliver over the Dean of St. Asaph into the hands of the Judges, humane and liberal indeed, but who could not betray *their* oaths, because you had set them the example by betraying *yours*, and who would therefore be bound to believe him criminal, because *you* had said so on the record, though in violation of your opinions—opinions which, as ministers of the law, they could not act upon—to the existence of which they could not even avert.[88]

83. 21 *State Trials.* cols. 847-1044.
84. Sir Patrick Devlin. (1991) 'The Conscience of the Jury.' 107 *Law Quarterly Review.* London, Stevens and Sons. p. 401.
85. William Shipley. (1783) *The Principles of Government in a Dialogue between a Gentleman and a Farmer.* London, John Stockdale.
86. 21 *State Trials.* col. 891.
87. Lord John Campbell. (1847) *Lives of the Lord Chancellors.* London, John Murray. vol. vi. p. 430.
88. James Ridgway. (1847) *Speeches of the Rt. Hon. lord Erskine at the Bar and in Parliament.* London, J. Ridg-

The jury, he added, should preserve their independence by judging the *intention* which was the essence of every crime.[89] And a man's motives 'only an English jury shall judge. It is therefore impossible, in most criminal cases, to separate law from fact, and consequently whether a writing be or not be a libel, *never can be an abstract legal question for judges.*'[90]

As expected, Mr. Justice Buller told the jury in his summing up that, there being no doubt as to the libel, the only question they had to decide was whether the defendant had or had not published the pamphlet. The jury retired for half an hour. On their return to court, they found the dean guilty of publishing only. After bruising exchanges between Erskine and the judge around the word 'only', the judge seemed nonplussed about what to do and the jury, confused by what they had heard, withdrew again and eventually returned to enter a verdict of, 'Guilty of publishing, but whether a libel or not we do not find.' The judge then declared the dean to be guilty on all counts.

Erskine subsequently moved the King's Bench to set aside the verdict on the ground that the judge had misdirected the jury. He was granted an order to show cause why there should not be a new trial and the matter came before Lord Mansfield, the Lord Chief Justice. Here Mr. Bearcroft conceded that it was the *right* of the jury to judge of the whole charge when Mansfield interrupted to say he meant the *power* and not the *right*. Interestingly, Bearcroft demurred saying,

> I did not mean merely to acknowledge that the jury have the *power*, for their power nobody ever doubted; and, if a judge was to tell them they had it not, they would only have to laugh at him, and convince him of his error by finding a general verdict which must be recorded: I meant, therefore, to consider it as a *right*, as an important privilege, and of great value to the Constitution.[91]

Lord Mansfield then quoted, from memory, from a ballad of 1754,

> For Sir Philip well knows,
> That his *innuendoes*
> Will serve him no longer
> In verse or in prose;
> For 12 honest men have decided the cause,
> Who are judges of fact, though not judges of laws.

In fact, with what was perhaps a Freudian slip, he was mistaken. The last line actually reads:

---

way. vol. i. pp. 138–40.

89. Lord John Campbell. *Lives of the lord Chancellors. Op. cit.*

90. 21 *State Trials*. col. 924.

91. *Ibid.* col. 973.

Who are judges alike of the facts, and the laws.[92]

Eventually the court found the indictment against the dean was defective and the case against him was abandoned.[93]

FOX'S LIBEL ACT

The Dean's case had widespread repercussions and led to the moving in the House of Commons in 1792 of a Libel Bill by Charles James Fox. When enacted the Bill became known as Fox's Libel Act[94] and fully established the right of juries to decide as a matter of law whether or not a writing was a libel and not merely that it had been published. They could reach a general verdict of guilty or not guilty without any requirement that they give their reasons for so deciding. It was enacted despite all the judges in the House of Lords declaring that it was inconsistent with the Common Law—which was, of course, the point of it. As the Act said, in trials for seditious libel the, 'jury sworn to try the issues may give a general verdict of guilty or not guilty upon the whole matter put in issue … and shall not be required or directed … to find the defendant or defendants guilty, merely on the proof of the publication.' It underlined trial by jury as a form of defence against executive tyranny, with the jury as lawmaker—in effect Sir Patrick Devlin's 'little Parliament'.[95]

LIBERTY SAFEGUARDED

In the last decade of the eighteenth century the rulers of England were seized with fear induced by the mayhem and wars of the French Revolution and its aftermath. Revolutionaries were believed to infest the land and conspiracies to destroy the Constitution took over the imagination and were seen everywhere. As a consequence, in 1794, *habeas corpus* was suspended and 800 warrants of arrest were prepared. Simultaneously, three treason trials were mounted at the Old Bailey as a prelude to trials of the whole 800 suspects. The eminent Victorian historian, J. R. Green, described the government's excesses in prosecutions and attacks on freedom at this time as the 'English Terror'.[96] In similar vein, Lord John Campbell described the frenzied attempts at repression, a 'Reign of Terror.'[97] The three trials, held separately,

---

92. *Ibid. cols.* 1037-38.
93. *Ibid.* col. 1044.
94. 32 Geo. 3, c. 60. [1792].
95. Sir Patrick Devlin. (1966) *Trial by Jury.* London, Methuen & Co. Ltd., p. 164.
96. J. R. Green. (1874) *A Short History of the English People.* London, The Folio Society. p. 818.
97. Lord John Campbell. *The Lives of the Chancellors. Op. cit.* p. 460.

were of Thomas Hardy,[98] a shoemaker and secretary of the London Corresponding Society, John Horne Tooke,[99] a philologist and John Thelwell,[100] an avowed Jacobin. Despite the moderation of at least Hardy and Tooke, all three were charged with high treason in compassing the death of the king, although it was never suggested that they actually threatened his life or intended to use any force whatever. They were eloquently defended by Thomas Erskine and each was found not guilty by a jury. The remainder of the 800 warrants for arrest were silently discarded.

If these trials were the tip of the iceberg of a prospective reign of terror then, in defence of liberty, the acquittals were prime examples of the spirit of the English jury in action in defence of liberty for all. After all, in similar cases in Scotland, juries proved subservient to the uncouth Lord Braxfield and there was a great deal of repression at lower levels of society in England by magistrates. For instance, a few years later, following the Peterloo massacre, an outwardly Christian clerical magistrate used his position on the bench to say to a defendant, 'I believe you are a downright blackguard reformer. Some of you reformers ought to be hanged, and some of you are sure to be hanged—the rope is already round your necks.'[101]

SPECIAL JURIES

Essentially, special juries were of three principal kinds each having different functions. The first, employed from the thirteenth century onwards, were judges of facts requiring knowledge of some special non-legal field. There are medieval cases recorded of self-informing juries of cooks and fishmongers in London summoned to try people accused of selling bad food, and many instances of mercantile disputes being settled by merchants of the trade in question.[102] As Cornish says, 'This was natural in a system under which jurors were expected to decide the case by applying their own knowledge.'[103] Hence, even later, in 1645-6 in the King's Bench,

> The court was moved that a jury of merchants might be retained to try an issue between two merchants, touching merchants' affairs, and it was granted, because it was conceived they might have better knowledge of the matters in difference which were to be tried than others could who were not of that profession.[104]

And, where a female defendant who was found guilty of a capital crime claimed

---

98. 24 *State Trials*. cols. 199-1408.
99. 25 *Ibid*. cols. 1-748.
100. *Ibid*.
101. *The Times*. 27 September 1819.
102. W. R. Cornish. (1968) *The Jury*. London, Allen Lane. pp. 31-3.
103. *Ibid*. p. 31.
104. J. B. Thayer. (1898) *A Preliminary Treatise on Evidence at the Common Law*. Boston, Little Brown and Company. pp.94-5.

she was pregnant, she could have an all-female jury 'inspect her belly' and, if she was indeed pregnant, execution would be delayed to allow the child to be born and, occasionally, she might be permitted to live.[105]

The second type of special jury, which came to prominence in the latter half of the seventeenth century and was sometimes known as a 'struck jury', was formed by the sheriff attending the master of the Crown Office, with an agent for each party, and selecting 48 names of prospective jurors. Each party was then allowed to strike out the names of 12 of them.[106] To an extent this allowed the parties to choose the jury and the procedure was regulated by an Act of 1730.[107]

The third type of special jury involved jurors of higher social status than those who made up petty juries. According to Blackstone, such special juries were originally introduced when causes, 'were of too great nicety for the discussion of ordinary freeholders; or where the sheriff was suspected of partiality in choosing trial jurors.'[108] The first reason appears to reflect a clear case of government special pleading. A feature of these special jurors, apart from their names appearing on special lists, was that they had to be paid a fee.[109] They were called frequently by the Crown, particularly, though not exclusively, in state and political trials and, indeed, following *Bushell's Case*[110] when judges lost control of 'perverse' juries, sometimes in cases of felony. There is no doubt hand picking of jurors occurred with court officials collaborating with the Crown Solicitor for the purpose.[111] Quite well-known were the 'guinea men' who were regular special jurors who lived off the fee in each case, commonly a guinea but sometimes as much as five guineas or more, and who knew that continuance of this income depended on bringing in verdicts for the Crown.[112]

As Oldham has confirmed, members of special juries were almost always of a much higher social status than the common jurors and in the counties such juries were composed of wealthy landed gentlemen, many of whom would have been justices of the peace.[113] Indeed, the County Juries Act of 1825 required that they should be persons, 'who shall be legally entitled to be called an esquire, or shall be a person of higher degree or shall be a banker or merchant.'[114] Then, in 1870, property qualifications were added that prescribed certain minimum rateable values above

---

105. James C. Oldham. (1983) 'The Origins of the Special Jury.' Chicago, Chicago University Press. 50 *The University of Chicago Law Review.* p. 171.

106. William Garrow MP. *Hansard.* (April-July 1816) First series. vol. xxxiv. col. 395.

107. 3 Geo. 2. c. 25.

108. Sir William Blackstone. (1830) *Commentaries on the Law of England.* London, Thomas Tegg. vol. iv. pp. 357-8.

109. J. Oldham. 'The Origins of the Special Jury.' *Op. cit.* p. 204.

110. Ante. p.124.

111. W.R. Cornish. *The Jury. Op. cit.* p. 131.

112. *Ibid.* pp. 131-2.

113. J. Oldham. *The Origins of the Special Jury. Op. cit.* p. 209.

114. 6 Geo. 4, c. 50.

those for common jurors.[115]

Nonetheless, such men were not always happy to be kept away from their businesses and pursuits. In the City of London in 1867 it was found that a Charles Mayhew, who had access to the jury list, ran a lucrative business in getting men excused from jury service. In return for paying him a guinea a year, any man not wanting to serve could send him the summons, and he would swear a false affidavit to get him excused. Although Mayhew was uncovered and put on trial at the Old Bailey, he died before the case came to court.[116] What is surprising is that special juries were not abolished until the Juries Act of 1949.[117]

There was also another kind of special jury prior to the late nineteenth century. This was known as a *jury de mediate linguae* (of half-tongue) and it was not unusual. Where a prisoner was a foreigner he could require that half his jury be of the same nationality as himself. For instance, in January 1784, a John Henry Aikles was prosecuted at the Old Bailey for theft and claimed he was a Hessian from Hesse in Germany a jury was sworn with one-half its members Hessians.[118] Since the existence of such juries suggested that, without such a device, the English legal system was prejudiced against foreigners they were eventually abolished, but not until 1870.

GRAND JURIES

Mention should also be made of the grand jury from which, as we have seen, the trial jury emerged in the thirteenth century. It survived until the twentieth century as the body deciding whether a person who was accused of an offence would be sent to trial. It was justified as being a shield against unfounded and oppressive prosecution and giving ordinary members of the public an opportunity to participate in the administration of justice. In reality it failed on both counts. Unlike the trial jury it could have up to 23 members. It met in secret and heard only the prosecution case without the defendant being present. Furthermore, it reached its decision by a majority if all its members could not agree.[119] members of grand juries were meant to be—and usually were—men of substance, although such men were not always willing to accept unpaid responsibility. There was no bar on their being related to the accused and, according to John Bellamy, in Tudor times at least, some definitely were.[120] If they found there was not a *prima facie* case against the accused they

115. W. R. Cornish. *The Jury. Op. cit.* p. 32.
116. Michael Lobban. (2002) 'The Strange Life of the English Civil Jury, 1837-1914.' In Cairns and McLeod (eds.) *The Dearest Birthright of the People of England: The Jury in the History of the Common Law.* Oxford, Hart Publishing, p. 200.
117. 12 & 13 Geo. 6. c. 27.
118. OBP Online. (www.oldbaileyonline.org) 14 January 1784. Ref: t17840114-80.
119. Radcliffe and Cross. ((1964) *The English Legal System.* London, Butterworths. p. 199.
120. J. Bellamy. (1979) *The Tudor Law of Treason: An Introduction.* London, Routledge & Kegan Paul. p. 128.

marked the indictment with the word *ignoramus* or 'not a true bill'. In the event they found such a case the indictment would be marked, *billa vera,* a 'true bill'.

Through the centuries there is little evidence of grand juries asserting independence in the way trial juries often did, although Lambarde drew attention to the tendency of grand jurors in Kent in the sixteenth century to, 'usurp the functions of both trial jury and judge, and to the criticism of this development by both local magistrates and assize judges.'[121] Moreover, he was critical of them as being, 'wont to pass over the huge heaps of offences, that they may seem rather to have conspired with evildoers … than to have come with prepared minds to have wicked men made good by deserved punishment.'[122]

Zachary Babington, an Oxford Circuit Associate, in his *Advice to Grand Jurors in Cases of Blood* in 1677 wrote of grand jurors,

> (as if they were judges of both law and fact) … finding the indictment sometimes manslaughter, when they should find it murder, contrary to the sense and direction of the learned judge … whereby a murderer many times escapes.[123]

Furthermore, according to Herrup, 'Grand jurors represented the legal conscience of the shire; their very presence could be a restraining influence on local malice and on magisterial highhandedness.'[124] Nevertheless, too much should not be made of their independence.

Throughout the Middle Ages, grand jurors were chosen by two men nominated in each hundred or town by the bailiffs, except when a powerful magnate or the government decided to deal with the selection themselves. For an example of the latter, in May 1537 the Duke of Norfolk told Henry VIII that he had appointed two grand juries at York and had declared his mind to them. This presumably meant telling them that since he and the king believed in the truth of the Bills of Indictment before them, they should also.[125]

By the nineteenth century, both the secrecy and the prosecution bias of grand juries were causing concern. Blackstone had claimed that the rule that the grand jury heard only the evidence for the prosecution was justified because the indictment was merely an accusation.[126] On the other hand, the growth of defence counsel cross-examining prosecution witnesses and magistrates discharging prisoners where guilt was in doubt also undermined the role of the grand jury. As did the establishment

121. Conyers Read (ed.) (1962) *William Lambarde and Local Government. His 'Ephemeris' and Twenty Nine Charges to Juries and Commissions* Ithaca, New York, Cornell University Press. pp. 119-20.
122. *Ibid.* p. 112.
123. J. S. Cockburn. ((1972) *Introduction to Calendar of Assize Records, Home Circuit Indictments Elizabeth I and James I.* London, HMSO. pp. 51-2.
124. Cynthia Herrup. (1987) *The Common Peace: Participation and the Criminal Law in Seventeenth-century England.* Cambridge, Cambridge University Press. p. 93.
125. J. Bellamy. *The Tudor Law of Treason. Op. cit.* p. 128.
126. Sir W. Blackstone. *Commentaries on the Law of England. Op. cit.* vol. iv. p. 302.

of police forces investigating the facts on which prosecutions were based. It was no surprise, therefore, when the Criminal Law Commissioners set on foot an inquiry into the grand jury in 1845.[127] In preparing their report the Commissioners sought opinions from what they described as, 'many persons of high eminence and great legal acquirements.' These included Lord Chief Justice Denman and William Samuel Jones, who had 51 years of Crown Office experience. There were many members of the legal profession, including recorders, magistrates, barristers, Clerks of the Peace and attorneys. They submitted written answers to a questionnaire sent to them by the Commissioners and made many important suggestions. Other topics dealt with in the questionnaires were Indictments, public prosecutions, the unanimity of juries and criminal appeals.

The function of the grand jury, it was said, was to protect falsely accused persons against the stigma, risk and expense of a criminal trial. However, it was alleged in evidence given to the Commissioners by R. Leigh, Clerk of the Peace for the borough of Wigan, and J. Pitt Taylor that the grand jury was often abused by deliberately being given too little of the available evidence (after bribery of witnesses) with the result that guilty people were set free. The secrecy of the proceedings prevented such misconduct from coming to light. Pitt Taylor actually answered the Commissioners' questions publicly in an article in *The Law Magazine* which appeared as Appendix C of the report.[128] He wished to abolish grand juries not only because they were 'utterly useless' but also because they defeated the ends of justice, were instruments of oppression, were expensive and created inconvenience.

Nonetheless, most respondents favoured the retention of grand juries, although not with much enthusiasm, and, in all, 42 of the witnesses favoured retention against 36 who opposed grand juries. The Commissioners were completely silent on grand juries in their report, which is surprising even if they were disappointed in the figures. In the event, grand juries were not abolished until 1933.[129]

PARDONS

Not only juries but judges also had considerable powers of discretion. Once an offender was convicted they could reprieve him and recommend him for a royal pardon. Further, after a felon had been condemned to death the judge might reprieve him to allow the king to show mercy if he chose or if such a course were recommended by the judge. He might do this if he thought the verdict was not satisfactory or if the prisoner had a previously good character. If a pardon were granted it was

---

127. *Parliamentary Papers.* (1845) Eighth Report. vol. xiv. p. 161.
128. *The Law Magazine.* (1844) vol. 131. pp. 245-75.
129. Administration of Justice (Miscellaneous Provisions) Act, 1933. 23 & 24 Geo. 5, c, 36,

sent to the court where the prisoner had to plead to it.

In this regard an interesting case occurred at the Old Bailey in 1789.[130] A number of women convicted of felony were brought up before the judge to be granted a royal pardon, on condition of being transported for life. All agreed except a Sarah Cowden who said she would accept the death penalty unless the sentence of death on Sarah Storer, who was innocent, was mitigated. After clearing the court, the judge told her she had forfeited her life and the king was being merciful in granting her a royal pardon. She replied that Storer was as innocent as a child unborn having merely entered the place where a robbery was committed to borrow a pair of bellows. She, Cowden, was willing to die with her although she was only 21 years of age. The judge thereupon ordered her execution for the following Thursday. At this point defence counsel asked permission to speak to Cowden and the judge raised no objection. She maintained her position, however, and the judge said she was trifling with the court. The matter was resolved only when counsel persuaded Cowden to plead to the pardon, after which she was sentenced to transportation for life.

Pardons were an essential part of the criminal law when the death penalty was so ubiquitous. They might be absolute in which case the prisoner would go free. They would be granted where the judge thought the jury's verdict of guilty was wrong or for reasons of age or infirmity. Alternatively, the pardon might be conditional upon the prisoner accepting transportation as an alternative to the gallows. So common did pardons become that at the conclusion of Assizes the judges would submit to the king a list of those considered suitable to be pardoned. Pardons were also granted more or less as a matter of course when requested for prisoners by persons of substance. It seems amazing but over the whole period from the Glorious Revolution of 1689 to the end of Queen Anne's reign in 1714, more than 60 per cent of the men and women convicted at the Old Bailey were pardoned.[131]

---

130. OBP Online. (www.oldbaileyonlone.org) 3 June 1789. Punishment Proceedings. Ref:t17890603-1.
131. J. M. Beattie.(2001) *Policing and Punishment in London, 1660–1750: Urban Crime and the Limits of Terror.* Oxford, Oxford University Press. p. 362.

CHAPTER 9

Punishment and Prisons

Although it is usual to speak of a system there is little theoretical framework for criminal justice in current government thinking and practice, except perhaps with restorative justice. And ethical considerations are rarely mentioned.

THEORIES OF PUNISHMENT

In the main, three objectives of punishment are usually, and have been for some time, put forward. First, deterrence, both of the criminal and potential criminals. Secondly, rehabilitation of the offender and thirdly, retribution or vengeance with incapacitation. Many people accept the validity of one or two of these but rarely all three. Deterrence is part of the utilitarian traditional belief that discouraging people from committing crime, by one means or another, makes for a stable society. Whether it can ever be achieved is open to question. Rehabilitation was the desired aim of John Howard, the defenders of the penitentiary and many modern prison reformers but has hardly proved to be a great success in practice however desirable in theory. Even probation has not proved to be an unmitigated success. As one writer has put it, 'With few and isolated exceptions, the rehabilitative efforts that have been reported so far have had no appreciable effect on recidivism.'[1]

Retribution, or vengeance, is commonly supported by wide sections of the public who consider it gives the criminal what he deserves. And the result is more easily seen than the effects of deterrence. Its history goes back to Aristotle who believed that just retribution involves a proportionate reprisal. More recently, Stephen wrote that the primary object of legal punishment was, 'the direct prevention of crime, either by fear, or by disabling or even destroying ... to gratify the public desire for vengeance upon such offenders as justify exemplary punishments.'[2] As will be seen, there was a great deal of that approach in the eighteenth century the reaction to which led ultimately to a more humanitarian attitude based upon deterrence and reformation. Nonetheless, the idea that the punishment should fit the crime and be in proportion to the amount of harm caused (the proportional approach, which is not easy to quantify accurately) has a long history in England. But so has the reformation theory that the punishment should only be enough to reform the offender.

Are there, however, other, less visible, motives for punishment? Undoubtedly,

---

1. Robert Martinson. (1974) 'What Works? Questions and answers about penal reform' 35 *Public Interest*. P. 25. Cited by Nigel Walker. (1991) *Why Punish?* Oxford, Oxford University Press.
2. J. F. Stephen. (1883) *A History of the Criminal Law of England*. London, Macmillan. vol. ii. p. 83.

crime and punishment vary according to time and place, as Bentham argued. They change with different levels of economic development, with changing cultural and social conditions and patterns of behaviour, with the needs of a given society and with the will of its governing class who make the law, define crime and determine punishments. The punishment for rape has been severe or lenient in different ages. Some activities which were not crimes in the past but have been made so today include drug abuse, white-collar crimes, drink driving and some types of pollution of the environment. Punishments for gambling, debt and for sexual immorality such as adultery were severe in the Puritan Commonwealth but are relaxed today, if they exist at all.

Protestants and witches are no longer burnt at the stake or, indeed, punished at all. The mere idea would seem ludicrous to the modern mind. Nevertheless, not only ancient lawgivers, but also such influential writers on penal law as Bentham and Stephen, have proceeded in the belief that punishments should be brought to bear on moral as well as legal guilt and this view has persisted until recent times and, indeed, still exists. Another viewpoint is that since it is one of the foundations on which ordered society rests, any system of criminal law and punishment must depend upon subtle methods of coercion, and *in extremis* upon force for its survival. This raises the question of whether punishment is merely a fluid *ad hoc* means of social control of the dangerous and politically dissident elements in society.

Hugo Grotius defined punishment as, 'the infliction of an ill for an ill done'[3] which tells us nothing about who is responsible for the punishing and why. It does, however, presuppose a victim who is in a subordinate position to the punisher. Clearly, in the Middle Ages, local social control was to the fore and punishments crudely reflected that fact. Subsequently, the philosophers of the Enlightenment concentrated on humanism and society's duty to protect the rights of man, property and personal welfare against the brutality of the still dominant feudal penal laws and institutions. In modern times should this not be extended to seeing the primary aim of punishment as resolving social frictions? Legal punishment often flows from the power of the state. But in a vibrant, democratic society the Rule of Law is far removed from being merely an expression of naked, arbitrary power. Punishments should reflect justice. Whether imprisonment and other secondary punishments have done so in the past we can now reflect upon alongside more recent opinions on the changing purposes of punishment.

One jurist has written:

Generally speaking, the increasing understanding of the social and psychological causes of crime has led to a growing emphasis on *reformation* rather than deterrence in the older sense, as the best way to protect both the individual criminal from himself, and society from the incidence of crime. In practical terms, this has meant the increasing use of corrective and educational measures, either in addition to, or in substitution for, punishment proper. The

---

3. H. Grotius. (1696) *De Jure Belli ac Pacis*. Ultrajecti. A.G. van de Water.

consideration of such alternatives has gradually spread from specialised categories of offenders to criminal offenders in general.[4]

This is particularly the case, he adds, in the treatment of juvenile offenders. H. L. Packer suggested a classification of sanctions into four categories. These are, compensation, regulation, punishment and treatment of socially condemned conduct as a disease rather than a crime.[5] The impact of such sanctions will be assessed later in the chapter on restorative justice.

Going even further, Baroness Wootton argues that, 'custodial sentences should be indeterminate in respect to the type of institution to which an offender should be committed, and indeed that the rigid division of institutions into the medical and the penal should be obliterated.' Essentially, 'decisions as to the treatment of offenders should be common administrative, instead of a judicial, matter.'[6]

CRIMINAL WARDENS

In the eighteenth century the conditions in most of England's prisons continued to be a disgrace to the nation with their extortions, ill-treatment and debauchery. Their story is appalling. Historically, they were places for holding men, women and children secure until their trial or until they paid their fines or debts. They were not meant to be places of punishment or for the rehabilitation of prisoners. At the Old Bailey, the major criminal court for London and Middlesex, imprisonment accounted for no more than 2.3 per cent of the judges' sentences in the years between 1770 and 1774.[7] Notwithstanding this, prisons indiscriminately took in felons and misdemeanants, the convicted and the unconvicted, the sane and the mentally ill, civil debtors, men, women and children. There was little segregation and all prisons were unheated, except for those who could afford to pay, unfurnished, except for straw, and had only the most primitive sanitary arrangements.[8]

According to Lionel W. Fox the only duty of the gaoler to the prisoners was to hold them, and his sole interest to make what he could from them.[9] The prison system was characterised by chaos in administration and indifference to the fate of inmates. Gaolers took a fee for the admission of prisoners and, if they were fortunate

4. W. Friedmann. (1972) *Law in a Changing Society*. Second edition. London, Penguin Books. p. 226.
5. H. L. Packer. (1968) *The Limits of the Criminal Sanction*. Stanford University Press. pp. 23, 205.
6. B. Wootton. (1963) *Crime and the Criminal Law: Reflections of a Magistrate and Social Scientist*. London, Stevens and Sons. p. 112.
7. Michael Ignatieff. (1989) *A Just Measure of Pain: The Penitentiary in the Industrial Revolution 1750–1850*. London, Penguin Books. p. 15.
8. Lionel W. Fox. (1952) *The English Prison and Borstal Systems* .London, Routledge & Kegan Paul Limited. p. 21.
9. *Ibid*.

enough to leave, another on their discharge. It was a common sight to see discharged prisoners dragged back to their cells until they could pay these fees. Although chaining in irons was illegal in theory, it was a frequent practice and the gaoler took a fee for hammering the irons on and another for knocking them off.[10]

Fees had to be paid for food and improved accommodation. Drink, tobacco, and women were in plentiful supply at a price.[11] Besides letting rooms to prisoners, the keeper usually 'maintained a coffee shop and tap for prisoners and visitors. At the Fleet and the King's Bench the keepers also sold to civil prisoners the privilege of living outside the walls of the prison. For eight guineas the debtor could purchase the right to live 'within the rules', that is within two-and-a-half miles of the prison.'[12] These prisons were houses of lechery, debauchery, moral corruption and the contagious pestilence of typhus, known as 'gaol fever'. At the 'Black Sessions' of the Old Bailey in 1750 four of the six judges, three counsel, an under-sheriff and several jurors and spectators all died of typhus contracted in court. According to Fox, it was computed that every year a quarter of all prisoners were thus destroyed.[13]

Newgate was the principle criminal prison in London, standing near the Old Bailey. It was:

[s]ynomynous with misery, despair, wickedness and death. 'The name of Newgate is a great terror to all', observed a prison officer in 1724, 'from its being a prison for felons ... and the blackest sort of malefactors'; the gaol's sinister reputation was further enhanced by public-spirited citizens who reviled it as a 'tomb for the living', 'the mansion of misery and even 'Hell itself'.[14]

Corruption in the Fleet prison

The Fleet prison was particularly notorious for the atrocious cruelty of its governors, then known as wardens. The prison had been built in 1197 off what is now Farringdon Street on the eastern bank of the Fleet river. It was destroyed in 1381 during the Peasants' Revolt and again in 1666 in the Great Fire of London. On each occasion it was rebuilt. Before the English Civil War it had been used to hold prisoners committed by the Star Chamber and was the scene of a great deal of torture. When the Long Parliament abolished the Star Chamber in 1640 it became a prison for debtors and persons guilty of contempt of court.

By the early eighteenth century the Fleet was under the control of judges of the High Court and London justices of the peace, although in practice that meant

10. *Ibid.*
11. For an interesting account of debauchery at Newgate see (1977) W.J. Sheehan. 'Finding Solace in Eighteenth-Century Newgate. In *Crime in England 1550-1800.* (ed. J.S. Cockburn) London, Methuen & Co. Limited. pp. 229-245.
12. Michael Ignatieff. *A Just Measure of Pain. The Penitentiary in the Industrial Revolution 1750-1850. Op. cit.* p. 30.
13. Lionel W. Fox. *The English Prison and Borstal Systems. Op. cit.* p. 21.
14. W.J. Sheehan. (1977) 'Finding Solace in Eighteenth- Century Newgate. In J.S. Cockburn (ed) *Crime in England 1550-1800.* London, Methuen & Co. Ltd., p. 229.

little for those incarcerated within its walls. In August 1728 the existing warden, John Huggins, sold his office to Thomas Bambridge for the huge sum of £5,000 which gives some idea of the income the new warden expected to obtain in the post. What made the office so valuable was that, contrary to law, Huggins had exercised arbitrary power to amass a fortune by extorting exorbitant fees from prisoners who wanted to avoid oppression and being chained in irons. By letters patent the warden also held the rights to, and could let, the Old Palace of Westminster, the shops in Westminster Hall (where the judges sat) and other properties which together produced a considerable income.

When he became warden Bambridge was known to assist prisoners to escape for a fee and he often refused to take in prisoners committed to him by the courts. Instead, he had them taken to a 'sponging house' which he owned and where he took from them huge payments for their accommodation and excessive charges for the plentiful liquor he plied them with. Sponging houses were so named after a sponge since once there debtors had all their available cash squeezed out of them. And it could be worse. One prisoner, named Robert Castell, decided he was unwilling to undergo further ill-treatment in prison and was transferred to the sponging house. There smallpox was raging which he caught and from which he soon died.

Parliamentary inquiry

In the Fleet, prisoners, held in irons, were loaded into a specially-built dungeon erected over the common sewer and adjoining a dunghill. The evil and sadistic Bambridge also personally attacked prisoners with his sword, chained them until their legs were broken and caused some to lose their sight. On one occasion he openly stated that his intent was to torture his victims, an aim which he certainly achieved, causing some of them to die. However, another prisoner, a Captain David Sinclair, who suffered terrible torments which damaged his limbs and his memory managed to get to court by a writ of *habeas corpus* and the full horror of the prison began to be exposed. As a consequence, a Committee of the House of Commons was appointed to inquire into the state of gaols in the country, paying particular regard to the 'cruel usage of prisoners'. Bambridge treated the committee with contempt but it reported on what he (and Huggins) had been doing and recommended their arrest and trial.

The committee's examination of the Marshalsea Prison also resulted in the prosecution of its deputy warden, William Acton, on a charge of murder. The Marshalsea was in Southwark and in 1729 it held some 300 debtors. It was demolished in the early nineteenth century but rebuilt in 1811 and subsequently held John Dickens, the father of Charles Dickens.

In separate trials held in 1729, all three wardens (Huggins, Bambridge and Acton) were accused of unlawfully using irons, creating foul dungeons and treating prisoners in a barbarous and cruel manner. In addition, the committee asked for leave to have a Bill prepared for better regulation of the Fleet and punishment for any arbitrary practices of the warden. Bambridge was sent to Newgate prison for a short time on remand but whilst there was allowed to have prostitutes visit him frequently until the prison tapster, Anne Jones, joined him as his mistress.

'Half-human creature'

Huggins was the first to be tried. He appeared at the Old Bailey on 21 May 1729 before Mr Justice Page, Mr Baron Carter and other judges.[15] The charge was one of the murder of Edward Arne who was described by witnesses as a starving half-human creature. This was by aiding and abetting James Barnes, the warden's agent who had escaped abroad, in confining the victim in a damp and insanitary dungeon with no heat or light until he died. Huggins denied having ever seen Arne, although he was contradicted by two witnesses for the Crown, and he produced witnesses who testified to his good character. In summing up to the jury, Mr Justice Page agreed the prisoner's good character had been established but said that if he were guilty of an act which destroyed that character, it would count for nothing.

The jury found that Huggins was an accessory to the murder but had not acted with malice. The attorney-general responded that on the circumstances the law implied malice. The jury's 'special verdict' (i.e. one where certain facts have been proved but the law—the malice—is left to the court) was taken to the King's Bench by writ of *certiorari*. The court found Barnes guilty of murder with malice implied because of his breach of the trust the law placed in him. Huggins, on the other hand, was acquitted and discharged on the incredible ground that, although he knew of the condition of the dungeon, he did not know it was dangerous to a man's life.

Appeal of felony

The trial of Thomas Bambridge, on a charge of murdering Robert Castell, took place at the Old Bailey on 21 May 1729.[16] The judges were Sir Robert Baylis, Lord Mayor of the City of London, Mr Justice Page, Mr Baron Carter, some other judges and a number of justices of the peace. The trial was very brief and the main witness was Richard Corbett, the keeper of Bambridge's sponging house. He told the court that although he told Bambridge that Castell wanted to be moved out of the house he, Corbett, had not permitted the prisoner to have contact with any smallpox victim there. On the strength of this evidence Bambridge was acquitted.[17] Castell's widow, Mary, then decided to bring an appeal of felony (a private prosecution permitted despite the acquittal) against both Bambridge and Corbett for the murder of her husband. This was heard the following year at The Guildhall before Lord Chief

15. 17 *State Trials.* cols. 310-382.
16. *Ibid.* cols. 398-461.
17. OBP Online. www.oldbaileyonline.org. (21 May 1729) Trial of Thomas Bambridge for murder. Ref: t17290521-50.

Justice Raymond.

On this occasion, witnesses gave evidence that Castell had paid considerable sums of money to Bambridge when in the Fleet but that when he decided to pay no more he was sent to the sponging house. Evidence was given again as to the conditions in the sponging house and of Castell's desire to be moved. Further, his death-bed statement that he blamed Bambridge for his death was allowed by the judge to be introduced.

The accused denied the testimony, however, and claimed that the sponging house was a lawful place of refreshment. Witnesses were called to confirm his story. In his summing up to the jury the lord chief justice told them that Corbett had no knowledge of there being smallpox in the house. This was curious, to say the least, since the judge had sat on the examination of the verdict in the trial of Huggins in which Corbett had spoken of a smallpox victim named White being there and of approaching Bambridge with Castell's request to be moved out of the house for that reason. Now the judge told the jury that without that knowledge there was insufficient evidence to convict Corbett and the jury accordingly acquitted him. As to Bambridge, the judge said that as a matter of law all the allegations against him had to concur and on that the jury found Bambridge also not guilty. Despite this it is believed that eventually he committed suicide.

Torture at the Marshalsea Prison

On 1 August 1729 William Acton, deputy-warden and head turnkey at the Marshalsea Prison in Southwark, was charged at the Kingston Assizes with the murder of Thomas Bliss. The trial took place before Mr Baron Carter and a jury.[18]

Bliss was incarcerated in the Marshalsea for a small debt. He had tried unsuccessfully to escape and this brought down the wrath of Acton upon his head. The indictment set out that Acton, 'a person of an inhuman and cruel disposition', had assaulted Bliss and placed him in an insanitary and dangerous dungeon with a great weight of irons and fetters on his legs. It further set forth that an iron engine of torture known as the 'skull cap' had been tightened around his head and thumb screws used until his thumbs poured with blood. Mrs Anne Bliss, the widow of the dead prisoner, testified that she visited her husband in the gaol twice a day. She described the dungeon and the deplorable condition to which it reduced her husband. Acton, she explained, had forced her to watch when he ordered that the skull-cap, an iron collar and the fetters and thumb screws be put on her husband, all at the same time. The next day she saw him after he had been beaten so badly that the clothes had to be cut from his body.

Mrs Susannah Dodd was the next to give evidence. She testified that she ran errands in the prison and had seen Bliss there hundreds of times. On one occasion, she

---

18. 17 *State Trials*. cols. 462-510.

had gone to the dungeon to take him some food. There she witnessed that he had thumbscrews on his thumbs, an iron cap on his head and irons known as 'sheers' on his legs. Bliss had asked her to chew his food for him as his mouth was sore from also having an iron band around his neck. Out of compassion she had done as he asked. Mrs Ruth Butler, herself a prisoner at the Marshalsea until two weeks before the trial, swore that Acton had beaten Bliss with a 'bull's pizzle' (a flogging instrument made from a bull's penis), had flung him to the ground and then stamped on his stomach until it became badly swollen. Altogether, 16 witnesses of cruelty to Bliss gave evidence for the prosecution. Bliss could not give evidence himself since, by the time of the trial, he had left the prison, incapable of work, unable to eat properly and physically and mentally incapacitated. He died nearly 12 months later.

Humane turnkey

In his defence Acton made much of the injuries to Bliss's legs that he claimed he had received when he fell from a roof during an attempt to escape. He also produced a number of witnesses to say they had never seen Bliss in chains or assaulted. On the contrary, they said Bliss always had a good word to say for Acton. A number of witnesses were also called to give evidence of Acton's humane character.

In addressing the jury, Baron Carter said, 'There are great contradictions in the evidence. I scarce ever heard so great. It is a matter of great consequence and deserves your mature consideration'. He then went to dinner and the jury withdrew to consider their verdict. On their return they found Acton not guilty.

During the following two days, Acton was prosecuted at the same Assizes before the same judge for the alleged murder of three more prisoners on similar evidence and, in each case, he was again acquitted. The judge had ruled that the fact that there had been no coroner's inquest was of no consequence but in doing so he ignored the statutory requirement for such an inquest when any inmate died in prison.

These absurd acquittals of men who can only be described as monsters, as indeed the House of Commons Committee had found them to be, left a dark stain on the country's penal history. Although the men had been gaolers of debtors' prisons, the cases undoubtedly undermined progress in the reform of the criminal justice system by the failure of the courts to expose and deal with such malicious ill-treatment of prisoners that was widespread.

JOHN HOWARD

It was nearly half-a-century later that John Howard, as High-Sheriff for Bedfordshire, began to examine the prisons in his county. He had previously spent time in a French prison after being captured at sea and was appalled at the conditions in the dungeon in which he was kept. As a consequence he became deeply sympathetic to the fate of prisoners. When he inspected Bedford Gaol he thought their suffering was caused by the gaoler charging them fees for board and lodging. When he suggested to the Bedford justices that the gaoler should instead be paid a salary they complacently replied that the same system was used throughout the country. To see for himself if this was the case he set out on a three-year tour of prisons countrywide, travelling over 10,000 miles collecting information. On 4 March 1774 he gave his evidence to the House of Commons which was prompted to pass the Gaol Act of that year. This abolished gaolers' fees and proposed improved sanitary arrangements but although Howard had copies of the Act printed and sent to every prison in England it was largely ignored by the justices and gaolers.

Concerned about the scenes which had greeted him in England, Howard also travelled to inspect prisons in parts of Europe with a view to exposing the evils he saw and to propose remedies. In 1777 he published his conclusions in *The State of the Prisons in England and Wales with some Preliminary Observations, and an Account of some Foreign Prisons*.[19] His exposure revealed that often prisoners were so starved they could hardly move, that many slept on rags or on the floor and many, including women, were kept at all times in irons, even at night when asleep. The book made a powerful impact and when Howard, who was a nonconformist landowner with a developed social conscience, died of typhus on 20 January 1790 in a military hospital in the Ukraine after inspecting conditions there, Bentham said of him, 'he died a martyr after living an apostle.'

Howard, was an ascetic county squire who wished to reform criminals by discipline. He believed that spiritual values would change men and women, as much as material decencies and necessities. This meant he saw virtue in prisoners spending long periods in solitary confinement in order to reflect on their sins and achieve reformation. The whole purpose of his regime was reformation by punitive measures. Nevertheless, his plans for paid gaolers, supervising justices, separate cells for sleeping and useful work in proper workshops were incorporated into statutes. These were not mandatory, however, and were more inspirational than effective.

It was when Sir Robert Peel became Home Secretary in 1822 that real change commenced. He recognised the necessity for dealing with both the evils within the prison system and providing effective administrative control. His Gaols Act of 1823[20] consequently made mandatory Howard's four principles of providing secure and sanitary accommodation, making gaolers salaried servants of the local authorities, instituting a regime of reformation and ensuring the systematic inspection of all parts of the prisons by visiting justices. Above all, the Act made it the duty of justices to organize their prisons on a prescribed plan and to furnish quarterly re-

---

19. John Howard. (1777) *The State of the Prisons in England and Wales with some Preliminary Observations, and an Account of some Foreign Prisons*. 2 pts. Warrington.
20. 4 Geo. 4. c. 64.

ports to the Home Secretary upon every department of their prison administration. Unfortunately, although the statute had some persuasive effect, there was no central machinery available to enforce it.

ELIZABETH FRY

A good deal of the credit for the Gaols Act goes to Elizabeth Fry and her brother Joseph Gurney. Both were Quakers with a family background in banking that gave little indication that they would become outstanding prison reformers and philanthropists. Their father, Joseph Gurney, was a successful banker as a partner in Gurney's Bank and their mother, Catherine, was a member of the Barclay family who helped found Barclays Bank. Their family home as children was Earlham Hall, Norwich, now part of the University of East Anglia. Fry's brother-in-law was the reforming MP Thomas Fowell Buxton who helped her give evidence to a House of Commons committee on conditions in English prisons, which made her the first woman to testify in Parliament. Fry had visited Newgate Prison and was appalled at the conditions there. As a consequence she founded a prison school for the children imprisoned with their parents and, in 1817, helped establish the Association for the Improvement of the Female Prisoners in Newgate.

With her brother and Buxton she involved herself in the campaign for the abolition of capital punishment and, as Peel's prison reforms did not apply to debtors' prisons or local town gaols, like Howard before them, she and Gurney toured the prisons of Great Britain and published their gruesome findings—with conditions as bad as in Newgate—in a book.[21] In 1840 Fry opened a training school for nurses, a number of whom Florence Nightingale took with her to the Crimea. Fry's brother Joseph was educated at Oxford University but as a Quaker was not permitted to take a degree. In addition to working with his sister for prison reform he joined Buxton in the struggle against the slave trade. This involved visits to North America and the West Indies as part of his campaigning against slavery.

In February 1817 Fry and Gurney attempted to secure a pardon for two women prisoners, Charlotte Newman and Mary Ann James, who were sentenced to death for forgery but were unable to save them from the gallows. The same year they attempted to save from death a maidservant named Harriet Skelton. even visiting the Home Secretary, Lord Sidmouth, but to no avail. They had more success, however, in establishing night shelters in London and Brighton for the homeless. Fry's visits to comfort women in prison are famous, were recognised by Queen Victoria, and in the year 2002 she was depicted on the Bank of England five pound note.

---

21. Joseph Gurney and Elizabeth Fry. (1813) *Notes on Prisons in Scotland and the North of England.* London, The Pamphleteer.

SECONDARY PUNISHMENTS

Despite the foregoing pictures of horror in gaols, prior to the early nineteenth century imprisonment was still not much used as a punishment. The death penalty and transportation remained the prime punishments for felony. Peel saw that it was necessary to do something about secondary punishments; Bentham and his followers could also see nothing but evil in the gallows and transportation and looked for some alternative. However, the problem of secondary punishments remained as vexatious and intractable as ever. To the nineteenth century mind it was difficult to conceive of a real alternative to the punishment of death for felony. For instance, on 24 March 1826 Peel himself wrote a letter to Sydney Smith in which he admitted that, 'the whole subject of what is called secondary punishment is full of difficulty ... I despair of any remedy but that which I wish I could hope for—a great reduction in the amount of crime.'[22] Unfortunately, a dream too far.

THE HULKS

The suspension of the early transportation of convicts to the American colonies in 1775 raised a serious problem for those in charge of England's criminal justice system and there was no easy solution in sight. As a temporary measure, under an Act of 1776,[23] they brought to the Thames two old, rotting and disused warships, the *Censor* and the *Justitia*, to be moored near Woolwich and used as floating prisons. In charge of them was Duncan Campbell, a merchant with extensive experience of packing convicts into ships. They were soon known as 'hulks' and, proving inadequate to the size of the problem others were established at Gosport, Plymouth, Portsmouth, Chatham and Sheerness. By 1787 some 2,000 convicts in irons were employed on them, raising sand for ballast and constructing new dockyard facilities. Their cheapness kept them operative for 80 years. According to the Webbs they proved to be, 'of all the places of confinement that British history records ... apparently the most brutalizing, the most demoralising and the most horrible.'[24]

The hulks were intended as staging posts pending the transportation of prisoners to the colonies but they often proved to be a more permanent home for the unfortunate wretches confined in them. They were overcrowded and ridden with disease, with the convicts given only intermittent labour on shore and having to spend most of their time under battened hatches.[25] Confinement in a dark cell and whipping were common pun-

---

22. C. S. Parker. (1891) *Sir Robert Peel from his Private Correspondence.* London, John Murray. vol. i. p. 402.

23. 16 Geo, 3, c. 43.

24. S. & B. Webb. (1922) *English Prisons under Local Government.* Vol. vi. of *English Local Government.* London, Longman, Green & Co. pp. 45-6.

25. [1778] 36 *H.C. Journals.* p. 926.

ishments. Diet was pitiful, including putrid meat and mouldy biscuits.

In 1847 Thomas Duncombe, one of the two radical MPs sitting for Finsbury, sent a statement to *The Times* in which he accused the superintendent of convicts, J. H. Capper, of gross neglect of duty and mismanagement of the hulks. Capper denied the charges but a prison inspector was appointed to inquire into the condition of the hulks at Woolwich. Although the inspector dismissed some of Duncombe's specific charges, his 29-page report, and the evidence he received, were devastating.[26] As he reported, even on the hospital ship the diet caused scurvy and the oatmeal was so bad that the patients threw it overboard. The great majority of the patients were infested with vermin. The earnings of the prisoners, who worked on building the Royal Arsenal at Woolwich, were mismanaged and lunatics were confined with other prisoners. One insane inmate was flogged. It was found that the assistant-surgeon was unqualified and a student. Cleanliness was non-existent and the brutal life on the hulks was described as a 'Hell on Earth'.

So grim was the report that the government was forced to take action and, after a life of some 80 years, the hulks were gradually phased out of use. During those years they had held tens of thousands of prisoners in such wretched conditions.

TRANSPORTATION

This was favoured by governments as removing criminals from British society and because of its allegedly low budget. It was considered to be a suitable substitute for the gallows since it fulfilled a similar function in removing the criminal from the society he knew.[27] Although it was not illegal for someone transported to return to Britain after the expiry of his sentence, few did so. For instance between 1810 and 1820 only 389 left New South Wales.[28]

Transportation had commenced with a Privy Council Order in 1615 for sending vagrants and criminals to the American colonies. In some cases convicts could choose transportation as an alternative to the gallows. They were transported by private merchants who paid the sheriff 'a price per head that included jail fees, the fees of the clerk of the appropriate court, fees for drawing up the pardon, and so on.'[29] After 1718, however, instead of merchants being charged to transport convicted felons they were offered a subsidy of three pounds per person. Following the War of Independence transportation to America was no longer possible (although it had lasted for twice as long as the subsequent transportations to Australia) and as a

---

26. PP. (1847) *Report on Inquiry into the Hulks at Woolwich.* xlviii. p. 831.
27. W. R. Cornish. (1978) 'Criminal Justice and Punishment'. In *Crime and Law in Nineteenth Century Britain.* Dublin, Irish University Press. pp. 22-3.
28. *Ibid.* 22-23.
29. J. M. Beattie. (1986) *Crime and the Courts in England 1660-1800.* Oxford, The Clarendon Press. p. 479.

short-term alternative, by an Act of 1776, the convicts who would have been transported were crammed into old warships converted into hulks, the ghastly, disease-
ridden dungeons referred to in the last section.

However, by 1787, the convict settlement of Botany Bay had been established
and transportation began again in earnest. As a result, between 1788 and 1853,
152,170 convicts were sent out, of whom 149,507 arrived alive. [30] Death was not the
only terror, however. Miserable wretches—hundreds of men, women and children—
were crammed into a floating prison in which they faced the risk of famine, disease
as well as death only to reach a life of slavery, suffering and misery at the other end.
On the journey convicts were confined, ill-fed, kept in irons and rarely allowed on
deck. On arrival large numbers of them were found to be unable to walk or even
move a hand or foot. Once put to work, if they were thought to be idle they suffered
up to 500 lashes and were kept in double irons if so ordered by a magistrate[31]—that
is if they survived the whipping.

Although conditions for the transported convicts were extremely harsh and often cruel, as the number of free immigrants grew, convicts with a record of good
behaviour were leased out (assigned) to them as servants and agricultural labourers.
But, maintaining discipline was a major problem. Hence, under governor Macquarie (1809-1821), as an inducement to good behaviour, assignments increased
and grants of land were made to those whose sentences had expired. Transportation
even for seven or 14 years, began to be seen in England as a less harsh penalty than
imprisonment. As a consequence, after a proposal to admit ex-convicts into legal
practice, a Commissioner (later governor) Bigge, was sent out to New South Wales
to investigate. He proved hostile to Macquarie although he did approve of much of
what he had established.[32]

Leaving aside the effect it had on Australia, in Britain transportation failed as a
deterrent. As A. G. L. Shaw has written, it failed:

> partly because it was misunderstood at home, partly because it is hopeless to rely solely on de-
> terrence to get rid of crime ... [I]n fact transportation and assignment was the most effective
> reformatory punishment that was widely adopted before 1850; but at that time few accepted
> the principle that the aim of punishment and prison discipline should be reformation rather
> than the infliction of suffering, and most men would have agreed with Sir James F. Stephen
> that the 'criminal law is mainly a system of licensed revenge'.[33]

But the story was not quite over. Some people in prison preferred to be transported. In Britain transportation was replaced with a national system of convict

---

30. A. G. L. Shaw. (1966) *Convicts and the Colonies: a Study of Penal Transportation from Great Britain and Ireland to Australia and other Parts of the British Empire*. London, Faber. Appendix.
31. *Ibid*. pp. 72, 108.
32. See *Report on the State of the Colony of New South Wales*. (1822) 448. xx. IUP Australia 1.
33. *Ibid*. pp. 358-9.

prisons but some inmates had earlier resented the lost chance of a new start in Australia. According to Ignatieff, between 1853 and 1859 a small group of women convicts in Brixton and Millbank:

> waged a dogged protest against the conversion of their sentences from transportation to imprisonment. They tore up their bedding, set fire to their uniforms, banged on their cell doors, stripped naked before their astonished matrons and broke the silence with swearing and chants ... They seemed to resist dark cells, straightjackets, and bread and water punishments. In 1859, the director of convict prisons ... admitted they had a real grievance in that on their release they suffered more stigma than men and consequently found it much more difficult to secure employment.[34]

The women were conscious of this, said Ignatieff, and were determined to pressure the prison directors to let them go to Australia.[35] The women may also have had a false idea of what lay ahead in Australia. In the event, their demands were not met but in 1856 new legislation was passed standardising penal servitude and transportation sentences.[36]

Transportation could be for seven, ten or 14 years or for life. Those imposing the penalties had little idea of what was involved for the unfortunate victim. Lord Chief Justice Ellenborough, for instance, in standing firm for the retention of the death penalty, claimed that transportation was, 'only a summer airing by an easy migration to a milder climate'.[37]

Bentham, on the other hand, was totally opposed to this form of punishment and regarded it as a complete failure. He believed it resulted, at an enormous expense of money, labour and suffering, in the foundation of a community basically vicious and miserable and growing every year more depraved and more wretched. It could hardly be said to be exemplary, so great was the disproportion between the real and the apparent suffering. The community in England saw a convict sent on a long voyage to a fertile country with a fine climate. That, he wrote, was the example. The reality was that, after rotting in the hulks for a year or two, the miserable wretch was crammed with hundreds of others into the floating prison in which he faced the risks of famine, disease and death, only to reach a life of slavery, suffering and misery.

In a letter dated 9 August 1802, Bentham wrote to Charles Bunbury of the, 'utter repugnance' with which he viewed Botany Bay.[38] The next day he presented him with a long summary of his comments covering several large pages in tabulated

34. P.P. (1859) xiii. p. 308.
35. Michael Ignatieff. *A Just Measure of Pain. The Penitentiary in the Industrial Revolution, 1750-1850. Op. cit.* p. 203.
36. 20 and 21 Vic. c. 3.
37. Samuel Romilly.(1842) *Memoirs of his Life.* London, John Murray. vol. ii. pp. 333-4.
38. B. M. *Add. Mss.* 33,109. f. 331.

columns under the title: *Panopticon v, New South Wales, August 10, 1802.*[39] After long lists of objections to transportation he concluded that its real purpose was incapacitation by distance and that it could involve little deterrence or reformation.

Shaw, in contrast, believes that transportation at first offered what seemed to be the only alternative to capital punishment and, although finally abandoned as insufficiently deterrent, it provided an essential means of punishment at a time when the unreformed gaols made long terms of imprisonment virtually impossible.[40] In the end, transportation to New South Wales was suspended in 1840, to Van Dieman's Land in 1846 and Australia finally closed its doors in 1867. Thus ended this mockery of penal justice.

JEREMY BENTHAM

Bentham had been born on 15 February 1748 in Houndsditch, East London. He had a feeble, dwarfish body but a dazzling mind. An infant prodigy, at the age of three he was found seated at a desk reading Rapin's huge folio *History of England* with a lighted candle on each side of him. He was called to the Bar by Lincoln's Inn at the age of 16, having been the youngest graduate at Oxford until that time. But, in opposition to Blackstone and his contentment with 'this noble pile', as he called the Constitution, Bentham came to despise the unwritten Common Law with its judicial law-making. He decided to set out to replace it with a science of law based upon logic and clarity of expression, seasoned with humanity.

With his Utilitarian philosophy of the pursuit of happiness (the greatest happiness of the greatest number), he encouraged Romilly, Brougham and Peel in law and penal reform and, starting from first principles, turned his own inventive mind to the task of codifying the rules of government and law in their entirety. His works on law and government are prodigious. As Brougham said, 'the age of law reform and the age of Jeremy Bentham are one and the same.'[41] His was a seminal influence in a time which saw the birth of modern manufacturing industry, the establishment of the United States, the French Revolution, Adam Smith's *Wealth of Nations,* the Enlightenment and the Reform Act of 1832. It was a fitting end to his tireless efforts for reform that he actually died in his 85th year on the day the Reform Bill received the royal assent—7 June 1832. His influence on law reform was far-reaching throughout the nineteenth century and he remains a serious intellectual force for any critique of the English legal system.

39. *Ibid.* See also letter to Lord Pelham under the same title on 17 December 1802. Bentham. *Works.* vol. iv. pp. 173-248.
40. A. G. L. Shaw. *Convicts and the Colonies. Op. cit.* p. 360.
41. Henry, Lord Brougham. (1838) *Speeches.* Edinburgh, Adam and Charles Black. vol. ii. pp 287-8.

Bentham's panopticon

Bentham had long been concerned about prison reform. He studied the work and ideas of John Howard and thought his writings on prisons, 'supplied a rich fund of materials, but that a quarry was not a house.'[42] He was deeply interested in the punishment of imprisonment and began to ask himself whether its use could be extended as a secondary punishment by making it more effective, more humane and, at the same time, cheaper. His over-active mind now conjured up a novel type of prison to be called the panopticon or 'inspection house'.[43] In March 1792 he laid a proposal before Parliament to undertake the custody of 1,000 convicts in such a prison. Parliament approved the scheme and passed an Act two years later which adopted it.[44] The prison was to be distinguished by three striking new features.

First, from the form of the building, a circular iron and glass cage of open cells, the governor would be able to see each prisoner (and gaoler) at all times without being seen by them and could give them orders without leaving his central inspection tower. 'The spider in his web!', exclaimed Edmund Burke of such a governor,[45] but the scheme was approved by Charles James Fox and William Pitt.

Secondly, the management of the prison was to be exercised under contract. The government would pay a fixed sum for the total expense of each convict, who would work in his cell for as long as 16 hours a day, and, in return, the contractor would have the profit after a proportion had been paid to the prisoner. This would replace the still existing system of fees paid to gaolers by the prisoners.

Thirdly, all accounts would be available for public inspection and the prison open at all times to every magistrate, and at certain hours to the public generally.

The cost factor for the scheme was of primary importance. Parliamentary reports had estimated that transportation was costing over £1m every ten years, approximately £38 for each convict. Under Bentham's contract, he calculated that each convict would cost the government a mere 13 shillings and ten pence, including one shilling and ten pence for the building and land. Also included would be a fund to indemnify persons injured in the course of the convicts' crimes.

Bentham saw the panopticon as a civilising influence on society. Morals would be reformed, health preserved, industry invigorated, public burdens lightened, economy seated on a rock, the Gordian knot of the poor law not cut but untied—all, he said, by a simple idea in architecture. More recently critics have accused Bentham, Howard and Fry of desiring to control prisoners' minds with 'machines for grind-

---

42. C. Phillipson. (1923) *Three Criminal Law Reformers. Beccaria, Bentham, Romilly.* London, J.M. Dent & Sons Ltd., p.127.
43. Jeremy Bentham. (1791) *Panopticon or The Inspection House. The Works of Jeremy Bentham.* Edinburgh, John Bowring. vol. iv p. 37.
44. 34 Geo. 3, c. 84.
45. Gertrude Himmelfarb. (1968) 'The Haunted House of Jeremy Bentham'. In *Victorian Minds* London, Weidenfeld & Nicolson.

ing men good.' And although Parliament agreed to Bentham's cyclopic monster in 1794, it was never built at the Millbank site purchased for it where the Tate Britain Gallery now stands. One was built in the United States and another at Breda in Holland which still exists. Bentham was eventually paid 23,000 pounds in compensation by Parliament for his efforts in working on the project for many years, but he never lost the bitterness he experienced from the rejection of his scheme and the many wasted years involved.

On imprisonment generally, Bentham saw some disadvantages but thought it perfect in regard to disablement, eminently divisible in duration and very susceptible to different degrees of severity. Whilst prisoners were not seen, which did not help to deter others, the prison itself was visible and might well strike terror in the beholder. Indeed, he went on to suggest that prisons which held medium and long-term offenders should exhibit on the outside various figures such as a monkey, a fox and a tiger to represent mischief, cunning and rapacity. Inside, should be placed two skeletons to represent the abode of death. All these devices indicate how clearly impressed Bentham was by the utility of visual aids.

THE RISE OF THE PENITENTIARY

Once transportation to North America had ceased abruptly after the War of Independence, the Westminster government appointed a Commission of three, John Howard, William Eden (later Lord Auckland) and William Blackstone, to consider the long-term treatment of prisoners. Their labours resulted in the Penitentiary Act 1779 and, following the example of the earlier houses of correction, it expressed a puritanical enthusiasm for disciplined work. Public and violent punishments were being replaced by private punishments inside prisons which were equally violent and cruel. It declared in section 5 that:

> If many Offenders, convicted of Crimes for which Transportation hath been usually inflicted, were ordered to solitary Imprisonment, accompanied by well regulated labour, and religious Instruction, it might be the means, under Providence, not only of deterring others from the Commission of the like Crimes, but also of reforming the Individuals and inuring them to Habits of Industry.[46]

The Act provided for two penitentiaries to be built in London, one for male and another for female prisoners. In place of transportation the prisoners were to be confined for up to two years in solitary cells, but labouring in association during the day. They were to wear uniforms to 'humiliate' them as well as making them easier to discover if they escaped. Surprisingly, it was believed this type of imprisonment

---

46. 19 Geo. 3, c. 74.

would improve their morals and deter others from a life of crime.

Prisoners' work was to be, 'of a base nature, such as treading the wheel, sawing stones and beating hemp.'[47] The tread-mill could be used for pointless labour and in the early nineteenth century was to cause considerable controversy over the physical and mental dangers of such exhausting and degrading work.[48] Work, of course, might not be sufficient. Additional means had to be found to ensure discipline and remorse. Some authorities pressed for a separate cell system in the prisons where the prisoners could work (the 'separate system'). Others called for the enforcement of strict hard labour, in silence to enable the prisoners time to consider their crimes and repent (the 'silent system'). The separate system is considered shortly. The silent system would mean that prisoners were required to maintain total silence at all times. This would be made more difficult because they were not to be separated. They would work and sleep together in large open areas and dormitories where the turnkeys could keep a lookout and punish them if they spoke. In the event, at the time no penitentiary was built when the government lost interest, largely because of the potential cost.

In 1816, however, a penitentiary was built at Millbank in place of the doomed panopticon. The inmates were carefully chosen and in the main were young first offenders. A principal purpose was rehabilitation or reform of offenders and prisoners were given separate cells, vocational employment and religious instruction. The normal practice in prisons of flogging those who offended against discipline was strictly forbidden. Prisoners were paid for their work, although this was not given to them until their discharge, when they also received a gratuity of three pounds. All this represented new thinking about what prisons should be.

However, not surprisingly, there was a debit side as the prison resembled a Gothic fortress with damp underground punishment cells. The staff were corrupt and violent and the food, consisting of bread, gruel and thin soup, was not only not nourishing but was inadequate. There were constant troubles with prisoners and when the medical superintendent put these down to over-eating, the diet was cut. In consequence, typhus and scurvy broke out and, after 31 inmates had died, the remaining 400 were either released or transferred to the hulks. Subsequently, reopened, trouble flared again and, in 1844, the Millbank was finally closed as a failed experiment. The perceived need for a regime which combined reform with strict discipline led next to separate confinement and Pentonville.[49]

To encourage the separate system a large new prison was built at Pentonville in 1842 to hold 450 prisoners. There they suffered solitary confinement, hard labour in

---

47. W. R. Cornish. 'Criminal Justice and Punishment.' In *Crime and Law in Nineteenth Century Britain. Op. cit.* p. 28.
48. *Ibid.*
49. For a full and interesting treatment of Pentonville and its context see Michael Ignatieff. *A Just Measure of Pain. The Penitentiary in the Industrial Revolution 1750-1850. Op. cit.*

their cells and religious instruction, all to bring about their rehabilitation. Cells were identical being 13.5' by 7.5'. Each cell contained a table, a chair, a bench, a hammock, a broom and a bucket. Pentonville was a model for all new penitentiaries, of which 54 were built in the following six years. This alone gave the country a total of 11,000 separate cells that were meant to provide an alternative to transportation. By 1856, returns made to Parliament showed about one-third of the prisons in England employing the separate system exclusively and another third employing it partially. Presumably, the remainder had insufficient cell accommodation to follow suit.

In a sense these new prisons reflected the social discipline of the extending factory environment outside, despite being seen by some, notably Thomas Carlyle and Charles Dickens, as 'palaces for felons'.[50] For the government, however, the strains of industrialisation, including a perceived increase in criminality, called for more stringent modes of social control to protect society from crime. Hence, when a penitentiary opened each prisoner was to spend 18 months in solitude in his cell, in contrast to the silent association system. As the awful effects of the 18 months' solitary confinement became clear to the authorities the period was reduced to 12 and then nine months after which the prisoner was sent to public works prisons at Portland, Chatham and a refurbished Dartmoor or was transported. Even the daily exercise period was spent alone in a small yard in which he had to march around in quick time. Prisoners were masked, wearing what was called a 'Scottish cap', to prevent them seeing one another or communicating, and there were separate stalls in chapel to prevent even the slightest conversation during religious services.[51] As a consequence of the successes of movement for the abolition of the death penalty and the building of new prisons, in the second half of the nineteenth century, imprisonment ceased to be a secondary punishment and replaced the gallows and transportation as the primary means of disposal for those committing serious crimes.

SOCIAL NEED

The stated purpose of the whole 'Pentonville Policy', and in particular the cruel separation system, was to improve the minds of the prisoners with a view to reformation. This was to be achieved by a combination of hard labour, instruction by the chaplain and an opportunity in the cells to reflect on, and repent of, their crimes. The regime was highly punitive; there were many suicides and a great deal of mental derangement. As late as 1877 the suicide rate in English prisons was 17.6 per 1,000 inmates. The serious effects of this repressive regime caused considerable public dis-

---

50. *Ibid.* p. 3.
51. L. W. Fox. *The English Prison and Borstal Systems. Op. cit.* p. 43.

quiet and, by statute in 1850,[52] under Sir Joshua Jebb, the architect of Pentonville and by then the Director of Convict Prisons, Pentonville ceased to be a penitentiary and became instead a convict prison. An association exercise yard was provided and the partitions in the chapel were removed.

Nevertheless, despite the public disquiet, support for the penitentiary had been persistent because it rested on social need. It was presented as a response, 'not merely to crime, but to the whole social crisis of a period, and as part of a larger strategy of political, social and legal reform designed to re-establish order on a new foundation ... It was seen as an element of a larger vision of order that by the 1840s commanded the reflexive assent of the propertied and powerful.'[53] Nevertheless, some historians, such as Ignatieff, Bentham and Foucault, regarded the penitentiary as a means of training the 'dangerous classes' into accepting the discipline of labour.

An Act of 1853[54] to some extent replaced the declining punishment of transportation with sentences of penal servitude. Four years penal servitude was set as the equivalent of the minimum sentence for transportation of seven years. The punishment involved hard labour on public works and was intended to act as a deterrent, both to the convict himself and other potential offenders. The statute also provided that, after a certain period, for good behaviour a convict could be granted a ticket-of-leave which enabled him to live outside the prison for the remainder of his term provided he behaved himself. This provoked widespread fear among the public but led eventually to the modern parole system.

Where, as in Ipswich, sufficiently arduous hard labour was not considered to be available, the tread-mill, or 'everlasting staircase', was introduced into local prisons by the magistrates. This was invented around 1818, after earlier more primitive types, by Samuel Cubitt, a native of Ipswich. Intended originally for his local magistrates, by 1824 the idea was adopted enthusiastically by other justices throughout the country. It comprised a huge revolving wheel with steps which the prisoners continuously mounted to make it turn. Six, 12 or 18 prisoners would step side by side from morning to night, treading some 8,640 feet in distance to grind corn or raise water or even simply air, until they were half-dead.[55] People with bad legs, pregnant women, and men with hernias joined other prisoners indiscriminately as a consequence of the general intoxication of the magistrates by the machine.[56] As this 'wholesome influence', as the prisons inspector called it, continued to maim and kill, it also put additional power into the hands of the warders who could tighten the

---

52. 13 and 14 Vic. c. 39.
53. M. Ignatieff. *A Just Measure of Pain. The Penitentiary in the Industrial Revolution, 1750–1850. Op. cit.* p. 210.
54. 16 and 17 Vic. c. 99.
55. Sydney and Beatrice Webb. *English Prisons under Local Government. Op. cit.* p. 98.
56. For the attitude of the justices who adopted the tread-wheel, see their opinions in correspondence with Peel. 1823 (113), xv. 1824 (45,247) xix. Dublin, Irish University Press. Prisons, p. 11.

spring to make it unbearably painful. This led to the origin of the slang term 'screw' for prison warder. Incredible as it may seem, hard labour was not abolished until the Criminal Justice Act, 1948.

CHAPTER 10

Nineteenth-Century Crime and Policing

A PERIOD OF TRANSITION

Apart from the adversarial revolution in procedure, the criminal justice system in the early nineteenth century remained in the grip of the medieval criminal law. It was still brutal, arbitrary and haphazard. Death remained the penalty for felony, mitigated only by pardons, jury nullification and, until it was abolished by the Criminal Law Act 1827,[1] benefit of clergy. To a large extent the criminal law was personal with the victims of crime being the actual private prosecutors in almost all criminal trials. The position remained the same as in the previous century when,

> not only assaults but virtually all thefts and even some murders were left to the general public. That meant that responsibility for the initial expense and entire conduct of the prosecution was thrown on the victim and his or her family ... As late as the mid-nineteenth century no public official was responsible for ensuring that even the most serious offences were prosecuted.[2]

Hence, even though lawyers were beginning to appear to prosecute and defend more often, the trial was still frequently a personal confrontation between the prosecutor and the defendant.

On the other hand, the Industrial Revolution was creating many new urban areas where poverty and crime were growing, the two things perceived to be linked. At the same time, with the aftermath of the Napoleonic wars producing unemployment among returned soldiers alongside food shortages, there was an upsurge in rioting and political protest. To meet what was believed to be a serious threat to government control, new thinking was required that in time would produce an effective police force and a strengthening of the concept of the Rule of Law as a binding force in society. As part of this, and in line with a growth in the market economy came the development of adversary trial as well as the impact of Beccaria and Bentham and the setting up of paid police forces as outlined later in this chapter.

---

1. 7 & 8 Geo. 4, c. 28.
2. D. Hay, and F. Snyder. (1989) *Policing and Prosecution in England, 1750–1850*. Oxford, Oxford University Press. p. 27.

TREASON

By the early years of the nineteenth century nothing had been done to improve the law of treason, indeed it had been extended by ever more constructive treasons. And, one or two cases of substantive treason allegations stand out in this period. In April 1820 Arthur Thistlewood and ten other men were put on trial before a Special Commission at the Old Bailey on a charge of treason in attempting to overthrow the government by murdering the entire British cabinet, including Lord Liverpool, the Prime Minister, at one of their periodic dinners.[3] The men had been arrested by a group of Bow Street Runners and soldiers in a dilapidated room in Cato Street, a back street parallel to the Edgware Road in London. Hence the name, the Cato Street Conspiracy.

The story is complicated in that the cabinet did not meet for dinner on the night in question (such dinners having been discontinued as a mark of respect for George III who had died on 29 January 1820) but a special notice of a fictitious 'Grand Cabinet Dinner' had been planted in a newspaper by the Home Office and 'discovered' by George Edwards, one of the conspirators. During the trial it was revealed that Edwards was a government spy and *agent provocateur* who had initiated the conspiracy but could not be found when required to give evidence and be cross-examined. In fact, he had been spirited away to Guernsey by Sidmouth's Home Office with whom he corresponded in subsequent years.

Although they denied the charge, Thistlewood and four other defendants were duly found guilty and sent to the gallows outside Newgate Prison on May Day 1820 in the presence of enormous crowds who were sympathetic to the prisoners and had to be held in check by two troops of the Life Guards. The remaining prisoners were also found guilty but were transported for life.

The other substantive treason trial of the time was that of John Frost for his part in the Newport Rising of 1839.[4] The Chartist movement was at its height but divided between a 'moral force' group who wanted to rely upon meetings, petitions and education to secure the 'Peoples' Charter' and a 'physical force' group who talked of insurrection. When a monster petition containing the six points of the Charter and bearing 1,280,000 signatures was rejected by the House of Commons on 12 July 1839, the physical force group thought their time had come. They were said to have decided upon a general insurrection, with a rising in South Wales to operate as a starting signal to activists in other parts of the country.

South Wales miners were a depressed community and were particularly inflamed that one of their leaders, Henry Vincent, was being held in appalling conditions in

---

3. OBP. Online. (www.oldbaileyproceedingsonline.org) Trial of Arthur Thistelwood and Ors. (1820). Ref: t18200416-1.
4. See David Jones. (1985) *The Last Rising: The Newport Insurrection of 1839*. Oxford, The Clarendon Press.

Monmouth Gaol. For some reason the miners decided to march on Newport, not Monmouth, in an attempt to secure his release. John Frost was a tailor and draper in South Wales who had been appointed a magistrate in Newport in 1835 and was elected mayor of the town a year later. He was a moral force Chartist but when the march of Newport was decided upon he felt it his duty to join the miners. He became the leader of one of the miners' contingents marching down the valleys on a wet, dark night but it is doubtful that the move was part of a general insurrection and certainly one never took place. Nevertheless, the march on Newport was met by armed soldiers when the men reached the town and in the firing that followed a number of miners were shot dead, the estimates ranging from 11 to 33.

Frost, and 12 other prisoners, were charged with high treason in waging war against the queen and their trial opened before Special Commissioners sitting at Monmouth on 31 December 1839. At the end of the hearing the judge, Chief Justice Tindal, appeared to favour an acquittal but Frost and some of the other prisoners were found guilty by the jury and sentenced to death. In their support a large number of enormous demonstrations were held throughout the country and, subsequently, they were reprieved on the recommendation of the judge and transported to Van Diemen's Land. Frost received a full pardon in 1856 and returned to Wales, where he wrote and lectured on the horrors of transportation until he died aged over 90. What he did not do was clear away the fog that surrounds the true purpose of the rising, which is still shrouded in mystery to this day. The case remains, however, the last tried in Britain for waging war against the monarch within the realm.

CONSTRUCTIVE TREASON

In the nineteenth century a riot or an unlawful assembly with a private purpose remained a felony. Once the motive was public or general, however, the participants were held to be guilty of treason, even though never guilty of a disloyal thought or intention in their lives. The case of *Damaree and Purchase*[5] from 1710 was still considered the leading case on the subject. Then the lord chief justice and several other judges at the Old Bailey had held that an assembly to demolish all meeting houses was an act of high treason against the queen. In his defence Damaree claimed he was drunk at the time and had been physically pressured to join a crowd in Lincoln's Inn Fields where a meeting house had been set on fire. None of the Crown witnesses could link Damaree with the arson, and even had he been, his lawyer argued that the offence was participating in a riot. However, he was found guilty of treason in levying war as the purpose of the assembly was to destroy meeting houses in general. Fortunately, Damaree avoided the barbaric sentence for treason on being granted a pardon by Queen Anne. It is interesting that during Anne's reign of 12 years no

---

5. (1710) MS. Tracy. pp. 16, 17.

person who was found guilty of treason suffered death.

This type of case was, of course, based on construction of the law by the judges and was heavily criticised by the early nineteenth century Criminal Law Commissioners.[6] In the actual cases the commissioners considered they believed the offenders acted out of excitement, without premeditation, and without any general project in mind. Constructive extensions of the penal law, they said, were always dangerous and objectionable, and should be replaced by positive enactments. The great error, they suggested, had originally been in making the criminality of an act depend upon its consequences rather than on its nature.

In the reign of George III, because jurors were more and more unwilling to convict for constructive treasons, a statute was passed which incorporated such constructions into the enacted law.[7] And, as Lord Ellenborough observed in the trial of James Watson, who was unsuccessfully charged with treason by levying war in the Spa Field Riot in 1817,[8] the statute

> did not so much introduce any new treasons, as declare to be substantive treasons those acts which had been, by successive constructions of the Statute of Treason, determined to be the strongest and most pregnant overt acts of the several treasons specified in that statute.

Yet, indictments for high treason continued to contain counts founded on the old constructions. This occurred frequently and, in the trial of Watson, Lord Ellenborough expressly approved the practice in his summing up to the jury.

HOMICIDE

In the nineteenth century, in order to establish culpable homicide there had to be a killing and an 'evil disposition of mind' on the part of the offender. For a killing to be criminal, death had to be caused by some external act or a failure to perform a legal duty. Hence, deliberately killing another by mental excitement was not punishable by law. Intention had to be manifested by an act of physical violence, or some criminal intent. Necessity and self-defence were still valid defences in law. And, implied malice, a relic of the old doctrine of strict liability for homicide, still survived. This showed there was no true malice and was, indeed, a legal fiction which was heartily condemned by the Criminal Law Commissioners.[9] They complained that it raised manslaughter to murder although it was left wholly undefined and its existence was held to be a matter of law for the judge and not fact for the jury. Stephen,

6. (1849) Fifth Report. PP. xxi. p. 477.
7. 36 Geo. 3. c. 7.
8. (1817) *R. v. Watson.* 32 *State Trials.* 579.
9. See their Fourth Report. (1839) PP. xix. 235.

on the other hand, was prepared to accept it, thinking that the harsh constructions by judges on malice had occurred because benefit of clergy made the punishment for aggravated manslaughter inadequate.[10] Juries appear to have thought otherwise. 'There were 93 spouse murder trials during the 1860s in which the defendant was not declared to be insane. These resulted in 35 verdicts of manslaughter, 12 of them in opposition to the instructions or clearly expressed views of the judge.'[11]

The crime of murder continued to require premeditation or malice aforethought, which are perhaps the same thing. There had to be a motive of ill-will against, and an express intention to destroy or injure, the victim. But it could also include cases where there was no express malice, only malice in a legal sense by construction of law, i.e. again implied malice. Provocation was also important since it involved cases in which the question arose whether the offence amounted to murder or manslaughter depending upon implied malice as a question of law. Indeed, juries found provocation useful as a means of mitigating the harshness of the law. It should also be remembered, as shown in *Chapter 14*, that at this time once a killing was proved the presumption of innocence was replaced by a presumption of guilt. In other words, the prisoner had to prove accident, necessity or infirmity since the law presumed malice, unless the contrary was shown.

Provocation could still reduce a verdict of murder to one of manslaughter. But after the end of the century the new Court of Criminal Appeal established in 1907 began to confine the circumstances that could amount to provocation. They required that the act of antagonism would have 'provoked a reasonable man—a man indeed of teutonic stoicism; and insisted that the killing should have been a reaction so immediate as to allow no chance for second thoughts.'[12]

THEFT

As earlier, the offence of feloniously taking the personal property of another was either larceny or robbery if accompanied by violence, threats or terror to the person. The taking, or carrying away, was still an important aspect. In the case of *R. v. Henry Cozlett*[13] the prisoner picked up a parcel in a wagon and carried it from one end of the wagon to the other with intent to steal it. It was never taken out of the carriage, but this was held by all the trial judges to be a sufficient carrying away. Where,

---

10. J. F. Stephen. (1883) *A History of the Criminal Law of England.* London, Macmillan. vol. iii. p. 46.

11. Martin J. Wiener. (1999) 'Judges v. Jurors: Courtroom Tensions in Murder Trials and the Law of Criminal Responsibility in Nineteenth-Century England'. University of Illinois Press. *American Society for Legal History.* vol. 17. No. 3.

12. W. R. Cornish and G. de N. Clark. (1989) *Law and Society in England, 1750-1950.* London, Sweet and Maxwell. p. 622.

13. (1782) MS. Buller J.

however, William Cherry[14] had picked up a wrapper in a wagon and set it up in one end of the wagon for greater ease in extracting its contents, and cut it open for that purpose, all the judges agreed on this occasion that, although his intention to steal was clear, there was no larceny. This was a curious decision since for a carrying away there had to be a removal of the goods from where they were, and the prisoner must, for an instant at least, have had the entire and absolute possession of them. Both of these requirements were met in this case.

Certainly they appear to have been satisfied in *R. v. Lapier*[15] where the prisoner snatched a diamond earring from a Mrs Hobart as she left the opera house. Although her ear was injured, the lady's earring fell into her hair where it was found when she returned home. All the judges held that the prisoner had momentarily had possession.

With robbery also something had to be taken, since an assault with intent to rob was a less serious offence. The essence of the offence of robbery was the use of force and terror which was not confined to an apprehension of bodily injury. It was sufficient if it was likely to cause a person to part with his property against his will. In *R. v. Jones, alias Evans*[16] the prisoner followed a man out of a theatre, seized him by the arm, told him he had earlier offered the prisoner an indignity not to be borne, and threatened to raise the mob if he attempted to run. The victim was terrified and on being asked for money handed over three guineas and 12 shillings. The jury held that the accusation made of an unnatural crime would strike a man with as much or more terror than if he had a pistol at his head, and accordingly they found the prisoner guilty. The opinion of the judges was then sought and they decided the conviction for highway robbery was proper since there was no need to use a weapon or real violence when the victim was placed in a situation which rendered him an unfree man.

These cases occurred in the late eighteenth century but they remained binding precedents throughout the nineteenth century. The Larceny Act 1861[17] was one of a group of statutes passed in that year to consolidate the law. It repeated Common Law rules and perpetuated the confusion they caused. In effect it eliminated a few inconsistencies but largely left the law as it was. It did not define theft but did reiterate the abolition of the distinction between grand and petty larceny. Its arrangement, said Stephen,

> is so strange that a person who, with no previous knowledge of the subject, attempted to find our from it what was the English law relating to the punishment of theft and other similar

---

14. (1781) MS. Gould & Buller Js.
15. (1784) MS. Gould.
16. (1776) MS. Gould J.
17. 24 & 25 Vict. c. 96.

offences would be simply bewildered.[18]

In the end, it was left until the Theft Act 1968 for the law of theft was clarified.

RAPE

With the growth of industrial capitalism in the nineteenth century there arose a contradiction in the position of women. More and more working class women were drawn into work in the factories but at the same time the range of occupations open to middle and lower middle class women narrowed. One consequence of the latter was the growth of a domestic home life which was obscured from the view of the criminal justice institutions, including the police. This began to affect working class women as well, when conditions began, relatively at least, to improve. All this led to more sexual violence in the home but by law, at the time, a husband was not deemed to able to rape his wife whatever the circumstances. Her consent to intercourse was implied in another example of legal construction by the judges.

The law on rape remained, in the main, as it had been earlier and was still a capital crime after the reduction in the incidence of the death penalty in 1837. After all, there can be no satisfactory compensation for rape. An anomaly existed, however, by the statutory provision that the rape of a girl between ten and 12 years was only a misdemeanour.[19] In another example of law-making by judges, (this time more suitable) in 1882 the Court of Crown Cases Reserved held in *R. v. Ratcliffe*[20] that the Act did not operate to prevent a conviction for felony, which carried a more severe penalty than for a misdemeanour.

An important landmark in the law of rape came with the Criminal Law Amendment Act of 1885 which was intended to protect women and girls and suppress brothels.[21] Prior to the Act the age of consent had been 12 and it was a felony to have consensual sex with a girl under ten, and, as above, a misdemeanour with a girl between ten and 12. The original Criminal Law Amendment Bill had provided for raising the age of consent to 16 years and for increased penalties for sexual offences. It passed the House of Lords in 1883 but did not get through the Commons mainly because it contained other provisions that were regarded as distasteful and breaching civil liberties.

Then, with the express object of ensuring the return of the Bill to Parliament, on 23 May 1885 Wickham Stead, editor of the *Pall Mall Gazette,* purchased a 13-year-old girl, named Eliza Armstrong, from her parents for money and wrote about it

18. J. F. Stephen. *A History of the Criminal Law of England. Op. cit.* vol. iii. p. 146.
19. 38 & 39 Vict.
20. (1882) 10 QBD. 74.
21. 48 & 49 Vict. c. 69.

sensationally in his articles exposing the white slave traffic under the title, 'Maiden Tribute of Modern Babylon'. He was successful in creating a storm of protest and as a consequence the Bill was brought before Parliament again and was finally passed on 14 August. Among other things it provided that:

- it was a criminal offence to abduct a girl under 18 years for
- purposes of carnal knowledge;
- the age of consent was raised from 12 to 16 years;
- it was a criminal offence to procure girls for prostitution by administering
- drugs, intimidation or fraud;
- householders who permitted under-age sex on their premises would be
- punished;
- the courts could remove a girl from her legal guardians if they condoned
- her seduction; and
- summary proceedings could be taken against brothels.

By a last minute insertion, and without any debate upon it, a clause was also inserted which created a new offence of homosexual acts between male adults in private. This was the clause that led to Queen Victoria's famous intervention denying the possibility of female homosexuality. Known as the 'blackmailer's charter', this was this statute under which Oscar Wilde was prosecuted and sent to Reading Gaol with hard labour for two years—a sentence that caused his gradual disintegration but produced *De Profundis* and the *Ballad of Reading Gaol* before he died a broken man in Paris. The Act was not amended until 1967 after the Wolfenden Report had recommended that homosexual behaviour between consenting adults should cease to be a criminal offence.[22]

CONSTABULARY

When the nineteenth century opened England had no professional police force. Outside of the towns, law and order was in the hands of the parish constable. He was elected annually but was unpaid and played only a minor role in the enforcement of the law. His duty was to preserve the peace and he had powers of arrest but his office was archaic and largely unproductive. Even with serious crimes a victim endeavouring to bring an offender to justice was expected to pay the constable for his assistance. Furthermore, many parishes permitted constables to buy themselves out. On the other hand, behind the constable were the justices of the peace who

---

22. HMSO. (1957) *The Wolfenden Report on Homosexuality and Prostitution.*

could order the arrest of persons suspected of committing crimes. They could also, in serious situations, swear in special constables, read the Riot Act and call in the military[23], as happened with the Peterloo Massacre on 16 August 1819 when eleven people were killed and over 400 injured.[24] They were also merciless when dealing with Luddites, the followers of 'Captain Swing'[25] and food rioters on many occasions. It was this power of the magistrates that caused the gentry (many of whom sat as JPs) to struggle bitterly to prevent the creation of a centralised police force which would interfere with their position of power in the shires.[26]

At the start of the nineteenth century trial procedure and the law of criminal evidence were formed by the Common Law. Prior to 1723 this was also true of those serious crimes which were defined by the Common Law. And, 'despite the exceptionally rigorous laws enacted during the reigns of the Tudors and Stuarts, no more than about 50 offences then carried the death penalty.'[27] In 1723, however, Parliament passed the notorious Waltham Black Act[28] which added some 50 new capital offences to the criminal law to make a total of over 200 for which death was the penalty. Thus was born what became known as the penal law's 'Bloody Code.' As a consequence, in 1810 Sir Samuel Romilly was to say, 'there is probably no other country in the world in which so many and so great a variety of human actions are punishable with loss of life as in England.'[29]

In fact, the offences at which the statute was directed were already adequately covered by existing law and included going armed and disguised (a handkerchief over the mouth was sufficient) to stealing fruit from trees, damaging orchards and killing a deer.[30] In essentials it was simply an Act to provoke terror and was used against persons who were not disguised and were not criminals. In the main it was to secure the conviction of small farmers and tenants endeavouring to protect their customary forest rights. It endured into the nineteenth century and was followed by, 'an ever-increasing volume of statute law specifying particular offences ... much designed primarily to impose death as the penalty for crimes against property.'[31]

23. See R. Vogler. (1991) *Reading the Riot Act: the Magistracy, the Police and the Army in Civil Disorder.* Milton Keynes, Open University Press.

24. E. L. Woodward. (1954 edn.) *The Age of Reform 1815-1870.* Oxford, The Clarendon Press. p. 62.

25. E. J. Hobsbawm and George Rudé. (1969) *Captain Swing.* London, Lawrence & Wishart. p. 253.

26. See T. A. Critchley. (1967) *A History of Police in England and Wales 900-1966.* London, Constable.

27. L. Radzinowicz. (1974) *A History of the English Criminal Law and its Administration from 1750. The Movement for Reform.* London, Stevens & Sons Ltd. vol. i. p. 4.

28. 9 Geo. I. c. 22.

29. *Parliamentary Debates.* (1810). [15] col. 366.

30. For prime minister Robert Walpole's responsibility for the Act to preserve his hunting rights see E.P. Thompson. (1975) *Whig and Hunters: The Origin of the Black Act.* London, Allen Lane.

31. W. R. Cornish & G. de N. Clark. *Law and Society in England: 1750-1950. Op. cit.* p. 545.

BOW STREET RUNNERS

Policing urban crime was a different matter. Prior to the nineteenth century many towns and cities, including London, had obtained Improvement Acts. These enabled them to employ watchmen whom they paid from a local rate. That was, however, quite insufficient in London where gangs of robbers and highwaymen were endemic. In any event, the watchmen, known as 'Charleys', were generally of low calibre and were frequently mocked. As a consequence, Bow Street was established in 1729 and was given a stipendiary magistrate. By 1749 the then magistrate, Sir Henry Fielding, novelist and reforming JP, employed a small body of full-time thief-takers known as 'Bow Street Runners'. Initially they were only eight in number.

In 1753, after five murders were committed in one week, Fielding was given £200 with a promise of another £400 to put an end to the gang responsible. Within a few weeks it was dispersed and its leaders arrested. The 'Runners' were transformed into a professional force and after Fielding's retirement they were continued by his brother, blind Sir John Fielding known as the 'Blind Beak of Bow Street', who succeeded him as the stipendiary magistrate. By 1815 Bow Street had 70 plain-clothed foot runners and a uniformed horse patrol known as 'Robin Redbreasts' or 'Raw Lobsters' because of their scarlet waistcoats. They patrolled London, were sent to discover dangerous murderers, and, on one occasion, to collect information relating to the robbing of the Bishop of Bath and Wells at Maidenhead. Their services were sought as far away as Bristol and Portsmouth as travel became safer.[32] Eventually, however, some of them were found to be receiving money and goods as bribes to cast a blind eye over the activities of certain criminals. They had, however, shown that professionalism and control of street life were possible and as crime was considered to be increasing their role and public concern meant that the way was open for the reforms of Sir Robert Peel.

WIDESPREAD VIOLENCE

At the beginning of the 1830s England was in the throes of violent transition. The rejection of the Reform Bill by the House of Lords in October 1831 was received in the country as a national calamity. *The Times* could barely contemplate the enormity of what had happened. 'What have the Lords done?' it asked and then answered, 'They have done what they can never undo … the 400 or so Lords have drawn a line between them and 22 million people.'[33] In the same month Nottingham Castle was fired and the Bristol riots exploded with the gaols forced open, the town hall

---

32. L. Radzinowicz. *A History of English Criminal Law and its Administration from 1750. Op. cit.* vol. iii. p. 57.
33. *The Times.* 10 October 1831. p.4.

set alight and the bishop's palace burned to the ground. Whilst Bristol was burning riots also occurred in Bath, Coventry, Warwick and Worcester while in London angry crowds manhandled the king's carriage. On Guy Fawkes night effigies of bishops were hanged and burned on many bonfires in place of the usual guy.

In point of fact these extreme outbreaks were an expression of the revival of spiritual and political life taking place among the middle and working classes after decades of repression. They transformed the battle for reform. There was now to be a fight to the finish with either reform or revolution triumphant. The Duke of Wellington spoke of two engaged armies in the reform struggle[34] and John Croker, influential Secretary to the Admiralty, claimed the struggle was no longer between two political parties for the Ministry, but between the mob and the government.[35] A third way was no longer possible.

'MIGRATION INTO TOWNS'

The growth in the size of towns, pressured by the development of an industrial society as part of the Industrial Revolution, was a central cause of the agitation both for a new style police force and for reform of the medieval criminal law. It was crystallised in an influential article by Sir Archibald Alison, the Sheriff of Lanarkshire, in *Blackwood's Edinburgh Magazine* entitled, 'Causes of the Increase of Crime'.[36] He claimed that, 'destitution, profligacy, sensuality and crime' had advanced with unheard of rapidity in the manufacturing districts, whilst, at the same time, the 'dangerous classes' were able to mass together in general strikes and insurrections which excited universal fervour. Two million people, he added, had been brought together in the manufacturing towns in a space of 40 years which he described as, 'an astonishing migration without precedent in history.' And, he continued, nine-tenths of all crime was committed by the lowest class in society, 'this dismal substratum, this hideous black band of society' which was composed of the most unfortunate from all classes. But this gave reason for hope. Alison claimed that about 60,000 persons were annually committed for serious offences and about double that number for summary offences. Of these, 150,000 he thought, came from the three million who comprised the lowest and most squalid classes, and only 30,000 from the remaining 24 million who lived in comparative comfort.

Thus the remedies for the unprecedented increase in crime had to be applied only in a limited sphere and all that was needed was for the general population to agree to the introduction of efficient laws and punishments. In this way Alison

---

34. PRO. (1878) Wellington Dispatches. Second Series.
35. The Croker Papers. (1885) *Correspondence of John Wilson Croker* London, John Murray.
36. (July 1844) vol. 56, pp1-14.

expressed the widespread pressure for law and order and the widely felt need for professional policing and discipline through law.

The violence aroused around the Reform Bill had been preceded by the Luddite riots of the 1820s and widespread burning of ricks and barns by the followers of 'Captain Swing' in 1830[37]. Then came the violence aroused by the House of Lords' rejection of the Reform Bill which subsided when the Lords finally backed down. After the Reform Act received the royal assent on 7 June 1832 there was little political violence until it flared again with the 'Rebecca Riots', against heavy turnpike tolls in Wales, where gangs pulled down the toll-houses justifying themselves with the prophecy that Rebecca's seed should possess, 'the gates of those which hate them.'[38] Behind the riots was the fact that turnpike trusts were rapidly being made bankrupt by the rapid growth of the railways. Sections of the Chartist Movement took to arms and threatened violence that culminated in the attempt on Newport, South Wales in which up to 33 men were killed and many more injured. All this led to strong public disquiet and a new determination in government to recruit new police forces which could not only do battle with such insurgency but collect intelligence about the organizations involved, their leaders, their strategy and tactics and their intentions. Then there could be a general preventative campaign. Gradually the strategy began to bear fruit although the change in temper of the working class in the latter half of the nineteenth century in the face of rising prosperity and the advance of democracy also had a significant effect. Violence might still occur but the threat to law and order receded as the century advanced.

PEELERS

As indicated, the early nineteenth century saw considerable social unrest following the end of the French wars and the repressive nature of a government held in thrall by the horrors of the French Reign of Terror. Yet policing was in a deplorable state, in part because of the example of the police in France. In regard to watchmen, each parish in London was entirely isolated from its neighbours. Some did not have any night watch at all. And, although the need for a professional police force for London might have been clear, a public fear of the despotism and surveillance at all levels of society as perceived to exist in France was a serious obstacle. A system other than local policing it was believed would strengthen Westminster government and infringe liberty. Nevertheless, as Home Secretary, Peel, following his experience with the Royal Irish Constabulary from 1812 to 1818, set out to tackle the problem in the face of fierce opposition. In 1820 he presented to Parliament a revolution-

37. See E. J. Hobsbawm and George Rudé *Captain Swing. Op. cit.*
38. The Old Testament. Genesis, xxiv, 60.

ary proposal for a unified police force in London directly under the control of the Home Office. Gaining acceptance was not easy but eventually he succeeded and the Metropolitan Police Act became law on 19 June 1829.[39] The heads of the new force, known as commissioners, were Colonel Charles Rowan and Richard Mayne, a young barrister, who was to be particularly effective.

The objects of the new force were laid down as, 'the Preservation of the Peace, the Prevention of Crimes, the Detection and Committal of Offenders.' The first was directed at what Sir Archibald Alison called the 'dangerous classes' who were particularly active at this time and caused the government to fear insurrection. As Philip Rawlings has put it:

> while the new police emphasised crime prevention, this was not in terms of deterring potential criminals by the certainty of detection, which had been at the core of John Fielding's work … rather they looked to the moralisation of the poor and the continual harassment of those identified as the least moral sections of the poor—the 'trained and hardened profligates,' the people of St Giles, the vagrants and the drunks.[40]

This was, in fact, the beginning of the 'civilising' process of the new industrial population of England that continued throughout the nineteenth century as democracy and a culture of human rights took hold.

Among other things, further objects of the Act meant that penalties could be more appropriate to the crime and more uniformly enforced instead of being simply physically cruel and arbitrary. Henceforth the criminal law could deal with each offender as an individual although, it must be said, with scant sympathy for him. Rehabilitation of the offender was about to become the new watchword in place of deterrence.

The office of the new police was established in a small Whitehall courtyard known as Scotland Yard, soon with a force of some 3,000 men organized into seventeen divisions. Known as 'peelers' they were initially extremely unpopular and it took two or three decades before they acquired some degree of authority and success.[41] One consequence of the antipathy was that the City of London secured a statute in 1839 to establish its own force of 500 men.

It was next necessary to tackle the remainder of the country where, similarly, there was considerable opposition to the idea of county and borough forces. Attempts to set up borough forces under Watch Committees in 1835 failed against the power of the gentry. As a consequence, and following Chartist disorders, a Royal Commission was appointed in 1836 to, 'inquire into the best means of establishing

---

39. 10 Geo. 4. c. 44.
40. Philip Rawlings. (1999) *Crime and Power: A History of Criminal Justice 1688-1998*. London, Addison Wesley Longman. p. 81.
41. Peter Ackroyd. (2000) *London, The Biography*. London, Viking. p. 288.

an efficient Constabulary. Force in the counties of England and Wales.'[42] The 1839 Act which followed allowed for the creation of new county police forces but was permissive rather than mandatory and had little effect. The Home Office sometimes declined to assist counties that did not set up police forces and this had some impact although it was limited. However, in 1856 continued government concern brought about the County and Borough Police Act[43] which finally made the setting up of county police forces mandatory. Thirty-two years later, in 1888, control of them passed from Quarter Sessions to Standing Joint Committees comprised of magistrates and county councillors. All the new police forces were organized on a military basis. There were grades of rank, a distinctive uniform of top hats, red waistcoats and helmets, as well as the imposition of drill and strict discipline.

In London, the Bow Street Runners had been disbanded in 1839 and replaced three years later by a small detective group at Scotland Yard which soon grew in size and importance.[44] As the nineteenth century proceeded the idea grew that the police should fight crime by detective work. Such investigative activity was seen as the most effective means of preventing crime and maintaining order.

POLITICAL ACTION

Apart from working class distrust of the police, and disinclination to help them, political disorder continued to raise its head in London. In particular, serious rioting broke out in Hyde Park in 1866 and at Trafalgar Square in 1886 and 1887. The year 1866 saw the stirring verbal battles in the House of Commons between Gladstone and Disraeli over reform of the parliamentary franchise. On the defeat of Gladstone's Bill and the resignation of the government that year the National Reform League called for a meeting in Hyde Park on 24 July. So huge was the meeting expected to be that Sir Richard Mayne, Chief Metropolitan Police Commissioner, had the gates to the park closed at 5 p.m. Many thousands of demonstrators, estimated at over 100,000, marched to the closed gates at Marble Arch where they were confronted with 1,700 police officers. In the ensuing struggle park railings were knocked down over a length of 1,400 yards. Fighting between demonstrators and the police then continued for two more days. Considerable damage was caused and many policemen were injured. Some 40 to 50 people were arrested and sentenced to imprisonment or payment of fines.[45]

---

42. First Report. (1839) *Parliamentary Papers*. vol. 19, p. 1.
43. 19 and 20 Vic. c. 69.
44. David Bentley. (1998) *English Criminal Justice in the Nineteenth Century*. London, The Hambledon Press. p. 6.
45. *The Times*. 25 July 1856. p. 9.

The background to other Trafalgar Square disturbances 20 years later was the sharp rise in unemployment in 1886. The Social Democratic Federation decided to call a protest meeting in Trafalgar Square for 8 February. It was addressed by John Hyndman, a Cambridge scholar who played cricket with W. C. Grace but had become a disciple of Karl Marx, and John Burns, then a fiery young socialist but later a Liberal Cabinet Minister. When the meeting ended the aristocratic Hyndman, wearing his frock coat and top hat, and Burns, who made a striking figure with his black beard and red flag, together led a large crowd up Pall Mall towards Hyde Park. Along the route violence erupted after marchers were taunted from the windows of members' clubs. In response the marchers threw stones at the clubs and this was followed by widespread looting of shops in London's West End during the next two days. Hyndman, Burns and others were prosecuted for seditious conspiracy at the Old Bailey but acquitted by the jury.

The police, who had been conspicuous by their absence during the rioting and looting, followed them up by going to shopkeepers and warning them to expect further trouble. This led to their being severely criticised for failing to protect property and for spreading alarm. As a consequence the Metropolitan Police Commissioner, Sir Edmund Henderson, was replaced by Sir Charles Warren who had an excellent military record but little imagination. In a futile step he closed Trafalgar Square to all meetings.

The times were troubled with economic depression and coercion in Ireland; more serious clashes were gathering. One sparking point was to be another socialist demonstration about Ireland which was called for Trafalgar Square on 13 November 1887. An estimated 10,000 people, mostly unemployed and Irish, attended the meeting on the day which became known as 'Bloody Sunday'. Two thousand police, 200 mounted Life Guards and a detachment of Grenadier Guards attacked and clashed violently with the demonstrators of whom hundreds were injured and three died from their injuries. At the funerals of the dead men the streets were lined with vast crowds and at the end of the ceremonies sympathisers sang William Morris's 'Death Song' to the music of Malcolm Lowson. Yet, although the day became an important symbol in working class history, Sir Charles Warren and the police were soon to be diverted by the Jack the Ripper murders and a new focus on crime and poverty.

CHAPTER 11

Victorian Images

HANGING BY THE NECK

Once capital punishment was reserved only for the most serious crimes it was open to reformers to campaign for its total abolition. Foremost in the field was William Ewart, ably supported by John Bright. After they had made several unsuccessful attempts to persuade Parliament to abolish the death penalty altogether, a Royal Commission on Capital Punishment was appointed in 1864. Despite the title of the commission, its terms of reference did not include a consideration of whether the death penalty should be done away with or not, but simply whether the number of crimes classified as murder should be reduced. The commission, of which more later in this chapter, took a great deal of evidence but, not surprisingly in the light of its terms of reference, could not agree on the abolition or retention of the death penalty. Its report[1] came out in favour of dividing murder for the purpose of punishment into degrees, with death only for the first degree, as in the United States. The first degree was to be murder committed with malice aforethought and death was also to be the penalty if the murder was committed in, or with a view to, the perpetration of the felonies of arson, rape, burglary, robbery or piracy.

Other murders would fall into the second degree and be punished with life imprisonment or with imprisonment for a period of not less than seven years, at the discretion of the court. In the event the proposals fell on stony ground and no action was taken. The commission also recommended that executions should no longer take place in public and this gave further impetus to those advocating abolition of the death penalty, as will be seen in the next section. After this failure of nerve on the part of the government which had appointed the commission, little serious effort was made to secure abolition until the twentieth century.

Public spectacle

Historically, executions in England took place in public. The most notorious gallows for hangings was Tyburn Tree (near Marble Arch) in London. It was named after the village where it stood, known originally as Ty Bourne. This meant two brooks and they formed a tributary of the Thames which entered the river at Vauxhall. It still exists but now flows underground. The tree had commenced its gruesome role as early as the year 1108 when the Normans considered the scaffold to be the tree of justice. Aside from justice, however, it provided evidence—as with the Coliseum

---

1. PP. (1865) Report of the Capital Punishment Commission. lxxiii. p. 232.

at Rome—that there are always people in all classes of society who enjoy witnessing spectacles of cruelty. In early modern England it had three triangular shaped beams on which as many as 24 felons could be hanged at one time. Every Monday the prisoners left Newgate Prison in open ox carts, often sitting on their own coffins with a rope hanging from their necks. Their slow journey over three miles took more than two hours. The procession would stop at the Hospital of St. Giles in the Fields where the condemned were offered 'a great bowl of ale to drink as their last refreshment in life.' Hence came the expression 'One for the road'. As their guards were not allowed to drink they were said to be 'On the wagon'.

These were public spectacles drawing huge crowds which often exceeded 100,000 men, women and children. They were described by the author Arthur Griffiths as a

> ribald, reckless, brutal mob, violently combative, fighting and struggling for foremost places, fiercely aggressive, distinctly abusive. Spectators often had their limbs broken, their teeth knocked out, and sometimes they were crushed to death.[2]

They were there for the spectacle, to listen to the dying speeches and confessions from the gallows and to see the criminals hanged.

In the first half of the nineteenth century most people still believed that hangings in the public eye had a deterrent effect. However, this had not always been the case. In 1725, Bernard de Mandeville portrayed the behaviour of those condemned to death on the gallows as 'either drinking madly, or uttering the vilest ribaldry, and jeering others, that are less impenitent.' He drew the conclusion that spectators came to believe 'that there is nothing in being hang'd, but a wry Neck, and a wet pair of Breeches.'[3]

Henry Fielding, who supported capital punishment as a deterrent, was nevertheless opposed both to the processions from Newgate to Tyburn and to public executions. He claimed that the purpose of carrying out the execution in public was 'to add the punishment of shame to the punishment of death.' Significantly, however, he made it clear that the opposite was often the result when he wrote:

> The day appointed by law for the thief's shame is the day of glory in his own opinion. His procession to Tyburn, and his last moments there are all triumphant; attended with the compassion of the meek and tender-hearted, and with the applause, admiration and envy of all bold and hardened ... And if he hath sense enough to temper his boldness with any degree of decency, his death is spoken of by many with honour, by most with pity, and by all with approbation.[4]

---

2. Arthur Griffiths. (1884) *The Chronicle of Newgate*. London, Chapman and Hall. 2. vols.
3. Bernard de Mandeville. (1725) *An Enquiry into the Causes of the Frequent Executions at Tyburn*. London, J. Roberts. pp. 19 and 37.
4. Henry Fielding. (1751) *An Enquiry into the Causes of the Late Increase of Robbers: with some Proposals for Remedying this Growing Evil*. Dublin, G. Faulkner. p. 265.

Undoubtedly, the elevating of murderers to the status of popular heroes must have had a detrimental effect on public morality. But with thieves it was a different matter. The public well knew that many of them were condemned to death for trifling and poverty-induced offences. As Fielding understood, the object of the state ritual was not always accepted by the condemned or the crowds, and this contradiction was to bedevil the issue for generations. The world and his wife would gather in festive mood but public feeling against hanging was vividly portrayed in many widely-sung ballads and ever-popular Punch and Judy shows where, after much crude mayhem, Punch finally outwitted and hung the archetypal hangman, Jack Ketch, himself. At that time these shows were not children's entertainment but were watched principally by adults who had seen public hangings.[5] Their pleasure at seeing Punch escape the gallows and knock down the Lord Chief Justice, representing the majesty of the law, gives us a fascinating insight into public attitudes of the time.

Although it is more likely that they had the opposite effect and generated more crime, the pomp and circumstance attending executions were believed by the authorities to create a shock and awe that helped deal with criminal activity. When the first motion to abolish public executions and avoid releasing 'fierce hungry passions' was introduced in Parliament by Henry Rich on 16 February 1841, it was greeted with laughter and rejected outright.[6] Even William Ewart opposed the motion, but in his case only from a reasonable and persistent fear that taking away the public exhibition might weaken the pressure for total abolition of capital punishment, as indeed proved to be justified when executions were later carried out in private.

The position of Peel's government of the day was made clear in 1844 when, after the execution in Nottingham of William Saville for the murder of his wife and children, a large number of people were trampled to death and injured in a stampede by the watching crowd. It was urged by the mayor of the town that the area for executions in front of the county gaol was too restrictive for the purpose. A new location was suggested to the Home Secretary, Sir James Graham, whose permission was required for any change of venue. The proposed new site was certainly large enough but the Nottingham magistrates were concerned that the gallows could be viewed only from a distance. In their support Graham sent the magistrates some guidelines for performing executions. 'The principal object of capital punishment', he said in his memorandum, 'is the terror of the example.'[7] It was necessary, he continued, for the purpose that a large multitude of spectators should assemble sufficiently near the scaffold to recognise the criminal. Some of them should also be able to hear any words of warning about the consequences of crime that the criminal might wish to address to them.

5. V. A. C. Gatrell. (1994) *The Hanging Tree: Execution and the English People 1770-1868*. Oxford, Oxford University Press. p. 120.
6. *Hansard*. 3rd series. (1841).[56] cols . 647-66.
7. Public Record Office. HO. 45. 681.

Charles Dickens intervenes

Public sentiment was beginning to change, however, as the country began to benefit materially from the Industrial Revolution and its position as the 'workshop of the world'. Prosperity for many was spreading and a new sensibility about what was humane was arising. William Makepeace Thackeray made clear his despair at the spectacle of a hanging he attended and Charles Dickens publicly expressed the loathing of the middle class when he proposed ending public executions with their 'odious levity'. Six years after attending the execution at Newgate of Francois Courvoisier, who had been found guilty of cutting the throat of Lord William Russell in his bed, Dickens was disgusted with what he saw of the surging throng from his window above the multitude. 'I did not see', he wrote, 'one token in all the immense crowd of any emotion suitable to the occasion. No sorrow, no salutary terror, no abhorrence, no seriousness, nothing but ribaldry, debauchery, levity, drunkenness and flaunting vice in 50 other shapes. I should have deemed it impossible that I could have ever felt any large assemblage of my fellow-creatures to be so odious.'[8]

It was later, in the year 1849, after attending the executions of Maria and Frederick Manning, that Dickens,[9] who seems to have been drawn to watching such spectacles,[10] became publicly ready to support executions being carried out in private. In an indignant letter to *The Times* he described in detail the crude behaviour in what he said he believed was, 'a sight so inconceivably awful as the wickedness and levity of the immense crowd collected at that execution this morning could be imagined by no man, and could be presented by no heathen land under the sun.' As a consequence, he said, the government should make the infliction of capital punishment a private solemnity within the prison walls.[11] The paper, however, could not agree. Although it declared that an execution was horrid—indeed an act of judicial slaughter—it believed pubic executions could ensure 'useful terror and a convenient humility.'[12]

Select committee

Although in 1845 Dickens had written of his aversion to capital punishment as such,[13] by 1849 he had confirmed Ewart's worst fears by breaking with his support for abolition as a consequence of his conversion to private executions.[14] He claimed to have whipped up a roaring sea of controversy but it was not until 1856, which saw the end of the Crimean War, that the House of Lords was persuaded to appoint

---

8. Letter to the *Daily News* 28 February 1846.
9. Dickens used Maria Manning, who was Belgian, as the model for Hortense, the murderous Frenchwoman in *Bleak House.*
10. He also attended a public execution by guillotine in Rome. Charles Dickens. *Pictures from Italy*, (1846)
11. *The Times.* 14 November 1849.
12. *Ibid.*
13. Letter to Macvey Napier , (28 July 1845) In 'Mamie Dickens and Georgina Hogarth', *The Letters of Charles Dickens.*(1882) Leipzig, B. Tauchnitz vol. iii. pp. 78-9.
14. *The Times.* 19 November 1849.

a Select Committee to inquire into 'the mode of carrying into effect capital punishment.' The proposal was made by Samuel Wilberforce, bishop of Oxford and son of the anti-slavery crusader, William Wilberforce. The bishop feared that public executions were threatening to undermine capital punishment altogether. 'A few more such scenes,' he had earlier told their Lordships, 'would have the effect of making men's minds recoil from that which I believe to be essential to the highest principles of justice as well as to the necessities of human expediency.'[15] Subject to certain safeguards, so that those executed were seen to have been actually executed, on 7 July the committee recommended the introduction of private hangings. However, under pressure against the recommendation from both the press and abolitionists— although from opposing positions—the House took no action.

Royal Commission

Almost a decade later, in 1864, a sea change in popular perceptions about public executions occurred when three controversial hangings caused scenes of deep disgrace by the crowds. The press and MPs swayed with the wind, but not the government which, attempting to stem the storm, pointed out that the judges favoured retention of both the death penalty and public executions. John Bright immediately responded that every amelioration in the criminal law had been carried against the advice of the judges.[16] The pressure on the government remained intense and in May, in an attempt to thwart a motion by Ewart for a Select Committee to consider abolition, it announced the appointment of the Royal Commission mentioned earlier to inquire into public executions and capital punishment.[17] Pointedly, as already indicated, its terms of reference did not include the issue of total abolition but whether the number of crimes classified as murder could be reduced.

Whilst the commission was sitting came the hanging of young Franz Muller at Newgate on 14 November 1864 for robbery and murder on a London railway train. He was the first to be known to have committed murder on a train, and the first to be arrested by use of the Atlantic cable after he had fled to the United States. His incarceration in Newgate and his hanging both revealed how little had changed. Spectators could still assemble at the prison to gape into the cells of the prisoners who were due to be executed. Whilst Muller was in prison awaiting execution, his church minister complained to the authorities about 'a cruel and crying evil in Newgate. Again and again', he said, 'on Monday morning in those last solemn moments our prayers were interrupted by the savage yells of the multitude assembled to witness the execution.'

Present at the execution itself, *The Times* reporter filed the following:

---

15. *Hansard.* [Lords] [133] col. 311. 15 May 1854.
16. *Ibid.* [174] col. 2092. 1864.
17. PP. xxi. (1866)

Before the slight slow vibrations of [Muller's] body had well ended, robbery and violence, loud laughing, oaths, fighting, obscene conduct and still more filthy language reigned round the gallows far and near. Such too the scene remained with little change till the old hangman (Calcraft) slunk again along the drop amid hissing and sneering inquiries of what he had had to drink that morning. After failing once to cut the rope he made a second attempt more successfully, and the body of Muller disappeared from view.[18]

Also present (for the *Morning Star* newspaper) was the respected radical George Jacob Holyoake who expressed sentiments of disgust similar to those voiced by Dickens in 1840. In his *Public Lessons of the Hangman*, published as a penny pamphlet in 1864 and in part included in his memoirs, Holyoake wrote that the crowds saw 'the frame quiver and the blood rush to the neck. A thrill passes through the congregated scoundrels whom the government had thus undertaken to entertain.'[19] Those scoundrels, he wrote, were the knave and the burglar, the pickpocket, the prisoner on leave, the drunkard and the wife-beater, all of whom had 'found means to profit (in education) by this great State opportunity ... An influence stronger than lust, more alluring than vice, more tempting than plunder is exercised by this seductive instructor [the gallows]. Why,' asked Holyoake, 'did the Archbishop of York condemn sensational novels and utter not one word against this vile, this real, this overriding villainous sensation provided by the government in every county of the Kingdom?'[20]

Meanwhile, among the distinguished members of the Royal Commission were its chairman, the Duke of Richmond, John Bright, Charles Neate, MP for Oxford, Dr. Stephen Lushington and William Ewart himself. Most of the members favoured retention of the death penalty but supported the ending of public executions. Over a period of two years, extensive testimony was taken from judges, prison governors, police officers, clergymen and a former Home Secretary as well as the then current holder of the office, Sir George Grey.

James Fitzjames Stephen always had a consuming interest in the definition of murder and the retributive theory of punishment. As a consequence he appeared as a witness before the commission on no less than three separate occasions. He strongly advocated the retention of the death penalty as a deterrent but he wanted a new definition of murder, confining it to felonious homicides of great enormity and treating all other homicides as manslaughter. Radzinowicz has suggested that if this advice, together with that Stephen gave on the *M'Naghten Rules*, had been adopted there would have been a significant reduction in capital punishments.[21] In the case of constructive murder, for which death was the penalty, he proposed the judge

18. *The Times*. 16 November 1864.
19. G. J. Holyoake. (1902 edn.) *Sixty Years of an Agitator's Life* London, T. Fisher Unwin. vol. ii. p. 117.
20. *Ibid.* (1864) *Public Lessons of the Hangman.* pp. 6-7.
21. Sir Leon Radzinowicz. (1957) *Sir James Fitzjames Stephen 1829-1894 and his Contribution to the Development of Criminal Law.* Selden Society lecture. London, Quaritch. p. 35.

should be allowed to pass a sentence of one day's imprisonment if he thought it proper. The judge, he said, already had that discretion with manslaughter, burglary, forgery, arson and other crimes and experience showed it was beneficial.

Eventually, although saying that they forbore to enter into the abstract questions of the expediency of abolishing or retaining capital punishment on which there were differences of opinion among them, the majority of the commissioners found it, 'impossible to resist such a weight of authority' received on the desirability of private executions. Accordingly, they recommended that public executions be brought to an end and their report, which included other proposals not relevant here, was published on 8 January 1866.[22] Then on 23 March the government introduced the Law of Capital Punishment (Amendment) Bill in the House of Lords.[23] Among other things it included provision for executions within prisons. In the debate Lord Malmesbury urged that private executions be rejected, with the curious reasoning that, 'We must not give way to the natural sentiments which civilisation prompts.'[24] In contrast to the abolitionists he also feared the move would lead to the end of the death penalty itself. In the event the government withdrew the Bill on 30 July.

It was not until the following year that the government introduced two new and separate Bills. The first was the Murder Law (Amendment) Bill which was soon abandoned because of the complications surrounding its proposal for degrees of murder. The second was the Capital Punishment Within Prisons Bill which set out the measures considered necessary to ensure that executions in private would be carried out with sufficient precautions to satisfy the public that they were genuine. This too was withdrawn, which seems to indicate divisions within the government about the whole question of capital punishment.

However, in May 1867 Garthorne Hardy was appointed Home Secretary and the picture began to change. He had been a member of the Royal Commission and later became Earl Cranbrook. Although he favoured retention of the death penalty, he re-introduced the Capital Punishment Within Prisons Bill on 26 November. Private executions, he argued,[25] would act as a more effective deterrent than public hangings because the consequent, 'mystery and indefiniteness attending the punishment serves only to increase its terrors in the eyes [of the people].'[26] Moreover, he added, public executions attracted the very worst classes, many of whom were themselves on the road to the gallows. They attended only to make a jest of what to every worthy person was a matter of gravest regret. Far from absorbing a moral message they kept one another's courage up by singing low songs and laughing at low jests, he added. An amendment in the Commons for a complete end to the death penalty

---

22. PP. (1866) xxi.
23. *Hansard.* [Lords] (1866) [182] col. 837.
24. *Ibid.* col. 243.
25. PRO. HO. 144/18/46237.
26. *Hansard.* [190] col. 1128. (1867)

was opposed, among others, by Gladstone, Disraeli, and John Stuart Mill, a former abolitionist, and it was defeated.

Mill's position is interesting in the light of his reputation as the personification of liberalism. He believed abolition would produce an 'effeminacy in the general mind of the country' and was it, he asked, so dreadful a thing to die? He not only thought a man were better off dead than suffering a long term of imprisonment but also gratuitously advocated flogging as a punishment for brutality. Despite considerable evidence to the contrary he did not accept that innocent people were sometimes sentenced to death and he believed that the rules of evidence were too favourable to prisoners. Curiously, coming from him, he said that he was opposed to what he regarded as the position of advanced liberal opinion.[27] Editorially, *The Times*[28] concluded that what it correctly described as Mill's 'remarkable speech' had considerably helped secure the defeat of the amendment for abolition which was lost by 127 votes to 23.[29]

HANGING IN PRISONS

About this time five men and a woman were charged at the Old Bailey with murder arising from the dynamiting of Clerkenwell Gaol in an endeavour to rescue some Irish Fenian prisoners held there. Only one man, Michael Barrett, was found guilty and he was hanged outside Newgate Prison on 25 May 1868—the last person to be hanged publicly in England. Four days later the Bill received the Royal Assent and a relic of medieval barbarism had finally been brought to an end. As Sir Leon Radzinowicz has put it, 'The spectacle once thought so essential and potent a deterrent had dwindled to little more than a notice and a certificate on the gate of a prison.'[30]

The first person hanged inside a prison was Thomas Wells at Maidstone, Kent on 13 August 1868. He was an 18-year-old Dover railway porter who had murdered his station-master after a reprimand. His execution, whilst he proudly wore his railway uniform, was generally disapproved of because of his age. Furthermore, after the drop he still took two minutes to die. The first hanging inside Newgate took place 26 days later, on 8 September, when another 18-year-old, Alexander Mackay, was executed for murdering his master's wife. Both were part of the depressing statistic that 90 per cent of people executed at the time were aged under 21.

Home Office records reveal dissatisfaction with the requirement of the 1868 Act that the prison bell should be tolled to ensure that it was known outside the prison that an execution was taking place. The bell had to be tolled for 15 minutes before

27. *Ibid.* [191] col. 1054. (1868)
28. 22 April 1868.
29. *Hansard.* [191].
30. L. Radzinowicz. (1968) *A History of English Criminal Law and its Administration from 1750: Grappling for Control.* London, Stevens & Sons. vol. iv. p. 353.

a hanging and for 15 minutes following. An advantage one person wrote, was that those who heard it could offer up a prayer for the, 'poor wretch who is to be hurried into eternity.' The general view, however, was that whilst it did nothing for the man dazed with 'the awful certainties of his next few minutes', its effects on other prisoners was to bring about a 'brutal levity.'.[31] It also undoubtedly produced among them reactions of fear and depression. As a consequence, the tolling of the bell during an execution was abandoned in March 1901.

JUVENILES

Another reform in the nineteenth century of the criminal justice system related to the treatment of juveniles. In the early years of the century the criminal law was both chaotic and bloody with periodic use of hanging, use of the dreaded infested, rotting hulks and transportation as punishments for most offences, including many of a trivial nature. Children and young persons were treated no differently from adults. The case of Nicholas White, mentioned later, was quite typical.[32]

Reformers believed that harsh law bred crime. In 1815, a Society for Investigating the Causes of the Alarming Increase of Juvenile Delinquency in the Metropolis had been founded by Peter Bradford, known as the 'Spitalfields Philanthropist'. Included on its committee were also Dr Lushington, Fowell Buxton, James Mill and David Ricardo. In their view, the causes of delinquency were the severity of the criminal law, the mixing of children with 'atrocious' adult criminals on remand in prison and the defective state of the police. They wanted to see much imprisonment and corporal punishment replaced by '…mildness of persuasion and gentleness of reproof…'[33]

This approach led, in 1821, to a parliamentary Bill for the 'Punishment, Correction and Reform of Young Persons'. It provided that, instead of committing children to prison to await trial at Quarter Sessions, or even Assizes, for such petty offences as stealing apples or tarts, they should be dealt with summarily by two justices with a view to their reform. Unfortunately, the Bill received scant support from MPs and was defeated, although the idea of summary trial for juveniles was to be revived later in the century.

Another proposal was made by the 'Select Committee on Criminal Law in 1828 which had concluded that lengthy imprisonment awaiting trial was degrading and led to vice.[34] Again, nothing was done since the authorities, including many JPs, felt little disquiet at such lengthy imprisonment or the awful punishments inflicted

31. PRO. HO. PCOM. 8/210.
32. post, p.200.
33. Committee Report. (1816) pp. 26-7.
34. PP. (1828) vi. p. 12.

upon a large number of young children and saw no process of cause and effect.

Then, in 1833, the Criminal Law Commissioners were appointed and were asked to consider if it were desirable to distinguish the modes of trial of juvenile and adult offenders.[35] In accordance with their usual practice they decided to question professional witnesses before preparing their report. The replies given to them by the generally enlightened men they approached are surprising. They reveal some compassion but a startlingly hard-headed attitude to young offenders, including small children.

For example, Richard Mayne, the young barrister recently appointed a Commissioner of the Metropolitan Police, considered existing punishments were often too lenient. They should particularly be increased, he said, where, even though proof of an offence was not complete, the accused were convicted under the Police Act as *reputed* thieves or *suspected* persons. Henry Gawler, a magistrate at Southampton, was opposed to summary trial for juveniles even though he agreed that young persons sent to prison on remand would mix with bad company.

Some other witnesses had more vision. Sir Eardley Wilmot, a magistrate for the county of Warwick, concluded that early imprisonment of children was a direct cause of crime. He recommended immediate and summary review of offences committed by the young to avoid the stigma and contamination of prison and the publicity of trial. Moreover, larceny by a juvenile should be made a minor offence, to be dealt with by two magistrates with power to punish, or discharge without punishment, rather than put a child who stole a bun into gaol for three months on remand.

Dr Lushington strongly opposed corporal punishment. In his experience, for larceny to the amount of a few pence a first offender would often receive from a month to three months' imprisonment with hard labour along with whipping and solitary confinement. As a result, children could end up in a state 'horrible to contemplate'. And it produced no benefit or good at all—only callousness.

Other witnesses gave evidence on both sides and the commissioners, in their report, argued for summary trial of juveniles, instead of trial by jury, to avoid long periods of imprisonment for weeks or months on remand which was destructive of morals. Moreover, they said, the formality of a solemn trial at Quarter Sessions or Assizes for slight offences derogated from the dignity of such courts. Indeed, they added with a mixture of compassion and realism, that where theft resulted only from incitement by others it might often be less mischievous to society to pass over the offence altogether.

In the event, the government refused to implement the report it had sought on the ground, stated by Lord John Russell, the Home Secretary, that it would vio-

---

35. PP. (1837) xxxi. p. 1.

late the principle of trial by jury.[36] However, the work of the commissioners came to fruition with the enactment of the Juvenile Offenders Act in 1847.[37] This gave magistrates increased powers, if they saw fit and a parent or guardian of the child consented, to deal summarily with juveniles so that any child aged 14 or less be either whipped or discharged without any other punishment. The age of 14 years in the statute was increased to 16 by the Juvenile Offenders Act 1850.[38] Although it was correct that juveniles should be treated differently from adults, in this way the commissioners may be said to have unwittingly started the process whereby summary trial in the magistrates' courts of both adults and juveniles gradually took over most cases from trial by jury.

HOUSE OF LORDS SELECT COMMITTEE

The year 1847 also saw the setting up of a House of Lords Select Committee to inquire into the law relating to juvenile offenders and transportation.[39] It sat under the chairmanship of Lord Brougham. The first witness was Charles Ewan Law QC, who had succeeded Lord Denman as Recorder of London. Not a great many children under the age of nine had been convicted of felony before him, he said, but some under ten years had been and a great many under 12. Incredibly to modern eyes, he had sent some to the hulks and sentenced others to three years' imprisonment. Another witness, John Adams, a judge who had been chairman of the Middlesex Sessions from 1836 to 1844, told the committee that a large number of boys had been brought before him whose ages ranged from seven to 15. He said he blamed 'the Jews' who would get children to steal and reward them with a few pence which at first they spent on 'gingerbread and cakes.' They then became frequenters of penny theatres and were trained until they became regular thieves. There was almost unanimity among the witnesses in their opposition to short sentences and for retention of capital punishment for serious offences.

Captain Hall, the Governor of Parkhurst Prison, indicated that he took in boys of all ages from ten to 18. He claimed that the regime was educational for two to three years after which they were transported. Nearly all the witnesses agreed that transportation for children could not safely be abandoned since it invoked a terror greater than all other punishments except death. The committee believed that imprisonment was not an efficient punishment, even with hard labour and separation or silence, since it had no deterrent effect after a second sentence. And for young offenders it resulted in a fatal contamination so that one saw a frightful picture of boys

---

36. *Hansard*, (April 1837) [37] col. 962.
37. 10 & 11 Vict. c. 82.
38. 13 & 14 Vict. c. 37.
39. PP. (1847) viii. 2 Reports.

under 12 returning to prison within three or four years as often as 15 times and on average nine times. The committee concluded, therefore, that young first offenders should be sent to reformatory asylums on the principle of Parkhurst. Presumably, as with the later borstals, the sentences there were longer to admit of training.

These appalling attitudes to young offenders, and what were considered to be appropriate punishments for them, were at odds with the position taken by some of the witnesses who gave evidence to the Criminal Law Commissioners but nothing further was done for young people until the Children Act 1908 which forbade the imprisonment of children under 14 years.

GARROTTING

Crimes of violence were perceived to be on the increase in the 1850s and panic set in when an outbreak of garrotting occurred in various parts of the country in the period from 1856 to 1862. Garrotting involved choking, suffocating or strangling a victim, often using a length of wire, in the course of committing an indictable offence—usually robbery. During these years *Punch* magazine carried a whole series of cartoons and lengthy jokes about the crime, including many eccentric means of defence. One advertisement appeared offering the public an 'anti-garrot collar'. This was a steel collar to be hand-fitted round the neck with a large number of sharp steel spikes pointing outwards. Despite such bizarre forms of protection, the offence caused a great deal of fear among the public and it was generally regarded as a very serious threat to law and order. Letters to *The Times* began to appear from gentlemen who had been so attacked and robbed. In response the judges began to order severe floggings in addition to penal servitude in an attempt to stem the growth of the crime. Their example was then followed by Parliament which, against the wishes of the government, enacted the Security from Violence Act 1863.

This permitted judges to order flogging once, twice or thrice in addition to imprisonment or penal servitude. For offenders over the age of 16 this could mean 150 lashes and for those under that age, 75 lashes. Ironically, in the event, the epidemic of garrotting died out before the statute became law. Although the judges claimed all the credit for the demise of flogging, it is more likely that penal servitude for life was the true deterrent.

CHAPTER 12

A Century of Criminal Law Reform

CRIME AND PUNISHMENT

In 1764 the Italian Count Cesare Beccaria published to an astonished world his renowned book, *Dei Delitti e delle Pene* (Of Crimes and Punishments). This powerful work was not the first protest against the bleak inhumanity of the criminal law nor was it merely a plea for some change. It gave expression to a *cri de coeur* for a complete reform of the penal law which drew strength from an intellectual movement for a more rational and enlightened society based on the social contract philosophy.[1] Although Beccaria was only 26 and had little legal background when he wrote his book in just a few months, it became the inspiration of a new philosophical movement for the reduction of all punishments, which quickly spread across Europe. In England it attracted a number of influential writers, including Blackstone, William Eden, Romilly and Jeremy Bentham. All four of them agreed with Beccaria and poured scorn on the concept that the same punishment of death should apply to totally different types of offence.

The book was first published anonymously for fear of serious reprisals and was a brilliant indictment from which the crusade against capital punishment was to take off. Not surprisingly, the Inquisition forbade its publication under pain of death and called Beccaria a madman and a stupid imposter. It stigmatised the work as having, 'sprung from the deepest abyss of darkness, horrible, monstrous, full of poison.' The Church even argued that torture was a mercy to the criminal since it purged him in his death from the sin of falsehood. In response, Beccaria exposed torture to ridicule and asked how the truth could reside

in the muscles and fibres of a wretch in torture? By this method the robust will escape, and the feeble be condemned ... These are the inconveniences of this pretended test of truth worthy only of a cannibal.[2]

As a result of his persuasive message torture was soon abolished in Lombardy, Austria, Portugal, Sweden, Russia and France.

Considering that the only reasonable basis for punishment was its effectiveness as a deterrent, Beccaria considered that the death penalty was useless. It was in it-

---

1. For a wider view of Beccaria and his work see C. Phillipson. (1923) *Three Criminal Law Reformers: Beccaria, Bentham, Romilly.* Part 1. pp. 3-106.
2. Cesare Beccaria. (1769 edn.) *Of Crimes and Punishments.* London, F. Newbery. p. 58.

self a barbarous act of violence and injustice since it rendered an act legitimate in payment for an equivalent act of violence. Furthermore, if punishments were very severe men were led to commit other crimes to avoid punishment for the first. He continued:

> Countries and times most notorious for the severity of punishment, were always those in which the most bloody and inhuman actions and the most atrocious crimes were committed for the hand of the legislator and that of the assassin were directed by the same spirit of ferocity.[3]

To avoid being an act of violence, he concluded, every punishment 'should be public, immediate and necessary; the least possible in the case; proportioned to the crime, and determined by the laws.'[4] Its primary purpose was to benefit society, not to torment offenders. Moreover, punishments should be imposed by law not by judicial discretion. The so-called 'spirit if the law', by which the law was replaced by the point of view of the judge, he considered dangerous. Judges in criminal cases had no right to interpret laws as they were not legislators. There should be a fixed code of laws drawn up in the vernacular, free from obscurity, and made known to the public at large. 'Ignorance and uncertainty of punishments,' said Beccaria, 'lend assistance to the eloquence of the passions. Every citizen ought to know when his acts are guilty or innocent.'

At the time the book was translated into English, Beccaria's influence in England was muted but eventually it had a significant effect on policing and punishment. As we have seen, in the nineteenth century police forces would be established first in London then in the remainder of the country. And, in place of the death penalty came transportation and imprisonment at home which in due course replaced transportation entirely. All the theoretical premises of Beccaria's work, and in particular his proposals regarding grades of punishment to fit the offence, were adopted by the Criminal Law Commissioners who inspired a great deal of nineteenth century criminal justice reform. Hitting at the heart of penal practice in England, Beccaria claimed that the certainty of a small punishment made a stronger impression than the fear of one more severe with a hope of escaping. He considered it in the nature of man to be terrified at the approach of the smallest inevitable evil, whilst hope dispelled fear of a greater evil, especially if backed by examples of impunity.

DETERRENCE VERSUS RETRIBUTION

The ethical approach to capital punishment involves asking the question whether the execution of criminals is ever justified. In legal philosophy, corrective justice

---

3. *Ibid.* p. 99.
4. *Ibid.* p. 179.

distinguishes two major theories of punishment, utilitarian and retributive. The first involves considering whether punishment produces greater happiness by deterrence of offenders and potential offenders. Deterrence is the key to reducing the incidence of crime but the punishment should be appropriate and not excessive. Those favouring retributive punishment believe criminals not only deserve punishment but that it should be equal to the harm done. Compensation is possible but some retributionists continue to believe in *lex talionis* or the biblical 'eye for an eye'. In other words that the punishment should fit the crime. And, to many this can be expressed in one word—vengeance. Stephen, for example, not only thought hatred of criminals and vengeance were not wicked in themselves but went on to say,

> The infliction of punishment by law gives definite expression and a solemn ratification and justification to the hatred which is excited by the commission of the offence ... The criminal law thus proceeds upon the principle that it is morally right to hate criminals.[5]

He continued by asserting, 'Death, flogging and the like emphatically justify and gratify the public desire for vengeance upon such offenders as justify exemplary punishments.'[6] However, for many today that has been modified to a demand for 'just deserts', and for retributionists, other considerations, such as a future reduction in crime, are not the most important thing. They believe incapacitating the offender by death or long-term imprisonment is what is required.

The philosopher, John Locke, defended capital punishment by combining the two approaches. He attempted to justify the death penalty by arguing that criminals deserved punishment (retributive) and society needed to be protected by deterrence which meant preventing crime by threatening people with pain (utilitarian). Under the influence of this theory England endured what continentals (and Peel) called the 'Bloody Code,' the primary purpose of which was to sustain and legitimise the existing, social and political order. The Italian Count, Cesare Beccaria, on the other hand as we have seen, contended that people did not sacrifice their right to life when entering into the social contract. In fact, the death penalty is immoral, inhuman, unjust and undignified. Judicial murder sets the wrong example and, indeed, innocent people are from time to time executed in error. On top of this statistics consistently show that it is not a deterrent to murder.

In England, the reduction in the incidence of capital punishment was the key expression of criminal justice reform in the nineteenth century. After all, it had been a central element in the criminal law for centuries and under the 'Bloody Code' more than 200 offences, many of them minor, were capital. It is a sobering thought that our criminal laws were the most sanguine in Europe. And, although not all who were sentenced to death were executed, in 1785 the Rev. Martin Madan, a barrister,

---

5. J. F. Stephen. (1883) *A History of the Criminal Law of England.* London, Macmillan. vol. ii. p. 81.
6. *Ibid.* p. 83.

a Surrey magistrate and a cousin of William Cowper, demanded an end to all re-
prieves and pardons so that severity could act as an effective deterrent. In his eyes all
capital laws had to be rigidly enforced. Severity, he asserted, produced fear and made
an example of the guilty. He dedicated his pamphlet, *Thoughts on Executive Justice*,
to the judges of Assizes and sent each of them a copy.[7] Lord Ellenborough was full
of praise for it but Sir Samuel Romilly, in contradiction, claimed that its influence
accounted for the very large number of offenders hanged in 1785.[8]

A contrary view was taken by William Paley, MA., DD, Archdeacon of Carlisle.[9]
He believed that there could be only two methods of applying the penal law. The
first was to provide capital punishment for only a few offences but invariably inflict
it. The second, to utilise such punishment for many different kinds of offences, but
inflict it upon only a few examples of each kind. He favoured the second approach
By means of the danger of death hanging over the crimes of many, he said, 'the ten-
derness of the law cannot be taken advantage of.'

At this time the political debate on penal policy was divided into two philoso-
phies. One group wanted certainty in the law and included liberal Tories, utilitari-
ans, evangelicals and the 1833 Criminal Law Commissioners. Romilly and Bentham
wanted more rule-bound law. They believed the discretion of judges and juries made
the criminal law unpredictable and they wanted it minimised.[10] The other group
desired an interventionist style of government responding to public opinion about
penal reform.

THE CRUSADE AGAINST THE DEATH PENALTY

Over the ensuing years Sir Samuel Romilly developed his earlier attacks on Madan
into a more mature penal theory which he expressed fully in a memorable speech
in the House of Commons on 9 February 1810 when moving for leave to bring in
three bills to repeal certain statutes imposing the death penalty for larceny.[11] The
bills were defeated, largely because Lord Chancellor Eldon and Lord Chief Justice
Elllenborough opposed them in the House of Lords. However, Romilly's speech
made a deep and lasting impression in Parliament and in the country, and played a
crucial part in the growing movement for reform.

Romilly was born at 18 Frith Street in London's Soho district on 1 March 1757
with strong Huguenot antecedents. In adult life he constantly introduced Bills into

---

7. Martin Madan. ((1785) *Thoughts on Executive Justice.* London, J. Dodsley.
8. *Memoirs of the Life of Sir Samuel Romilly.* (edited by his sons.) (1840) London, John Murray. vol. i. p. 89.
9. W. Paley. (1785) *Principles of Moral and Political Philosophy.* London, T. & .J. Allman. c. ix. p. 526.
10. Lecture by Philip Handler. (6 February 2008) *Penal Reform and Trial Practice in England 1808-1861.*
    London, Institute of Advanced Legal Studies.
11. *Hansard.* [15] cols. 366-374.

the House of Commons to mitigate the rigours of the penal law and showed great perseverance and courage in the face of widespread and powerful opposition, particularly from the judiciary.

Following Beccaria's example, Jeremy Bentham argued that capital punishment was undesirable since, *inter alia*:

- it could not be used for compensation as its source was destroyed;
- executed men could not be reformed;
- the death penalty was unequal since men were unequal and it was not variable or remissible to meet individual cases; and
- judges and juries were not infallible and many innocent victims had perished.

Change of Mood

In the early years of the nineteenth century political tensions shifted the mood on capital punishment.

Those who were amassing the newest forms of wealth did not view the haphazard brutalities of the existing system as an adequate means of putting down crime and increasingly they were worried by the purloining of their manufactures and the forgery of bills, warrants and other commercial paper. The petitions of factory owners, bankers and insurers, which poured in upon Parliament, demanded that the death penalty be given up and adequate policing be instituted instead.[12]

The issue was raised in 1819 by Sir James Mackintosh who secured the appointment of a Select Committee on the criminal law relating to capital punishment[13] of which he became chairman. This was achieved against the strong opposition of Lord Castlereagh who wanted a committee with far wider terms of reference on the administration of the criminal law generally. The Committee's report, recommended that capital punishment be removed from numerous property offences but met with a good deal of opposition and achieved very little in changing the law. Nevertheless, it made a powerful impact upon public opinion.

SIR ROBERT PEEL AND THE PENAL CODE

Peel entered the Cabinet as Home Secretary in 1822 determined to improve the criminal law, but with a sensitive awareness of how far MPs would follow him. Although not prepared to go as far as Bentham on the death penalty, Peel did,

---

12. W. R. Cornish and G. de N. Clark. (1989) *Law and Society in England 1750–1950*. London, Sweet & Maxwell. p. 575.
13. PP. (1819) vol. viii. p. 1.

however, adopt the mantle of Beccaria with his promise to 'break the sleep of centuries'. This approach did not please Bentham and his followers, however, since they wanted nothing less than the whole loaf. Bentham wrote, 'Mr Peel is for consolidation in contradistinction to codification: I for codification in contradistinction to consolidation.'[14] And consolidation is what Peel achieved with his four statutes dealing with the law relating to larceny, malicious injuries to property, offences against the person and forgery. Well over 200 statutes were consolidated by these measures and more than three-quarters of all offences were covered. Peel would not go any further, however, and it was left to Lord John Russell to mount an even more serious onslaught a decade later with the assistance of the 1833 Criminal Law Commissioners.

Nonetheless, the most important effect of Peel's measures was that they severely reduced the incidence of capital punishment, and in this Peel was rewriting the law as perhaps Bentham could have recognised. Within a year of taking office he had replaced death with transportation or imprisonment for shoplifting and sending threatening letters. The Waltham Black Act was entirely repealed save for two provisions.[15] Assaulting a customs officer ceased to be capital in 1825. At the same time capital burglary and housebreaking were confined to entry into a dwellinghouse, no longer including its curtillage.[16] Benefit of clergy was abolished as was the distinction between grand and petty larceny.[17] Crimes that were non-clergyable, such as treason, remained capital but those that were became punishable with seven years' transportation or up to two years imprisonment.[18]

However, by this time public opinion had moved rapidly against the death penalty, except for murder, and Parliament was flooded with petitions indicating that Peel's reforms had not gone far enough. A number of books also appeared arguing for considerable further reform. To these were added the campaigns of the London liberal newspapers, the *Morning Herald* and the *Morning Chronicle* as well as the *Monthly Review* and the *European Magazine,* both of which favoured reform of the criminal law, the *Monthly Magazine,* which was wildly favourable, the Whig *Edinburgh Review,* and the *Quarterly Review,* which was had always been forceful in its aid to Romilly. It was at this point that William Ewart MP commenced his successful campaign for the revision of Peel's statutes and secured a further reduction in the number of capital offences.

The movement for abolition continued and 1829 saw the formation of the Committee for the Diffusion of Information on the subject of Capital Punishments under the chairmanship of Charles William Allen FRS. The names of some of the members of its London Committee make instructive reading. There was the ir-

---

14. J. Bentham. (1843) *Works.* vol. x. p. 594.
15. 4 Geo. 4, c. 53, 54.
16. 6 Geo. 4, c. 78 and 8 Geo. 4, c. 29.
17. 7 & 8 Geo. 4, c. 29.
18. 7 & 8 Geo. 4, c. 28.

repressible abolitionist, Fowell Buxton, MP., J. T. Barry, Leonard Horner FRS, Dr Stephen Lushington, LLD, MP, Basil Montague and J. Sydney Taylor, a prominent barrister. All these men spent the greater part of their lives in tireless agitation against the death penalty and Barry and Lushington appeared as witnesses before the 1833 Criminal Law Commissioners. Buxton and Horner were national figures and Basil Montague was instrumental in saving many convicted prisoners from the gallows. At the age of 60 he generalised his experiences in a book of wider implications than its title—*Thoughts on the Punishment of Death for Forgery*—suggests.[19]

As Peel may have anticipated, his early success and that of Ewart, far from satisfying the movement for abolition, raised its determination to new heights with Brougham and Lord John Russell joining Mackintosh, Buxton and Ewart in their parliamentary onslaughts. Further progress continued to be clamoured for by journals and newspapers, and by now so many petitions against capital punishment were flowing into Parliament that Brougham exclaimed that, 'the Table groaned with them.'[20] Perhaps the most significant petition was that from 214 cities and towns for the abolition of death for forgery.[21] It included the signatures of 1,000 bankers who claimed they suffered most from the crime, but had found from experience that the possibility of inflicting the death penalty for it prevented the prosecution, conviction and punishment of the criminal and thus endangered the very property which it was intended to protect.[22]

One of the reasons why these bankers suffered was because the notes of the Bank of England were easy to forge[23] and juries were reluctant to convict. In 1797 there had been 'an epidemic of forgeries and an avalanche of prosecutions.'[24] And, in the period 1818-21 the situation reached a crisis point. Two juries at the Old Bailey refused to convict any of the prisoners charged with the capital offence of uttering forged notes. The evidence was clear, the judge had given instructions to convict and yet the jurors, using their discretion to mitigate, acquitted.[25]

Peel himself led the opposition to the outcry for abolition. He knew much remained to be done, but was afraid that if Parliament proceeded too rapidly a strong prejudice would arise in the country against new measures and, as he had said earlier, the 'great object of justice and humanity might be defeated.'[26] He also made it clear he was concerned with wider aspects of reform including the establishment of

19. B. Montague (1830) *Thoughts on the Punishment of Death for Forgery* London.
20. *Hansard.* (New series) (1830) vol. 24. col. 1058.
21. *Journals of the House of Commons.* (24 May 1830) vol. 85. 463.
22. *Ibid.*
23. Cairns and McLeod. (eds.) (2002) `*The Dearest Birthright of the People of England': The Jury in the History of the Common Law.* Oxford, Hart Publishing. p. vi.
24. Philip Handler. (2002) 'The Limits of Discretion: forgery and the Jury at the Old Bailey 1812-21.' In Cairns and McLeod. *Ibid.* p. 155.
25. *Ibid.*
26. *Hansard.* N.S. (1826-7) vol. 16. cols. 635-6.

an effective police force, and the fierce opposition this aroused made him even more cautious and brought him strong support from the judges, including Lord Tenterden and Lord Chancellor Lyndhurst. Nonetheless, various measures were soon introduced to revise Peel's statutes. Ewart brought in a Bill on 27 March 1832 to repeal capital punishment for stealing in a dwellinghouse to the value of £5 and for horse, sheep and cattle stealing. This represented an importance advance since out of the 9,316 death sentences passed in 1825-31, as many as 3,178 related to these offences. On the 'principle' of flexibility 70 of these sentences were executed out of a total of 410 for all offences.[27]

Peel intervened no less than three times in the debates,[28] asserting that the proposal was 'a most dangerous experiment.' He now felt stronger than ever in his opposition since, 'as civilisation increased, the facility for the commission of crime increased more rapidly than the facility for the protection of it.' The Bill also met with angry opposition in the House of Lords, particularly from Lord Tenterden, by then lord chief justice, and Lord Wynford, and was only passed when an amendment was agreed by which the death penalty was replaced by one punishment only, transportation for life. Also in 1832 some forgeries ceased to be capital, although two new ones, relating to powers of attorney for the transfer of government stock and to the making of wills, were brought within the net, again on the prompting of Lord Wynford. His power had waned by the following year, however, when an Act to exclude housebreaking with larceny to any value was passed not only against his opposition, but that also of the Duke of Wellington.

On 2 August 1833, Lord Suffield introduced into the House of Lords a Bill to abolish the death penalty for simple housebreaking.[29] In the course of his speech he referred to a trial in the previous May of a boy named Nicholas White.[30] Nicholas, only nine years of age, whilst playing with some other children, was tempted by them to push a stick through a cracked window and pull out some printers' colours. Despite their value being only two pence the boy was prosecuted at the Old Bailey, where he pleaded not guilty but was convicted and sentenced to be hanged under the Act Lord Suffield's Bill was intended to repeal. Terrible as the case was, it served to highlight the gross inconsistency between the theory and practice of the law in that out of 1,100 persons convicted under that statute in the previous two years, only one had been executed. In a repeat performance, both Lord Wynford and the Duke of Wellington spoke against Suffield's Bill. It is significant, however, that neither of them cared to grapple with the facts produced by Suffield nor did they venture to press the Lords to a division. In the event, the Bill received the royal assent 12 days later on 14 August—a remarkably speedy enactment.

---

27. *Ibid.* 3rd series. (1932) vol. 11. col. 952.
28. *Ibid.* vol.11, cols. 952-3 and vol. 13, cols. 195-7 and 198-200.
29. *Ibid.* vol. 20, cols. 278-82.
30. OBP Online. (www.oldbaileyonline.org) May 1833. Trial of Nicholas White. Ref:t18330516-5.

Nevertheless, despite all these successes, since at the commencement of the century over 200 crimes had attracted the death penalty, a large number still remained. They included rape, buggery, murder, numerous types of forgery and attempted murder resulting in injury. It now fell to the new home secretary, Lord John Russell, to take a decisive step.

CRIMINAL LAW COMMISSIONERS

On the advice of Lord Chancellor Brougham, the Criminal Law Commissioners were appointed by King William IV in 1833.[31] They were John Austin, Henry Bellenden Ker, Andrew Amos, William Wightman and Thomas Starkie. They were all eminent lawyers and liberal reformers, well suited to the task they were set of codifying the whole of the criminal law and more than willing to innovate and act as a pressure group for law reform.[32] In all, their eight reports over the years contained over two million words in 2,324 large folio pages and although they did not result in a codification of the criminal law they were responsible for a whole number of reforms during the nineteenth century which became known as 'the century of law reform'.

At the request of Lord John Russell, the commissioners dealt with the death penalty in their Second Report.[33] They expressed their support for Beccaria's principles and rejected the theories of Paley which still remained influential. They questioned whether capital punishment could be of any use when it applied to many offences but was not normally inflicted. After careful inquiry they reached the significant conclusion that selection of a few culprits who alone suffered death did not diminish but, on the contrary, actually tended to increase the number of offenders. The fear of death was not strong when remote and uncertain, they said, as was evidenced by men who engaged in the most hazardous occupations without regard to danger to life. Or, as Russell put it in another context, 'Death itself, for many, has no terrors; the passions of revenge, honour, love, despair triumph over and despite it'[34]

After examining the Common Law and statutes and many witnesses largely, but not entirely from the legal profession, the commissioners concluded that the punishment of death should be confined to the crime of high treason and, with some exceptions, to offences which consisted in, or were aggravated by, acts of violence to the person, or which tended directly to endanger human life. As a consequence, a number of existing offences would cease to be capital and many classes of offences reduced, in their liability to capital punishment, to very narrow limits. The report

31. Their first Report. Parliamentary Papers (PP) (1834) xxvi.
32. For more details of the commissioners see J. Hostettler. (1992) *The Politics of Criminal Law: Reform in the Nineteenth Century*. Chichester, Barry Rose Law Publishers Ltd.
33. PP. (1836) xxxvi. p. 183.
34. *Hansard.* [37] col. 713.

was delivered to Lord Chancellor Cottenham on 9 June 1836.

Soon after, on 19 September of the same year, Lord John Russell, as Home Secretary, wrote to inform the commissioners that, following their report, it was likely that the government would introduce a Bill on capital punishment.[35] He wanted the commissioners to consider what the principal heads of such a Bill should be.

This official letter was followed, on 20 October, by a more personal letter in which Russell set out his own views on the proposals of the report.[36] For instance, he wanted more detail on the aggravations that would leave offences like robbery, arson and rape still capital. Further, he continued significantly, he would not altogether exclude from the commissioners' consideration the question of abolishing capital punishment to a still greater extent. He doubted, however, the concurrence of public opinion in the abolition of capital punishment in cases of burglary or robbery where great violence was used, and he was of the opinion that the shedding of a man's blood by premeditated violence could not cease to be capital without increasing the number of such crimes.

The commissioners replied to the Home Secretary on 19 January 1837. In response to his letters they had carefully considered how the principles of the second report might be carried into legislation at once. They submitted the heads of Bills which would decrease the number of capital punishments, classify crimes according to certain grades and introduce precise definitions of the offences to which different degrees of punishment should be assigned.

The first Bill proposed expressly to abolish capital punishment for eight specified crimes, substituting for it a discretionary punishment varying between transportation for life and imprisonment for five years.

Their second Bill proposed to abolish the punishment of death for certain forgeries which still remained capital.

The third Bill was intended to modify and restrict the application of capital punishment in the cases of malicious injuries, burglary, robbery, stealing from the person, burning or destroying buildings or ships and piracy.

So great an advance would these Bills represent that their combined effect was to remove the punishment of death from more than three-quarters of the existing capital offences.

Legislation
During the course of 1837 Russell, armed with the commissioners' drafts, sponsored Bills in the House of Commons to remove the death penalty from 21 of the 37 offences still capital, and for restrictions on the use of such punishment in

---

35. PP. (1837) xxxi. p. 1.
36. *Ibid.*

the 16 remaining.[37] William Ewart proposed an amendment that would have removed capital punishment from all offences short of actual murder. He reminded the House that where capital punishment had already been abolished crime had decreased after abolition.[38] Despite Russell's opposition Ewart's amendment secured 72 votes against 73.

Some voices raised in the debate called for complete abolition, including for murder. True to the caution expressed in his letter to the commissioners, however, Russell warned the House to move slowly to prevent a revulsion of public feeling against abolition. In reply, radical members urged that public opinion had supported Parliament in all the earlier changes towards greater leniency in criminal justice.

Russell's Bills became law with great speed and soon the death penalty was inflicted only in cases of murder and treason. The work of the commissioners had proved to be of considerable help to the government in securing the abolition of capital punishment to the great extent that it was achieved. It was a fitting climax to the work of reform started by Romilly. Nevertheless, the strong support in the House of Commons for Ewart's amendment revealed the desire of the newly enfranchised middle class for an even more substantial reduction in the use of capital punishment as part of its general endeavour to reduce crime and extend the work ethic in a fast expanding industrial economy. It was an important aspect of the general movement for reform of the criminal justice system—itself an integral element in the powerful changes taking place in British society which had produced the *Wealth of Nations,* Utilitarianism, classical liberalism and all that went with, and came from, the Great Reform Act of 1832.

ABOLITION OF DEODANDS

Deodands existed in Anglo-Saxon times, if not earlier. When men were engaged in cutting down trees and one fell upon a man and killed him, the tree was considered to be guilty and was given to the dead man's kin. Originally, it meant 'to be given to God'—from *Deo Dandum.* More significantly, if a moving object, such as a horse or a cart caused death it too was regarded as guilty of the killing and was forfeit to the king even if the true cause of death was the negligence of an owner who had taken too much drink. The custom was that the king's almoner would distribute the value of the deodand for charitable purposes, including compensating the family of the victim. However, it was not seen primarily as a form of restitution, for which it was clearly inadequate, but, according to Pollock and Maitland, 'as an object upon

---

37. *Hansard.* 3rd series. [37] col. 709.
38. *Ibid.* cols. 908, 911.

which vengeance must be wreaked before the dead man will lie in peace'.[39]

Deodands changed during succeeding centuries and only the offending wheel of a cart and not the vehicle was held responsible. On this basis they survived, although without being much used, until the nineteenth century when the Criminal Law Commissioners described them as, 'one of the last relics of very severe and repressive laws which were still occasionally imposed on persons not at fault and in an arbitrary and capricious manner' By this time, according to the research of Harry Smith, these 'hallowed mysteries enjoyed a revival in the nineteenth century' as a means of providing compensation for accidents caused by factory machines and death-dealing railway engines.[40] No longer was the offending wheel of a vehicle alone responsible for a person's death but an entire railway carriage or a coach and horses. This change appears to have occurred to enable the payment of more substantial compensation by the new capitalists to the widow of other relatives of a deceased through the coroner investigating the death.

In fact, the Industrial Revolution had given a fresh meaning to deodands since, following the harsh ruling in the case of *Baker v. Bolton* in 1808, there was no right of action for economic loss or solatium on the death of a breadwinner. The only hope of compensation was the deodand, although juries commonly awarded only small sums. This situation changed when Dr Thomas Wakley,[41] a coroner, campaigned to extend the value of deodands. Partly as a consequence of his efforts their values rose rapidly and in 1840 sums of £500 and £600 had been given. Then, in 1841, in a case against the newly opened London and Birmingham Railway Company a sum of £2,000 was awarded as a deodand. This case proved to be the turning point, however, as in the same year the Queen's Bench held in the *Sonning Railway Carriage case* that deodands could be awarded only in respect of wilfully committed crimes.

This led, in turn, to the compromise of 1846 when Lord Campbell's Fatal Accidents Act was passed, ostensibly to help the widows of men killed in accidents through the act or default of another. In fact, on 7 April 1846 Campbell had introduced his Fatal Accidents Bill in the House of Lords at the same time as a Bill for the Abolition of Deodands. The two Bills travelled together throughout their passage through Parliament. Clearly the first was intended to ensure the enactment of the second. Nevertheless, Campbell complained, on the Lords' second reading of the Fatal Accidents Bill, that he had heard that 80 members of the Commons could

39. Pollock & Maitland. (1968 edn.) *The History of English Law Before the Time of Edward I.* Cambridge, Cambridge University Press. vol. ii. p. 474.
40. Harry Smith. (1967) 'From Deodand to Dependency'. *The American Journal of Legal History.* North Carolina University Press. vol. 11. p. 389.
41. For more about Wakley see J. Hostettler. (1993) *Thomas Wakley: An Improbable Radical.* Chichester, Barry Rose Law Publishers Ltd.

be mustered by one railway company alone to vote against the Bill.[42] Presumably they wanted no compensation to be payable at all but that would not have been the result if deodands remained. On the other hand, they may have been mere figments of Campbell's imagination as his colleagues told him not to be so paranoid and the most severe criticism he actually received was from Wakley, who was also MP for Finsbury, in the Commons debate when he claimed that the Bill was crude and carelessly drawn. It was his opinion, he said ironically, that it must have been drawn by 'some legal gentleman who was practising as an amateur'.[43]

To Lord Denman, on the Lords' third reading, deodands were a remnant of a barbarous and absurd law, but as they were the only security against death caused by reckless conduct their abolition was a strong argument in favour of the other Bill.[44] After its enactment, however, the Fatal Accidents Act provided quite inadequate compensation in most cases and meant that, after the abolition of deodands, the relatives of victims of railway accidents were left with few rights at all against the railway companies who could often rely upon the defences of common employment and contributory negligence which could not be raised in answer to deodands. It seems curious that Campbell thought the companies were hostile to an Act that proved so advantageous to them.

THE PRISONERS' COUNSEL ACT 1836[45]

As just indicated, the nineteenth century saw a whole raft of reforms of the criminal justice system and this statute was one of the most significant. It may be useful to restate briefly the position of defence counsel before the passing of the 1836 statute. At Common Law a prisoner charged with treason or felony could not have counsel appear for him. That was remedied for treason by the Treason Trials Act of 1696[46] which permitted counsel to appear for the defence in treason trials. This statute was passed by the newly empowered Whigs who had suffered persecution and, in some cases death, at the hands of the judges of the late Stuarts at the end of the seventeenth century. No similar provision was made for prisoners in felony trials, however. On the other hand, prosecutors were paid by the state what became known as 'blood money' to secure the conviction of criminals but this led to widespread perjury and often the trial of innocent people. As a consequence the judges slowly

42. *Hansard.* Third series. (24 April 1846) [85] col. 967. This bears a curious similarity to Walter Bagehot's claim that 'There were said to be two hundred `members for the railways' in the present Parliament,' which he likened to a formidable sinister interest. (1905) *The English Constitution.* London, Kegan Paul, Trench & Co. p. 108.
43. *Hansard.* (22 July 1846) [87] col. 1372.
44. *Ibid.* (7 May 1846) [86] col. 174.
45. 6 & 7 Will. 4. c. 114.
46. 7 & 8 Will. 3. c. 3.

moved towards allowing counsel to appear for defendants to cross-examine prosecution witnesses but not to address the jury. This led during the eighteenth century to aggressive cross-examination, particularly at the Old Bailey, by astute barristers like Sir William Garrow who were also largely responsible for the introduction of restrictive rules of criminal evidence to help defendants. In this process adversary trial became meaningful and counsel sometimes managed to speak to the jury during cross-examination. Nonetheless, the situation for prisoners remained unsatisfactory and from time to time efforts were made to secure the right for defence counsel to address the jury.[47]

One of the problems was that the judiciary and sections of the Bar were hostile to the idea. According to Alyson N. May many members of the Bar had mixed feelings about the Old Bailey which in the early nineteenth century they, 'regarded as a forum for dishonest hacks', with even its outstanding advocates being regarded with a degree of suspicion.[48] However, from 1821 to 1834 liberal and radical MPs introduced a number of Bills in the House of Commons to give prisoners the right to have counsel address the jury, although they all suffered defeat. Then in 1836, William Ewart, the radical barrister MP for Liverpool, introduced a Bill which was passed in the Commons with a large majority. Nevertheless, it still faced the hostility of the lawyers and landed interests in the House of Lords.

At this point, Lord John Russell, as he also did with the death penalty, appealed to the Criminal Law Commissioners. Clearly he believed the right to counsel was inalienable and of great importance. Again the commissioners took evidence from selected witnesses and although there was some opposition, in their conclusion they submitted that:

- as a general position, the right of an accused to be heard prior to condemnation was founded upon principles of reason, humanity and justice recognised by the law of England;
- it was essential to this right that it should, at the option of the accused, be exercised through counsel;
- no reasonable distinction as to the exercise of the right could be made between felonies and other classes of crime [where the right already existed];
- the existing practice was in many respects detrimental to the interests of justice in regard to the conviction of the guilty, as well as the protection of the innocent;
- considerable inconvenience might follow a change, but the arguments urged

---

47. See J. Hostettler. (2006) *Fighting for Justice: The History and Origins of Adversary Trial.* Winchester, Waterside Press.
48. A. N. May (2003) *The Bar and the Old Bailey: 1750-1850.* Chapel Hill. The University of North Carolina Press. p. 133.

in favour of the anomaly, were insufficient to warrant its continuance;

- prisoner's counsel was in all cases to be entitled to the concluding address; and
- this was also to be extended to trials for misdemeanours.[49]

On 23 June 1836 Lord Lyndhurst, a commanding figure in the House of Lords, accepted the difficult task of winning over its members on their second reading of Ewart's Bill.[50] He repeated many of the arguments supporting the Bill contained in the report of the commissioners, which he described as 'most elaborate and learned', and cast the existing law as, 'remnants of a barbarous code of laws relating to felons.' His long and impressive speech was undoubtedly effective and for the first time a Bill on this question received a second reading in the House of Lords and was quickly enacted, although the Lords insisted on deleting from the Bill the clause which gave defence counsel the final right of reply. However, adversary trial was finally given parliamentary approval.

The concluding legislative step for adversariality was to come with the Criminal Evidence Act 1898[51] which finally made the accused competent to give sworn testimony, although he could not be compelled to go into the witness box. Since this Act came into force it is unusual for defendants to decline to give evidence even though they face the hazard of convicting themselves out of their own mouths. It is certainly fraught with the danger of what conclusions the jury might draw if they do so decline.

WHIPPING

Corporal punishment continued to be acceptable in English public life throughout the nineteenth century. It is true that whipping was withdrawn from public gaze as a deterrent in 1817 but it continued to flourish, particularly in prisons, the armed forces and for juveniles. Most prisons possessed a 'cat-o'-nine-tails' for use on erring convicts who were strapped to a large triangle with feet and arms asunder, as I myself witnessed in a British gaol in Aden in 1962. Such floggings were agonisingly painful and a sickening and demeaning spectacle for those present.

For violently resisting a constable, a 'rogue and vagabond' could be sent to prison and undergo whipping. This, said Peel in a sad moment, was a 'salutary terror, which checked the growth of such offences.'[52] Juveniles could be whipped instead of, or in addition to, going to prison and, indeed, large numbers were. By the Whipping

---

49. PP (1836). *Op. cit.* vol. xxxvi.
50. *Hansard.* 3rd series. [34] col. 760.
51. 62 Vict. c. 36.
52. *Hansard.* (3 June 1824) [11] col. 1085.

of Offenders Act 1862,[53] however, the number of strokes of the birch was restricted to 12 for juveniles and no young person was to be whipped more than once for the same offence. Nevertheless, in courts of summary jurisdiction the numbers ordered to be whipped rose from an average of 590 in the years 1858-60 to 2,900 in 1893 and nearly 3,400 in 1900.[54] It was not until the Criminal Justice Act of 1948[55] that Parliament finally declared that the whipping of young children (and adults) was forbidden.

Floggings in the army and navy were also a regular occurrence with up to 200 lashes with the cat. On 15 June 1846 Frederick John White, a private of the Seventh Hussars, received a severe and cruel flogging of 150 lashes at the Cavalry Barracks on Hounslow Heath after an enforced 17 hours fast. Several soldiers witnessed the flogging and fainted on the spot. White died from his wounds on 11 July. Without examining his back, three army doctors declared that his death had nothing to do with the flogging. The coroner for the district, Dr Thomas Wakley, heard of the death, attended the scene and summoned an inquest jury. He also called in a specialist, Erasmus Wilson of the Middlesex Hospital who, after examining the lacerated body, had no difficulty in convincing the jury that the death was caused by the flogging. The jury had also seen the body and in giving their verdict expressed their 'horror and disgust' at the law which permitted the 'revolting punishment of flogging to be inflicted on British soldiers.' As a consequence of public concern the case was debated in the House of Commons and flogging in the army largely fell into disuse until it was finally abolished by the Army Act of 1881.[56]

EXPANSION OF THE JURISDICTION OF MAGISTRATES

Traditionally, an accused who pleaded not guilty to an indictable offence was tried either at Quarter Sessions or Assizes before a judge and jury. Then in 1827, Peel's Larceny Act[57] recast the law of larceny and allied crimes and gave summary jurisdiction over some minor offences to magistrates sitting without a jury.[58] In such cases the accused had no choice in the matter but if the charge were at all grave he had jury trial by right. The first inroad into this system came, as we have seen, with the report made in regard to young offenders by the 1836 the Criminal Law Commissioners. The government refused to implement the report with the Home Secretary,

---

53. 25 & 26 Vict, c. 18.
54. Sir L. Radzinowicz. (1986) *A History of English Criminal Law and its Administration from 1750. The Emergence of Penal Policy.* vol. v. London, Stevens & Sons. p. 719.
55. 12 Geo. 6. c. 58.
56. John Hostettler. *Thomas Wakley: An Improbable Radical. Op. cit.* pp. 116-120.
57. 7 & 8 Geo. 4, c. 29.
58. R. M. Jackson. (1937) 'The Incidence of Jury Trial During the Past Century.' 1 *Modern Law Review.* London, Stevens and Sons. pp. 132-3.

Lord John Russell, saying that 'it would violate the principle of trial by jury,'[59] as indeed it would have done. However, the commissioners' suggestion did come to fruition in 1847 with the Juvenile Offenders Act mentioned earlier.

Then, in 1848 the Summary Jurisdiction Act[60] (commonly known as Jervis's Act after the Attorney-General, Sir John Jervis) was enacted. It both clarified and enlarged the powers and duties of magistrates and granted them a new power to issue a summons or warrant for every indictable offence committed within their area, or elsewhere if the suspect had entered the area of their jurisdiction.

An even more significant change for adults then occurred a few years later with the enactment of the Criminal Justice Act of 1855.[61] This paved the way for a huge expansion of the public judicial work of justices during the nineteenth and twentieth centuries which eventually was to result in their disposal of at least 95 per cent of all prosecutions in England and Wales[62] and a severe weakening of trial by jury. What the Act did was to enable magistrates to deal with simple larceny, or attempted larceny, where there was a theft of money or goods not over ten shillings in value, if the justices agreed and the accused consented. Previously, the cut-off point had been 12 pence. Many defendants chose summary trial because of its lower penalties than in the higher courts and the police were happy to avoid the uncertainties of jury trial.

This change marked a turning point in the history of the criminal justice system. Prior to the Act, 'the distinguishing feature of the criminal process had been trial by jury; henceforth, there was to be a steadily increasing erosion of that 'palladium' of the liberties of the subject.'[63] Indeed, the immediate effect of the Act was a sharp reduction in the number of jury trials upon indictment.[64] In 1854 the number of such trials was 29,359, whilst for 1856 the figure was 19,437. Comparing the average of the five years following, the decrease amounted to 34.9 per cent.[65] No doubt, the government was suitably pleased with the financial savings involved.

It is interesting that such a fundamental change in criminal justice was treated with indifference by most members of Parliament. The Bill upon which the Act was based was introduced in the House of Lords by Lord Chancellor Cranworth in 1854.[66] Lord St. Leonards rose to say that he did not trust magistrates in Quarter Sessions and he did not see why he should do so in Petty Sessions. Furthermore,

---

59. *Hansard.* (April 1837) [37] 3rd series, col. 926.
60. 11 & 12 Vict. c. 43.
61. 18 & 19. Vict. c. 126.
62. Sir Thomas Skyrme. (1991) *The History of the Justices of the Peace.* Chichester, Barry Rose Publishers. vol. ii. p. 177.
63. A. H. Manchester. (1980) *A Modern Legal History of England and Wales 1750-1950.* London, Butterworth & Co. Ltd., p. 161.
64. *Ibid.* p. 94.
65. R. M. Jackson. 'Incidence of Jury Trial. Op. cit. p. 136.
66. *Hansard.* [136] col. 1871.

as someone could suffer two years in prison for committing a trivial offence he was entitled to a jury. Having thus unburdened himself St. Leonards went on to say that he would not oppose the Bill. Only one other peer spoke to the Bill and in a short statement supported it.

On 26 March 1855 the Bill received its second reading in the House of Commons where it was introduced by Sir George Grey who outlined its provisions.[67] Here, Seymour Fitzgerald, the member for Horsham, expressed 'great doubts as to the principle of the Bill, which would transfer the trial of one half' of cases before the judge and jury at Assizes or Quarter Sessions to magistrates in Petty Sessions. With some prescience he asked that once the policy was in force what was to prevent it being taken further? We must not, he concluded, 'infringe on the great safeguard of our liberties—trial by jury.' Robert Palmer, member for Berkshire, thought the Bill should cover only trivial offences such as 'stealing a couple of turnips.' Only two other members spoke in the debate and expressed a view repeated by governments today that the Bill should be supported because of the heavy financial costs of trial by jury.

When the Bill reached its third reading,[68] an alert T. Chambers, member for Hertford, said that although the Bill dealt with a great constitutional question it had reached the third reading without any discussion of its principle. It would abolish the 'great constitutional tribunal for trying criminals' and set up an entirely new tribunal in its place. No one could say why, and the Bill gave no answer for it had no preamble. He denied that there was any considerable degree of delay and expense with trials and claimed that to the extent that there were, for the offences covered, people should be allowed bail. The attorney-general, Sir A. E. Cockburn,[69] endorsed the Bill that he believed would be of 'great benefit to criminals, magistrates and the country.' Three other members agreed with him and the Bill received the royal assent on 14 August 1855. Thus was this great constitutional change introduced by Parliament, with only a handful of members bothering to discuss it.

In line with Seymour Fitzgerald's foreboding, this policy of replacing juries with magistrates was extended by the Summary Jurisdiction Act 1879, although in this case with more justification in that it was dealing with children. If the justices saw fit and the accused, or his or her parents or guardian, consented, summary trial was considered appropriate for a child under 12 for any offence other than homicide. There was summary trial also for offenders between 12 and 16 years of age for a wide variety of offences, and for adults charged with larceny to a value not exceeding 40 shillings. Once again there was a decline in the number of jury trials. Taking the annual average for five years preceding and following the statute, the number of

---

67. *Ibid.* [137] col. 1167.
68. *Ibid.* [139] col, 1866. (6 August 1855)
69. *Ibid.* col. 1879.

indictable offences tried summarily increased by 8,764 a year, or 23.3 per cent.[70]

Thus did the most significant assault on criminal trial by jury in English history to that time commence in the nineteenth century, and it should be borne in mind that,

> when a defendant exercises his election between summary trial and trial on indictment the choice he has to make will be influenced by more than a preference for a mode of trial. Committal for trial involves waiting (perhaps in prison) and the possibility of a longer sentence if convicted. The scales are weighed in favour of summary trial.[71]

The change has been justified on the ground that the country having by that time been transformed into an industrialised and somewhat more democratic society; it was believed that with new kinds of disputes there was a need for simpler and speedier processes to deal with the growing volume of work.[72] And behind the attack lay the perceived view that summoning juries caused inconveniences and delays, was costly, impeded the desire to keep court timetables flexible and cut down the length of trials.[73] Nevertheless, this clearly involved a considerable diminution of the basic human right of prisoners on indictment to trial by jury.

MORE REFORMS

The criminal law reforms mentioned above, together with a number of others, justify its description as a century of law reform. The century saw the changes in imprisonment described earlier and the ending of transportation to Australia. Among other reforms was a statute of 1837[74] which discontinued the use of the pillory. Lord Campbell's Libel Act 1843[75] reversed the rule used in the case of John Almon[76] that a printer was liable for the publication of a seditious libel by his servant without his knowledge. The fact that the matter published was true and for the public benefit became a defence and an apology admissible in evidence in mitigation of damages. Lord Denman's Act of 1846[77] gave increased power to judges to vary punishments in some cases to prevent injustices. A number of penalties and disabilities for beliefs of religion and conscience were removed and Jervis's Acts of 1848,[78] which in effect were a code of one branch of the criminal law, and dealt with procedure before justices

---

70. R. M. Jackson. 'Incidence of Jury Trial.' Op. cit. p. 136.
71. *Ibid.* p. 138.
72. W. R. Cornish. (1968) *The Jury.* London, Allen Lane.
73. *Ibid.*
74. 7 Will. 4 and 1 Vict. c. 23.
75. 6 & 7 Vict. c.96, s. 7.
76. Ante. p 135.
77. 9 & 10 Vict. c. 24.
78. 11 & 12 Vict. c. 43.

of the peace, defined the cases in which justices could issue a warrant of arrest and covered a whole number of other issues relating to their powers. An Act of 1870[79] abolished forfeiture for high treason and felony and introduced compensation for victims of fraud. Statutes also removed the incompetency of witnesses,[80] secured a lengthier interval between sentence and the execution of a convicted murderer,[81] and created a treason/felony offence that partially mitigated the treason laws.[82]

---

79. 33 & 34 Vict. c. 23.
80. (1843) 6,7 Vict. c. 85.
81. (1836) 6,7 Will. 4. c.30.
82. (1848) 11,12 Vict. c. 12.

CHAPTER 13

Criminal Incapacity

LIABILITY

With the exception of cases of strict liability, all allegations of crime are subject to specific defences such as self-defence. Of course, proving them is by no means always easy, indeed they frequently raise serious problems. Yet even more complex are the general defences based upon incapacity. If permitted at all, these apply to all cases including those of strict responsibility and, if successful, they secure exemption from punishment.

From a utilitarian point of view punishing offenders who have no ability to know they are doing wrong is unjust, since it can have no deterrent effect either on the actor him or herself or those similarly placed. Nonetheless, English law has always been slow to accept such defences as insanity, intoxication, compulsion and necessity as sufficient to secure acquittal on a charge of committing a crime. No doubt the possibility of fabrication is an important element contributing to this reluctance, and it has often been considered that incapacity should merely go to the mitigation of punishment.

Sir Matthew Hale devoted eight chapters of his *History of the Pleas of the Crown* to dealing with incapacity as a possible defence in capital cases although, in the context of legal theory in his time, in a rather rudimentary fashion.[1] It may prove interesting to consider some of these topics here.

CHILDREN

In Hale's day a young person over the age of 14 was considered capable of discerning between good and evil and was subject to capital punishment in the same way as an adult. Between the ages of seven and 14 very strong evidence of that ability was required before the jury could convict, but Hale mentioned cases where infants of eight, ten and 13 had been executed. Infants under seven could not be tried at all as there was a legal presumption that they were incapable of distinguishing between good and evil.

---

1. Sir Matthew Hale. (1736) *The History of the Pleas of the Crown.* London, E. & R. Nutt and R. Gosling. vol. 1. chaps. 2-9.

Today, no child under the age of ten years can be found guilty of an offence. The presumption, known as *doli incapax*, that he or she is not capable of committing a crime is irrebuttable. But, at Common Law there was a rebuttable presumption that a young person aged ten but not yet 14 could not be convicted of an offence unless the prosecution could prove that he or she understood the act or omission to be wrong. This rule was abolished by section 34 of the Crime and Disorder Act 1998.[2] As a consequence children between ten and 14 are now considered to be responsible for their actions.

INTOXICATION

In Coke's time drunkenness could never be a defence unless induced by unskilled medical treatment or the action of a man's enemies. This was summed up in the maxim, 'He that kyllyth a man dronk, sobur schal be hangyd.' Hale, however, believed that, 'the vice doth deprive men of the use of reason' and wanted to see the rule modified for an habitual drunkard who caused himself a permanently diseased intellect. He discussed the difficulties of proving the dementia of drunkenness and largely relied upon the jury to resolve the problems arising.[3]

By the nineteenth century the rigidity of the old rule had been gradually relaxed by judicial decisions. For his part, Bentham believed that 'perfect intoxication', like insanity, should exempt an offender from punishment on the utilitarian but thin ground that the penalty could not deter the offender from repeating his offence. He thought the existing law was hard and unthinking, but he saw the dangers of what he was advocating and diluted it by adding that anyone who knew by experience that wine rendered him dangerous deserved no indulgence for those excesses into which it might lead him.[4]

In 1819, in the case of *R. v. Grindley*[5] temporary insanity was held to excuse murder where the killing was on a 'sudden heat and impulse' caused by drunkenness. This doctrine was overruled, however, by *R. v. Carroll*[6] in 1835, when it was pleaded as a defence by a soldier who, when drunk, stabbed a man with his bayonet. Park J., in his judgment, declared of the doctrine that, 'there would be no safety for human life if it were to be considered as law.' His view was modified in three subsequent cases and in *R. v. Cruse* in 1838, where a drunken man knocked a child's head against a beam and killed her, it was left to the jury to decide whether the

---

2. 1998. c. 37.
3. Sir Matthew Hale. *The History of the Pleas of the Crown. Op. cit.* vol. i. pp. 32-3.
4. Jeremy Bentham. (1970 edn) *An Introduction to the Principles of Morals and Legislation.* (ed. J. H. Burns & H.L.A. Hart. London, Methuen & Co. Ltd. p.161.
5. W. O. Russell on Crimes. (2nd edn) (1826-28) London, p. 8.
6. 7 C. & P. p. 145.

prisoner had a murderous intent at the time of the attack. At the end of the trial he was acquitted of murder.

For reasons of policy voluntary intoxication is not a defence since it is believed that a person taking an excess of alcohol is acting recklessly in ignoring the possible consequences with violent behaviour and uncontrollable actions. In this sense it satisfies the requirement for the *mens rea* of a crime of basic intent (involving recklessness) although it can negate specific intent. In *Majewski,* [7] the accused was unaware of what he was doing because of alcohol and drugs. The House of Lords held that evidence of voluntary intoxication cannot negative *mens rea* in a crime of basic intent. Although the accused was not aware of what he was doing he could not be said to be acting involuntarily in the ordinary sense of the word and, therefore, he had the necessary basic intent.

Generally speaking, drunkenness remains no excuse for crime, except where it is involuntary or where it results in permanent or temporary insanity.[8] But it is of importance if it can be proved to negate a mental element essential to the charge. This particularly applies to crimes such as murder and theft where it may negate specific intent, recklessness or specific knowledge. The evidential burden is then on the prosecution to establish, where the offence requires such intent, that despite the evidence of intoxication, the accused had the necessary specific intent. However, recent cases show that the problems are still far from being resolved. It would appear, for instance, that provided a person had the requisite *mens rea*, the fact that involuntary intoxication led him to commit an offence which he would not have committed if sober, does not give rise to a defence,[9] although it may mitigate his punishment. The most recent case is *Attorney-General for Jersey v. Holley.*[10] Here the defendant killed his partner whilst he was intoxicated and after she had taunted him by telling him she had had sex with another man. It was said in his defence of provocation that his consumption of alcohol was involuntary as a result of chronic alcoholism and that this disease, and not mere drunkenness, had provoked him into doing what a reasonable man would do in the circumstances.

The Court of Appeal in Jersey agreed and the Attorney-General for Jersey appealed to the Privy Council which allowed his appeal. The Privy Council held that chronic alcoholism was not a matter to be taken into account. The Homicide Act 1957 set a purely objective standard by which the defendant's conduct should be evaluated and the standard of self-control—i.e. 'the ordinary powers of self-control'—was invariable. The statute did not leave each jury free to set whatever standard they considered appropriate.

---

7. *DPP. v. Majewski.* (1977) AC. p. 443.
8. Cf. *R. v. Kingston* (1993) and the reliance of the court of appeal on Hale's, 'classic statement of principle' on drunkenness as a defence.
9. *R. v. Davies.* (1983) Crim. LR p. 741.
10. [2005] UKPC 23 PC.

MADNESS

Insanity as a defence excuses the accused from trial as a matter of public policy. If it were otherwise, confidence in the penal system would be undermined. Nevertheless, by the law of England, wrote Hale, no man shall avoid his own act by pleading madness.[11] He was the first jurist, however, to distinguish between total and partial insanity. This, he believed, would enable a judge and jury to draw a line between an inhuman approach to the defects of human nature and too great an indulgence to serious crimes. According to professor Nigel Walker, Hale's exposition was 'to exercise the minds of lawyers, psychiatrists and Royal Commissions for the next three centuries.'[12]

Defences of insanity were sometimes successful in the seventeenth century. But the two succeeding centuries saw a change with a series of convictions in important trials after a number of murders, and attempts on the lives of royalty, prime ministers and noblemen. Some of these were considered by the judges when they attempted to set out a clear position following the *M'Naghten case* in March 1843.

The M'Naghten Rules[13]
In 1843 Daniel M'Naghten claimed that 'the Tories' were trying to kill him and in response he fatally shot Sir Robert Peel's private secretary in mistake for Peel himself. M'Naghten's defence was that partial insanity was within the law of insanity and that he was partially insane—it being impossible on the evidence to prove full insanity.

His counsel, Alexander Cockburn Q.C. (later lord chief justice) argued that M'Naghten's insanity consisted of a delusion directed to one or more persons which took away all power of self control. His brilliant conduct of the defence secured from the jury an acquittal which shocked the public. One M.P. even sought leave to introduce a Bill to abolish completely any plea of insanity in cases of murder or attempted murder. Parliament refused to be panicked, however, and the House of Lords proceeded to debate the issue in what Brougham called the 'present emergency.'

Lord Chancellor Lyndhurst and others asserted that despite the *M'Naghten* verdict there was no serious defect in the law on insanity. In a letter to Peel,[14] Lyndhurst wrote that the law of monomania had been correctly laid down in the case of Thomas Bowler who had been tried at the Old Bailey on 1 July 1812 for firing a loaded

---

11. Sir Matthew Hale. *The History of the Pleas of the Crown. Op. cit.*. vol. i. p. 29.
12. Nigel Walker. (1968) *Crime and Insanity in England.* Edinburgh, Edinburgh University Press.
13. *M'Naghten's Case.* (1843) H.L. 10 Clark &Finnelly. 200.
14. BM. *Add. Mss.* 40442. (1841–49) Peel Correspondence with Lyndhurst. fol. 138.

blunderbuss at a William Burrows and wounding him.[15] This was a curious case, however, since Bowler was found guilty and sentenced to death in the face of the testimony of witnesses that he was insane and a Commissioners' Report, admitted in court, that confirmed Bowler was insane at the time of the offence. Moreover, the judge had told the jury that it was for them to determine whether the prisoner, when he committed the offence, was under the influence of any illusion regarding the victim which made him at that moment insensible to the nature of the act he was about to commit. If he were, he would not be legally responsible for his conduct.

Lord Mansfield had said substantially the same thing in the case of John Bellingham who was sentenced to death for fatally shooting the prime minister, Spencer Perceval, in the lobby of the House of Commons on 11 May 1812.[16] Unfortunately the distinguished judge cried over the death during his summing up to the jury and told them that Bellingham was clearly sane at the time of the killing, neither of which was of any help to the accused or to justice. According to Stephen, Bellingham was arrested, committed, tried and hanged all in little more than a week in order to prevent him setting up the defence of madness.[17] In fact, the Old Bailey Sessions Report shows that the murder was committed on 11 May and the trial and conviction took place on 13 May which makes it perhaps the swiftest trial in the modern legal history of this country. Samuel Romilly, who considered Bellingham mad, but a danger to mankind who should not be exempt from punishment, nevertheless thought the defence application to put back the trial to give him time to bring witnesses from Liverpool was, 'very reasonable.'[18] But, after the example of Bowler, it may not have helped.

To return to the House of Lords' debate on the *M'Naghten case*, most of their lordships agreed with the Lord Chancellor that the existing law was satisfactory but, in order to placate public opinion, they agreed to summon the judges to give their opinion of the law. The House took the unusual step of submitting a number of questions to the judges whose replies, known to subsequent generations as the M'Naghten Rules, became binding law.

From that time onwards every person was presumed to be sane and responsible for their crimes until the contrary was proved. It was a defence to show that, at the time of committing the crime, the accused was labouring under a defect of reason due to disease of the mind based on either not knowing the nature and quality of the act (e.g. automatism or mistake of fact) or, if these were known, not knowing that they were wrong. This was not to mean, as before, morally wrong, but wrong according to the law of the land. However it was not until 1952, in the case of

15. OBP Online. (www.oldbaileyonline,org) 1 July 1812. Trial of Thomas Bowler. Ref: t18120701-11.
16. OBP Online. (www.oldbaileyonline.org) 13 May 1812. Trial of John Bellingham. Ref: t18120513-5.
17. Sir James Fitzjames Stephen. (1859) 'Cambridge Essays'. p. 38.
18. Samuel Romilly. (1840) *Memoirs*. (Edited by his sons). London, John Murray. vol. iii. p. 36.

Windle,[19] that the Court of Criminal Appeal finally confirmed this to be the test for the jury. In this case, after killing his wife in what he believed was a mercy killing, a man telephoned the police and said, 'I suppose I'll hang for this' on which it was held he knew what he had done was wrong in law.

Whether a particular condition amounts to a disease of the mind is, therefore, a legal and not a medical question and is decided within the ordinary rules of interpretation. It need not be a disease of the brain and covers internal but not external disorders which result in violence and are likely to recur. For example, in one case a diabetic committed an assault while in a state of hypoglycaemia caused by insulin, alcohol and failure to eat. These were held to be external factors and did not constitute a disease of the mind.[20] On the other hand, in another case, where a hardening of the arteries caused loss of control during which the accused attacked his wife with a hammer, it was held that this was an internal condition and thus a disease of the mind.[21]

If insanity were limited to a delusion, an accused would be free of punishment only if the delusion would have justified his act in law if it were true. On this basis M'Naghten would have been convicted and since that time judges have proceeded on the assumption that a deluded man or woman can be presumed to be normal in all other respects, unless there is evidence to the contrary. And whereas today many psychiatrists and clinical psychologists view most mental disorders in terms of differences of degree, the criminal law still expects diagnoses to fit a verdict of guilty or not guilty. However, by section 2 of the Homicide Act 1957, although irresistible impulse and mental disorder falling short of insanity are generally no defence on a charge of murder, a verdict of manslaughter must be returned if the accused is found to be suffering from diminished responsibility. This allows the judge a discretion as to punishment which is not available in cases of murder.

An insane person acting in a state of automatism would not know the nature and quality of his act.[22] This would also apply where a person cut the head off a sleeping man because, 'it would be great fun to see him looking for it when he woke up.'[23] It should be noted that insanity is not generally a defence to offences of strict liability.[24]

A jury may not return a verdict of 'not guilty by reason of insanity' except on the evidence of two or more registered medical practitioners of whom at least one has special experience in the field of mental disorder. However, they may disagree with the experts if there are facts or surrounding circumstances which, in the opinion of

---

19. *R. v. Windle.* (1952) 2 All ER. p. 1.
20. *R. v. Quick and Paddison.* (1973) 3 All ER , p. 397.
21. *R. v. Kemp.* (1957) 1 QB, p. 399.,
22. *R. v. Sullivan.* (1983) 2 All ER. P. 673.
23. Sir J. F. Stephen. (1883) *A History of the Criminal Law of England.* London, Macmillan. vol. ii. p. 166.
24. *DPP. v. Harper* (1997).

the court, justify them in coming that that conclusion.[25]

The M'Naghten Rules are often criticised for making no allowance for 'irresistible impulse'. This would permit a person to raise a defence of showing that, although he was aware of the nature and quality of his act and knew it to be wrong, he found, owing to insanity, that it was impossible to prevent himself committing the crime. Such a defence is allowed in a number of Commonwealth and United States jurisdictions and the defence of diminished responsibility admits it on a charge of murder. In 1975 the Butler Committee on Mentally Abnormal Offenders[26] found the Rules unsatisfactory and proposed a recasting of the law on the legal responsibility of mentally abnormal offenders. Its position was largely endorsed by a Report to the Law Commission ten years later[27] but nothing has been done to implement it by legislation.

NECESSITY

In theory this defence arises when a defendant is obliged by circumstances to transgress the criminal law. It involves an assertion that certain conduct promotes a higher value than a literal compliance with the law. An example might be destroying a house to prevent a fire from spreading. It has commonly been believed, however, that such a defence does not exist in English criminal law. For instance, in 1975 Lord Denning stated *obiter* that the driver of a fire engine was compelled to stop at a red traffic light even if he saw 200 yards down the road a blazing house with a man at an upstairs window in extreme peril of losing his life.[28]

Statutory exceptions now cover this position but, nonetheless, the concept has a long history. Bracton declared that what was not otherwise lawful was made so by necessity.[29] As long ago as 1499 Rede J. said that jurors might lawfully depart from the court without leave of the judge if an affray broke out and they were in peril of death, or if the courtroom fell down.[30] Nevertheless, Hale thought that killing an innocent person in peacetime could never be justified.[31] On the other hand, a good deal later, in 1815, the judges held that although it was a misdemeanour to expose an infected person in public, necessity would be a defence to the charge if, for example, a sick child was carried through the streets to a doctor.[32]

---

25. Criminal Procedure (Insanity and Unfitness to Plead) Act, 1991.
26. London, HMSO. Cmnd. 6244.
27. *Codification of the Criminal Law* (1985) Law Com. No. 143.
28. *Buckoke v. GLC.* (1975) Ch. 655.
29. Cited by Coke. (1797) 2 *Institute* London, E. & R. Brooke. p. 362.
30. Y. B. T. 14 Hen. 7. 196, pl. 4.
31. Sir M. Hale. *The History of the Pleas of the Crown. Op. cit.* vol. i. p. 51.
32. *Vantandillo.* (1815) 4 M. & S. 73.

It is not surprising, therefore, that Stephen was to say that the law on the defence of necessity was vague and the judges could lay down any rule they thought expedient.[33] The law had been modified, he believed, since Hale's treatise. But then, in 1884, came the celebrated case of *R. v. Dudley and Stephens* [34] which highlighted both the difficulties and the danger of framing a general defence of necessity. In this case shipwrecked sailors killed their cabin boy for food. The jury found that if the men had not fed on the body of the boy they probably would not have survived to be picked up and rescued, and that the boy, being in a much weaker condition than the others, would have died before them. Nevertheless, the sailors were found guilty of murder and sentenced to death, although the judge did not wear the normal black cap for such sentences and the Crown reduced them to six months imprisonment.

It was long held that where duress induced a well-grounded fear of death or grievous bodily harm it should excuse a person from punishment from crimes other than treason or homicide. However, in the leading case of *Tyler and Price* in 1838[35] Lord Denman held that duress could be no defence to any illegal act. Today, on the contrary, duress can be a defence in itself since the harm sought to be avoided proceeds from another's wrongdoing, and is, therefore, unlike necessity which may arise from an infinite variety of circumstances.

In the case of *R. v. Willer* in 1986[36] the defendant had driven recklessly to escape from a crowd who appeared intent upon causing physical harm to the passengers in his car. The court of appeal ruled that the defence of necessity was permitted and this was confirmed in *R. v. Conway* in 1988[37] where the driver drove recklessly from what he thought was an assassination attempt. But necessity cannot be a defence to a charge of murder and in *R. v. Howe* in1987[38] the House of Lords affirmed *Dudley and Stephens.* Among the reasons given by their lordships, in line with the view of Hale, was that the protection of the life of an innocent person is of supreme importance and that a person should be required to sacrifice his own life rather than be permitted to decide who should live and who should die.

An interesting case was heard by the Court of Appeal who gave judgment on 15 October 2007.[39] The appellants, who acted lawfully throughout, were detained by police in a cordon at Oxford Circus for over seven hours during a demonstration on May Day 2001. In consequence they claimed under Common Law and section 7 Human Rights Act 1998 for the tort of false imprisonment contrary to Article 5 of the European Convention On Human Rights (ECHR), one of them merely being

33. Sir J. F. Stephen. *A History of the Criminal Law of England. Op. cit.* vol. ii. p. 108.
34. 14 QBD. p. 273.
35. 8 C. & P. p. 616.
36. 83 Cr App R p. 225.
37. 3 All E R p. 1025.
38. AC 417.
39. *Austin and Another v. Commissioner of Police of the Metropolis* (15 October 2007) *The Times.* 29 October 2007. p. 62.

in the area on his employers' business. The court held that, although the police did not reasonably suspect that the claimants were about to commit a *breach of the peace*, containing the crowd was necessary in order to avoid an imminent breach of the peace by others outside the cordon. It was lawful although the test of necessity could only be justified in truly extreme and exceptional circumstances. In addition, said the Master of the Rolls, Sir Anthony Clarke, the action taken had to be proportionate and reasonably necessary.

These tests, he said, derived from *O'Kelly v. Harvey*[40] and *R. (Laporte) v. Chief Constable of Gloucestershire Constabulary*[41]. Further, the Strasbourg cases on article 5 of the ECHR had drawn a distinction between a restriction of liberty of movement as opposed to a deprivation of liberty.[42] Mere restrictions on liberty were governed by article 2 of Protocol 4, not by article 5 of the Convention. The difference between the two was merely one of degree or intensity, not one of nature or substance. As to article 2 of Protocol 4, it had not been ratified by the United Kingdom and its provisions were not part of the law of England and Wales.

On the whole, in regard to defences of incapacity, legislation is not very prolific and the complexities of this aspect of the law are still left to the courts to resolve, if they can. In connection with necessity it is worthy of note that the Law Commission has changed its mind on a number of occasions. In 1974 it declared in favour of a general defence of necessity only to change its mind three years later when it rejected the idea and proposed that, in so far as it existed at law, it should be abolished. Then in 1985 it turned again. This time it proposed a defence of necessity called 'duress of circumstances', and in its draft Criminal Law Bill in 1993 proposed extending it to all crimes including murder.[43]

STIGMATA

It may be useful to mention here the theory, connected in the main with the Italian university professor and criminologist Cesare Lombroso (1835-1909) and those following him, that criminals are a distinct physical type who can be recognised by distinct physical traits or characteristics, known as stigmata. As a consequence, they argue that punishment should be based upon the danger the offender presents to society and not be proportionate to the gravity of the crime.[44] Lombroso was highly influential in Europe and he also advocated humane treatment of criminals and

---

40. (1883) 14 LR Ir 105.
41. (2007) 2 AC 105.
42. See *Guzzardi v. Italy* (application No. 7367/76) (1981) 3 EHRR 333 and *HM v. Switzerland* (30187/98) (2004).38 EHRR 17.
43. Law Com. (1993) No. 218, clause 26.
44. Sir Leon Radzinowicz and Roger Hood. (1986) *A History of English Criminal Law and its Administration from 1750. The Emergence of Penal Policy.* London, Stevens and Sons. vol. v. pp. 3-4.

limitations on the use of capital punishment. His theory of criminal anthropology and atavistic stigmata involved among other things:

- measuring for deviations in head size and shape to reveal an atavistic criminal;
- observing the shape and size of the ears;
- observing the facial bones, the forehead and the nature of lips, hair and teeth;
- looking for receding or short and flat chin, 'as in apes';
- consideration of hawk-like noses or shifty eyes; and
- consideration of scanty beard or baldness.

The point made was that crime was inherited and could be evaluated by such tests.[45] At first he saw the criminal as a throwback with a more primitive type of brain structure and of behaviour. But, in attempting to predict criminality in this way he created a new pseudoscience of forensic phrenology. He believed white people were superior to black people and in social progress from primitive to modern. In 1871 he said, 'Only we white people have reached the ultimate symmetry of bodily form.'[46] After years of contact with critics, Lombroso modified his views to some extent to include more social, economic and environmental data and he concluded that perhaps less that half the criminal population were born to crime. As an army doctor and director of a mental hospital in Pesaro, Italy he also came to attach a considerable importance to the effects of mental illness in causing criminality.

In regard to female criminality, Lombroso carried out the same measurements and other criteria as for men and concluded that female criminals were rare. They showed few signs of degeneration because they had 'evolved less than men due to the inactive nature of their lives.'[47] This passive nature, he believed, inhibited them from acting illegally because they lacked the intelligence and initiative to do so. Nevertheless, there were women who were atavistic occasional criminals who were harder to detect than men and who were more vicious than men. Crime, he suggested, would wither away if atavistic people were prevented from breeding.

An important student of Lombroso's was Enrico Ferri (1856-1929) who modified his work and stressed the importance of environmental influences. Unlike Lombroso, he emphasised psychological characteristics rather than physiology. These included handwriting, slang, secret symbols, moral insensibility and, 'a lack of repugnance to the idea and execution of the offence, previous to its commission, and

45. Cesare Lombroso. (1876) *L'Uomo Deliquenti. (The Delinquent Man)* Milan.
46. A. Herman. (1997) *The Idea of Decline in Western History* London, The Free Press. p. 116.
47. *Ibid.* p. 110.

the absence of remorse after committing it.'[48] He also called for crime prevention methods as opposed to punishment of criminals after their crimes had been committed. He was a socialist member of the Italian Parliament and became a supporter of Mussolini.

Lombroso had a great deal of influence and it was not until 1893 in Germany and 1913 in England that scientific evidence was produced to discredit his theory of the physical criminal type. In London, in 1913, Dr Charles Goring, who was a prison doctor, published *The English Convict: A Statistical Study*.[49] Using statistical techniques, he completely disproved the idea that a criminal type could be identified by head measurements and other physical characteristics. He did this by comparing criminals with a non-criminal control group and the physical attributes on which Lombroso relied were found to be equally common in both groups. University staff and students were no different. Curiously, Lombroso's pseudo-scientific theories continue to hold a certain sway in parts of Europe.[50]

48. E. Ferri. (1895) *Criminal Sociology*. London, Fisher Unwin.
49. Charles Goring. (1913) *The English Convict: A Statistical Study*. 2 parts. London, The Prison Commission.
50. Hall Williams. *Criminology and Criminal Justice. Op. cit.* pp. 17-18.

CHAPTER 14

A Revolution in Procedure

RULES OF CRIMINAL EVIDENCE

In general, evidence is of great importance in the criminal law but to be acceptable it has to be relevant to an issue before the court. If it is irrelevant, insufficiently relevant or is prejudicial, it will be excluded. The law of evidence is extremely complex and it is significant that it is the exceptions that make up most of it. Until recent times the four main exceptions were hearsay, opinion, character and conduct on other occasions.[1]

According to legal historian T. A. Green, 'a great watershed in the history of trial practice was the increasing recourse to counsel and the development of a true law of evidence in the late eighteenth and early nineteenth centuries.'[2] Indeed, the criminal law of evidence grew along with adversary trial and changes in trial procedure as defence lawyers grappled to secure maximum protection for their clients. With counsel appearing more frequently for the defence they constantly appealed to evidential rules many of which, in the words of Beattie, were referred from the courts to the 'judges in their post-circuit meetings at Serjeant's Inn' which helped to form 'what amounted to a law of evidence in criminal trials.'[3] He adds that, '[i]n 1700 there were few treatises on this subject; by the early nineteenth century there was a substantial literature, a market having formed among lawyers at the criminal bar.'[4]

Sir Geoffrey Gilbert, Thomas Peake, William David Evans and S.M. Phillips all extolled exclusionary and adversarial rules of evidence. Gilbert, for example, as early as 1754 wrote, 'The attestation of the witness must be as to what he knows, and not to that only which he hath heard, for a mere Hearsay is no Evidence.'[5] And Peake included in his *Compendium of the Law of Evidence* an Appendix of some leading cases on evidence law, confirming that by the opening of the nineteenth century evidential rules were an important element in such cases.[6] This growth of a concept of rules of criminal evidence is in sharp contrast to the European situation where rules of procedure were more precise and largely reliant upon confessions. The system of

1. Sir Rupert Cross. (1974) *Evidence*. London, Butterworths pp. 16-18.
2. T. A. Green. (1985) *Verdict According to Conscience. Perspectives on the English Criminal Jury Trial 1200-1800*. Chicago, University of Chicago Press. p. 267.
3. J. M. Beattie. (1991) 'Scales of Justice: Defence Counsel and the English Criminal Trial in the Eighteenth and Nineteenth Centuries.' 9(2) *Law and History Review*. Illinois, University of Illinois Press. p. 233.
4. *Ibid.*
5. G. Gilbert. (1754) *The Law of Evidence*. Dublin, Sarah Cotter. p. 107.
6. T. Peake. (1801) *A Compendium of the Law of Evidence*. London, E. & R. Brooke and J. Rider.

roman-canonical proof, 'encouraged and, indeed, often required, the torture of the accused in order to produce a confession, which was considered of particularly high evidential value'[7] but regarded with much distaste in England. In fact, the medieval law of torture is considered by Langbein to be 'the great European blunder'.[8]

However, as the distinguished American jurist, John Henry Wigmore, indicated, the purpose of the rules of criminal evidence was to determine whether a given piece of evidence should be considered, not to establish the precise probative value to be attached to it. They were needed, he said, because adversary proceedings gave rise to dangers flowing from facts being the subject of controversy between human beings moved by strong emotions and tempted to gain their cause by deceiving the court.[9]

PRESUMPTION OF INNOCENCE

The Human Rights Act 1998 provides that everyone charged with a criminal offence shall be presumed innocent until proved otherwise. Unfortunately, there is an implication with the word 'until' that the defendant is guilty and the principle would be better expressed by saying that a person is presumed innocent unless proved guilty. In general, the burden of proving the defendant to be guilty lies on the prosecution and this proof must be beyond a reasonable doubt. This has not always been the case and, as we shall see, there are exceptions today with what are called cases of absolute liability.

The presumption, or something akin to it, may have existed for some time before the eighteenth century.[10] But, if so, it by no means applied generally and Beattie records that in Surrey in 1739 where a prisoner claimed he was not a thief the judge told him, 'You must prove that.'[11] It is Beattie's impression that, 'the engagement of lawyers on behalf of some prisoners over the second two-thirds of the eighteenth century began to shift the focus of the defence in a fundamental way by casting doubt on the validity of the factual case being presented against the defendant, so that the prosecution came increasingly under the necessity of proving its assertions.'[12] He continues,

7. George Fisher. (1997) 'The Jury's Rise as Lie Detector.' New Haven, 107 *Yale Law Journal*. p. 587.
8. J. H. Langbein. (1977) *Torture and the Law of Proof: Europe and England in the Ancien Regime.* Chicago, University of Chicago Press.
9. William Twining. (1985) *Theories of Evidence: Bentham and Wigmore.* London, Weidenfeld and Nicolson. p. 157.
10. Perhaps in the seventeenth century. See B. Shapiro (1991) *'Beyond Reasonable Doubt' and 'Probable Cause': Historical Perspectives on the Anglo-American Law of Evidence.* Berkeley, University of California Press. p. 40.
11. J. M. Beattie. (1986) *Crime and Courts in England, 1660-1800.* Oxford, The Clarendon Press. p. 349.
12. *Ibid.* pp. 374-5.

The involvement of counsel brought an elaboration of the rules under which trials were conducted and tended to shift the burden of proof from the prisoner to the prosecutor—to encourage the mental shift that is embodied in Sir Richard Phillips' *Golden Rules for Jurymen* (1820) in which he exhorts jurors to be careful in their judgments, to give the benefit of the doubt to the accused, to weigh all the evidence carefully, to guard against overbearing judges, and to regard the prisoner as innocent until he has clearly been proved guilty, that onus being squarely on his accuser.[13]

Moreover, in summary proceedings, many defendants had been obliged to struggle against a statutory presumption of guilt.[14] Indeed, Bruce Smith says that cases of suspected petty theft were sent for summary trial precisely because of, 'the challenges of securing convictions in the higher courts for the felony of simple larceny.'[15]

It was not until 1791 that William Garrow was the first counsel to express the presumption clearly in an English court.[16] In the trial at the Old Bailey of George Dingler on a charge of murder, he told the judge that it should be, 'recollected by all the bystanders (for you do not require to be reminded of it) that every man is presumed to be innocent until proved guilty.'[17] However, despite Garrow's remarks, judges did not feel bound to accept the principle and it was certainly not accepted by the judiciary in murder trials. As late as 1933, in *R. v. Lawrence*[18] the Judicial Committee of the Privy Council had confirmed that once a killing was established by the prosecution the burden of proof shifted to the defence who had to prove the prisoner's innocence. This was changed in *Woolmington's case* in 1935 but not before the court of first instance and the Court of Criminal Appeal had based their decision against the prisoner on the precedent of *Lawrence*.[19]

Woolmington appealed to the House of Lords.[20] He admitted shooting his wife but claimed he had merely been showing the gun to her when it went off. After hearing all the evidence, and conferring for a few minutes, the Law Lords decided to allow the appeal and give their reasons later. After a lapse of six weeks, the lord chancellor, Viscount Sankey, gave the judgment from which certain phrases have echoed down the corridors of time. Sankey gave an extended review of the history of the law of murder and with considerable skill was able to extract that:

---

13. *Ibid.* p. 375.
14. B. P. Smith. (2005) 'The Presumption of Guilt and the English Law of Theft: 1750-1850.' 23(1) *Law and History Review.* University of Illinois Press. p. 135.
15. *Ibid.* p. 136.
16. Interestingly, the presumption appears in the French *Declaration of the Rights of Man* in the same year of 1791.
17. OBP. Online. (www.oldbaileyonline.org) 14 September 1791 Ref: t19710194-1.
18. [1933] AC. 707.
19. For details about Reginald Woolmington and extracts from the House of Lords judgments see B. Block and J. Hostettler. (2002) *Famous Cases: Nine Trials that Changed the Law.* Winchester, Waterside Press.
20. Woolmington v. D.P.P. [1935] AC. 462.

Throughout the web of the English criminal law *one golden thread is always to be seen, that it is the duty of the prosecution to prove the prisoner's guilt* subject to what I have already said as to the defence of insanity and subject also to any statutory exception. If, at the end of and on the whole case, there is a reasonable doubt, created by the evidence given by either the prosecution or the prisoner, as to whether the prisoner killed the deceased with a malicious intention, the prosecution has not made out the case and the prisoner is entitled to an acquittal. No matter what the charge or where the trial, *the principle that the prosecution must prove the guilt of the prisoner is part of the Common Law of England and no attempt to whittle it down can be entertained.* [Italics added]

No presumption of murder

It is an axiom of the criminal law that the judges do not make law but merely declare what it is and always has been. Nonetheless, 'It was *Woolmington* that effected a revolution in the criminal law … for all that Viscount Sankey pretended that he was only stating the existing position.'[21] However, it had taken a very long time for the 'golden thread' to become visible to the judges in murder trials and it was a close thing and would not have been perceived then if the case had rested with the Court of Criminal Appeal.

It was also decided by *Woolmington* that there is no presumption of murder when a defence to a charge of murder is accident or provocation. The burden of satisfying the jury still rests with the prosecution.

Statutory exception to the presumption of innocence

Sankey mentioned that there were statutory exceptions to the presumption of innocence and in this connection the Court of Appeal cases of *R. v. Lambert, R. v. Ali and R. v. Jordan* are relevant.[22] Here the appellants claimed that the statutory burden placed upon defendants to establish certain defences on balance of probabilities and not beyond reasonable doubt was contrary to their right to a fair trial under the Human Rights Act 1998. The court concluded that the presumption of innocence was not breached by the provisions of section 2(2) Homicide Act 1957 or sections 5(4) and 28 of the Misuse of Drugs Act 1971 which provided defendants who could prove certain specified facts with a defence to a charge of murder or possession of drugs.

Also in the year 2000 *Woolmington* was still being explicitly invoked. A 15-year-old boy was convicted under section 1(1) of the Indecency with Children Act 1960 for inciting a child—a girl of 13—to commit an act of gross indecency with him. This was a strict liability offence and the Divisional Court upheld the justices' ruling that mistaken belief in the complainant's age did not amount to a defence. On appeal five Law Lords, including the current and immediate last lord chancellors, ruled otherwise.[23] They stated that not only was an honest but mistaken belief that the girl was over the age of 14 a defence, the belief need not be a reasonable one.

---

21. Glanvillle Williams. (1988) 'The Logic of Exceptions'. Cambridge, *Cambridge Law Journal.* p. 47.
22. *The Times.* 5 September 2000.
23. [2000] *B (a minor) v. DPP.* 1 WLR 452.

Accordingly, for a conviction under section 1(1) of the Act it was necessary for the prosecution to prove the absence of a genuine belief on the part of the accused, which did not have to be on reasonable grounds that the victim was 14 or over. The leading authority in favour of strict liability, *R. v. Prince* of 1875[24], the court said, was unsound—'a relic from an age dead and gone.'

Strict liability itself is not dead and gone, but this case represents a leaning towards the presumption of innocence which Parliament has considerably eroded by statute. As Lord Cooke of Thorndon, an eminent New Zealand judge, declared in his Hamlyn lecture 'One Golden Thread?' in 1966, 'It does seem odd that in the home of *Woolmington* absolute (or strict) liability is so extensively accepted by the courts, and with some equanimity.'[25] Perhaps he would qualify that in regard to the courts after the case of *B (a minor) v. DPP* in the year 2000.

Lord Goddard for one was never well-disposed to Viscount Sankey's historic ruling but Sir John Smith has well-said of *Woolmington*, 'Never, in my opinion, has the House of Lords done a more noble deed in the field of criminal law than on that day.'[26]

Infringements of the presumption of innocence

The presumption of innocence may be infringed in practice. For instance, in France prisoners may be held for long periods on remand while inquiries are made. In the United Kingdom, however, there is *habeas corpus* and there are statutory limitations on long periods of custody before charge, although the latter has been extended for suspected terrorists. Another example of infringing the presumption arises where the courts prefer the testimony of the police or persons of certain status or ethnicity, although this is now far less likely to occur than in the past. Again, the use of a screen in cases of rape or sexual assault to prevent the complainant being distressed at the sight of the accused may suggest to the jury that a crime has indeed been committed by the defendant. These potential infringements need to be addressed but, overall, in the United Kingdom the presumption is a fundamental right of every person accused of a crime, unless strict liability is prescribed by statute.

HEARSAY

In general hearsay evidence is inadmissible although there are many exceptions to the rule. Such evidence is oral or written testimony that is second-hand and not given by a witness in court. In other words, a statement other than one made by a person while giving oral evidence in proceedings is inadmissible as evidence of any

---

24. [1875] LR 2 CCR. 154.
25. p. 47.
26. 39 *Northern Ireland Law Quarterly*. p. 224.

fact stated.[27] It is considered not to be 'best evidence'. Prior to the 1730s, although hearsay evidence was always unpopular, there had been little restriction upon its introduction in criminal trials. For example, in a trial in 1721 it was alleged that the prisoner, Christopher Atkinson, had beaten Alice Peak to death. A prosecution witness, a Mrs Hart testified that the deceased told her that the prisoner had thrown her down some stairs and had 'stampt on her Belly in the coach, and that she laid her Death to him.' No objection was raised to this evidence but fortunately for the prisoner a surgeon found no injuries on the body of the deceased and an apothecary testified that she died of a fever. Not surprisingly, the prisoner was acquitted.[28]

By the 1730s, however, the situation was beginning to change and there were a number of cases at the Old Bailey where hearsay evidence was no longer allowed, usually because it was not given on oath to which great importance was attached. At the same time counsel were beginning to appear for the defence and were quick to object when hearsay evidence made an appearance. It was once barristers were acting for prisoners that the dangers of hearsay were fully appreciated, since it precluded cross-examination which was counsel's strongest weapon in securing a not guilty verdict when an accused person was not competent to give evidence on oath. With serious consequences, often death, flowing from a criminal conviction it takes little imagination to see the dangers in so-called 'second-hand' evidence. Repeating what another person has said may involve changes of emphasis or intended meaning or even miscomprehension of what was expressed and towards the end of the eighteenth century the exclusionary rule was being applied more commonly.

Historically, it was in the early eighteenth century that the dangers of hearsay were beginning to be fully appreciated, as precluding cross-examination as well as not being on oath. As the eminent jurist, Serjeant Hawkins, put it:, an out of court statement was 'in Strictness no Manner of Evidence either for or against a prisoner, not only because it is not upon Oath, but also because the other Side hath no Opportunity of a cross-Examination.'[29] Further, repeating what another person has said may involve changes of emphasis or intended meaning or even miscomprehension of what was expressed.

Old Bailey proceedings of the eighteenth century reveal that defence lawyers persistently asked that hearsay be excluded and gradually the judges, who decide whether evidence is hearsay or not, also began to think it wrong and decided not to allow its introduction. One example, is the case of William Jones charged on 10 December 1783 with receiving stolen goods.[30] Giving evidence, a Mr Isaacs told the court that he saw a quantity of locks and asked Mrs. Dunn whose they were. When defence counsel, William Garrow, acting for Jones told Isaacs that he must not tell

---

27. Sir Rupert Cross. *Evidence, Op. cit.* p. 6.
28. OBP Online. (www.oldbaileyonline.org) 6 December 1721. Ref: t17211206-9.
29. Serjeant W. Hawkins. (1716) *Treatise of the Pleas of the Crown.* London, J. Walthoe, vol. ii. p. 431.
30. OBP Online. (www.oldbaileyonline.org) 10 December 1783. Ref: t17831210-105.

the court what she said, counsel for the prosecution, John Silvester, intervened to say, 'He must tell his story'. Garrow appealed to the court and was upheld by Mr Baron Hotham who appears from this and other trials to have viewed exclusionary evidential rules with favour.

Yet, by the Criminal Justice Act 2003, hearsay has now become admissible in some cases,[31] having been seen recently as another area ripe for change.[32] Cross-examination is at the heart of our trial system and the change means that when hearsay is admitted the loss of the fundamental value of a witness being cross-examined and having his or her veracity assessed by the jury—something that Sir Matthew Hale insisted upon four centuries ago.[33] It raises the question: why did these exclusionary rules exist? The eminent jurist, John H. Langbein, who on the whole opposes them, has put it clearly:

> The danger that inexperienced laymen rendering conclusory and unassailable judgments might err in matters of life and death has led to the development of prophylactic safeguards at the trial stage. The information about the case that is allowed to reach the jurors is filtered through rules of evidence that are meant to exclude types of information whose import the jurors might misapprehend. The hearsay rule and the rule excluding evidence of past criminal convictions typify this exclusionary system.[34]

These hard-won safeguards have now been severely diminished. It is little wonder that *The Times*[35] wrote in dismay that some of the proposals of the 2002 White Paper *Justice for All*[36] risked corrupting the justice system. They would deny human rights, increase the chance of miscarriages of justice and lead to sloppier police and prosecution work. Since then the Criminal Justice Act 2003, incorporating many but not all of the proposals of the White Paper, has become law. Moreover, those proposals that were not included in the Act may well resurface in the future.

Written records

In general, written records are inadmissible evidence of the matters they contain. However, public documents are often admitted as evidence of the truth of their contents. This is because, 'In public documents, made for the information of the Crown, or all the king's subjects who may require the information they contain, the entry by a public officer is presumed to be true when it is made, and it is for that reason receivable in all cases, whether the officer or his successor may be concerned

31. Criminal Justice Act, 2003. Part 11, chap. 2.
32. HMSO. White Paper. (2002) *Justice for All.* chap. 4.60.
33. Sir M. Hale. (1736) *The History of the Pleas of the Crown.* London, E. & R. Nutt and R. Gosling. vol. ii. pp. 276-7.
34. John H. Langbein. (1978) 'The Criminal Trial Before the Lawyers'. Chicago, 45 *The University of Chicago Law Review.* p. 273.
35. 18 July 2002.
36. HMSO. (2002) White Paper. *Justice for All.* c. 40.

in such cases or not.'[37] Despite that, for a document to be classified as an admissible public record it must satisfy four requirements:

- the document must be available for public inspection;[38]
- the person compiling the document must be under a public duty to satisfy himself of the truth of the statement;[39]
- it must concern a public matter, e.g. a company's statutory returns; and[40]
- the document must have been created to be permanent, not temporary.[41]

At the end of the twentieth century the hearsay rule meant that only a statement given by a witness orally in court proceedings was admissible as evidence of the facts the witness was presenting. Evidence had to be oral, written statements were not admissible and a witness could not repeat what others had said. Then, on 19 June 1997 the Law Commission issued a report on evidence in criminal proceedings dealing with hearsay and other topics.[42] This was followed by the Auld Report, *Review of the Criminal Courts of England and Wales,* in 2001,[43] and the White Paper, *Justice for All,* in 2002[44]. The Criminal Justice Act, 2003, based upon Auld and the White Paper, largely implemented the report and virtually abolished the previously existing Common Law on hearsay. It preserved certain Common Law rules such as those relating to public documents, confessions and expert evidence but abolished all the remainder. The Act also provided, for the first time, that hearsay evidence would be admitted where all parties in the case so agreed. Furthermore, any hearsay evidence may be admitted by the court if it is, 'in the interests of justice to do so.' Here it sets out, in section 114(2), criteria in determining whether the interests of justice test are met (although other considerations can be taken into account). They are:

- how much value the statement has in proving a matter in issue in the trial (if the statement is true);
- what other relevant evidence has or can be given;
- its importance in the context of the case as a whole;
- the circumstances in which the statement was made;
- the creditworthiness of the maker of the statement;
- how reliable the evidence of the making of the statement appears to be;

---

37. Baron Parke in *Irish Society v. Bishop of Derry* [1846] 12 Cl & Fin 641.
38. *Lilley v. Pettit.* [1946] KB 401.
39. *Doe d France v. Andrews* [1850] 15 QB 756.
40. *R. v. Halpin.* [1975] QB 907.
41. *White v. Taylor.* [1969] 1 Ch. 150.
42. LC 245. (www.lawcom.gov.uk/docs /lc245.pdf)
43. [2001] HMSO.
44. [2002].HMSO. c. 5563.

- the reason why oral evidence cannot be given;
- the difficulty involved in challenging the statement; and
- the extent to which that difficulty would be likely to prejudice the party facing it.

Unavailable witnesses

By section 116 of the 2003 Act, first-hand hearsay evidence, whether oral or documentary, is admissible where the witness is unavailable for one of the following reasons:

- he or she is dead;
- he or she is unfit by reason of bodily or mental illness;
- he or she has disappeared;
- he or she is absent abroad; and
- through fear he or she cannot give (or continue to give) oral evidence in the proceedings. Here the court must be satisfied it is in the interests of justice, including whether special measures (such as video live-link) would assist and whether it would be unfair to the defendant in not being able to challenge the evidence.

There have been two recent cases on this last provision where much of the prosecution case has rested upon evidence by a witness who is absent from court. In *Luca v. Italy*[45] it was held that a conviction based on evidence of witnesses whom the accused had had no opportunity to cross-examine was in breach of article 6 of the European Convention on Human Rights which provided for a right to a fair trial. On the other hand, in *R. v. Arnold*[46] it was said that the rule permitted some exceptions as otherwise it would provide a licence to intimidate witnesses—each application had to be weighed carefully. Then, on 30 July 2007, the Court of Appeal, Criminal Division held that the hearsay evidence of a witness who could not be cross-examined could be admitted in evidence, even where it was the sole or the decisive evidence against a defendant, if that was compatible with a fair trial. The lord chief justice, Lord Phillips of Worth Matravers, in giving judgment of the court said that the *Luca* case must give way the governing criterion of the fair trial test and article 6 imposed no absolute embargo on the admission of hearsay evidence.[47]

Section 118 of the 2003 Act preserves certain Common Law categories of admissibility. These include *res gestae*. The reason is based on the belief that because certain statements are made naturally and spontaneously during the course of an event, they

---

45. [2003] 26 EHRR 46, European Court of Human Rights.
46. [2004] 6 Archbold News 2, CA.
47. *R. v. Cole* and *R. v. Keets*. (30 July 2007) CA Criminal Division. (2 October 2007) *The Times Law Report*.

leave little room for misunderstanding upon hearing by the person who will give evidence in court. It means that reported words closely connected to a relevant event are deemed capable of forming reliable accounts in certain circumstances. However, one of the following pre-conditions must be met:

- the person making the statement was so emotionally overpowered by an event that the possibility of lying can be discounted; or
- the act does not make sense without the statement; or
- the statement relates to a physical sensation or mental state, such as an intention or emotion.

Other Common Law categories of admissibility include, public documents (dealt with above), a statement made by one party against another engaged in a common enterprise and expert evidence.

DOUBLE JEOPARDY

The double jeopardy rule is a human right and was a basic principle of the English criminal justice system from the thirteenth century until the Criminal Justice Act 2003. Its purpose was to prevent the state retrying a person for an alleged crime of which he or she had already been acquitted. In some countries, including the United States, it is not only a rule of evidence but a constitutional right. Because jeopardy 'attaches' at the outset of a criminal trial, in modern times the double jeopardy rule has prohibited the prosecution or the court from interrupting a trial that was going badly for the prosecution in order to try it afresh on another day before another jury. Once there is a second trial, the defendant is in jeopardy a second time for the same offence. However, in the seventeenth century jeopardy did not attach until the jury's verdict was entered.[48] Hale noted that whilst Coke's *Institutes* say that a case cannot be withdrawn from a jury,

> Yet the contrary course hath for a long time obtained at Newgate and nothing is more ordinary than after the jury is sworn, and charged with a prisoner, and evidence given, yet if it appear to the court, that some of the evidence is kept back, or taken off, or that there may be a fuller discovery, and the offence notorious, as murder or burglary, and that the evidence, though not sufficient to convict the prisoner, yet gives the court a great and strong suspicion of his guilt, the court may discharge the jury of the prisoner, and remit him to the jail for farther evidence, and accordingly it hath been practised in most circuits of *England*, for otherwise many notorious murders and burglaries may pass unpunished by the acquittal of a person probably guilty, where the full evidence is not searched out or given.[49]

---

48. John H. Langbein. 'The Criminal Trial before the Lawyers,' *Op. cit.* p. 287.
49. Sir Matthew Hale. *The History of the Pleas of the Crown. Op. cit.* vol. ii. p. 295.

Of course, in Hale's day the presumption of innocence and the test of guilt beyond a reasonable doubt had not yet emerged.

The principle of double jeopardy has now been withdrawn retrospectively by the 2003 Act in certain cases. Where someone has been acquitted of a serious offence such as murder, kidnap, armed robbery or rape, the Court of Appeal may quash the acquittal and order a retrial if it is in the interests of justice to do so and there is compelling new evidence that is reliable, substantial and makes it highly probable that the defendant is guilty.[50] It is difficult to see how, notwithstanding the direction of the judge, the second jury will remain untainted, especially in high profile cases. Both a new police investigation and a retrial will be subject to the personal consent of the Director of Public Prosecutions.

The arguments against the rule were re-inforced after the *Stephen Lawrence case*, which followed his murder aged 18 on 22 April 1993. Here four defendants were acquitted of an allegedly racist murder. The subsequent Macpherson Report led to a campaign for at least some of the accused to be tried again after new evidence had come to light. Indeed, DNA testing now makes it possible to re-open old files of so-called 'cold cases' long after the event and in some cases persons once acquitted have been found guilty on re-trial—but not those acquitted of murdering Stephen Lawrence. New evidence is defined under to 2003 Act as evidence not adduced in the proceedings in which the person was acquitted. It is 'compelling' if it is reliable, substantial and, in the context of the outstanding issues, it appears highly probative of the case against the acquitted person.[51] Clearly, there remains a danger that introducing *compelling* new evidence may give a strong indication to the jury that the defendant is guilty.

Perhaps the best argument for opposing this breach of a fundamental right was given by Mr Justice Black in a case in the United States when he said:

> The underlying idea ... deeply ingrained in at least the Anglo-Saxon system of jurisprudence, is that the State with all its resources and power should not be allowed to make repeated attempts to convict and individual for an alleged offence, thereby compelling him to embarrassment, expense and ordeal and compelling him to live in a continuing state of anxiety and insecurity as well as enhancing the possibility that even though innocent he may be found guilty.[52]

BAD CHARACTER

In modern times the situations in which evidence of an accused person's bad character has been admissible have been closely restricted, until the Criminal Justice

---

50. Criminal Justice Act 2003. ss. 75-80.
51. *Ibid.* sect. 78(2) and (3).
52. 355 U.S. 184, 2 L. Ed. 199, 78 S Ct. 221, 61 ALR 2d 1119.48.

Act 2003 which abolished existing legal rules in favour of a new code.[53] Prior to the Act the character rule prevented the prosecution from introducing evidence of the defendant's bad character, especially evidence of former crimes, except by way of rebuttal.[54] In other words, the prosecution could not adduce evidence of the defendant's bad character unless the defendant enabled him to do so by bringing evidence of his good character, or by attacking the character of the prosecutor.

Nevertheless, in earlier times it was not considered improper to adduce evidence of a defendant's bad character. As Stephen wrote of a trial for perjury in 1653, 'at this time it was not considered irregular to call witnesses to prove a prisoner's bad character in order to raise a presumption of his guilt.'[55] There are also a number of cases reported in the Old Bailey Sessions Proceedings in which evidence of bad character was admitted and determined the outcome against the prisoner. An example is the case in December 1684 of Anne Gardener charged with obtaining silk by fraud. She pleaded not guilty, but being shown to be a notorious cheat and shoplifter she was found guilty, fined ten pounds and imprisoned for one month in the Bridewell prison.[56]

Bad character was clearly revealed when a prisoner was visibly seen to have been branded with hot iron as a consequence of having pleaded benefit of clergy to avoid the gallows for a capital crime. In the case of William Sims, charged with grand larceny on 16 July 1685 it was reported, 'The prisoner appeared to be an old Offender, and Burnt in the Hand, having no evidence in his defence, was thereupon brought in Guilty by the jury.'[57] No burden of proof on the prosecution there. In the following year, John Thacker, George Drury and William Clark were charged with grand larceny on 24 February 1686. Here, it was reported, 'The prisoners giving a slender account of themselves, and Clark and Thacker having been formerly Branded in the Hand they were all found Guilty',—which appears to have been even harder on Drury than on the other two.[58]

Under section 99(1) of the Criminal Justice Act 2003 'The Common Law rules governing the admissibility of evidence of bad character in criminal proceedings are abolished.' 'Bad character' is defined by section 98 of the Act as meaning evidence of, or of a disposition towards, misconduct on a person's part, other than evidence that, '(a) has to do with the alleged facts of the offence with which the defendant is charged, or (b) is evidence of misconduct in connection with the investigation or prosecution of that offence.'

---

53. Criminal Justice Act, 2003. Part 11.
54. J. H. Langbein. (2003) *The Origins of Adversary Criminal Trial*. Oxford, Oxford University Press. p. 179.
55. J. F. Stephen. (1883) *A History of the Criminal Law of England*. London, Routlege/Thoemmes. vol. i. p. 368.
56. OBP Online. (www.oldbaileyonline.org) Ref:t16841210-35.
57. OBP Online. (www.oldbaileyonline.org) Ref: t16850716-8.
58. OBP Online. (www.oldbaileyonline.org) Ref: t16860224-20.

By section 101(1) of the Act evidence of the defendant's bad character is admissible if:

(i)   all parties agree;

(ii) the evidence is adduced by the defendant himself or is given in answer to question in cross-examination;

(iii) it is important explanatory evidence;

(iv) it is relevant to an important matter in issue;

(v) it has substantial probative value in relation to an important issue between the defendant and a co-defendant;

(vi) it is evidence to correct a false impression given by the defendant; or

(vii) the defendant has attacked another person's character.

However, by section 101(3) and (4) the court must not admit evidence under (iv) or (vii) if, on a application by the defendant to exclude it, it appears that its admission would have an adverse effect on the fairness of the proceedings. And, on an application by the defendant to exclude evidence under (iii) the court must consider the length of time between the matters to which the evidence relates and those which form the subject of the offence.

Other sections of the Act deal with co-defendants, attacking another person's character and contaminated evidence. In general, this part of the Act (as with some other parts) has proved controversial in that inappropriate conclusions may be drawn from such evidence as is now permitted and this could cause abuse and miscarriages of justice. A case in point is *Musone v. The Queen.*[59] Here a prisoner in Ryehill Prison named Reid was stabbed to death in his cell by another prisoner. The question was: which of three other prisoners who went into the cell did the deed? One of them, Musone, wished to put in evidence an alleged confession made by another, named Chaudry, to Musone a year before the trial that he had been guilty of a murder 12 years earlier. Section 101(1)(e) of the Act allows evidence of bad character to be admitted if it has substantial probative value in relation to an important matter between the defendant and a co-defendant. On this basis the Court of Appeal was prepared to allow the evidence although it excluded it on other grounds. This seems a dangerous interpretation of the section that allows an alleged confession to be admitted so many years after the act was alleged to have taken place.

---

59. (2007) EWCA Crim. 1237.

PREVIOUS CONVICTIONS

Before the 2003 Act a defendant could be cross-examined on his or her previous convictions only if he had attacked the character of the prosecutor or his or her witnesses.[60] The question of previous convictions is a difficult one as is shown by the convoluted law of similar fact evidence and the difficulty in arriving at judicial agreement as to what 'similar facts' are. Nevertheless, in general it is considered by the judges that similar previous acts can be submitted in evidence. They have also decided that whilst evidence of a propensity to commit certain types of crimes is not permissible, previous convictions which show a method or habit can be introduced in evidence.

A case that has worried many people is that of Nicholas Edwards heard at the Old Bailey in September 2000.[61] Edwards, aged 39, was found guilty of raping Miss D, aged 25, after the jury were allowed by a House of Lords ruling to hear evidence (i) from four women who had earlier gone to court claiming Edwards had raped them even though he was acquitted; and (ii) from a woman whom he was jailed for raping. The ruling was based on the ground that the women's testimonies established a pattern of behaviour that was strikingly similar to the evidence in the present case and outweighed any prejudice against the accused, despite the fact that it could be argued that the prejudicial value of four women giving evidence that he had raped them was so overwhelming that it could never be outweighed.

This trial set a new precedent not only on similar fact evidence, but, to some extent, although not in theory, in also overruling the principle of double jeopardy. The Law Lords held that the rule of double jeopardy would not be breached by allowing the women to give evidence since the defendant was not charged with, and would not be at risk of conviction of, the earlier rapes but only on the alleged rape for which he was standing trial. Their evidence was relevant and admissible as similar fact evidence despite the previous acquittals.

Nevertheless, it remains a principle that in general a verdict should be based on the evidence given in court and not on what the defendant has done on other occasions. Otherwise what has happened to the presumption of innocence and the charge the judge gives to the jury to try the case only on the facts before it? And might not the police arrest suspects on the basis of the knowledge of previous offences and hope that the revelation of past convictions (or even acquittals) would be a substitute for evidence? But the White Paper proposed that not only the judge (as previously) but juries also should be told of a defendant's previous convictions and acquittals, 'or anything else suggesting a criminal tendency', if sufficiently relevant

---

60. Criminal Evidence Act, 1898. sec. 1 (f) (ii).
61. Reported in *The Times* 22 September 2000 and *The Guardian* 25 September 2000.

in the view of the judge.[62] This approach is included in the 2003 Act under the rubric, 'evidence of bad character'.[63]

The White Paper conceded that research undertaken for the Law Commission showed that knowledge of previous convictions might prejudice a jury unfairly against the defendant.[64] A recent experiment examining the effects of revealing a previous conviction to simulated jurors concludes that its results clearly confirm that the evidence of previous convictions can have a prejudicial effect and that, 'If we assume that amongst defendants with similar previous convictions, some are innocent of the current offence, we have good grounds to infer that routinely revealing previous convictions would indeed increase the risk of convicting an innocent man.'[65]

Under the Act there is a new approach in that *each* previous conviction must be treated as an aggravating factor. The magistrates' court can now be made aware of the defendant's previous convictions when deciding whether it will hear a case or send it to the Crown Court for trial. The Home Office, in its guidance notes to the Act, asserts that, 'Any previous convictions that are recent and relevant should be regarded as an aggravating factor which should increase the severity of the sentence' and this applies whether such convictions are serious or minor. Furthermore, the previous ban on magistrates sitting to hear a case after having learned details of a person's previous convictions during a bail application has been abolished by the Act.[66]

THE RULE AGAINST SELF-INCRIMINATION

This is a right that is often believed to have been won at the time of the English Civil War. It is true it was proclaimed and exercised by the Leveller John Lilburne but it did not become a serious rule until taken up by defence counsel in the course of establishing adversarial trial in the eighteenth century. Indeed, what Langbein has characterised as the 'accused speaks' form of trial before the eighteenth century was in part the reason for the refusal of counsel to the defence.[67] It was considered important that the prisoner should speak in his own defence. Far from remaining silent, virtually the only hope for an accused was to respond to the prosecution's allegations—difficult as that was for most prisoners who were untrained, overawed by the court atmosphere and trappings, and usually illiterate. Yet, without counsel, not to speak meant no defence. It was the subsequent capture of the criminal trial

62. HMSO. White Paper. (2004) *Justice for All. Op. cit.* c.4. p.54.
63. Part 11. Chapter 1.
64. HMSO. White Paper. *Justice for All. Op. cit.* c.4, p. 55.
65. Sally Lloyd-Bostock. (2000) 'The Effects on Juries of Hearing About the Defendant's Previous Criminal Record: A Simulation Study.' *Criminal Law Review.* London, Sweet and Maxwell. p. 755.
66. Sch. 3. para. 14. Criminal Justice Act, 2003.
67. John H. Langbein. *The Origins of Adversary Trial. Op. cit.* p. 48.

by the lawyers that made it practical for a prisoner to decline to bear witness against himself.

The essence of the rule against self-incrimination is that neither a prisoner nor a witness should be required to accuse himself of, or admit to, a crime. Yet, as we have seen, the Marian Committal Statute of 1555[68] required that a justice of the peace should conduct a pre-trial examination of a defendant promptly after he had been arrested. Anything the defendant, or witnesses, said that was relevant was to be recorded and sent to the trial court to be used in evidence against the accused. The victim and other accusing witnesses were to be bound over to appear at the trial and give evidence against the prisoner. In other words, the statute was designed to collect prosecution evidence with the justice acting as the chief prosecution witness at the trial and with the accused having been given no advice that he need not answer questions or that what he did say would be used against him. The statute was still in use in the eighteenth century and Beattie put the position under it clearly when he wrote:

> The magistrates were not being asked to act impartially or judicially, to investigate and dispose of the case as they thought the facts warranted, committing some accused to trial and discharging others. Indeed they were clearly forbidden to discharge anyone brought before them accused of committing a felony. All suspects were to go on to trial, and the magistrate's task was to ensure that they got there and that the strongest evidence of their guilt would be contained in the depositions and examination that they were required to send in to the court. In the Marian procedure the magistrate was more a policeman than a judge.[69]

Hence, the pre-trial procedure of the time was designed to induce the accused to bear witness against himself promptly. As Beattie also confirmed, 'There was no thought that the prisoner had a right to remain silent on the grounds that he would otherwise be liable to incriminate himself.'[70] In the eighteenth century Michael Dalton advised Justices of the Peace that, 'even though it shall appear to the Justice that the Prisoner is not guilty' the magistrate should commit him for trial, 'for it is not fit that a Man once arrested and charged with Felony (or suspicion thereof) should be delivered upon any Man's Discretion, without further Trial.'[71] In effect, this was inquisitorial trial. It is partly for this reason that pious perjury grew substantially in the eighteenth century against the background of the death penalty for serious and trivial offences alike.

The privilege against self-incrimination is part of the adversary system of criminal procedure. Only when the modern style of defence counsel cross-examination

---

68. 2 & 3 P. & M. c. 10.

69. J. N. Beattie. *Crime and Courts in England 1660-1800. Op. cit.* p. 271.

70. *Ibid.* p. 348.

71. M. Dalton. (1746 edn.) *The Countrey Justice: containing the practice of the Justices of the Peace out of their Sessions.* London, The Company of Stationers. p. 260.

in criminal trials displaced the 'accused speaks' style did the prisoner acquire an effective right to decline to speak to the charges against him.[72] And, alongside the protection against self-incrimination grew the idea that the accused should remain silent and allow his counsel to do the work. This was a revolutionary change from Langbein's 'accused speaks' form of trial. Of course, before the Criminal Evidence Act 1898[73] a prisoner was not competent as a witness but he could make an unsworn statement to the court. In one case in 1784, defence counsel William Garrow, after cross-examining the prosecution witnesses, told his clients, after the prosecution had concluded its case, 'Prisoners, if you take my advice, I advise, you to leave the case where it is, it is in perfect good hands.' The defendant took the advice, re-mained silent, and were acquitted by the jury.[74] Garrow knew that a prisoner could be his or her own worst enemy when speaking in a criminal trial. In a handwritten note made in the margin of a copy of the 1784 Old Bailey Proceedings where he had prosecuted in a forgery trial, he wrote, '[t]his prisoner was one of the innumerable Instances of Persons who by making a Speech occasion their own conviction.'[75]

RIGHT TO SILENCE

This means that from the moment a suspect is arrested by the police until the end of his or her trial he or she has the right to remain silent in the face of police ques-tioning and at his of her trial without adverse comment from the judge or oppos-ing counsel. However, in a trial it meant little until the enactment of the Criminal Evidence Act in 1898 since prior to that statute a prisoner would not be testifying on oath anyway. The right was claimed by John Lilburne and others at the time of the Star Chamber and the High Commission when refusal to answer questions was considered to be an admission of guilt. To some extent this changed with the advent of adversary trial and the rise of counsel for the defence who often advised their cli-ents to say nothing. Nonetheless, the right to remain silent was not fully recognised until the formulation of the Judges' Rules in 1912. These required the police, on making an arrest, to inform the suspect that he need say nothing but that anything he did say might be used in court against him. It is, of course, consistent with the presumption of innocence with the burden of proof resting on the prosecution.

It was laid down in 1992 by Lord Mustill in *R. v. Director of Serious Fraud Office, ex parte Smith,* that the right 'does not denote any single right, but rather refers to a

72. R. A. do Amaral and E. de Lima Veiga. (1998) *The Right Against Self-Incrimination.* Instituto Cultural Minerva, Institute of Brazilian Issues. p. 11.

73. 62. Vict. c. 36.

74. OBP Online. (www.oldbaileyonline.org.) 7 July 1784. Trial of Thomas Isham and Others for Theft. Ref: t17840707-74.

75. OBP Online. (www,oldbaileyonline.org) 20 October 1784. Trial of Thomas Freeman. Ref:t17841020-70.

disparate group of immunities, which differ in nature, origin, incidence and importance.' Within that context he identified six different rights as follows:

1. A general immunity, possessed by all, from being compelled on pain of punishment to answer questions posed by others,
2. A general immunity from being compelled on pain of punishment to answer questions if the answers will incriminate,
3. A specific immunity, possessed by all persons under suspicion of criminal responsibility whilst being interviewed by police officers or others in similar positions of authority, from being compelled on pain of punishment to answer questions of any kind,
4. A specific immunity, possessed by accused persons undergoing trial, from being compelled to give evidence or answer questions put to them in the dock,
5. A specific immunity, possessed by persons who have been charged with a criminal offence, from having questions material to the offence addressed to them by police officers or persons in a similar position of authority,
6. A specific immunity possessed by accused persons undergoing trial, from having adverse comment made on any failure (a) to answer questions before trial, or (b) to give evidence at the trial.

This detailed yet succinct outlining of the essence of the right to silence appears to have set alarm bells ringing for governments who claimed that the right was being exploited by professional criminals—as indeed all the rules to protect defendants might be. Consequently, the Criminal Justice and Public Order Act 1994[76] modified the right for persons under police questioning. Prior to the Act juries were told not to assume a defendant was guilty because he or she failed to answer an accusation at the time of arrest or later at a police station. The Act allows for such negative inferences as 'seem proper' (such as subsequent fabrication) to be made if a defendant fails to mention something which he relies on in his defence provided it reasonably could have been mentioned earlier.

The Act also changed the wording on the caution to be given by police to a suspect. He must still be told that he need not say anything and it is his right to remain silent. However, that must be qualified by an additional statement that it might harm his defence if he does not mention when questioned something which he later relies on in court, and anything he does say might be given in evidence. The law remains, however, that a defendant cannot be convicted solely because of his silence.[77] In fact the Act so specifies but its subsequent interpretation has somewhat

---

76. HMSO. (1994) c. 33.
77. [1993] HL *R. v. Kevin Sean Murray.*

undermined that. A *Practice Direction* by the Court of Criminal Appeal in 1995[78] provides a form of words to be used pursuant to section 35 of the Act. This indicates that if a defendant declines to give evidence the judge should, in the presence of the jury, ask the defendant's lawyer if he has told his client that if he chooses not to give evidence or refuses without good cause to answer questions, the jury 'may draw such inferences as appear proper from his failure to do so.' If the lawyer has not done so the judge will direct him to.

If the defendant maintains his right of silence the judge will direct the jury in the following terms:

> His silence in this trial may count against him. This is because you may draw the conclusion that he has not given evidence because he has no answer to the prosecution's case, or none that would bear examination. If you do draw that conclusion, you must not convict him wholly or mainly on the strength of it, but you may treat it as some additional support for the prosecution's case.

In *R. v. Cowan* in 1996[79], Lord Chief Justice Taylor said, 'The effect of section 35 is that the … jury may regard the inference from failure to testify as, in effect, a further evidential factor in support of the prosecution case.' Thus, has yet another fundamental right of an accused person been undermined by a government that appears to take a cavalier attitude to the full meaning of the Rule of Law.

---

78. [1995] 2 Cr App R 192.
79. [1996] 1 Cr App R 7.

CHAPTER 15

Early Twentieth Century

By the end of the nineteenth century such faith as there had been in the military-style prison regime had evaporated. Contrary to official expectations, recidivism was growing and both separate confinement and the rule of silence were widely seen to be too harsh and cruel. In 1890, one observer, echoing Oliver Goldsmith over a century earlier, wrote that the English prison system was 'a manufactuary of lunatics and criminals'.[1]

THE GLADSTONE REPORT ON PRISONS

As usual, there were wide differences of opinion between those responsible for the prison service as to who was to blame and what should be done. The chairman of the Prison Commission, Sir Edmund Du Cane, was severely criticised for the failure of the system by those who perceived a new policy of reformation and rehabilitation of individual prisoners to be the solution. Du Cane's penal philosophy had been summed up as, 'Hard labour, hard fare and hard bed'. During his reign as head of the prison service the conditions of prison life were deplorable with the treadmill, poor and inadequate food and wooden planks for sleeping on in place of hammocks.

Widespread public disquiet led the Conservative government of Lord Salisbury to appoint what became a notable Departmental Committee on Prisons under the chairmanship of Mr Herbert Gladstone. The *Gladstone Report on Prisons* was published towards the end of the Victorian era in 1895[2] and, setting the tone for future penal policy, firmly placed on the agenda the twin themes of 'deterrence and rehabilitation' by means of training and treatment. These goals were to remain the objective for the greater part of the twentieth century with its attempts at penal reform to include improving life in the prisons and the reform of prisoners in an attempt to reduce recidivism.

Among other measures, the Gladstone Report recommended the abolition of the treadmill, less solitary confinement and a better diet. This was backed by a strong belief that it was desirable to keep as many offenders as possible out of prison altogether. Recidivism, the report declared, was 'a growing stain on our civilisation'. It also recognised that separate confinement led to moral and mental deterioration and that the silence rule was unnatural. This belated acknowledgment overturned at a blow nearly a century of a more harsh penal philosophy. A new chairman of the

---

1. A. W. Renton. (1890) 6 *Law Quarterly Review*. London, Stevens & Son. p. 338.
2. C. (7702) PP. (1895) vol. 56. p.1.

Prison Commission, the cultured civil servant, Sir Evelyn Ruggles-Brise, replaced Du Cane who was retired and Ruggles-Brise was told by Prime Minister Asquith, 'the view of the [Gladstone] Committee should, as far as practicable, be carried into execution'.[3]

As a consequence of that mandate and the new broom, the opening of the twentieth century saw a spate of improving statutes. These were directed at giving effect to the new thinking which was part of the political change taking place in the country. The turn of the century was witnessing a decline in the economic fortunes of Britain and widespread industrial unrest. They were accompanied, however, by the birth of the welfare state under Lloyd George as Chancellor of the Exchequer, the growth of trade unionism among the unskilled, the formation of the Labour Party, and the Parliamentary successes of the Liberal Party. The stultifying hand of late-Victorianism was replaced by a new vitality in the country, coinciding with the advent of the new century.

The forerunner of the statutes was the Prison Act of 1898.[4] This reduced the number of offences for which flogging could be inflicted, shortened the length of hard labour, introduced a new 'useful industrial labour', established a system for classifying offenders and introduced remission for good conduct. The statute also handed the detailed regulation of the system to the Secretary of State who was given power to make all rules necessary for the government of both local and convict prisons. This made it possible for changes to be effected under a code of rules without fresh legislation.[5] The Bill had had a stormy passage through Parliament, however, since it did not go as far as the Gladstone Report had suggested. Omitted were the major radical recommendations for the treatment of young adult habitual offenders and habitual drunkards. There was to be no independent Prison Inspector and no special Prison Commissioner 'skilled in mental diseases'. But the Act laid down the principle that the Prison Rules should have regard to the 'sex, age, health, industry and conduct of the prisoners'.[6]

PROBATION

Three other statutes were soon enacted to give effect to the desire to avoid giving some offenders the stigma of imprisonment. The first, in 1907, was the Probation of Offenders Act which established the Probation Service and empowered the courts to suspend a sentence for a period between one and three years on condition the

3. Sir E. Ruggles-Brise. (1921) *The English Prison System*. London, Macmillan. p. 77.
4. 61 and 62 Vic. c. 41.
5. L. W. Fox. (1952) *The English Prison and Borstal Systems*. London, Routledge & Kegan Paul. p. 58.
6. Sir Leon Radzinowicz and Roger Hood. (1986) *A History of English Criminal Law and its Administration from 1750. The Emergence of Penal Policy*. London, Stevens & Sons. vol. 5, p. 581.

offender was placed under the supervision of a probation officer. It was considered that crime would be reduced as a consequence of the probation officer assisting and befriending, advising and supervising the offender in a welfare-type agency. The aim, with punishment suspended for a time, was the reformation of the offender and the reduction of crime with the offender drawn to leading an honest and industrious life. As portrayed by Radzinowicz and Hood, the Act could be seen as a 'charter for the establishment of social work within the system of criminal justice'.[7]

CHILDREN'S CHARTER

In the late nineteenth century 'baby-farming' was a minor industry. In the absence of legal adoption poor mothers would often farm out a newborn baby to 'baby-farmers' and an official enquiry in 1871 found that most of the children handed to them met an early death. 'It was estimated that between 70 and 90 per cent of 'farmed' children in the big towns died, as compared with a national death rate among children of about 16 per cent.'[8] Subsequently, convictions of baby-farmers for offences including murder led, in part, to the enactment, in 1908, of Asquith's Liberal government's Children Act,[9] known as the 'Children's Charter'. The Act was considerably wider, however, and was primarily concerned with child protection. It defined a 'child' as a person under the age of 14 years and a 'young person' as one who was 14 years of age and over but under 16. It then forbade the imprisonment of children under 14 years of age. It also established juvenile courts as distinct units of summary jurisdiction for offenders under 16 and provided that those between 14 and 16 could be sent to prison only if a court granted a special certificate stating that they were unruly and depraved. As a consequence, whereas 572 young people of under 16 years were sent to prison in 1907, the number was reduced to 18 by 1925.[10] The Act further raised the minimum age for execution by hanging to 16 and granted powers to local authorities to keep poor children out of the workhouse and protect them from abuse—a provision that led later to social services. Children were also to be prevented from working in dangerous trades and from buying tobacco and alcohol.

A Departmental Committee on Young Offenders in 1925-1927 considered the merits of rival theories on the treatment of juveniles and its recommendations led to the welfare provisions of the landmark Children and Young Persons Act of 1933.[11]

---

7. *Ibid.* 634.
8. W. R. Cornish and G. de N. Clark. (1989) *Law and Society in England: 1750-1950.* London, Sweet & Maxwell. p. 405.
9. E Edw. VII, c. 67.
10. *Report of Committee on Treatment of Young Offenders.* Cmd. 2381.
11. 23 & 24 Geo. V. c.12.

Juvenile courts were retained but the justices sitting on them now had to show a genuine interest in dealing with young people. They were to be specially trained and the words 'conviction' and 'sentence' were dispensed with. A 'young person' was now defined as someone between the ages of 14 and 17 and all children, those aged 10 to 13 inclusive, and young persons were brought within the jurisdiction of the juvenile court. Reformatory and industrial schools for delinquents were abolished and replaced by 'approved schools' to be provided by county and county borough councils. The restrictions on the imprisonment of children and young persons imposed by the 1908 Act were re-enacted for children and young persons as re-defined.

At the same time, enlarged powers of guardianship were given to local authorities for dealing with cases that did not warrant the intervention of the juvenile court. The age below which sentence of death could not be pronounced was raised from 16 to 18 and an offender under 17 could be committed to a remand home if his offence was one for which the court could sentence an adult to imprisonment and if the magistrates considered that no other way of dealing with him or her was suitable. The term was not to exceed one month or the maximum sentence available for the offence, whichever was the shorter.

INFANTICIDE

Prior to 1922 infanticide was a capital offence. It was treated as murder although there was a tendency to avoid the death penalty by substituting the offence of concealing a birth. However, the Infanticide Act 1922 created a separate non-capital offence of a mother causing the death of her child. By providing a partial defence to murder it abolished the death penalty for a woman who wilfully killed her newborn child while her mind was disturbed as a result of giving birth. This was followed some 16 years later by the Infanticide Act 1938. This statute provided, by section 1, that where a woman by any wilful act or omission caused the death of her child under the age of 12 months she was guilty of infanticide. This made her subject to punishment as for manslaughter if her mind was disturbed by the effects of giving birth. The mother has to give sufficient evidence to raise the defence but the burden of disproving it rests on the Crown, unlike the defences of insanity and diminished responsibility where the burden of proof is on the accused (on a balance of probabilities). Nowadays it is very unusual for a mother who kills her infant child to be sent to prison although there have been a number of high profile cases, including where more than one child has been involved, e.g. in a cot deaths, and a number of miscarriages of justice following too great a reliance on expert opinion. However, generally, such convictions tend only to occur if the circumstances are exceptional.

When a mother kills her child who is over one year old the Infanticide Act does not apply but the defence of diminished responsibility is available. In the case of *R.*

v. Budden[12] in 1960 a mother killed her child of eight. The medical evidence was that she did not know her act was wrong as a consequence of which she was convicted of manslaughter on the ground of diminished responsibility and placed on probation with hospital treatment for 12 months.

PREVENTION OF CRIMES

The year 1908 also saw the enactment of the Prevention of Crime Act which ensured that young offenders aged 16 to 21, who were liable to imprisonment, should be sent to a borstal instead. Sentences were to be indeterminate, and often as a practical result longer than they would otherwise have been since these young men and women were to receive between two and three years training followed by a year under supervision. The ideal was the replacement of the former policy of treating young offenders with force and violence. As Alexander Paterson put it:

> Once upon a time the method employed to deal with them consisted simply in the use of force. The lad was regarded as a lump of hard material, yielding only to the hammer, and was, with every good intention, beaten into shape. Sometimes there were internal injuries, and the spirit of the lad grew into a wrong shape, for sometimes the use of force produces a reaction more anti-social than the original condition.[13]

All that was to change, with 'hard and honest' work the underlying basis for character training in classes of about 12. The trades taught included carpentry, farming, bricklaying, sheet metal work, motor mechanics and a number of others. Every boy or girl was also required to spend at least six hours a week in evening education and to join clubs for producing live art.[14] By 1938 the number in male borstal institutions was over 2,100 and, despite all the odds against it, borstal treatment as it developed was considered to be a success, until the experienced and caring staff (and many of the inmates) were required for other duties in World War II.

After the war the borstals became overcrowded with young adult offenders they had not been intended for. One consequence of this was that many inmates were released early and before they had completed their training. The borstals ceased to continue their pre-war successes and in 1982 the Criminal Justice Act[15] abolished them for offenders under 21 and they were replaced by detention centres and youth custody orders.

Another, and more controversial, provision of the 1908 Act was that which enabled habitual criminals to be sentenced not only to penal servitude but also to an

---

12. *The Times*. 14 October 1960.
13. L. W. Fox. *The English Prison and Borstal Systems. Op. cit.* p. 355.
14. *Ibid.* pp. 373-8.
15. HMSO. (1982) c. 48.

added period of preventive detention for up to ten years. When Winston Churchill became Home Secretary in 1910 he expressed deep concern about the potential dangers of this provision. He declared that he had:

serious misgivings lest the institution of preventive detention should lead to a reversion of the ferocious sentences of the last generation. After all preventive detention is penal servitude in all essentials, but it soothes the consciences of Judges and of the public and there is a very grave danger that the administration of the law should under softer names assume in fact a more severe character.[16]

It might be said that the provision was itself imposing ferocious sentences and Churchill's forebodings proved justified and many cases of injustice resulted. Some of them Churchill was able to mitigate until later his view prevailed and preventive detention sentences were gradually phased out. He also used his position at the Home Office to visit prisons and urge the need for improvements in conditions. In one case he ordered the immediate release of a number of incarcerated juveniles whom he met on one such visit.

On Ruggles-Brise's retirement in 1910, he was replaced as Prison Commissioner by Alexander Paterson, the first person in that role from outside the Prison Service or the Home Office. As a consequence, prison earnings were increased and the rule of silence was modified. Allegations that prisoners were being pampered emerged but were met with the response that pampering was not the object nor was it the result.[17]

In the years after World War I, the effects of the legislation inspired by Gladstone were tested. So far as prison conditions are concerned they were revealed still to be appalling in 1922 from the first-hand experiences of them related by Hobhouse and Brockway.[18] Despite the improvements mentioned above convicts continued to have their hair cropped, were still dressed in clothes covered with broad arrows and still spent as many as 17 out of 24 hours in their cells. They were humiliated, treated like caged animals and suffered the indignity of degrading and filthy sanitary arrangements.

Many of these horrors were to be remedied by the prison reforms of the humanitarian Sir Alexander Paterson while he was a Prison Commissioner between 1922 and 1947. Soon after his appointment the convict crop and the broad arrows had gone, a substantial breach had been made in the rule of silence, new cell furniture and clothing were planned and visitors could be received in more congenial conditions.[19] It was Paterson who coined the phrase, 'men are sent to prison as a

---

16. HO 144/1002/134165.
17. L. W. Fox. *The English Prison and Borstal Systems. Op. cit.* pp. 67-8.
18. Hobhouse & Brockway. (eds) (1922) *English Prisons Today: being the Report of the Prison System Enquiry Committee.* London, Longmans, Green & Co.
19. L. W. Fox. *The English Prison and Borstal Systems. Op. cit.* p . 67.

punishment not for punishment', and that summed up his underlying philosophy which did so much to alleviate the deplorable lot of prisoners in his time. Separate confinement was soon abolished except as a last resort and adult education courses for prisoners were commenced. Regular shaving was introduced and continuous supervision was reduced.[20]

Apart from the improvement in prisons, there was little call for penal reform in the inter-war years, although useful research was undertaken which would have led to some new measures had World War II not intervened. One example was the work of the Cadogan Committee on corporal punishment in 1938.[21] This Committee analysed the records of 440 prisoners convicted of robbery with violence between the years 1921 and 1930. It compared the subsequent careers of those who had been flogged as a punishment against those who had not. Those flogged were found to have the worse records of further crime. The report is a reminder that in 1938 the birch and the cat-o'-nine-tails were still in use, although with a maximum of 36 strokes. Reform was delayed by World War II, however, and whipping as a punishment was not finally more or less abolished until the Criminal Justice Act 1948 although, even then, it was retained for grave assaults on prison officers and mutiny in prison.

APPEALS

Throughout the history of the English Criminal Justice System until the 20th century there was no effective system of appeal from a conviction. Occasionally over the centuries all the judges would meet in Serjeants Inn, London, to discuss what was in effect an appeal but this was a rare occurrence and in no way affected the general rule. In 1848 the Court for Crown Cases Reserved heard questions of law referred to it by the higher criminal courts but not questions of fact. In the last half of the nineteenth century over 40 Bills to introduce a Court of Criminal Appeal floundered in Parliament.[22] The 1833 Criminal Law Commissioners had invited lawyers and others to give their views in writing on the question in 1845.[23] Of 44 respondents who replied, 35 were in favour of some improvement but many were hesitant about what they believed would be an adverse effect on the right of juries to decide cases on the basis of fact. Later in the century James Fitzjames Stephen's draft Criminal Code took the bull by the horns and proposed a Court of Criminal Appeal, but a

20. *Ibid.* pp. 68-69.
21. Cmd. 5684.
22. L. Radzinowicz and R. Hood. (1986) *A History of English Criminal Law. The Emergence of Final Policy.* vol. v. p. 758.
23. P.P. (1845) vol. xiv. p. 161.

change of Ministry meant the code was dropped.[24]

Ultimately, against the wishes of judges, many lawyers and the Home Office, a Court of Criminal Appeal was established in 1907[25] in response to the miscarriage of justice in the case of Adolph Beck and the likely miscarriages in the trials of Birmingham solicitor, George Edalji, and the alleged poisoner, Florence Maybrick. The court was given the power to uphold or quash a conviction, but not to order a re-trial. However, the Act allowed a convicted offender to appeal not only as of right on questions of law but also challenge the jury's verdict on questions of fact, or seek a reduction in his sentence. In the years 1909 to 1912, the new court heard an annual average of 450 applications to appeal and 170 actual appeals. With the appeals it quashed 20 per cent and varied the sentence in 22 per cent.[26] Once established the court also took the opportunity of improving the treatment of those under trial and 'its record must be accounted very real progress towards procedural fairness.'[27]

About the same time, the King's Bench judges conferred official status on the Judges' Rules which laid down the proper procedure for police questioning of suspects, including when a caution should be given that what is said may be taken down and used in evidence. It fell to the Court of Criminal Appeal to oversee the Judges' Rules in practice, through the doctrine that confessions made by prisoners were inadmissible in evidence not because of compliance with the Rules but on the basis whether the confession was made voluntarily.[28] The fact that confessions were not necessarily excluded because of the rules led to some difficulties for both the police and defendants. The police said it made their task on occasions unduly difficult and defendants complained that it did little to stop them being pressured and mistreated in police stations.[29]

24. John Hostettler. (1992) *The Politics of Criminal Law: Reform in the Nineteenth Century* Chichester, Barry Rose. p. 164.
25. Criminal Appeal Act, 1907. 7 Edw. 7, c. 23.
26. W. R. Cornish and G. de N. Clark. *Law and Society in England 1750-1950. Op. cit.* p. 620.
27. *Ibid.*
28. (1972) *R. v. Prager.* 1 WLR. 260.
29. *Ibid.* p. 621.

CHAPTER 16

Improvement After World War II

After six years of war the newly-elected Labour government of 1945 promised great social and political changes in which the Criminal Justice System was not entirely forgotten. The emphasis was to be on rehabilitation of prisoners rather than deterrence. The Attlee government's Criminal Justice Act 1948[1] attempted to continue the reforming spirit of Paterson. Corrective training along the lines of the borstals was introduced for those over 21 years. For persistent offenders there was imprisonment with corrective training for between two and four years. And, in a regression to past 'penal philosophy', provision was made for another attempt at preventive detention. This time it was for a fixed term of between five and 14 years for a person aged 30 or over whose current crime was serious and who had three previous convictions on indictment, two of them involving a custodial sentence. This, the statute said in repeating the argument of the 1908 Act, was for the protection of society, although the Cadogan Committee in 1938 had questioned whether it was ethically sound to make an example of individuals for the benefit of the community. More importantly, on a happier note the Act abolished both penal servitude and hard labour and replaced them with straightforward imprisonment.

Some 20 years later the Criminal Justice Act 1967 abolished both corrective training and preventive detention which, it was belatedly decided, were special punishments for persistent offenders who were being penalised for previous offences already punished. In their place it introduced the extended sentence. This empowered a court to extend a sentence beyond the normal length (or even, in limited circumstances, beyond the statutory maximum) where the offender's record justified a term to protect the public. This provision, which was hardly an improvement, was, however, little used. The Act further abolished the ancient distinction between felony and misdemeanour which had caused so much injustice in the past.

One of the major changes introduced by the Act, against the advice of the Advisory Council on the Treatment of Offenders, was to empower the courts to suspend a sentence. As a consequence, a sentence pronounced but suspended was only activated or modified if a further offence was committed during the period of the suspension. This was one of several measures introduced in this period to avoid imprisonment where possible. Others included partial suspension of a sentence, attendance centre orders and community service.

---

1. 11 & 12 Geo. VI, c. 58.

YOUNG PERSONS

It has been said,

> In attempting to uncover the roots of juvenile delinquency, the social scientist has long since ceased to search for devils in the mind or stigma of the body. It is now largely agreed that delinquent behaviour, like most social behaviour, is learned and that it is learned in the process of social interaction.[2]

This is reflected in the fact that, so far as the treatment of children and young persons are concerned, the criminal law has come a long way in the last 150 years. In 1849, for instance, 10,703 young persons under 17 years of age were transported whilst a similar number languished in prisons. Today we have police cautions to avoid bringing some young people before the courts at all. Youth courts have replaced juvenile courts but have retained all their powers—discharge, binding over, fines, compensation orders, supervision orders and now referral panels as part of the search for restorative justice, of which more later. A custodial sentence can be passed on a young offender today only if he or she has a history of failure to respond to non-custodial penalties. The sole exceptions are where the court concludes that only a custodial sentence is adequate to protect the public from serious harm or the offence is so serious that a non-custodial sentence cannot be justified.

WOMEN AND CRIME

Generally speaking, over the centuries, the number of men charged with crimes has greatly exceeded the number of women charged. This, no doubt, resulted in part because women were less involved in violent conduct and their position in the family would have been a discouragement to crime or their greater confinement to the home a denial of opportunities or temptation to commit offences. At the same time, juries and the courts to some extent sought to ameliorate the punishment of women who were seen as more delicate and vulnerable than men. Those women who did offend tended, in a pre-politically correct era, to be categorised as being 'deviant' from the norms and expectations of the fairer sex and thus, sometimes, more deserving of censure. Nonetheless, the quarter century after the Glorious Revolution of 1689 was almost certainly unique in the history of crime in London in that more women than men were charged with crimes against property at the Old Bailey in that period. This probably involved stealing to ameliorate poverty and distress and to provide food for children. The unusually high levels of prosecutions in the 1690s, and the

---

2. G. M. Sykes and D. Matza. (1957) 'Techniques of neutralization: a theory of delinquency.' 22 *American Sociological Review*. pp. 664-70.

prominence of women among the defendants, together help to explain some of the sense of panic in those years about the levels and character of property crime and the anxiety to improve policing, encourage prosecutions, and find more effective punishments.[3] Beattie shows that in London in this period 1690-1713 some 51.2 per cent of the defendants in property offences at the Old Bailey were female.[4]

By Victorian times femininity was idealised and ironically this resulted in criminal women being condemned more harshly than male criminals who were portrayed as exercising man's natural sense of adventure.[5] 'During the second half of the 19th century over one-fifth of those convicted of crime were women—today they make up only one-eighth. And whilst 100 years ago women made up 17 per cent of the daily average local and convict prison population, today the figure is less than four per cent.'[6] A deeply rooted patriarchal attitude to women saw, in particular those who were unmarried and independent, as a threat. Accordingly, when Sir George Jeffreys (the infamous Judge Jeffreys of the Bloody Assize) was Recorder of London at the Old Bailey, he ordered public whippings for a group of women convicted of petty larceny and chastised them as having 'the impudence to smoke tobacco, and gustle in Ale-houses'.[7] It was a common belief that all prostitutes were also thieves.

In reality, women criminals pose less of a danger to society than criminal men in that, in general, their crimes are less violent and they are less likely to re-offend. It is unfortunate, therefore, that, in recent times, there has been a growing tendency to consider female crime to be a product of mental deficiency. Holloway Prison for women exemplified that approach. As James Callaghan, then Home Secretary, said in 1968, Holloway would be 'basically a secure hospital to act as the hub of the female system. Its medical and psychiatric facilities will be its central feature and normal custodial facilities will comprise a relatively small part of the establishment'.[8] Of course, a mother's separation from her children will usually have more emotional effect upon her than upon a father but, awful as such effect may be, it has nothing to do with mental deficiency.

In the year 2004 a Women's Offending Reduction Programme was launched by the government. Its purpose is to enhance community services and support greater use of community sentences in place of short sentences of imprisonment.

3. J. M. Beattie. *Policing and Punishment in London 1660-1750.* Oxford, Oxford University Press. p. 338.
4. *Ibid.* p. 65.
5. Lucia Zedner. (1991) *Women, Crime and Custody in Victorian England.* Oxford, The Clarendon Press. p. 40.
6. *Ibid.* p. 1.
7. J. M. Beattie. *Policing and Punishment in London 1660-1750. Op. cit.* p. 64.
8. Alison Morris. (1987) *Women, Crime and Criminal Justice* .Oxford, Basil Blackwell. p. 109.

INCHOATE OFFENCES

There are three auxiliary, or inchoate, crimes, namely incitement at Common Law (now replaced by Part 2 of the Serious Crimes Act 2007)[9] and the statutory offences of attempt and conspiracy.

To incite a crime a person must counsel, command or advise its commission and it is an offence to solicit or incite another person to commit any offence, other than conspiracy, whether the offence is committed or not. This is similar to the law relating to being an accessory before the fact except that one cannot be an accessory unless the crime is committed.

The Common Law offence of attempt to commit an indictable offence was abolished by the Criminal Attempts Act 1981. Section 1 of the Act provided an alternative statutory offence of attempt. Accordingly if, with intent to commit an offence, a person does an act which is more than merely preparatory to the commission of an offence, he or she is guilty of attempting to commit that offence.

At Common Law there was a legal conspiracy if there was an agreement:

(i)   to commit a criminal offence,

(ii) to defraud,

(iii) to commit certain torts,

(iv) to pervert the course of justice, or

(v)   to corrupt public morals or outrage public decency.

Historically, the act which it was conspired to do did not have to be criminal. This was changed by the Criminal Law Act 1977[10] which abolished Common Law conspiracy, except for conspiring to defraud, and introduced the statutory offence of conspiracy. Nonetheless, there is a conspiracy among the participants only if agreement is reached but, once it is, it becomes illegal even if there is no attempt to put the plan into effect. The 1977 Act was amended by the Criminal Attempts Act 1981 section 1(1) of which reads:

> If a person agrees with any other person or persons that a course of conduct shall be pursued which, if the agreement is carried out in accordance with their intentions, either—
>
> (a) will necessarily amount to or involve the commission of any offence or offences by one or more of the parties to the agreement, or
>
> (b) would do so but for the existence of facts which render the commission of the offence or any of the offences impossible,

---

9. HMSO. (2007) c. 27.
10. *Ibid.* (1977) c. 45.

he is guilty of conspiracy to commit the offence or offences in question.[11]

It is interesting that the crime of conspiracy originated in the Star Chamber. It seems to be unknown on the continent and it has always been contentious in England. It is sometimes justified on the ground that a combination may be more dangerous than comparable conduct by a lone individual, but it must be recognised that one man can often do as much harm as a group can. On the other hand, for prosecutors it is sometimes possible to prove a conspiracy to commit an illegal act where there is no evidence beyond a possible doubt of it being effected. This sometimes leads to conspiracy law being used in an odious manner in political and civil liberty prosecutions.

PAROLE

After World War II, against a background of emphasising the rehabilitation of non-violent prisoners, it was widely believed that at some time during his sentence a prisoner reaches a stage at which his continued detention leads to mental decline. This fuelled a demand for some kind of parole system whereby a prisoner might be released before the end of his term. At the same time it was also perceived that releasing a prisoner too early might pose a risk to the public and care would have to be taken in preparing a suitable scheme. In response, in December 1965 the government issued a White Paper announcing its intention of introducing a parole system. It said,

> A considerable number of long-term prisoners reach a recognisable peak in their training at which they may respond to generous treatment, but after which, if kept in prison, they may go downhill. To give such prisoners the opportunity of supervised freedom at the right moment may be decisive in securing their return to decent citizenship.[12]

To meet both sides of the debate, however, the White Paper continued, 'release on licence would be limited to those who were likely to respond to generous treatment and who were not regarded as a risk to the public'.[13] Following the White Paper, parole was introduced into the penal system of England and Wales with the establishment of a Parole Board by the Criminal Justice Act 1967.

It might be thought that, like Caesar's wife, the concept of parole was beyond criticism. Yet, it has been said:

---

11. HMSO. (1981) c. 47.
12. HO (1965) *The Adult Offender.* Cmnd. 2852, London, HMSO. p. 4.
13. *Ibid.*

The parole system in England and Wales was constructed upon shaky theoretical foundations, its procedures have always reflected a tendency to place administrative convenience above the requirements of 'justice', and it has been subject several times to manipulation by Home Secretaries to ease immediate political pressures. Not surprisingly, it has generated cynicism and discontent among prisoners, unease among Parole Board members, and continued criticism from academics about its lack of principle and consistency. It has also been the subject of challenges in the domestic and European courts, mainly on the grounds of breaches of the principles of natural justice.[14]

Under the parole scheme there is a Local Review Committee (LRC) at each prison where parole is possible and this makes decisions for a wide range of short-term offenders, subject to scrutiny by the Ministry of Justice (formerly by the Home Office).[15] Prisoners recommended for parole may be released on licence by the Lord Chancellor without consulting the Parole Board. Other offenders, whose crimes include violence, sex offences, drugs offences and arson where their sentence is in excess of four years, must be referred to the Parole Board. The Board sits in panels of four or five members who include judges and recorders, psychiatrists, probation officers, criminologists, lay magistrates, social workers, businessmen and trade unionists. The panels sit three or four times a week, mostly in London.

The prisoner has to make an application for parole and set down in writing his reasons for wanting early release although the latter requirement can be dispensed with. He will be interviewed by a member of the LRC who reports to the Board. Under the system, by 1981 prisoners serving a fixed term of imprisonment might, on the recommendation of the Board, be released on licence under the supervision of a probation officer after serving not less than one-third of their sentence or 12 months, whichever was longer.[16] Seven years later the government appointed a Review Committee, under the chairmanship of Lord Carlisle, to review the whole system.[17] The committee's terms of reference included deciding whether a parole scheme should be retained and, if so, what its objectives should be and if any changes were necessary. Their report discussed the history and philosophy of parole and remission, the release mechanisms in other countries; how the parole and remission system worked in England and Wales and the case for change.

The committee found that overall the number of people on parole was rising, although the proportion of people with sentences longer than two years was reducing. Nearly 20 per cent of people on parole re-offended, but only five per cent had their licences revoked. The evidence of the long-term effectiveness of parole was, in the view of the committee, not clear cut, but they did think it reduced the likelihood

14. Mike Maguire. (1992) 'Parole'. In Eric Stockdale and Silvia Casale. (eds) *Criminal Justice under Stress.* London, Blackstone Press Ltd. p.179.
15. See J. E. Hall Williams. (1982) *Criminology and Criminal Justice.* London, Butterworths. pp. 222-24.
16. HO (1981) *Review of Parole in England and Wales.* Summary.
17. HMSO. (1988) Cm. 532.

of re-offending. In any event, the majority of prisoners were not eligible for parole, because their sentences were too short to qualify. Statistics seemed to indicate that relatively minor offending was a phase which many young men went through and, therefore, the committee welcomed the priority given to crime prevention and schemes for diverting youngsters away from the Criminal Justice System.

The committee's report argued for sending fewer people to prison and that once there people should be held for the shortest period consistent with their offence. But parole should not be seen as a right rather than a reward. There was a strong case for restoring some meaning to the full sentence imposed by the court. All in all, the report set out rather a hotchpotch of ideas and, possibly, not the kind of trenchant proposals for which the government had hoped.

Figures issued more recently by the Parole Board may prove more useful.[18] In one year alone (2002/3) the board considered applications from 6,012 long-term prisoners serving sentences of four years or more. Of these, 53 per cent were granted parole and 5.8 per cent were recalled for a further offence, which represents 188 people out of over 6,000. For the vast majority of those recalled the basis was an arrest or charge rather than a conviction. The average period on parole is 18 months, which is insufficient time for most cases to be evaluated but 25 per cent of those to whom parole was refused were recalled for re-offending.

Whilst the figure of 5.8 per cent is relatively low, say the board, it represents a significant increase from the previous year's lowest ever figure of three per cent recall of parolees for a further offence. This key figure had remained in the region of four per cent over the previous five years, while the percentage of prisoners granted parole had gradually risen from 38 per cent in 1997/8 to just over 50 per cent in the next two years.

Under the Criminal Justice Act 2003 prisoners serving a fixed term sentence of 12 months or more for offences committed after 4 April 2005 are released automatically after serving half their sentence, but on licence.

On 1 February 2008, the Court of Appeal held that the Board's relationship with the Executive was such that it did not have the independence required when determining whether convicted prisoners should remain in prison or be released on licence.[19] 'Both by directions and by the use of his control over the appointment of members of the Board' said the Lord Chief Justice, Lord Phillips of Worth Matravers, 'the Secretary of State [the Minister for Justice] had sought to influence the manner in which the Board carried out its risk assessment.' He added that, 'Their Lordships had no doubt that the Secretary of State was in a position to ensure that the Board was so placed within the sponsorship responsibility of his ministry that its independence was not open to question'.

---

18. www.parolegboard.gov.uk/newsPage.asp?id=38
19. R. (Brooke and Another) v. Parole Board and Another. CA. (2008)

POLICE

The second half of the twentieth century saw a shortage of police officers in a period of rising crime, high profile police scandals and growing allegations of police corruption. Accordingly, in 1960 a Royal Commission, under the chairmanship of Henry Willink, was appointed to examine the relationship between the Home Office, chief constables, local police authorities and the public as well as police pay, disciplinary procedures and the possible amalgamation of forces. In November of that year it issued an interim report[20] dealing with remuneration. This stated that from 1949 to 1959 there had been a 45 per cent rise in crimes reported to the police and that there were two-and-a-half times more reported crimes of violence. Conceding that the causes of crime were complex the report argued that, while the police were the main weapon against this rising tide, there was a 14 per cent deficiency in the national police strength. It concluded that increasing the pay of police officers was an important factor in attracting a significant number of new recruits.

The final report, published on 31 May 1962, proposed that no national police force be formed but that central government should exercise more power over local forces than before. This led to the Police Act 1964[21] which gave the Home Secretary a more supervising role than before. Police authorities were to consist of two-thirds elected members and one-third magistrates and would lose some powers to the Home Secretary. At the same time a whole number of forces throughout the country were amalgamated. The general effect was to subordinate local police forces to central government.

Nothing was said about police corruption which continued to grow as exemplified by the appalling case in 1964 of Detective-Sergeant Challenor of the Metropolitan Police. Challenor and three constables from Saville Row police station were tried for ill-treatment and fabricating evidence against demonstrators. Challenor was found to be suffering from a severe mental illness and was admitted to a mental hospital whilst the constables were convicted and sent to prison. Ten other cases, involving 29 complaints against Challenor and other officers, were investigated and settlements were made out of court.[22]

The police did not accept, however, the findings of Lord Scarman after the Brixton riots in 1981 that they were out of touch with the community. And when the Police and Criminal Evidence Act (PACE) was passed in 1984[23] they initially resented it bitterly, claiming it made their task more difficult because of its procedures to protect suspects. But, the passage of the Act was a watershed for the police and in

20. (1960) HMSO. Cmnd. 1222.
21. (1964) c. 48.
22. Mary Grigg. (1965) *The Challenor Case*. London, Penguin Books.
23. post. p 274.

time they came to regard it in a more favourable light. The explosion came, however, with the murder in a racist attack on 22 April 1993 of Stephen Lawrence, a black British teenager aged 18. The then Home Secretary, Jack Straw, asked Sir William Macpherson of Cluny to head an inquiry which found that the Metropolitan Police investigation into the crime had been incompetent and listed a series of failures they had committed.[24] Significantly he also found that the police were institutionally racist and, on 25 July 2006 the Independent Police Complaints Commission asked the Metropolitan Police to enquire into alleged claims of corruption, involving drugs, that may have been involved in the killers not being caught. To this day no one has been brought to justice for the murder.

By the end of the twentieth century there were contrasting approaches about the role of the police. In 1993 the Conservative government of John Major issued a White Paper entitled, *Police Reform: A Police Service for the Twenty-First Century.* Whilst this stressed the need for a partnership between the police and the community it declared unequivocally that, 'the main job of the police is to catch criminals'. In contrast, the main purpose of the police for the Labour government of Tony Blair in 1997 was, 'to build a safe, just and tolerant society, in which the rights and responsibilities of individuals, families and communities are properly balanced, and the protection and security of the public are maintained'.

What seems agreed on most sides is the importance of community policing. Yet, as one commentator has put it:

> community policing sees the protection of the community and the individual, primarily, in terms not of establishing rights but of preventing and detecting crime. So, although legislation such as the Police and Criminal Evidence Act 1984 introduced 'safeguards' for suspects, it has proved difficult to integrate into policing and, indeed, into the criminal justice system generally, mechanisms to prevent the abuses inflicted by the police and that system on individuals and communities—not just those seen as suspects, but also those who are the victims of crime.[25]

The present position of the police in England and Wales will be considered in the next chapter.

ABOLITION OF THE DEATH PENALTY

Having been the core element, and the worst feature, in the Criminal Justice System for nine centuries from 650 A.D., the end of the death penalty in the 20th century was the most radical and important change in the entire history of that system.

---

24. (24 February 1999) *The Macpherson Report.* HMSO. Cm. 4262-I.
25. Philip Rawlings. (1999) *Crime and Power: A History of Criminal Justice 1688-1998.* London, Addison Wesley Longman pp. 170-171.

Capital punishment was the ultimate sentence that could never be revoked. During a life of more than a thousand years the penalty of death on the gallows was often said to be justified because it brought retribution and acted as a deterrent to others. But, as we have seen, by 1837, after a virtual crusade against it, although it remained a public spectacle it was restricted in practice to the crimes of murder and treason. After that landmark, advocates of total abolition received scant support during the succeeding 100 years and more. In the twentieth century, for instance, Sir Alexander Paterson, a progressive Prison Commissioner, agreed with John Stuart Mill that death was more humane than 20 years' imprisonment which, he said, would often, 'permanently impair something more precious than the life of the physical body'. Only if life imprisonment were reduced to ten years as an alternative to capital punishment would he accept abolition.[26]

Nevertheless, some advance was achieved when, in 1930, a Select Committee of the House of Commons to which Paterson gave evidence, recommended abolition for an experimental period of five years. This was not acceptable to the government of the day but a clause giving effect to it appeared in the name of Sydney Silverman and others[27] in the Criminal Justice Bill of 1947. However, that was rejected by the House of Lords, with many judges voting against in a count of 181 to 28.[28]

In the Autumn of 1948 Labour's Home Secretary, Chuter Ede, announced the setting up of a Royal Commission to study the *possible limitation* of the death penalty.[29] (Italics added). The terms of reference were:

> To consider and report whether liability under the criminal law in Great Britain to suffer capital punishment for murder should be limited or modified, and if so, to what extent and by what means, for how long and under what conditions persons who would otherwise have been liable to suffer capital punishment should be detained, and what changes in the existing law and the prison system would be required. And to enquire into and take account of the position in those countries whose experience and practice may throw light on these problems.[30]

The members of the Royal Commission—two women and ten men—were announced on 28 April 1949 with its chairman being Sir Ernest Gowers who had had a distinguished career in public service. Once appointed, the commission was slow in getting under way but its work was completed by May 1951 when Gowers left for the USA saying that its report would be ready by Christmas.[31] In fact it was not published until September 1953[32] and not debated in Parliament until February 1955—a delay of over six years from Chuter Ede's statement. Despite its narrow

---

26. S. K. Ruck (ed.) (1951) *Paterson on Prisons*. London, F. Muller. p. 143.
27. *The Times*. 22 November 1947.
28. *Hansard*. [Lords] [156] cols. 176-7.
29. *Ibid*. [Commons] [458] col. 565.
30. *Ibid*. [460] col. 329. (20 January 1949).
31. *Ibid*. 7 May 1951.
32. HMSO. Cmd. 8932.

terms of reference, the commission wisely considered that there was only a fine distinction between the evidence given to it with regard to restriction on the one hand and abolition on the other. This was the issue declared the report.

Nonetheless, the report made certain other recommendations. It proposed that the doctrine of 'constructive malice' be abolished; that provocation by words be accepted provided it was sufficient to deprive a reasonable man of his self-control; that with suicide pacts there should be a crime of aiding or abetting suicide, unless the survivor had himself killed the other party. Further, by a majority the commissioners proposed raising the age limit for capital punishment from 18 to 21. As to insanity and mental instability the report recommended that the M'Naghten Rules should be abrogated with the jury left free to decide whether at the time of the act the prisoner was suffering disease of the mind or mental deficiency to such a degree that he should not be held responsible.[33] It also rejected the idea of dividing the crime of murder into degrees.[34] It would be some years, however, before any action was taken to bring about abolition, and then only because a change in public perception was eventually precipitated by four cases that caught the imagination.

Walter Rowland

In the 1930s Walter Rowland was convicted of murdering a child but he was reprieved from death and sentenced to imprisonment on the grounds of having an abnormal mentality.[35] During World War II he was released after serving eight years of his sentence in order that he might join the army. However, the army soon found he was unfit for service and he was discharged. Then, in October 1946, he was charged with murdering a prostitute named Olive Balchin by means of hammer blows to the head. The body was found near a bombsite in Manchester with the murder weapon nearby. The description by a local shopkeeper of the man who purchased the hammer from him together with eyewitness accounts of the man last seen with Balchin led the police to Rowlands whose clothes showed bloodstains matching her blood type and dust particles from the bomb site. Rowlands was arrested and charged with murder at Manchester Assizes. He was found guilty and hanged at Strangeways Prison on 27 February 1947 by hangman, Albert Pierrepoint.

Prior to the hanging, a man named David Ware voluntarily confessed three times to having murdered Olive Balchin and he was later convicted of attempting to murder a prostitute with a hammer. A Home Office inquiry concluded that Ware, who had been a patient in a mental hospital, had made a false confession and there had been no miscarriage of justice.[36] Nevertheless, many people continued to believe

---

33. Royal Commission Report. (1953) pp. 275-6.
34. *Ibid.* p. 278.
35. For this case see Elizabeth Orman Tuttle. (1961) *The Crusade Against Capital Punishment in Great Britain* London, Stevens and Sons. p. 90.
36. (1946-7) HO. Cmd. 7049. xiv, 515.

Rowland should have been reprieved, particularly as some thought the facts had been twisted to secure a conviction against him.[37]

The Trial of Bentley and Craig

During the long delay in publishing the Report of the Royal Commission, a murder was committed which had a profound impact on attitudes towards the death penalty by the public and in Parliament. This was the trial of Derek Bentley and Christopher Craig which commenced at the Old Bailey on 9 December 1952.[38] Craig, an illiterate youth aged 16, had shot and killed Sydney Miles, a police officer, on the roof of a warehouse in Croydon, south London. After firing at the police officer Craig had reloaded his gun and fired again showing that his actions were quite deliberate. Derek Bentley was with him and it was alleged he had urged Craig to shoot, although he denied any knowledge of Craig having a gun at all. In any event as they were engaged in a joint enterprise both were guilty of murder in the eyes of the law. What engaged public opinion was the decision to hang only Bentley who was not guilty of any direct violence and whom the jury recommended for mercy. In fact Bentley, who was simple-minded had been arrested and was thus in police custody, albeit still at the scene, before the shooting occurred.

The Lord Chief Justice, Lord Goddard, who presided at the trial, told Craig he was the more guilty of the two and when he passed to the Home Secretary the jury's recommendation of mercy for Bentley he told him that Craig was one of the most dangerous young criminals that had ever stood in the dock. In the meantime, as he was obliged to do by law, he sentenced Bentley to death and Craig, because he was under age, to be detained during His Majesty's pleasure. Bentley appealed unsuccessfully and the Home Secretary, Sir David Maxwell Fyfe, declined to advise a reprieve as he had failed to find any sufficient grounds to advise the Queen to interfere with the due course of the law.[39] Of course, had he been inclined to find grounds there were plenty available and with hindsight his reluctance can be seen as political act at a time of rising post-Second World War violence by young men. Those grounds included Bentley's age, his mental age, the fact that he did not fire the fatal shot and had no gun, that he was under arrest when the shot was fired and the jury's recommendation for mercy. As a consequence, there arose a groundswell of public support but despite this he was hanged at Wandsworth Prison at 9 a.m. on 28 January 1953. The case had a deep effect on public feeling about the death penalty at the time and support for a posthumous pardon remained strong over the following 40 years.

---

37. See Arthur Koestler. (1956) *Reflections on Hanging*. London, Victor Gollancz. pp. 114-17 and 119-120.
38. *The Times*. 10 December 1952.
39. *Ibid*. 22 Janary 1953.

An innocent hanged

The trial of Bentley and Craig was followed by that of John Christie who on 15 April 1953 was charged with the murder of six women whom he buried at a house, 10 Rillington Place, Notting Hill, London where he and Timothy Evans both lived.[40] Evans, aged 25, had been hanged in March 1950 for the murder of his daughter, Geraldine, to which he had pleaded his innocence. The outrage here was that she, and Evans' wife, were both killed by Christie who had given evidence against Evans. Three years after the Evans case Christie was tried before Mr Justice Finnemore at the Old Bailey for the murder of the six women, including his own wife, and burying them at 10 Rillington Place. When Christie had been charged with the murder of his wife he had said in a statement to the police,

> I sat up [in bed] and saw she appeared to be convulsive. Her face was blue and she was choking. I did what I could to restore breathing but it was hopeless ... I got a stocking and tied it round her neck to put her to sleep.[41]

As the Attorney-General, Sir Lionel Heald QC, MP pointed out, there is no such thing as mercy killing known to English law.

As the Howard League for Penal Reform explained:

> Here are two murderers, one is asked to believe, at work in the same small house, killing in the same way, hiding the bodies in the same place. Here was Evans, without knowing anything of the murders committed by Christie, accusing—just by chance—the one person in the whole of London who was murdering people in this way. And there was Christie, the principal witness for the prosecution in the Evans case, actually confessing to one of the murders for which Evans was hanged.[42]

In the event, the unsuccessful defence was insanity.

Thus, whilst the government prevaricated over the publication and debate on the Royal Commission Report the public were treated to two cases where men had lost their lives on the scaffold when they should still have been alive. In the circumstances, they did much to accelerate the cause of the abolitionists.

Before long, the Homicide Bill of 1956 was introduced and was welcomed by many in both Houses of Parliament. It became law in the following year[43] and restricted the types of murder for which a person could be hanged to:

---

40. *Ibid.* 16 April 1953.
41. Brian P. Block and John Hostettler. (1997) *Hanging in the Balance: A History of the Abolition of Capital Punishment in Britain.* Hook, Waterside Press. p. 143 *et al.*
42. Annual Report of the Howard League for Penal Reform, (1952-3) p. 5.
43. *Hansard.* [567] col. 584.

(i)   those in the course of theft;

(ii) those caused by shooting or an explosion;

(iii) killing a police or prison officer acting in the execution of his duty; and

(iv) second or subsequent murders.

Ruth Ellis

The climate of opinion with regard to capital punishment was also affected by the trial of Ruth Ellis in June 1955.[44] Two months earlier, on April 10, she had fired six shots from a .38 calibre revolver at her former lover, David Blakely, outside a public house in Hampstead. The shots killed him. She made no attempt to leave the scene and was arrested and charged with murder. At her trial at the Central Criminal Court she admitted that when she shot Blakely she intended to kill him. However, her counsel, Melford Stevenson QC, argued that there was no malice and the jury could return a verdict of manslaughter rather than wilful murder. This was not accepted by the judge, the jury took a mere 23 minutes to find her guilty and she was sentenced to death. She was hanged by Albert Pierrepoint in Holloway Prison on July 13 and proved to be the last woman hanged in England. It is interesting that of 145 women in Britain convicted of murder and sentenced to death in the twentieth century only 14 were hanged: a reprieve rate of over 90 per cent.

Prior to her execution there was widespread condemnation of the sentence and a petition to the Home Office asking for clemency was signed by over 50,000 people. The trial had unfortunate family repercussions with her husband, George Ellis, hanging himself in 1958. Her son Andy, who was aged eleven at the time of her execution, suffered psychological damage and committed suicide in 1982. Apparently, the trial judge, Sir Cecil Havers, sent money every year for his upkeep and Christmas Humphreys, who prosecuted at the trial, paid for his funeral.

There seems to be some question as to whether Ruth Ellis committed the murder. She was driven to the public house in Hampstead by another former lover, Desmond Cussen, who strongly disliked Blakely and who, the day before her death, she said had supplied the gun. How she learned to use a gun was never explored at the trial. It was a heavy Smith and Wesson revolver and she was only 5 feet 2 inches tall, weighed seven stone and had a gnarled left hand as a consequence of contracting rheumatic fever when a teenager. In the magistrates' court hearing before the trial Lewis Nickolls, Director of the Metropolitan Police Laboratory stated:

> On receipt the Smith and Wesson revolver was in working order, and during the course of firing in the Laboratory, the cylinder catch broke as a result of a long standing crack in the shank ... In order to fire these six cartridges, it is necessary to cock the trigger six times [and] to pull a trigger of ten pounds requires a definite and deliberate muscular effort.

---

44. B. Block and J. Hostettler. *Hanging in the Balance: A History of the Abolition of Capital Punishment in Britain Op. cit* p. 163.

At the Old Bailey trial this evidence was not given.[45]

Because of Ruth Ellis's age (she was 28), her children, the fact that the killing was impulsive rather than planned and because she was a woman, the case brought her widespread sympathy and undoubtedly strengthened public support for the abolition of capital punishment.

At the same time the public had become aware of problems with the criminal justice system. Not only had Timothy Evans been executed when he was innocent but a number of wrongful convictions had come to light. Although these did not involve people being sent to the gallows, they strengthened the belief that Evans might not have been the only innocent executed, and focussed the public's mind on the flaws in the system that made retention of the death penalty dangerous. It was in this situation that a general election was called and a change of government occurred which raised the hopes of abolitionists.

Abolition comes true

In October 1964 a Labour government was elected with a Prime Minister, Harold Wilson, who favoured abolition and a Lord Chancellor, Lord Gardiner, who was treasurer of the Howard League for Penal Reform and on the committee of the National Campaign for the Abolition of Capital Punishment. Nevertheless, in recognition of his years of effort to bring abolition about, it was left to Sydney Silverman to introduce in the House of Commons the Bill that began the sudden rush to end of the road for hanging after a life of over a thousand years. While the Bill was debated there were no prisoners awaiting execution, and it was declared that no executions would take place. Once it was enacted, after a great deal of debate in Parliament, the Murder (Abolition of the Death Penalty) Act 1965 ended the death penalty for a trial period of five years. It succeeded in making the punishment for all murders imprisonment for life, with the judge able to declare a minimum period.

After the compromise period of five years was brought to an end capital punishment was permanently abolished on 18 December 1969. The Archbishop of Canterbury, Michael Ramsey, summed up a great deal of feeling in saying, 'the abolition of capital punishment once and for all would help to create a more civilised society in which the search for the causes of crime and experiments in penal reform could be continued.'[46] Perhaps that was to expect too much.

Whenever a proposal to reinstate hanging has since come before Parliament it has been rejected on every occasion by a large majority. The last people to be hanged in Britain were Peter Allen and Gwynne Evans on 13 August 1964 at Manchester and Liverpool Prisons. The last woman to be executed was Ruth Ellis. Thus finally ended the lynchpin of the old law of felony whereby 'hanging by the neck until dead' was

---

45. http://en.wikipedia.org/wiki/Ruth_Ellis.
46. *The Times.* 19 December 1969.

the penalty for all serious crimes from the reign of Henry I. Indeed, hanging went back to Anglo-Saxon times but without the formula. However, the statute was not quite the end of the story. After the 1969 Act it was still theoretically possible for a person to be hanged for the offences of treason, piracy with violence and arson in the royal dockyards. That came to an end on 27 January 1999 when the Home Secretary signed the Sixth Protocol of the European Convention on Human Rights which ended all capital punishment in peacetime. That was extended to wartime as well by the Thirteenth Protocol which was only finally ratified by the UK in 2002.

TREASON

Historically, many of those executed for treason had honourable motives but suffered the misfortune of being on the losing side in whatever struggle they were involved. Such motives are less likely to be to the fore today but the law of treason is now hardly ever invoked, although it might be if there were an armed insurrection. Generally the criminal law is adequate to deal with cases where treason is alleged. However, the trial of William Joyce ('Lord Haw Haw') in World War II was held to be an exception because of wartime and even that was much criticised because of his disputed nationality.[47] Joyce was born in New York on 24 April 1906, the son of an Irishman who had become a naturalised American citizen. After a sojourn in Ireland he settled in England with his parents in 1921 and in 1933 he was granted a British passport after claiming to be a British subject. During World War II he was resident in Germany where he was granted German nationality and a German passport. Throughout the war he broadcast subversive, and largely false, propaganda to England over German radio.

He was tried at the Old Bailey in 1945 under the Treason Act of that year (passed to deal with his case) which abolished the rule that two witnesses were required to prove an overt act. His defence was that he was a citizen of the USA but the prosecution based its case on his owing allegiance to the Crown from his possessing a British passport even though resident in Germany. Joyce's lawyer argued that a passport was merely a means of identification and that, in any event, the one issued to Joyce was a nullity since a passport could not be given to an alien. The case went to the House of Lords which finally confirmed that Joyce was under the protection of the Crown and was properly held to be a traitor guilty of treason. He was sentenced to be hanged. On 3 January 1946, whilst in Brixton Prison awaiting the hangman Joyce wrote to his wife, 'I salute you, Freja, as your lover for ever; Sieg Heil! Sieg Heil! Sieg Heil!' This outburst of his true feelings did not, however, dispel the widely felt

---

47. *Joyce v. DPP.* (1946) AC. p. 347.

disquiet about the legal verdict.[48]

Today, in law, subject to the exceptions which follow, anyone who owes allegiance to the Crown can commit treason in any part of the world. This excludes citizens of the Commonwealth and the Republic of Ireland who can commit treason only by acts in the United Kingdom or colonies. However, outside of the war there have been no prosecutions for treason in the UK in modern times.

HOMICIDE

Murder occurs when a person causes the death of another where he intends to kill or death is virtually certain to arise from his conduct and he knows this. Equally, he is guilty of murder where he kills with the intention of causing serious bodily harm or this is a consequence of his conduct and he knows it.[49]

Where a person kills as above, the conviction will be reduced to voluntary manslaughter by reason of provocation,[50] of diminished responsibility[51] or because he killed in pursuance of a suicide pact provided, in the latter case, that he or she had a settled intention to die. [52]

Provocation is not a defence to any charge other than murder although it may serve as mitigation where a particular sentence is not mandatory. It is thus possible to make allowance for provocation in the sentence in all cases except murder or other situations in which sentence is fixed by law. Such a defence, if successful in a charge of murder, reduces liability to manslaughter. It requires that the defendant was provoked by things said or done that cause him suddenly to lose his self-control, where a reasonable person would have been similarly affected. Section 3 Homicide Act 1957 provides:

> Where on a charge of murder there is evidence on which the jury can find that the person charged was provoked (whether by things done or things said or by both together) to lose his self-control, the question whether the provocation was enough to make a reasonable man do as he did shall be left to be determined by the jury; and in determining that question the jury shall take into account everything both done and said according to the effect which, in their opinion, it would have on a reasonable man.

The issue is purely a question of fact but the reasonable man must share any characteristics that bear on the seriousness of the provocation,[53] e.g. a physical disability.

---

48. Alan Wharam. (1905) *Treason: Famous English Treason Trials.* Stroud, Alan Sutton Publishing. chap. 11.
49. Vickers. [1957] 2 QB 664. Wooling [1998] 3 WLR 382.
50. Sec. 3 of the Homicide Act 1957.
51. Sec. 2 of the Homicide Act 1957
52. *Ibid. sec.* 4.
53. *R. v. Camplin* [1978] AC. 705. HL.

And, a reasonable person must be of the same age and sex.[54] Unlike self-defence, it is not necessary that the accused believed his life to be in danger. It is sufficient if he has suddenly lost self-control. Also, although the accused himself must have been provoked the provocation need not have come from the victim.

For diminished responsibility the defendant must show, that at the time of the offence, he was suffering from a condition of arrested or retarded development of mind, or an inherent cause or injury, such as brain disease or mental illness, which caused an abnormality of his mind.[55] For example, if he has a reduced ability to distinguish between right and wrong provided this substantially impairs his mental responsibility for his acts. The controversial question of life sentences for murder is dealt with in the next chapter.

Today, unlawful homicide which is not murder is manslaughter. This can be voluntary manslaughter where a person is suffering from diminished responsibility as above, but it is not the same as insanity. It is a mitigating factor which enables the court to use its discretion in punishment unlike murder where the sentence is mandatory life imprisonment. Manslaughter is not an offence which requires a specific intent.[56] Involuntary manslaughter arises when the accused lacks an intention either to kill or cause grievous bodily harm. It is sufficient if the killing is by a reckless act or omission, or an act which is unlawful and dangerous.

Reform of the law of homicide is overdue and once again there are strong demands that degrees of murder be introduced. Some offences are determined by motive (provocation) whereas motive appears to be irrelevant in determining guilt in other cases such as mercy killing. Furthermore, a paedophile who kills to cover up his crime, or a serial killer who kills out of hatred for women, is treated in the same manner as a person involved in a fight who intends to cause serious injury. All these criminals are murderers and are treated the same, each receiving the mandatory life sentence. Nonetheless, their tariff as set by the judge, the minimum period before they can be considered for parole at all is likely to be different. There are also about 40 prisoners with a whole life tariff.

Against this background, on 28 November 2006 the Law Commission introduced proposals for the reform of homicide law.[57] Their plans, if adopted, will comprise the biggest shake-up of homicide law for 50 years. They propose three tiers of illegal killing—first and second degree murder and manslaughter. First-degree murder would arise if a person who kills intended to cause serious injury and was aware of a serious risk of death, instead of intending serious bodily harm as at present. There is no distinction between premeditated and spontaneous murder. If the killer, intending to harm but not kill, or being provoked, is not aware of the risk of death

54. *Att-Gen. for Jersey v. Holley.* [2005] UKPC 23 PC.
55. *R. v. Byrne.* [1960] 2 QB 396.
56. *R. v. Lipman.* (1970) 1 QB 152. CA.
57. (2006) Law Commission. *Murder, Manslaughter and Infanticide.* Report No. 304.

he would, under these suggestions, be guilty only of second degree murder and not be sentenced to life imprisonment.

At present duress is no defence to murder. The commission propose that duress be a complete defence to murder, whatever the degree. Killing as a result of gross negligence would be manslaughter if the defendant is aware of a serious risk of injury from his act. Under the proposals some killings now classed as manslaughter would be upgraded to murder, with offenders facing harsher sentences. At the time of writing the Home Office is consulting on the commission's proposals and it is not clear what, if any, action will result.

THEFT

Section 1(1) of the Theft Act 1968[58] provides that a person is guilty of theft if he dishonestly appropriates property belonging to another with the intention of permanently depriving the other of it. The offence is triable either way[59] and is punishable with a maximum of ten years' imprisonment on conviction on indictment. Prior to the Theft Act 1968, theft and similar offences were covered by a mass of conflicting laws which were extremely complex. The Act is a code of the law of theft, based on the eighth report of the Criminal Law Revision Committee,[60] which replaced all the earlier complicated common and statute law. Naturally, it could not foresee and resolve the problems its own definitions might produce and it has had to be supplemented by the Theft Act 1978 and the Theft (Amendment) Act 1996 but only Bentham believed a code would need no revision for 100 years.

The 1968 Act was an heroic attempt to cure the old defects and constructions of the Common Law. It changes the necessity for a 'taking' into one of 'appropriation', and property need no longer be specific corporeal things and can include land and wild creatures. The definition of theft in the Act replaces all the various types of larceny, embezzlement, and fraudulent conversion of the Larceny Act 1916.[61] Robbery is comprised of theft involving the threat or use of violence. Burglary includes housebreaking and shopbreaking. New offences of deception replaced false pretences and obtaining credit by fraud. The old problem that a person in possession could not steal, which gave rise to so many legal constructions, can no longer arise and the distinction between an employee's custody or possession of his employer's property is no longer required to secure a conviction. Generally speaking the Act has considerably reduced the technicality of the old law relating to theft and allied offences.

---

58. HMSO. (1968) c. 60.
59. Magistrates' Courts Act 1980, section 17(1) and schedule 1.
60. HMSO. (1966) Cmnd. 2977.
61. 6 & 7 Geo. 5, c. 50.

The 1978 and 1996 Acts brought up to date the law concerning the obtaining of a money transfer or services by deception, evasion of liability by deception, dishonestly retaining a wrongful credit and making off without payment. However, the Fraud Act 2006 has repealed most of the offences of deception. Under this Act there are offences of committing fraud (i) by false representation, (ii) by failure to disclose information and (iii) by abuse of position, all in order to make a gain for oneself or another or to cause loss to another.[62] Conviction on indictment can result in imprisonment up to ten years or a fine or both.

RAPE

Rape is still defined as sexual intercourse without the valid consent of one of the parties involved. The relevant statute is the Sexual Offences (Amendment) Act 1976. It is an offence, triable only on indictment, the maximum punishment being life imprisonment. Unfortunately in some cases with a female victim, under cross-examination she herself and her behaviour are under scrutiny as much as the alleged rapist. The 'lack of consent' does not necessarily mean an explicit refusal of consent. Generally it is not considered genuine if the person allegedly giving it is under duress (including violence and blackmail), is incapacitated by drugs or alcohol, is mentally impaired or is under the age of consent. Rape of a minor is known as statutory rape and is illegal, even if consensual.

A terrifying result emerged from one Home Office survey which revealed that most rapes are committed by family members, with only about a quarter involving strangers.[63] It may be that this is one of the reasons why rape is the least reported violent crime in this country, since the victim is often unwilling to involve members of the family and also feels somehow responsible in the family context. It is, however, now possible in England, since 1992, for a wife to claim that her husband raped her. Formerly rape within marriage was not a crime. Hale had laid it down that, 'The husband cannot be guilty of a rape committed by himself upon his lawful wife, for by their mutual matrimonial consent and contract the wife hath given up herself in this kind unto her husband, which she cannot retract.'[64] This approach was followed by the courts, eventually with reluctance, until marital rape was made a crime by legislation.

It is worth noting that the international Criminal Tribunal for Rwanda has defined coercive rape as an institutionalised weapon of war and a crime of genocide.

---

62. HMSO. (2006) c, 35.
63. L. Watson. (1996) *Victims of Violent Crime Recorded by the Police, England and Wales, 1990-1994.* Home Office Statistical Findings, Issue 1/96. London, HMSO.
64. Sir Matthew Hale. (1736) *The History of the Pleas of the Crown.* London, E. & R. Nutt and R. Gosling. vol. i. p. 629.

DRUG ABUSE

Another problem that became a serious issue in the late twentieth century was that of drug abuse. Earlier there had been no sanctions against taking drugs for pleasure, including opium which severely affected the health of James Fitzjames Stephen in his later years when he sat as a judge.[65] Governments seek to control harmful drugs and prevent their abuse and since about 1980 a great deal of effort has gone into attempting to prevent the importing and dealing in proscribed drugs. Possession of a proscribed substance is itself a criminal offence. But criminalising drugs often produces more organized crime. Offences can also be committed by a person who is under the influence of drugs and drug addicts often resort to theft and burglary to raise the money needed to feed their habit. As a consequence, some senior police officers have argued that decriminalisation of drugs would reduce drug abuse and drug related crime. On the other hand, the Home Office's Crime and Drug Strategy Directorate directs seven units to control drug crime although their tasks are far too great to be detailed here.

Among other things, drugs cost society huge sums of money. In February 2002 Home Office Minister Bob Ainsworth told the House of Commons Home Affairs Select Committee that research revealed that in England and Wales drug abuse cost £18.8bn a year—or more than £300 per person. This figure included the costs of crime, social security and bringing drug offenders to justice, as well as the bill to the National Health Service. It was necessary, he added, for the government to focus its efforts against Class A drugs like heroin and cocaine. He also stressed the importance of treatment schemes saying, 'We know treatment works: for every £1 spent, £3 is saved in criminal justice costs.' One important aspect of tackling the problem of drug abuse is the effort to wean prisoners away from drugs prior to their release into the community although it must be said that attempts to prevent drugs getting into prisons are largely unsuccessful.

ROAD TRAFFIC CRIME

The widespread ownership of motor vehicles has brought a new dimension to the lives of many people. It has also seen an increase in fresh crimes as set out in various Road Traffic Acts and a plethora of associated regulations plus the introduction of thousand of 'speed cameras' up and down the country. Normal penalties for breaches of most traffic laws are those familiar for other offences. But there are also a number of strict liability offences and fixed penalties. Speeding caught on camera

---

65. John Hostettler. (1995) *Politics and Law in the Life of Sir James Fitzjames Stephen.* Chichester, Barry Rose. pp. 250-51.

results in a fine on each occasion and penalty points endorsed on the licence of the driver. As a driver accumulates points he or she may be required to attend fresh driving lessons, re-take his or her driving test or even lose the licence.

Driving whilst under the influence of alcohol is operating a motor vehicle with a blood alcohol content that is higher than the legal limit which has been set at a level at which the government considers a person cannot drive safely. Drivers are given a breathalyser test by the police but the police must not make a test randomly but only if they see an offence or erratic driving. A combination of narcotics and alcohol can classify as being under the influence but if the driving is on private property there is no offence. However, sitting in a stationary vehicle with the ignition turned off may qualify.

The penalty points system is intended to deter drivers from following unsafe driving practices. The court *must* order points to be endorsed on the offender's license according to the fixed number or range set by Parliament. Three points are fairly common and there is a fine the lowest maximum of which is £1,000. However, if the offender responds within one month to a police notice he may have a fixed penalty of a £60 fine and his license endorsed with three points, but without having to appear in court. A driver who accumulates 12 or more penalty points within a period of three years must be disqualified from driving for a minimum period of six months, or longer if he or she has previously been disqualified. Worst offenders may be made to re-take the driving test.

In every offence which carries penalty points, the court has a discretionary power to order that the license holder be disqualified. This may be for any period the court thinks fit, but for minor offences will usually be between a week and a few months. In the case of serious offences, such as dangerous driving and drink driving, the court *must* order disqualification. The minimum period is 12 months, but for repeat offenders or where the alcohol level is high, it may be longer. For instance, a second drink-drive offence in the space of ten years will result in a minimum of three years' disqualification.

Moreover, in some serious cases, the court must, in addition to imposing a fixed period of disqualification, order that the disqualification should not end until the offender passes a driving test. The test may be of an ordinary length or an extended test according to the nature of the offence.[66]

The Road Safety Act 2006[67] introduced new offences of causing death by careless or inconsiderate driving; causing death by driving while unlicensed, disqualified or uninsured; and keeping a vehicle that does not meet insurance requirements. It also increased the maximum penalties for various road traffic offences and provided for the graduation of fixed penalties for specified offences and circumstances. And,

---

66. Some of the law in this section is contained in the Road Traffic Act 1991 sections 28, 29, 34, 35 and 36.
67. 2006. c. 49.

in an effort to help prevent fatigue-related accidents the Act allowed for a pilot of motorway rest areas similar to French *aires*.

Special rules apply to new drivers. These are drivers within two years of the date of passing their driving test if they passed the test after 1 June 1997 and held nothing but a provisional license before passing the test. If the number of penalty points on their license reaches six or more as a result of offences they commit before the two years are over (including any they committed before passing the test) their license will be revoked. They must then reapply for a provisional license and may drive only as learners until they pass a fresh theory and practical driving test.[68]

Where an offence is punishable by imprisonment (and many are) then the vehicle used to commit the offence may be confiscated. Drivers disqualified for drinking and driving twice within ten years, or once if they are over two and a half times the legal limit, also have to satisfy the Driver and Vehicle Licensing Agency's medical branch that they do not have an alcohol problem and are otherwise fit to drive before their license is returned at the end of their period of disqualification. This also applies to those who refuse to give a specimen of blood. Persistent misuse of drugs or alcohol may lead to the withdrawal of a driving license.

Some of these laws are deeply resented by many of the millions of motorists on our roads since the punishments involved can have serious consequences, not least for the guilty driver's employment and the livelihood of himself, or herself, and their family. Nevertheless, the crimes, for crimes they are, have to be dealt with and discouraged vigorously.

---

68. Road Traffic (New Drivers) Act 1995.

CHAPTER 17

Twenty-first Century Regression?

Modern-day criminal justice is as much about its processes and the rights of citizens whether as victims or offenders and is governed by a huge volume of legislation.

POLICE AND THE CRIMINAL EVIDENCE ACT 1984[1]

The Police and Criminal Evidence Act (known as PACE) was passed to extend police powers to combat crime and, at the same time, provide codes of practice to cover the exercise of those powers. Failure to abide by the codes while the police search, detain, arrest or interview a suspect may make evidence obtained inadmissible in court. The Act re-introduced police powers of 'stop and search', infamously known earlier as 'sus', meaning 'on suspicion'. Despite the suspicion having to be 'reasonable', such powers were particularly resented by black people who regarded themselves as being unfairly targeted by the police. Indeed, in 1981 there were over 700,000 recorded stop and searches in London alone and only 67,275 of these led to arrest.[2] In these circumstances it is essential that police powers of interrogation and detention are limited by law.

Yet, on 25 September 2007 Scotland Yard issued figures to show that between the months of April and August 2007 some 32,000 people were stopped and searched on suspicion in London under the terrorist legislation. Of those 17,348 were white and 11,042 black (some were not recorded). But, of course, these are actual figures and not proportions according to the size of the white and black populations of London. Indeed, the police admitted that black people formed a much smaller proportion of the population than whites. What is interesting is the large numbers of people stopped and searched under terrorism legislation alone in just a few months and the fact that how many were arrested was not revealed.

Under PACE a police officer may now stop and search a person or a vehicle where there are reasonable grounds for suspecting that they hold stolen goods or weapons or articles for use in offences such as theft and burglary. Where an arrest is improperly made an officer may be liable in damages to the wrongfully arrested person. Section 8 of the Act further allows an officer to obtain a search warrant from a magistrate when he reasonably believes that premises contain drugs or stolen property. Warrants for search and arrest are provided for by section 17, and section 32

1. 1984. c. 60.
2. A. Sanders and R. Young. (1994) *Criminal Justice*. London, Butterworths. p. 35.

allows an officer to search a person who has been arrested, for evidence or for articles that might help them escape or with which they might harm themselves.

The codes cover the requirements for the detention, treatment and questioning of people in police custody and the exercise by police officers of statutory powers to search a person or a vehicle without first making an arrest. They also cover police powers to search premises and to seize and retain property found on persons and that property. Tape recordings of interviews in police stations are also covered and one code deals with the detention of terrorist suspects. In effect, the Act established time limits for police detention and investigation and protection for those arrested in stop, search and seizure actions. And, although swiftly diluted by the Criminal Justice Act 2003, the right to silence was confirmed. Cases following the Act included:

- *R. v. Longman* (1988) where police entry on to premises to execute a search warrant for drugs was held to be lawful, even though deception had been used to gain entry and they had not identified themselves or shown a warrant. This is a curious decision in the light of the provisions of the Act but the following two cases are more in line with its intent;
- *O'Loughlin v. Chief Constable of Essex* (1998) where the entry by police on to premises to arrest O'Loughlin's wife was unlawful since no reason was given for the entry; and
- *Osman v. DPP* (1999) where a search was held unlawful because the police did not give their names and station.[3]

PACE was modified in 2005 by the Serious Organized Crime and Police Act[4] which replaced most existing powers of arrest with a new general power of arrest for all offences.

The principle aims of the police today are seen by the public as being to uphold the law and bring to justice those who break the law. It is important that officers should be drawn from the community and be responsible to the community as well as to the state. In a sense this was the purpose of PACE but the wide powers of arrest caused unrest among some sections of the community and, in particular, among ethnic minorities who widely believe they suffer unjustly from these powers. Furthermore, central government control of police forces has increased and is likely to increase further under the threat of terrorist attacks.

During Tony Blair's ten-year tenure of 10 Downing Street the Labour government passed 50 crime and punishment statutes and created some 3,000 new crim-

---

3. For these three cases see J. Martin. (2005) *The English Legal System.* (4th edn.) London, Hodder Arnold. pp. 129-33.
4. 2005. c. 15.

inal offences.[5] Many of them were statutes dealing with criminal justice matters requested by the police to assist in the fight against terrorism. Contrary to previous law they were given the increased powers to stop and search individuals and enter premises indicated above. Such powers can, however, if used improperly seriously undermine hard-won civil liberties of the citizen. Nevertheless, PACE, which was initially unpopular with the police, did also provide protective measures against over-zealous police officers in carrying out arrest, stop and search and seizures of property as well as the right to free legal advice from a solicitor. Fortunately, today the police appear to recognise its merits for suspects and police alike. However, some more devolved structure with a democratic content should be developed to be effective in our modern diverse society.

POLICING

There is still no national police force in England although certain functions are carried out on a national basis. Scotland Yard—the Metropolitan Police Service—still exists in London, and in other parts of the country there are 43 police forces and police authorities. The latter are democratic and are comprised of magistrates, councillors and other representatives of the community. However, police forces rely upon the Home Office for a large part of their funding and resources. As a consequence, although they often have their own specialist squads there are now a number of national police bodies with a national policing plan. Among other things, the purpose of the plan is to co-ordinate major national projects. Moreover, the Police Reform Act 2002[6] permits the Home Secretary to give directions to police authorities, to amend police powers and to take over police responsibilities when police forces fail in their duties. It also gives him the power to remove police officers.

Furthermore, there are a number of national units including the Serious and Organized Crime Agency which deals with major crimes of drug trafficking, criminal finance, people trafficking, terrorist finance and money laundering. This body is sponsored by, but operates independently of, the Home Office and is sometimes referred to as the 'British FBI'. It has a board of eleven members and, at the time of writing, its non-executive chairman is Sir Stephen Lander, a former head of MI5. Affiliated to it is the Child Exploitation and Online Protection Centre which tackles child sex abuse both at home and abroad.

Of course, the police do not always act responsibly and the Police Reform Act 2002 also set up the Independent Police Complaints Commission in place of the former Police Complaints Authority. The new body is entirely independent of the

---

5. Sir Menzies Campbell. (11 July 2007) House of Commons.
6. HMSO. 2002 c. 30.

police and the government, being a non-departmental public body although funded by the Home Office. Its duty is to oversee the whole of the police complaints system and deal with complaints effectively.

TERRORISM

A glance into the past shows that terrorism has a long history. Certain Roman emperors were not slow to employ it, nor were the Spanish Inquisition or the Ku Klux Klan after the American Civil War. More recent examples abound but the word took on a new dimension with the attack on the World Trade Centre in New York on 11 September 2001. Terrorism then came to London in the United Kingdom with the underground and bus bombings of 7 July 2005. Subsequent attempts have been thwarted by the police and security services but more attacks seem to be inevitable.

By the Terrorism Act 2000[7] 'terrorism' means the use of violence for political ends, and includes any use of violence for the purpose of putting the public or any section of the public in fear. The Act covers the disruption or interference with the supply of water or power where life, health or safety may be put at risk. It also deals with the disruption of vital computer systems and the assassination of key individuals. The proscription of organizations is also provided for.

A later statute, the Terrorism Act 2006, extended the scope of the 2000 Act and defined terrorism to include the following:

- using serious violence against a person or serious damage to property;
- endangering a person's life (apart from that of the terrorist);
- causing serious risk to the health and safety of the public or a section of the public;
- seriously interfering with or seriously disrupting an electronic system;
- threatening to influence domestic or foreign governments for the purpose of advancing a political, religious or ideological cause;
- using radioactive materials or devices; and
- encouraging terrorism—this is aimed, although not solely, at bookshops and other disseminators of terrorist publications.[8]

Other statutes relating to terrorism include:

- the Anti-Terrorism, Crime and Security Act 2001[9] which allows foreign nationals

---

7. HMSO. (2000). c. 11.
8. *Ibid.* Terrorism Act 2006. c. 11.
9. *Ibid.* c. 24.

who are suspected of terrorism to be detained for extended periods and aims to ensure the security of nuclear and aviation industries; and

- the Prevention of Terrorism Act 2005[10] which brought about a new system of control orders imposing obligations on individuals, such as prohibitions on the possession or use of certain items and restrictions on movement to or within certain areas.

Police terrorism arrest statistics from 11 September 2001 to 31 March 2007 show that 1,165 arrests were made under the Terrorism Act 2000 and 63 arrests under other legislation where a terrorist investigation was conducted.[11] Of the total 1,228 arrested:

- 132 were charged with terrorism offences only;
- 109 were charged with terrorism offences and other criminal offences;
- 195 were charged under other legislation for murder, grievous bodily harm, firearms, explosives offences, fraud, false documents;
- 76 were handed over to immigration authorities;
- 15 were on police bail awaiting charging decisions;
- 1 warrant was issued for arrest;
- 12 people were cautioned;
- 1 was dealt with under youth offending procedures;
- 11 were dealt with under mental health legislation;
- 4 were transferred to Police Service of Northern Ireland custody;
- 2 were remanded in custody awaiting extradition proceedings;
- 669 were released without charge; and
- 1 case was awaiting further investigation.

Of those charged:

- there have been 41 Terrorism Act convictions;
- 183 were convicted under other legislation;
- 110 at or awaiting trial; and
- 4 at or awaiting trial for terrorism related offences only.[12]

It goes without saying that anti-terrorism laws are bound to infringe upon civil liberties to some extent. For instance, under the 2000 Act the police can in effect

---

10. *Ibid.* c. 2.
11. www.homeoffice.gov.uk/security/terrorism-and-the-law/
12. *Ibid.*

stop and search anyone without giving a reason and at random. It has even been suggested that alleged terrorists should be held for up to 90 days before being released or charged: in effect, a form of internment without trial. According to Amnesty International, in the year 2005 ten foreign nationals were being held without charge in the UK under the 2001 Act. However, they pointed out that in December 2004 the Law Lords had ruled that such detention breached European human rights law, on the ground that the persons in question could not be deported to their home country as they faced torture or death there. What is clear is that, although the threat of terrorism is real, all anti-terrorist legislation needs to be subjected to public scrutiny to ensure the least possible infringement of civil liberties and human rights.

THE CRIMINAL JUSTICE ACT 2003

This Act represents a landmark in the evolution of criminal justice in England and Wales. Arising from the 2002 White Paper, *Justice for All*,[13] 'It is by far the most wide-ranging statute of its kind of modern times ... Some changes are fundamental, including those to the law of criminal evidence which replace Common Law and statutory rules that have served for over a century.'[14]

The background to the Act was the government's belief that a number of changes in evidence and procedure were needed to strengthen the hand of prosecutors. Accordingly, judges in the Crown Court are now allowed to hear trials sitting alone without a jury where there is a 'real and present' danger of jury tampering and it is in the interests of justice to do so.[15] Moreover, judges are given powers to dismiss a jury during the course of a trial if the jury is being intimidated or possibly where there is a 'serious risk that the jury will be subject to bribery or intimidation.' Although the government has declared that the defendant's existing right to elect for trial by jury will be retained as an issue of principle, it also ominously says it will be kept under review.

Rules of criminal evidence relating to double jeopardy, previous convictions, character, hearsay and the serious effect the 2003 Act has had upon all of them are dealt with earlier in *Chapter 14* of this book.

However, the Act goes much further than even those controversial provisions. It potentially affects every criminal trial as it progresses through the system. Some of the proposals herald a more flexible approach to the management of cases but those relating to juries and the rules of evidence do, as we have seen, undermine many of the protections for defendants built up over centuries. It can even be argued that

---

13. HMSO. Cm. 5563.
14. Bryan Gibson. (2004) *Criminal Justice Act 2003: A Guide to the New Procedures and Sentencing.* Winchester, Waterside Press. p. 9.
15. Criminal Justice Act 2003. sec. 44.

defendants are often to be regarded as guilty before their case is heard—how else can the giving of previous convictions before trial be interpreted? And where does this leave the presumption of innocence? Moreover, in the magistrates' courts the decision on whether this is to be done is made by a judge who will not be involved in the case and knows very little about it. What has happened to the requirement that the prosecution must prove its case beyond reasonable doubt if the magistrates know before hearing the case that the defendant has previous convictions? As a matter of principle the court should decide the case only on the evidence before it.

So far as juveniles are concerned it is intended that the welfare principles of the Children and Young Persons Act 1933[16] will continue. They are, however, changed by the provisions for restorative justice dealt with in the next chapter which are an attempt to improve the position for young people. Juveniles remain subject to the warnings and reprimands provided by the Crime and Disorder Act 1998, which introduced several measure openly based upon restorative justice, and are unaffected by the adult scheme for conditional cautions.[17]

MAGISTRATES

As early in the twentieth century as 1925, a large number of cases which were previously triable only by a judge and jury had been brought within the jurisdiction of magistrates at Petty Sessions.[18] Fifty years later, in 1975, the James Committee reached the 'firm conclusion' that the choice of venue by the defendant should not be removed because of its long existence and widespread public support.[19] Notwithstanding this decided view, in 1977 the government introduced the Criminal Law Act of that year which, based in fact on some of the James Committee's own proposals, took away from defendants the right to choose trial by jury in the case of certain public order offences and those where criminal damage below £200 was alleged,[20] even though this meant that a new raft of accused persons might be sent to prison without an opportunity to exercise their previous right to elect trial by their peers.

With the Criminal Justice Act 1988 the powers of magistrates were further extended by increasing summary offences to include, among others, common assault and battery and taking a conveyance without consent.[21] Five years later, the Royal Commission on Criminal Justice suggested that the prosecution and defence could agree on the mode of trial but that otherwise the magistrates court should decide

---

16. 23 and 24 Geo. V. c. 12.
17. Bryan Gibson. *Criminal Justice Act 2003. Op. cit.* p, 157.
18. Sir Thomas Skyrme. (1979) *The Changing Image of the Magistracy.* London, The Macmillan Press., p. 5.
19. The James Committee. (1975) *The Distribution of the Criminal Business between the Crown Courts and the Magistrates' Courts. Report of the Interdepartmental Committee.* Cmnd. 6323. paras. 60-61.
20. Criminal Law Act 1977. ss. 15 and 22 schedule 4.
21. Ss. 37-39.

upon the venue.[22]

Magistrates' courts are mainly served by volunteer justices of the peace known as lay magistrates who are unpaid but trained and advised by a legally qualified clerk also known as a justices' clerk or court legal adviser depending on his or her status. Some courts have a professional district judge. In the year 2006 magistrates' courts dealt with 2.3 million defendants in criminal cases. With serious cases, however, the courts deal only with the initial remand proceedings before the case is committed to the Crown Court. The Crown Court will decide if the accused is to be bailed or kept in custody pending his or her trial and the court, with a judge and jury, will hear and determine the case.

EITHER-WAY CASES

Such cases may be tried summarily in the magistrates' court or by indictment before a jury in the Crown Court. The official aim is to ensure that cases are dealt with in the appropriate court and reach it as soon as possible.

At present, where a defendant has been charged with an offence which is triable either way, the magistrates' court must hold a mode of trial hearing to decide whether they will hear the case or send it to the Crown Court.[23] It is essential that the defendant be asked where he or she wishes the case to be heard and his or her presence at the mode of trial hearing is required unless their behaviour is too unruly for the court to proceed, or the court considers there is good reason to proceed in their absence and their legal representative consents.[24]

If the defendant pleads guilty at the mode of trial hearing, the prosecution will present a summary of its case and suggest which court is suitable to give sentence. The justices will then decide whether to deal with sentence themselves or commit to the Crown Court. If the defendant pleads not guilty, the prosecution and the defendant will be asked whether summary trial or trial on indictment is more suitable. Taking both views into account the justices will then decide where the case should be tried. They will have to consider the nature of the case, how serious it is and whether the penalty they can inflict would be adequate. The defendant still has to agree to summary trial if the court so decides and he retains the right not to do so and to elect a Crown Court trial with a jury. If the court decides the offence to be suitable for trial by indictment the defendant cannot insist on summary trial.

Today there are some 30 main types of either-way offences, comprising about 700 individual crimes including offences of violence, threats to kill, burglaries and

---

22. Royal Commission on Criminal Justice, 1993. Cm. 2263.
23. The Magistrates' Courts Act 1980. s. 19.
24. *Ibid.* ss. 18(2) and 23(1).

thefts, arson not endangering life and causing death by aggravated vehicle taking.[25] According to the White Paper, *Justice for All,*[26] most either-way cases are dealt with by magistrates—'87 per cent in the year 2000, with 9 per cent going to the Crown Court because the magistrates declined to take the case and 4 per cent because defendants elected.' It added that the proportion of cases heard by magistrates has increased since the year 2000.

As was to be expected changes have been made by the Criminal Justice Act 2003. The new 'allocation' procedure gives the prosecutor an opportunity to inform the magistrates of previous convictions when it is deciding whether to try an offence or send it to the Crown Court. And, once it has accepted jurisdiction it can no longer commit a defendant to the Crown Court for sentence even if it regards its own powers as insufficient. Thus, the previous position where a defendant who was tried summarily and then found to have a bad prior record could be sent to the Crown Court for sentence no longer applies. However, as previous convictions are aggravating factors that serve to increase the seriousness of the alleged offence, they will often influence the court's decision as to the suitable venue for trial and sentence in favour of the Crown Court.

MODE OF TRIAL HEARING

In 1999 and 2000 the government introduced two Criminal Justice (Mode of Trial) Bills[27] to provide that courts not defendants should decide whether either-way cases should be dealt with summarily without the defendant having the right to trial by jury (nowadays also known as 'allocation and sending'). The purpose, it was said, was to secure an annual reduction of about 1,200 Crown Court trials, producing a net yearly saving of £105 million. The cost of the criminal justice system is a frequent preoccupation of governments even if their proposals deny fundamental rights to defendants. These Bills were supported by those least inclined to approve of jury trial including some judges, magistrates and police. As that would have meant for those affected putting one's livelihood and reputation in the hands of a single judge it was vehemently opposed by lawyers involved in criminal work, civil liberties organizations and ethnic minority groups including the Commission for Racial Equality. After all, any offence serious enough to involve a sentence of imprisonment is serious enough to justify allowing the defendant to choose trial by his or her peers.

However, both Bills passed in the House of Commons, where the government

---

25. The Magistrates' Courts Act 1980, as amended.
26. (2002). White Paper. *Justice for All.*
27. HMSO. AJ1000150 and AJ1000225.

had a large majority, but were defeated in the House of Lords. Only three peers on the government benches spoke in support of the second Bill which suffered a heavy defeat on 28 September 2000.[28] Among other things, it was argued that the procedure would be expensive to administer and its effects would be racially discriminatory. Subsequently, the government promised similar legislation in the future and also, if necessary, the use of the Parliament Act 1911 to secure its enactment.

OTHER CHANGES INTRODUCED BY THE 2003 ACT

Bail
Section 4 of the Criminal Justice Act 2003 amended section 30 of PACE to allow instant bail to be granted by a police officer at the scene of a person's arrest where there is no immediate need to take the arrested person to a police station. This is known as 'street bail' and the arrested person has to attend at a station later. At the time of the arrest he, or she, must be given a notice in writing setting out both the offence for which the arrest has been made and the reasons for it. By section 17 the right of a defendant to make a bail application to the High Court has been abolished. Judicial review remains possible but this is more difficult and stringent tests have to be satisfied. Only an appeal to the Crown Court is now really practicable.

Stop and search powers
Section 1 of the Act extended police stop and search powers for 'prohibited articles' by adding offences of damaging or destroying property. As a consequence police officers may now stop and search someone on reasonable suspicion that he or she is carrying an article that can cause such damage. Examples include paint sprays for creating graffiti and petrol cans carried for the purpose of arson. By section 2, people who accompany constables on a search of premises may now take an active part in the search, as long as they remain accompanied at all times.

Jury service
Those ineligible to serve on a jury prior to the Criminal Justice Act 2003 included judges, justices of the peace, men and women involved in the various aspects of the legal system and in professions and occupations concerned with the administration of justice. The last category included barristers, solicitors, police, prison and probation officers. Added to them were clergymen, the mentally ill and people on bail. In general, ineligibility arose because it was believed that most of the people in these categories might have an undue influence on other jurors. This was rejected by the 2003 Act and, with the exception of mentally disordered people, all those involved

---

28. *Hansard.* [Lords] [616] cols. 961-1033.

are now eligible under Schedule 33. Two other groups can no longer claim to be excused from sitting. First: peers, MPs and full-time members of the armed forces and secondly: medical practitioners, dentists, nurses, midwives, vets and pharmaceutical chemists. People with a criminal record involving certain types of sentence continue to be disqualified.

Trials without a jury

In addition to the powers of a judge to sit without a jury mentioned above, the Act provided that cases of serious or complex fraud should be tried without a jury if a judge was satisfied that, 'the complexity of the trial or the length of the trial (or both) is likely to make the trial so burdensome to the members of a jury hearing the trial that the interests of justice require that serious consideration should be given to the question of whether the trial should be conducted without a jury' (section 43). That was the intention, but on 28 November 2005 the then Attorney-General, Lord Goldsmith QC, announced in the House of Lords that the government had scrapped the plan.[29] He admitted that the government was about to lose the vote in the Lords and later, on 20 March 2006, he said, it had proved impossible to negotiate with opposition parties to abolish the right to trial by jury using order-making powers under the Act.[30] A group of peers, including Law Lords and a former Attorney-General, had insisted that prosecutors and judges were responsible for a number of celebrated fraud cases collapsing and insisted that, if cases were presented properly, juries could cope. Nonetheless, Lord Goldsmith added that the government planned primary legislation to push the abolition through.

A trial can still be conducted without a jury where a judge is satisfied that there is evidence of a 'real and present danger that jury tampering would take place.' The risk had to be so substantial, despite any steps that might be taken, including police protection, as to make it necessary to dispense with a jury in the interests of justice (section 44).

Prosecution appeals

Historically, the prosecution had the right to appeal decisions in the magistrates' courts on grounds of error of law or unreasonableness, and the right under the Criminal Justice Act 1988 to appeal an 'unduly lenient sentence.' Under the Criminal Justice Act 2003 they have the right to appeal a judge's decision to proceed without a jury and against some grants of bail. Part 9 of the Act gives a prosecutor a right to appeal against a judge's decision in a trial on indictment to order an acquittal before the jury has been asked to consider the evidence, in order to 'balance the defendant's existing right of appeal against conviction and sentence.' By section 58

---

29. *Hansard*, [Lords} [676]
30. *Ibid.* [680].

leave to appeal has to be obtained either from the trial judge or the Court of Appeal and the ruling terminating the trial will not take effect while the prosecutor is considering whether to appeal, or until the conclusion of any appeal or its abandonment.

Advance disclosure

Section 32 of the Criminal Justice Act 2003 amends the defence disclosure require-ments of section 5 of the Criminal Procedure and Investigations Act 1996[31] by obliging the accused to provide a more detailed defence statement than before. This substantially extends the information available to prosecutors. Briefly, the accused must in advance of the trial:

- set out the nature of the defence on which he or she intends to rely; and
- indicate any point of law that he or she wishes to raise, including the admissibility of evidence or abuse of process.

The accused person must also provide details, including names and addresses, of the witnesses he or she intends to call and of any experts consulted. In a new departure, the police may now interview potential defence witnesses. In the Crown Court, the judge has a discretion to disclose the defence statement to the jury if it differs from what is put forward in court. The prosecutor already had a continuing duty to disclose material that might reasonably be considered capable of undermin-ing the case for the prosecution or assisting the case of the accused.

Sentencing

Part 12 of the Criminal Justice Act 2003 made substantial amendments to nearly every part of sentencing practice. In another new departure, the general purposes of sentencing are declared to be:

- punishment;
- crime reduction (including deterrence);
- reform and rehabilitation;
- public protection; and
- reparation.

There are now 'generic community orders' for offenders aged 18 and over. With the intention of tailoring sentences more closely to the offender's requirements, such orders include unpaid work, supervision, activity, curfew, exclusion and residence alone or in combination with each other. There are no longer provisions limiting

---

31. HMSO. (1996) c. 25.

the use of some community orders to situations where the offence is punishable by imprisonment. Provision is, however, made for sentences of intermediate custody and custodial sentences followed by a period of community work and supervision.

In general, a court must not pass a custodial sentence unless the offence is so serious that neither a fine alone nor a community sentence can be justified for it. (section 152(2)). Notwithstanding that, as indicated below, under the Act danger- ous offenders are subject to compulsory life sentences or minimum sentences for over 150 violent or sexual crimes provided such offenders pose a significant risk to the public of serious harm occasioned by further specified offences. The Act created a new kind of life sentence called 'imprisonment for public protection' (or 'deten- tion for public protection') for those aged under 18 which may even be imposed for offences which otherwise carry a maximum sentence of ten years. (Sections 224-230 and Schedule 15). Such sentences are indeterminate in nature.

By section 167 the Act also created a Sentencing Guidelines Council with seven members drawn principally from the judiciary but with a minority of four non- judicial members. It is chaired by the lord chief justice and the non-judicial mem- bers must have experience in policing, criminal prosecution, criminal defence, the promotion of the welfare of victims of crime or more than one of these areas. It can issue statutory guidelines to all criminal courts which are required to have regard to them and give reasons for any departure from them.

Life sentence for murder
Section 269 of the Criminal Justice Act 2003 provides that for mandatory life sen- tences for murder the court must make an order specifying a period that the pris- oner will have to serve before the Parole Board can consider release on licence under section 28 of the Crime (Sentences) Act 1997,[32] i.e. a minimum term.

Life sentences may be mandatory for murder but they do not mean 'life' and Sched- ule 21 of the 2003 Act sets out the minimum terms for those convicted of murder. These terms are known as 'starting points' since the judge is required to start from them before increasing or diminishing the actual term. The starting points are:

> *Whole life*: This is imposed on an offender over 21 at the time of the offence, where the offence involves the murder of two or more persons with premeditation or abduction or sexual or sadistic conduct. It is also the starting point where such abduction or conduct involves the murder of a child, if the offender has been previously convicted of murder or if the murder is for the purpose of advancing a political, religious or ideological cause.

> *30-year minimum*: imposed on an offender over 18 at the time of the offence for:
> (i) the murder of a police officer or prison officer in the course of his duty,;
> (ii) a murder involving firearms or explosives;

---

32. *Ibid.* (1997) c. 43.

   (iii) a murder done for gain,

   (iv) a murder intended to obstruct or interfere with the course of justice;

   (v)   murder involving sexual or sadistic conduct;

   (vi) the murder of two or more persons;

  (vii) a murder racially or religiously aggravated or aggravated by sexual orientation; or

 (viii) a murder normally resulting in a whole life tariff committed by someone under 21.

   15-year minimum: any murder not covered by another category.

   12-year minimum: murder committed by a person under the age of 18.

In 2002 in *R. v. Secretary of State for the Home Department, ex parte Anderson* the House of Lords ruled that the Home Secretary was not permitted to set minimum terms for life sentences. They said that in order to have a fair trial under article 6 of the European Convention on Human Rights a defendant should be sentenced by an independent judge and not a politician who has extraneous concerns which may affect his or her judgment. The Home Secretary of the time, David Blunkett MP, responded in the House of Commons on 25 November 2002 with the following statement:

> The case of Anderson deals with the Home Secretary's power to set the tariff, or minimum period a convicted murderer must remain in custody until he becomes eligible for release. This power has ensured ministerial accountability to Parliament within the criminal justice system for the punishment imposed for the most heinous and serious of crimes … As is proper in a democracy, Parliament will continue to retain the paramount role of setting a clear framework within which the minimum period to be served will be established … I intend to legislate this session to establish a clear set of principles within which the courts will fix tariffs in the future. In setting a tariff, the judge will be required, in open court, to give reasons if the term being imposed departs from those principles.

Prison sentences

The new short forms of custody for adults are known as 'custody plus', 'intermittent custody' and the 'suspended sentence'. All three are prison sentences of less than 12 months and can thus be passed by magistrates as well as the Crown Court (although the first two have never been brought into force).

By section 181 of the Criminal Justice Act 2003 *custody plus* involves the following stages:

- the court must set an overall term of imprisonment which must be at least 28 weeks and not more than 51 weeks is respect of any one offence;
- it must specify a custodial period of at least 2 weeks and not more than 13 weeks at the end of which the offender will be released on licence,
- it must specify the licence period of at least 26 weeks; and

- it must set licence conditions to be observed on release from prison.

For sentences under 12 months only, *intermittent custody* means 'part-time custody' at weekends or other times determined by the court rather than continuous imprisonment. It represents an endeavour to save costs and reduce the numbers in prison but also to enable the offender to be employed and keep his family and community ties. In contrast with custody plus there is no minimum licence period at the end of a sentence.

The *suspended sentence* is a variant of custody plus (but currently operates as an amended form of a what can be styled 'old-style' suspended sentence until the underlying custody plus provisions are brought into force). By section 189 of the 2003 Act, once the court has determined the overall term of imprisonment and the custodial and licence periods, it has a discretion to order that the offender comply with stated requirements and if he or she does so the sentence of imprisonment is not to take effect. The requirements are the same as those for a generic community order and they may be reviewed periodically.

An important part of the correctional process in prison today is the establishment of training and career programmes for prisoners. Such training can include literacy classes, social and work skills and help can be given in obtaining work on release.

Indeterminate sentences

In a sense indeterminate sentences have existed since the introduction of parole but in their full sense they were provided for in the Criminal Justice Act 2003 as measures to protect the public from dangerous criminals, although in practice they have come under a great deal of justified criticism. They have been in use since April 2005. Known as indeterminate sentences for public protection (ISPPs) they can be imposed on a person convicted of a serious offence (defined by section 224 as an offence which is punishable by imprisonment for life, or imprisonment for a determinate period of ten years or more) where the court finds there is a significant risk to the public of serious harm from the commission by the defendant of a crime drawn from a list of 153 separate violent and sexual offences. Such a person will have to serve a minimum term and then remain behind bars until the Parole Board decides he is no longer a threat to society. In reality it has meant that people are being sent to prison even though their crime was relatively minor. For instance, in December 2005 Christopher Brown, aged 18, was sentenced to imprisonment for life for setting two wheelie bins on fire in north Devon. Although he caused only a few pounds worth of damage he was given an indeterminate sentence after threatening to commit more crimes if he was released.

Defendants given such a sentence must serve the minimum term set by the court and there has been criticism that some such terms given so far are much too lenient if the defendant is a danger to society. A further problem arises from the fact that after serving the minimum sentence a prisoner has to attend courses to enable him to present evidence to the Parole Board that he is no longer a risk and often such courses are not available. If he cannot show that he is no longer a danger he might remain behind bars indefinitely. But if no course is available, his detention after the minimum sentence has been held by a High Court judge to be unlawful and this could mean hundreds of dangerous prisoners being released prematurely.[33] On 1 February 2008 the Court of Appeal criticised Jack Straw, the Justice Secretary, for inadequately funding rehabilitation courses for prisoners serving open-ended sentences. It held that the Secretary of State acted unlawfully in failing to allow prisoners serving indeterminate sentences for public protection show the Parole Board by the expiry of their minimum terms that it was no longer necessary to confine them. At the same time the court overturned the earlier High Court finding that it was unlawful to hold prisoners serving such sentences after their minimum recommended term.[34]

There is also the case of *Wells v. The Parole Board*.[35] Wells was convicted of the attempted robbery of a taxi driver in November 2005 and sentenced to 12 months less 58 days. The sentence was due to expire on 17 September 2006. Parole Board hearings were not arranged until 18 January and 29 March 2007. Both hearings were adjourned for lack of a quorum and a fresh hearing was arranged for 9 May 2007. Using Article 5(4) of the European Convention On Human Rights, Wells applied for judicial review seeking a mandatory order that his case be heard by the Board forthwith. Nevertheless, it was not until eight months after the expiry of his sentence, that Wells' case was at last reviewed on 9 May. The board acknowledged that it was not his fault that, although he had wished to, he had not undertaken any course since such courses were not available at his prison. Yet, on the basis that they could not make up for deficiencies in the prison service they found he should not be released.

On Wells' appeal to the High Court, Lord Justice Laws stated that legislation allows 'the indefinite detention of prisoners beyond the date when the imperatives of retributive punishment are satisfied.' But, he added, this further detention was not arbitrary. It was imposed to protect the public and as soon as it was shown to be unnecessary for that purpose, the prisoner must be released. There must be material at hand to show whether the prisoner's further detention is necessary or not:

Without current and periodic means of assessing the prisoner's risk the regime cannot work as Parliament intended, and the only possible justification for the prisoner's further detention

---

33. *The Times*. 21 August 2007.
34. *R. (Walker (David) v. Secretary of State for Justice: R. James (Brett)) v. Same*. 1 February 2008.
35. EWHC. QB. (2007)

is altogether absent. In that case the detention is arbitrary and unreasonable on first principles and therefore unlawful.

At the time of writing, so many indeterminate sentences have been handed down by the courts that the numbers in custody who may never be released is causing a serious crisis of overcrowding in the prison service. By February 2007 the number of prisoners serving such sentences had reached 8,700, i.e. 140 prisoners a month since its introduction. After the term has been served, if the prisoner can demonstrate that he or she has undertaken necessary courses (if available) this will assist him or her to convince the Parole Board that he or she is fit for release and does not pose a threat to society. The Board will calculate the risk with a forensic psychiatrist's report and on a specific assessment of the individual. If he or she is released they will be on licence for life and subject to conditions. The only right they will have is an opportunity every ten years to apply to be released from the licence.

One problem with indeterminate sentences is that people can be in prison for their characteristics rather than their crime. Moreover, vulnerable people with personality disorders may be locked away for years for trivial offences, they may be sent back to prison after their release and they face the ever-present danger of being criminally contaminated whilst in prison. According to Richard Garside, the director of the Centre for Crime and Justice Studies at King's College. London, 'This sentence was ill-conceived from the start. In implementation it has proved highly corrosive of the principles of a just, proportionate and effective sentencing framework.'[36]

Conditional cautions

Normal police cautions are unconditional and accordingly the defendant cannot subsequently be prosecuted for the relevant offence. The conditional cautions scheme aims to divert lower level offenders from appearing in court. Conditions are directed at rehabilitation, addressing the offender's behaviour, and/or reparation—i.e. making good the harm the offender has caused. They may include restorative justice measures and are not aimed at contested or more serious cases or at prolific or serious offenders.[37]

Section 22 Criminal Justice Act 2003 provides that in place of prosecution a conditional caution may be given to a person aged 18 or over provided the conditions have the object of facilitating the rehabilitation of the offender and/or ensuring that he or she makes reparation for the offence and each of the following five requirements is met:

---

36. *The Times.* 8 May 2007.
37. Criminal Justice System Online.

- the constable or other authorised person giving the caution has evidence that the offender has committed an offence;
- there must be sufficient evidence to charge the offender and a conditional caution is suitable;
- the offender must admit committing the offence;
- the effect of the caution must be explained to the offender and he or she must be warned that failure to comply with any of the conditions may result in he or her being prosecuted for the offence; and
- the offender must sign a document containing details of the offence, his or her consent to the caution and the conditions attached to it.

Further, the Police and Justice Act 2006[38] allows punitive conditions to be attached to a caution. Indeed, this Act is extremely far-reaching. It allows the police, in addition to judges, to impose draconian pre-charge bail conditions on suspects which could include curfews and electronic tags. Shami Chakrabarti, the director of the civil liberties organization Liberty, had said of the Police and Justice Bill as it passed through its Parliamentary stages that it, 'offers a game of musical chairs in which the politicians are policemen, people become prosecutors and the police replace the judges. Justice becomes the odd man out.'

PUBLIC ORDER AND RACIAL AND RELIGIOUS HATRED

The Common Law offences against public order were riot, rout, affray and unlawful assembly. These have now been replaced under the Public Order Act 1986 with riot, violent disorder and affray. The Act also deals with offences relating to threatening, abusive, insulting or disorderly conduct, to public processions and meetings and to aggravated trespass.

By section 1(1) of the Act riot occurs when 12 or more persons use unlawful violence for a common purpose and their conduct is such as would cause a person of reasonable firmness to fear for his personal safety. The offence is triable only on indictment, the consent of the Director of Public Prosecutions is required and the maximum penalty is ten years in prison. By section 2(1) violent disorder occurs where three or more persons use or threaten unlawful violence and their conduct is such as would cause a person of reasonable firmness to fear for his person safety. The offence is triable either way and the maximum penalty on conviction on indictment is five years in prison. By section 3(1) of the Act a person is guilty of affray if he uses or threatens unlawful violence causing another of reasonable firmness to fear for his

---

38. HMSO. (2006). c. 48.

safety. The offence is triable either way with three years as the maximum punishment on conviction on indictment.

Part III (sections 17-29) of the Act deals with racial hatred. This is defined by section 17 as hatred against a group of persons in Great Britain defined by reference to colour, race, nationality (including citizenship) or ethnic or national origins. It is essential to the offence that there is an intent to stir up racial hatred or that it is likely to be stirred up, but not that it is actually stirred up. What is essential is that the written material, words or behaviour involved are threatening, abusive or insulting. The term 'ethnic' is construed widely following the words of Lord Fraser of Tullybelton in *Mandla v. Dowell Lee,* where he said:

> For a group to constitute an ethnic group in the sense of the Race Relations Act 1976, it must, in my opinion, regard itself, and be regarded by others, as a distinct community by virtue of certain characteristics. Some of these characteristics are essential; others are not essential but one or more of them will commonly be found and will help to distinguish the group from the surrounding community. The conditions which appear to me to be essential are these:

1. a long shared history, of which the group is conscious as distinguishing it from other groups, and the memory of which it keeps alive;
2. a cultural tradition of its own, including family and social customs and manners, often but not necessarily associated with religious observance. In addition to these two essential characteristics the following characteristics are, in my opinion, relevant:
3. either a common geographical origin, or descent from a small number of common ancestors;
4. a common language, not necessarily peculiar to the group;
5. a common literature peculiar to the group;
6. a common religion different from that of neighbouring groups or from the general community surrounding it;
7. being a minority or being an oppressed or a dominant group within a larger community...

> A group defined by reference to enough of these characteristics would be capable of including converts, for example, persons who marry into the group, and of excluding apostates. Provided a person who joins the group feels himself or herself to be a member of it, and is accepted by other members, then he is ... a member.[39]

The other Law Lords agreed and the dictum applies, among others, to Sikhs, with whom the case was concerned, and Jews.

---

39. (1983) *Mandla v, Dowell Lee.* 2 AC 548. pp. 562 and 1066-7.

No prosecution under Part III of the Act can be instituted without the consent of the Attorney-General and offences covered by Part III are triable either way with a maximum penalty of two years in prison.

The Public Order Act 1986 has been amended by the Racial and Religious Hatred Act 2006[40] with the creation of a new offence of stirring up hatred against persons on religious grounds. The new offence covers the use of words or behaviour or display of written material including public performances of plays, recordings, broadcasts or possession with a view to doing so. Following amendments in the House of Lords which removed recklessness, for each offence the words or material must be threatening and intended to stir up religious hatred. Religious hatred is defined as hatred against a group of persons defined by reference to religious belief, or lack of religious belief by such as Atheists and Humanists. Equally branches or sects within a religion can be considered as religions or religious beliefs in their own right.

The offence is committed only by the use of threatening words or behaviour and there is a requirement for the specific mental element that the defendant intends to stir up religious hatred. There is a defence for the protection of freedom of expression in that

Nothing in this Part of the Act should be read or given effect in a way which prohibits or restricts discussion, criticism or expression of antipathy, dislike ridicule, insult or abuse of particular religions or beliefs or practices of their adherents or of any other belief system or the beliefs or practices of its adherents or proselytising or urging adherents of a different religious or belief system to cease practising their religion or belief system.

The offence is an either-way offence with a maximum of seven years' imprisonment on indictment.

The Act is in line with the freedom of religion guaranteed by Article 9 of the European Convention On Human Rights. Further, the Act, in section 29J of Part 3A of the Schedule, makes it clear that the offences are not intended to limit or restrict discussion, criticisms or expressions of antipathy, dislike, ridicule or insult or abuse of particular religions or belief systems. It is to be hoped that this will prove to be the case in practice. No prosecution under the Act can be commenced without the consent of the Attorney-General and the maximum penalty for a conviction for an offence of stirring up religious hatred is seven years in prison. Finally, the Police and Criminal Evidence Act has been amended so that the powers of a citizen to arrest ('citizen's arrest') cannot be used in regard to offences of stirring up religious and racial hatred.

---

40. HMSO. (2006). c. 1.

MINISTRY OF JUSTICE

On 9 May 2007 the Home Office was split in the sense that some of its functions were handed to a new Ministry of Justice which also took over the former work of the Lord Chancellor's Department which ceased to exist as such. Although the possibility of such a ministry had been mentioned in the past, the split was carried out with unusual speed and the new department launched without serious consultation with the judiciary or the public. It was a classic *fait accompli.* Such speed was criticised by former lord chief justice, Lord Woolf, who said it should have been subjected to serious study rather than rushed through.

No doubt the Home Office was overstretched and prisons at bursting point when, in May 2007, the then home secretary, Dr. John Reid, revealed that it was 'not fit for purpose'. As a consequence it was restructured and now deals, among other things, with: public safety, liberty, the police, crime prevention, safeguarding personal identity, terrorism and immigration and asylum. The new Ministry of Justice's functions include: the courts, sentencing, the prison and probation services and parole, as well as constitutional affairs and human rights.

In the past the Home Office saw its role as to balance individual rights against the protection of the public. However, in a period of change over the last decade we have seen, as already indicated, the passing of 50 crime and punishment statutes and the creation of some 3,000 new criminal offences. Moreover, the terrorist attacks on New York, London and elsewhere have had the effect of increasing the politicisation of criminal justice. In these circumstances some slimming down of the Home Office and the creation of a new Ministry of Justice were probably inevitable. Otherwise, the home secretary might well have been not only overwhelmed but suffering from a split personality when confronting major threats to security on the one hand whilst seeking to encourage initiatives such as restorative justice.

The Constitutional Reform Act 2005[41] had already separated the judiciary from the legislature and the executive, transferred the judicial functions of the Lord Chancellor to the Lord Chief Justice and provided for a new Supreme Court. Scheduled to open in October 2009, this will take over the judicial role of the House of Lords and become the final court of appeal for the United Kingdom. Not everyone approved of these changes to the historical institutions that are seen as the bedrock of civil liberties. In particular, judges expressed some concern that as a consequence undue pressure might be put on them and judicial budgetary resources might be reduced. However, it was encouraging that Jack Straw, the Justice Secretary and Lord Chancellor, stressed that his first priority was to protect the independence of the judiciary.

---

41. *Ibid.* 2005 c. 4.

In justifying the break up of the former Home Office, Lord Falconer, the UK's first Justice Secretary, said it 'made sense to bring together all the people involved in the justice system' and hailed it as 'a huge step forward in making sure we have a justice system that works for the public, punishes the guilty and offers a realistic prospect of rehabilitation for the contrite.'[42] It remains to be seen how far such aspirations will be met. Both new departments must not be overwhelmed by the undoubtedly serious problems they will face but must remain open, democratic and accountable to the public. With their strategic roles and responsibilities both face a fresh start in a new era and should be a catalyst for progressive change.[43] That this is a daunting challenge can be seen by the regressive nature of much of the recent plethora of legislation mentioned in this chapter.

42. CJS Online.
43. Bryan Gibson. (2nd edn. 2008) *The New Home Office: An Introduction*. Hook, Waterside Press. chap. 10.

CHAPTER 18

The Advent of Restorative Justice

Although deterrence has long been at the core of the criminal justice system it is now widely considered that harsh punishment is not the best antidote to criminal activity. Hence the importance in recent times of non-custodial sentences as a possible alternative for all but serious crimes. To that should be added the new reliance on the assistance of community volunteers and the establishment of prison, and community, based organizations to facilitate the successful reintegration of the prisoner into society.[1] Today there are a variety of sanctions that are not punitive in the traditional sense.

WHAT IS RESTORATIVE JUSTICE?

As part of this way of thinking, restorative justice is a philosophy of justice that emphasises repairing the harm caused or revealed by criminal behaviour. To achieve that it seeks both to make reparation to the victim of crime and to securing the offender in the community. It is best attained by co-operative processes that include all stakeholders. And, it is new. As a former Deputy Secretary at the Home Office has said, 'The approach known as restorative justice has come into prominence in western societies only during the last ten years.'[2] It is still gaining momentum and is subject to fierce debate, not least as to the extent to which punishment can be combined with its methods. This lack of clear overall definition have caused some commentators to describe it as a 'rallying' cry rather than a fixed method.

In a reversal of the concept that became dominant at the time of Henry II, the advocates of restorative justice view crime as an act not against the State but against another individual or the community. In a sense it is a return to the late Anglo-Saxon system that sought to protect both victims and offenders, with compensation taking the place of the blood-feud and revenge. In the field of criminal justice it is based on the idea, 'that the response to crime should be to put right the harm, as far as possible, and not, as hitherto, to inflict harm on the offender'.[3] In other words, it is a theory of justice with a stress on making amends for harm done. As a consequence the victim plays a prominent role and often receives compensation or some other type of restitution from the offender. On the other hand, it is also intended that the offender should plainly see the consequences of his crime and hopefully be less likely to re-offend.

---

1. 'Penology,' Microsoft® Encarta® Online Encyclopedia 2007.
2. David Faulkner. (2006) *Crime, State and Citizen: A Field Full of Folk.* Winchester, Waterside Press. p. 153.
3. Martin Wright. (1999) *Restoring Respect for Justice.* Winchester, Waterside Press. p. 173.

Restorative justice takes many different forms but in the main it stresses the need for a corrective approach to harm, problem–solving and violations of legal and human rights. It gives to those directly involved and affected by crime an opportunity to participate in the response. This can involve meetings of the parties and others to discuss the crime and its effects, to give offenders an opportunity to repair the harm they have caused and restore both victims and offenders to contributing members of the community.

In criminal cases, victims are enabled to express the full impact of the crime upon their lives and to participate in holding the offender accountable for his actions. Equally, the offender can attempt mitigation for the crime, express remorse and pay compensation or undergo community service. In social justice cases, involving children in care and others, restorative justice is used to help them solve problems and integrate into the community, although the community can sometimes be intolerant. As two writers have put it,

> When a crime is committed some of the problems that result are addressed by the criminal justice system; other needs are met by restorative justice ... Criminal justice might address the legal needs of a person who has been victimised, but it cannot solve all the problems that arise for them or the community.[4]

They go on to cite from a 1995 report of the Ministry of Justice in New Zealand on the role of restorative justice in responding to the emotional dimensions of crime:

> The criminal justice system seeks to deal with crime dispassionately ... Restorative justice recognises the emotional effect of crime on victims, offenders and the community ... Restorative justice seeks healing of the emotional effects of crime as an important part of putting right the wrong.[5]

Some people, including David Faulkner, believe that restorative justice has arisen as an alternative to adversary trial. Faulkner writes,

> its origins, can be found partly in dissatisfaction with the operation of the adversarial system of justice in Common Law countries, which coincided with increased recognition of its neglect of the circumstances and feelings of victims of crime and its failure to require offenders to engage with the seriousness and consequences of their offences. They can also be found in different religious and cultural traditions in various parts of the world. Writers in the Christian tradition approach restorative justice from their ideas of punishment, reconciliation, redemption and atonement.[6]

---

4. Kimmett Edgar and Tim Newell. (2006) *Restorative Justice in Prisons: A Guide to Making it Happen.* Winchester, Waterside Press. p. 9.
5. New Zealand Ministry of Justice. (1995) p. 21.
6. David Faulkner. *Crime, State and Citizen: A Field Full of Folk. Op. cit.* p. 153.

The first point is, however, not strictly accurate in that restorative justice measures are being introduced within the framework of the adversary system of trial. In the inquisitorial system the prosecution does not bear the burden of proof which rests on the tribunal and the defendant does not have the right (now diluted in England) to remain silent under police interrogation. Also, it needs to be borne in mind that, as already shown,[7] more and more non-Common Law countries are turning from inquisitorial trial to adversary trial as the best means available of seeking the truth by extracting it with vigorous cross-examination.

Restorative justice has many positive features and there can be little doubt that much of it is here to stay. However, it requires the consent of the parties which is by no means always available and generally seems most applicable to youth crime. Indeed, in March 2007 the Restorative Justice Consortium found that fewer than one per cent of victims of adult offenders had access to restorative justice. It is also dependent on the offender admitting that an offence has been committed and the facts of the case not being in dispute.

DIFFERENT TYPES OF RESTORATIVE JUSTICE

(a) In court
With petty or first-time offenders a case may be dealt with by a pre-trial panel, with charges dismissed after compliance with a restitution agreement. For more serious cases restorative justice may form part of a sentence that includes a prison term or other punishments. There seems to be considerable potential for restorative approaches within prisons in terms of making them more humane, improving safety and making the experience less hostile and damaging for all concerned.[8]

(b) Victim-offender mediation
This usually involves a face-to-face meeting between the victim of a crime and the offender in the presence of a trained mediator. Participation is usually voluntary although the offender may participate in order to avoid more severe sanctions. The parties are able to express their views of the crime and its consequences to them, which can assist in dispelling misconceptions about one another. No specific outcome is imposed by the mediator but the mediation often concludes with an agreement about what the offender will do to make amends and repair the harm done to the victim. Unexpectedly, research by the Centre of Criminological Research at Sheffield University[9] has revealed that although offenders tended to want to make reparation, this was not generally considered important by the victims.

---

7. Ante. p.121.
8. See Edgar and Newell. *Restorative Justice in Prisons. Op. cit.* p. 22.
9. http//ccr.group.shef.ac,uk/

(c) Family group conferences

In addition to the victim and offender these meetings may include their families, who are also affected by the offence, and they are particularly useful in cases involving young people because of the importance of family in their lives. To participate, the offender must admit the offence. Others may be invited to attend such as friends, teachers and the police to represent the wider community. Again, the aim is to make amends for the harm done and enable all involved to move on.

(d) Community restorative boards

Such a board is composed of a small group of citizens, trained for the purpose, who conduct face-to-face meetings with offenders sentenced by a court to take part. They discuss with the offender the nature of his offence and its consequences for the victim and the community. They then arrive at appropriate sanctions which they discuss with the offender and endeavour to reach agreement with him for making reparation for the crime. A time limit is set and the offender must document his progress in carrying out the agreed steps. The board then reports to the court who alone decide what is to be done.

(e) Youth justice

When young people first commit minor offences, they can often be dealt with by the police or local authority using a variety of orders and agreements. The aim is to keep them out of the courts and prevent them falling into the youth justice system too early. It also offers them help and support to prevent them offending.[10]

If a young person under the age of 18 is convicted of an offence for which an adult could receive at least 14 years in custody, he or she may be sentenced under Section 90-91 Powers of Criminal Courts (Sentencing) Act 2000.11 This sentence can be given only in a Crown Court. If the conviction is for murder, the sentence falls under section 90 and is to be 'detained during Her Majesty's pleasure'. Otherwise the sentence will be under section 91 and its length (in custody) can be any where up to the adult maximum for the same offence, which for certain offences may be life.

If, under section 91, a young person is sentenced to less than four years, he or she will leave custody at the halfway point of their sentence and be supervised on licence by their supervising officer until the three-quarters point. If certain conditions apply, the young person may be released on a tag up to 134 days earlier, under the home detention curfew scheme. For young people sentenced to four years or more, if they are successful at their parole hearing, they will leave custody at the half-way point. If they are unsuccessful, they will leave at the two-thirds point. In

---

10. www.yjb.gov.uk/en-gb/yjs/SentencesOrdersandAgreements/
11. *Ibid.*

both cases, they will be supervised by their supervising officer until the three-quarters point.

Details of the sentences and orders available in the Youth Justice System are available to parents and interested parties online or in specialist publications.

Of course, there are cases which are unsuitable for restorative justice. These include where a defendant denies having committed a crime or, if he or she admits it, they show no remorse. Equally, except with community service, if the offender is unwilling to participate the purpose is defeated as he or she cannot be made directly accountable to the victim.

VICTIMS' RELATIVES

On 24 April 2006, under a pilot scheme, the Old Bailey and Crown Courts in Birmingham, Cardiff, Manchester and Winchester were given a new historic role in their proceedings. For the first time, the relatives of victims of murder and manslaughter were able to address the court after a guilty verdict, but before sentence. At the time of writing the scheme is being extended in a diluted form to every criminal court in England and Wales and to include the offence of causing death by dangerous driving. The original scheme opened the door to emotional pleading to influence sentences and secure revenge and could have produced scenes hitherto foreign to English courts. How many would restrain their feelings and remember the rules of evidence? And what if there were multiple victims, as with the Shipman murders? Moreover, what was the purpose when there already existed a right of families to address the court in writing through a victim impact assessment which went to the judge and which he could read out and use in sentencing? These considerations appear to have been taken into account and victims' families, instead of addressing the court, will instead be permitted to have statements read in court on their behalf. Restorative justice programmes include assisting relatives of victims but there was no obvious need for the original scheme to be used in court to the potential detriment of justice.

COMPLEMENTING THE LAW

Restorative justice is seen by Edgar and Newell and many others as an ideal complement to the criminal justice system. It is claimed that it assists each of the system's theories in the following manner:

- for retribution (or just deserts), community and victim have a say in what should happen as a result of the crime;

- for deterrence and social defence, offenders report the process as more demanding than the court process but also more respectful;
- for rehabilitation, the community and the victim are involved with the offender, often in taking part in a treatment plan.[12]

Moreover, offenders are 'censured and called to account (i.e. it is retributive), they have issues to work on for the future (i.e. rehabilitative) and they have an opportunity to make amends to the victims they have harmed (i.e. reparative).' The whole point of restorative justice, they say, is to heal.[13]

That undoubtedly is so and it has widespread support although it is unsuitable where an offender shows no remorse and for offenders incapable of taking responsibility. Some of it will surely remain as part of a non-custodial means of dealing with certain—particularly young—offenders. But it sits uneasily with the growth of retributive thinking by governments in the last 20 years. There are also concerns that it is held in private, without lawyers, and with little or no monitoring of its quality.[14] Moreover, as mentioned earlier, in March 2007 the Restorative Justice Consortium convened a seminar to identify the extent to which restorative justice has gained a foothold in the adult criminal justice system. They found that fewer than one per cent of victims of adult offenders had access to restorative justice.[15] It remains to be seen whether it can develop and improve or whether it will come to be seen as a false panacea in another attempt to answer the age-old question, 'Why punish?'

---

12. Edgar and Newell. *Restorative Justice in Prisons. Op. cit.* p. 20.
13. *Ibid.* pp. 20, 22.
14. See Declan Roche. (2003) *Accountability in Restorative Justice.* Oxford, Oxford University Press.
15. Martin Gosling. (2007) *Justice of the Peace.* vol. 171, p. 564.

CHAPTER 19

Placing Criminal Justice in Perspective

Apart from what has been attempted here there is, so far as I know, no book dealing with the entire history of criminal justice in England from Anglo-Saxon times to the present day. It must be clear that if this approach fulfils a need, at the same time it is virtually impossible to cover everything that could be said on so vast a subject. Most of the topics touched on could maybe justify a book in their own right and many such books have been written and published. On the other hand, the history of criminal justice as a whole has a living quality of its own with themes that are often in conflict but almost always interacting. Too many books on criminal justice deal exclusively with how the law stands at present and ignore the historical perspective which is crucial to an understanding of the fascinating story of how crimes and punishments evolved.

I have focussed, therefore, on topics that seem to me to be critical to the progress of the Criminal Justice System—in a word its lifeblood. These include Anglo-Saxon law, the growth of the criminal trial jury, the changes in, and development of, substantive laws like homicide, theft and rape over the centuries, and the nineteenth century conversion to secondary punishments as alternatives to the death penalty and the gradual shift to finding alternatives, in appropriate cases, to and better methods than punishment itself. Additionally, the origin of the rules of criminal evidence, the birth and rise of adversary trial and the modern concepts of human rights and restorative justice are essential ingredients of the concept and add to its human interest. Background ethical and political dynamics as well as the culture of practitioners, not least the idea of adversary trial and traditional ways of doing things, have also to be taken into account in this complex process that is criminal justice.

PUNISHMENT

At the present time Britain faces a penal crisis with its overcrowded prisons, longer sentences, growing recidivism and a hand-to-mouth penal policy. By the middle of the year 2007 the prison population of England and Wales had reached an all-time high of 81,016 and rising. This meant 150 people were in prison per 100,000 of the population—the highest rate in Europe. Since many prisoners were also being held in police station cells, which were quite inadequate for the purpose, the government was proposing to build 9,500 more prison places by the year 2012. In the meantime, about 25,000 prisoners were being scheduled for early release to ease the overcrowding.

So far as punishment is concerned there remains conflict over whether crime is the result of individual wickedness by someone not like the rest of us to be dealt with by imprisonment or a social phenomenon to be dealt with by community measures and involvement of the victim. In a sense the idea of punishment embodies theories of retribution against those of deterrence and reformation and, in England at least, governments have usually been found, at different times, attracted to one or the other. But how much, and what kind of, punishment is a recurrent question facing those involved in the criminal justice system. To give a recent example, on 8 June 2007 the Prison Service hosted in Wakefield Prison a lecture entitled, 'Public Protection—Public Delusion'. Mitch Egan, one of ten regional offender managers created by the National Offender Management Service, argued that none but the most serious criminals should be sent to prison. That should be reserved for only the most dangerous offenders on the ground that prison is ineffective in reforming criminals.

This approach aroused intense antagonism and, in contrast, and despite restorative justice measure, there has been the recent increase in a punitive approach with the indeterminate sentences that can be passed under the Criminal Justice Act 2003 and the process of 'naming and shaming' offenders which is popular with sections of the public and is a growing feature in both the United States of America and England. The intense feelings, both public and private, that are aroused around issues of criminal justice and punishment are an expression of the political nature of the subject.

As we have seen the utilitarian tradition of punishment is the basis of the theory of deterrence that involves deterring both the offender and those who would follow his or her example by putting the offender where he or she cannot re-offend, at least for a time in a proportional manner. In contrast, the retributive tradition seeks revenge and an eye-for-an-eye. Yet, in England, at least, during the last three centuries there has always been a strong desire for reformation of the offender as exemplified by the work of John Howard and Herbert Gladstone. In a sense this has been the liberal tradition and in this context Radzinowicz, for his part, believed that liberalism meant:

> free will; criminal responsibility; proportionality between the gravity of the crime and the nature and degree of punishment; avoidance of indeterminate sentences and as much restriction as possible on administrative interferences in the enforcement of criminal law … the liberal ingredient in criminal justice in a country like Britain [has been] much less susceptible than the social ingredient to radical change or insidious manipulations, for the simple reason that it is grounded in the constitutional fabric of the country. But, even so, its historical stability should not be taken for granted.[1]

These different approaches have been dealt with in this book but criminal law changes in the last decade show the prescience of Radzinowicz in warning that lib-

---

1. Sir Leon Radzinowicz. (1999) *Adventures in Criminology*. London, Routledge. p. 116.

eralism should not be taken for granted. Our criminal law is already extremely wide-ranging and it is dangerous to allow governments to undermine it by using the threat of terrorism or the more mundane question of cost to the public purse.

As has been said earlier there is very little theoretical framework for criminal justice in modern governmental thinking and practice in present day England. Criminal justice is always political in the broad sense of the word but it has been more directly politicised in the last 20 to 30 years. Margaret Thatcher was elected in 1979 in part on a platform of 'law and order' and made it a central element in her political appeal. Police powers were increased, public order law strengthened and the retributive aspects of punishments emphasised with a resulting substantial increase in the prison population. Little thought was given to the backlash in rising crime that would follow when the inmates of the country's prisons returned to the community. Efficiency in the fight against crime was the watchword.

When Tony Blair became Prime Minister in 1997 he recognised public feeling and, following Thatcher, used the slogan, 'Tough on crime, tough on the causes of crime'. As there was no theoretical basis for the cry the emphasis in reality was on the first part of the formula. Only with young people was the welfare philosophy continued but even then with an emphasis on law and order as with the anti-social behaviour orders. Inexorably, this political approach adopted by a line of 'tough' Home Secretaries, Michael Howard, Jack Straw and David Blunkett, led to the repressive and regressive features of the Criminal Justice Act 2003, parts of which undermine concepts of justice for defendants. This politicisation of criminal justice, and increasing severity of punishments, were carefully structured by governments and have paid electoral dividends. There are, it has been said:

> Many reasons to think that criminal justice policy and the institutions through which that policy is realised have a particular importance in establishing the legitimacy and credibility of governments. For a start, leaving aside the example of war, the power to convict and punish represents the most vivid exercise of state force in relation to individual citizens. Furthermore, and partly because of this, the nature of criminal justice power may be seen as a telling index of how humane and civilised a society really is. This is why evidence about matters such as the racial inequalities which mark the enforcement of criminal law—evidence which is depressingly plentiful in this country—cause such widespread concern.[2]

Very little, if anything, has been achieved in recent years in reducing crime or the numbers of people in prison. Indeed, recorded crime has doubled in the 20 years following 1979[3] and prison numbers have reached a record high. But there is no government-inspired debate to analyse why. Michael Howard's attitude that

---

2. Nicola Lacey, (2003) 'Principles, Politics, and Criminal Justice'. In *The Criminological Foundations of Penal Policy: Essays in Honour of Roger Hood*. Oxford, Oxford University Press. p. 85.

3. Philip Rawlings. (1999) *Crime and Power: A History of Criminal Justice 1688-1998*. London, Addison, Wesley Longman. p. 168.

'prison works' expressed a typical and erroneous 'practical' answer. A theoretical approach to the perennial question of why punish? might instead produce some new thinking relevant to the modern age. Some people, known as 'abolitionists' believe that the criminal justice system is bloated and should be reduced with infinitely less punishment and a minimum of coercion and interference in people's lives. This is not a view that is widely held, however, although there is some feeling that the penal system is too harsh on people who are merely inadequate. Nevertheless, a useful starting point might be with Bentham's belief, along with Beccaria, that all punishment is in itself evil since it inflicts pain. It is a kind of 'counter-crime' committed with the authority of the law. Hence it should be indulged in only to exclude some greater evil.[4] Punishment has to be intrinsically fair and just and be seen to be so and not merely, as so often in the past, as an imaginary panacea to prevent crime.

THE RULE OF LAW

In the background to criminal justice is the Rule of Law under which our system operates. No person can be punished or restrained by the state without being prosecuted for a specified crime and proved guilty beyond reasonable doubt to the satisfaction of an independent jury. In effect, everything is legal that has not been declared illegal. As has been said by historian E. P. Thompson:

> The Rule of Law itself, the imposing of effective inhibitions upon power and the defence of the citizen from power's all-intrusive claims, seems to me to be an unqualified human good. To deny or belittle this good is, in this dangerous century when the resources and pretensions of power continue to enlarge, a desperate error of intellectual abstraction. More than this, it is a self-fulfilling error, which encourages us to give up the struggle against bad laws and class-bound procedures, and to disarm ourselves before power. It is to throw away a whole inheritance of struggle *about* law, and within the forms of law, whose continuity can never be fractured without bringing men and women into immediate danger.[5]

In the end, I have made an attempt to explain the criminal justice system under which we live today with some assessment of its strengths and weaknesses against the essence of its past. At any given time this system reflects the society in which it is found and, where practicable, I have sought to give the context in which it operates. What is of interest, and it is worth repeating, is that the modern ideology of restorative justice can be traced back historically to late Anglo-Saxon times when financial payments replaced the blood feud with its retaliation and revenge. It was a period when primitive criminal justice sought to protect both victims and offenders. Over succeeding centuries, in an almost ceaseless flow despite setbacks, the criminal law

4. Jeremy Bentham. (1830) *Rationale of Punishment*. In *Works*. Edinburgh, John Bowring. pp. 1-143.
5. E. P. Thompson.)1975) *Whigs and Hunters. The Origin of the Black Act*. London, Allen Lane. p. 266.

expanded and grew as society passed through phases of royal power, to aristocratic rule and gradually to democracy. The biggest blemish was the ubiquitous death penalty which lay at the very heart of political life. Yet, even that was modified by the genius of the people with the benefit of clergy and jury nullification that saved countless prisoners from the gallows.

Other punishments were also cruel and outrageous, and were considered 'normal' at various times, but were gradually ameliorated. And, at numerous stages in our history the Common Law, juries, some lawyers, Parliament and, sometimes through the latter, statesmen, proved to be standard bearers of liberty. Torture was never institutionalised as on the continent of Europe, and adversary trial and the beginnings of modern human rights were born here and became England's gift to the world. It is all the more regrettable that in recent times there has been a turn for the worse and crucial aspects of liberty under the criminal justice have been seriously diluted.

CRIMINAL JUSTICE UNDER ATTACK

Whatever the state of criminal justice at any given time it has always had its critics and its reformers. That is not surprising since society itself is always in a state of flux and usually changing rapidly, with the law lagging behind. Principle is also involved since people with power often seek to hold tenaciously on to what exists or, sometimes, to turn the clock back as with the Bloody Code which vastly extended the offences for which death was the penalty. Today we are faced with a similar problem. Partly for reasons of cost and partly from ideological, electoral and power motives, governments are successfully undermining cherished hard-won foundations of liberty. Some of these are set out in *Chapter 14* which reveals a serious and determined attack on vital rules of evidence. Furthermore, the whole system is undergoing sweeping changes with 50 crime and punishment statutes and 3,000 new criminal offences seeing the light of day in the last decade as government has increasingly undertaken to form criminal justice policy. As part of that process there have been fundamental changes to the system following the atrocities in the United State on 11 September 2001 and in London on 7 July 2005. At risk are fundamental principles of equality, the Rule of Law and human rights despite the Human Rights Act.

In a speech in Watford on 2 September 2005 the Prime Minister, Tony Blair said, 'The criminal justice system that we have in this country still asks first and foremost, 'How do we protect the accused from potential transgressions of the state or the police?' That is the attitude the criminal justice system has at its heart.' Saying he wanted to put the question the other way round, he continued, 'I think the question should be: 'How do we protect the majority from the dangerous and irresponsible minority?' In line with a major thesis of this book David Faulkner's response to that is:

> On that view, punishment and the rest of the apparatus of criminal justice can be treated as just another form of social intervention which the Government has at its disposal, and as having no particular authority of its own. Principles such as the presumption of innocence, the criminal standard of proof, the right to silence, disclosure of the case against the defendant and 'equality of arms' are no longer of much importance.[6]

He goes on to add that:

> The Government clearly intends that the state, through the criminal justice system, should intervene more actively and intrusively in controlling people's lives in the interests of public safety and comfort, in ways which rely on punishment but which go far beyond punishment as it is ordinarily understood. If the state is to punish people for who they are and not for what they have done, there is a serious danger that punishment will lose its legitimacy, and those who administer it will lose their moral authority.

As part of the government's ongoing changes to the criminal justice system, the Home Office no longer exists having been replaced by two departments one dealing with national security issues and the other a new Ministry of Justice. The lord chancellor no longer heads the judiciary or presides over the House of Lords from the Woolsack, his judicial functions now being performed by the lord chief justice, and the courts now determine the time to be served under a sentence of life imprisonment instead of the Home Secretary. A Commissioner has been appointed under the Domestic Violence, Crime and Victims Act 2004[7] which, in giving the police and courts wide powers to protect victims and prosecute abusers, has provided the biggest overhaul of domestic violence law in 30 years.

As the jury has become more democratic by including almost the whole adult population, so it has increasingly come under attack. The Auld Report[8] clearly expressed the view that the jury had largely outlived its usefulness. It is true that the government accepted only two of the report's recommendations affecting the right to jury trial. The first, to give judges power, in certain circumstances, to sit without a jury on fraud cases has temporarily been withdrawn. The second was for a judge to dispense with the jury where he considers there is a substantial danger of jury tampering. The government has also extended the power of magistrates to hear cases instead of trial by judge and jury. It is still possible that other proposals of the Auld Report will be adopted in the future to diminish or extinguish the right to jury trial.

---

6. David Faulkner. (2006) *Crime, State and Citizen: A Field Full of Folk* Hook, Waterside Press. p. 361.
7. HMSO. 2004, c.28.
8. (2001) *Review of the Criminal Courts of England and Wales.* Cm. 5563.

The Criminal Justice Act 2003, essentially based upon Auld, contains a whole raft of provisions that undermine the rights of prisoners on trial. Sometimes with certain limitations, the Act has reduced the rights of defendants in regard to hearsay, previous convictions, the presumption of innocence, double jeopardy, the right to silence and the exclusion of evidence of bad character. What an intimidating list, and what an indictment of deliberate government policy, is revealed there. Moreover, with magistrates hearing 94 per cent or more of all criminal cases, they themselves have come under subtle attack. In the past lay magistrates have had the function of deciding cases before them on their merits, acting as independent judges of fact and, with advice from their clerk, of law.

Historically the administrative and judicial powers of the magistracy have been the foundation of criminal law and practice, generally at an undocumented and un-lettered level, although in 1820 Chief Justice Abbott eulogised the magistracy and said that the country was under a great obligation to justices of the peace.[9] More recently, Lord Chancellor Hailsham, speaking to magistrates in 1981, referred to their influence out of court, as well as on the bench, and described them as 'one of the characteristic institutions holding our society together'.[10]

Now it is suggested that they are no longer capable of dealing with the increased volume and complexity of the cases before them. The alternative put forward is for more full-time stipendiary magistrates as part of a government policy of establishing a professional judiciary for all courts. Lay magistrates now receive intensive training and guidance which has had the effect of reducing their independent role and may well mean that they are more likely to act as the government of the day wishes.

Sir Thomas Skyrme served the magistracy for many years as secretary of commissions for England and Wales and in 1991 he expressed the opinion that the work of justices was becoming so complex and wide-ranging that it perplexed even the lawyer magistrates. He argued, therefore, that some reduction in the scope of the justices' duties was essential in the interests of efficiency. That word again rather than liberty! As a consequence justices' licensing duties were removed and, although Skyrme stated that the system of lay justice would remain for the foreseeable future because there is no feasible alternative, further alleviation of the pressure on them is necessary if they are to retain their credibility.[11]

The lay magistracy has a history going back 700 years. Of course, its character has changed over that time but it involves the people's participation as empowered citizens. Generally speaking it has the confidence of the public as a form of local, participatory democracy although some members of racial groups consider they are more likely to obtain a fair trial before a jury—another citizen-participating body. Whereas the government in

9. *R. v. Borron.* (1820) All E.R.R. (1814-23) 775.
10. Sir Thomas Skyrme. (1991) *The History of the Justices of the Peace.* Chichester, Barry Rose and the *Justice of the Peace,* vol. ii. p. 420.
11. *Ibid.* pp. 422-3.

1997 promised to be 'tough on the causes of crime', it can be seen to have adopted regressive measures which concentrate on the control of offenders rather than taking social measures to curtail the desire and the opportunity to commit crimes.

FREEDOM UNDER THE LAW

Some of the changes to the criminal justice system in the past decades have been of value in the administration of justice. According to the 2002 White Paper, *Justice for All,* they have the purpose of rebalancing the system in favour of victims and the community whilst ensuring the fair treatment of suspects and offenders. Other changes, however, have tended to strengthen the state and undermine liberty. In 1949 Sir Alfred Denning, as he then was, gave that year's Hamlyn Trust lecture which was reproduced in book form under the title, *Freedom Under the Law.*[12] Both the lecture and the book were well-received and the book went through eight impressions between 1949 and 1968. Denning maintained that certain aspects of criminal justice were fundamental to freedom in this country and he included the presumption of innocence, the right to a jury in all disputed criminal cases in the Crown Court, the unanimity of the jury, withholding previous convictions until sentence, the double jeopardy rule and the hearsay rule. It will be noticed from the foregoing that all of these have either been abolished or seriously diluted since his lecture was given. In all, it amounts to a gradual dismantling of the protections afforded in the past to defendants in criminal cases. Even the presumption of innocence is being questioned.

And, as was seen earlier in a preceding chapter, the 1999 and 2000 Mode of Trial Bills that would have taken jury trial away from some 12,000 defendants were both passed in the House of Commons and only defeated in the Lords. This poses a serious problem in that if the House of Lords were to be reformed in such a manner as to become a supporter of the government of the day, it might not be long before jury trial were lost altogether. What is also worrying is that these changes have brought forward so little opposition from the public. The concerns that motivated the people in fighting for these rights in the past seem absent today. The spark and exhilaration that fired huge groups of supporters of John Lilburne, William Penn, the shoemaker Thomas Hardy—to mention a few of those whose trials were beacons of liberty—must be re-ignited today if our freedom is not to come further under threat.

---

12. Sir Alfred Denning. (1949) *Freedom Under the Law.* London, Stevens & Sons Limited.

Select Bibliography

Official sources

British Library:
   Bentham letter to Charles Bunbury. *Add. MSS.* 33,109. f. 331.
   Cole, William. (1659) *A Rod for the Lawyers.* Thomason Tracts. E985 (15)
   Hardwicke Papers. *Add. MSS. 35863.*
   Hargrave Tracts. (1665) *Add. MSS.* 18, 234.
   Somers Tracts. (1688) London, Richard Janeway.
   Thomason Tracts. British Library.
   Report of Committee for Investigating the Causes of the Alarming Increase of Juvenile
   Delinquency in the Metropolis. (1816)
Criminal Justice System Online.
Criminal Law Revision Committee. (1966) Cmnd. 2977.
HMSO:
   (1888) *Calendar of the Manuscripts of the Marquis of Salisbury at Hatfield House.*
   (1960) *Royal Commission on Police.* Cmnd. 1222.
   (1965) HO. *The Adult Offender.* Cmnd. 2852.
   (1975) *The Distribution of Criminal Business Between the Crown Courts and the Magistrates'
      Courts.* Cmnd. 6323.
   (1981) HO. *Review of Parole in England and Wales.*
   (1988) HO. *Carlisle Review of Parole.* Cm. 532.
   (1993) Cm. 2263. *Royal Commission on Criminal Justice.*
   (1996) HO. Statistical Findings, Issue 1/96.Watson, L. *Victims of Violent Crime. Recorded by the
      Police, England and Wales, 1990–1994.*
   (1999) *The Macpherson Report.* Cm. 4261-1.
   (1999) AJ1000150 *Criminal Justice (Mode of Trial) No. 1 Bill.*
   (2000) AJ1000225 *Criminal Trial (Mode of Trial) No. 2 Bill.*
   (2001) Auld Report: *Review of the Criminal Courts of England and Wales.*
   (2002) White Paper. *Justice for All.*
House of Commons Journals. (1652) vol. vii. (1653) vol. vii. (1778) vol. xxxvi. (1830) vol. 85.
IUP. Australia. (1822) vol. xx.
Law Commission. (1997) 245. (2006) 304.
Old Bailey Proceedings Online. Various dates.
Parliamentary History. (1653), (1696)
Parliamentary Papers. (1810), (1816), (1819), (1823), (1824), (1828), (1836), (1837), (1839),
      (1841), (1845), (1847), (1849), (1854), (1859), (1864), (1865), (1866), (1867), (1895).
Parliamentary Proceedings. (1826), (1827), (1830), (1836), ('1837), (1846), (1854), (1855), (1864),
      1866), (1867), (1868), (1871)
Sir Robert Peel Correspondence. (1823) (113) xv. (1824) (45,247) xix. Dublin, Irish University
      Press, Prisons.
Public Record Office. File, JUST. 1/516. HO. 45. HO. PCOM. 8/210. Wellington Dispatches.
      2nd series. (1878)
Surrey Assize Proceedings. (1742)
United States Bill of Rights Institute.
West Sussex Record Office. Goodwood MSS 155/H42.

Other primary sources

Anon. (1888) *Calendar of the Manuscripts of the Marquis of Salisbury at Hatfield House.* part ii. London, HMSO.

Atkyns, Sir R. (1689) *A Defence of the Late Lord Russell's Innocency.* London, Timothy

Attenborough, F.L. (editor and translator) (1922) *The Laws of the Earliest English Kings.* Cambridge, Cambridge University Press.

Aubrey's *Brief Lives.* (ed. O.L. Dick) (1972) London, Penguin Books.

Beccaria, Count Cesare. (1764) *Of Crimes and Punishments.* London, F. Newbery.

Bentham, Jeremy. (1791) *Panopticon or The Inspection House. Works.* Edinburgh, John Bowring.

(1802) Letter to Lord Pelham. *Works.* vol. iv. Edinburgh, John Bowring.

(1830) *Rationale of Punishment.* Edinburgh, John Bowring.

(1843) *Works.* (edited by John Bowring).

Bracton, Henry de. (1256) *Tractabus de Legibus Consuetudinibus Angliae.* (Treatise on the Laws and Customs of England).

Brougham, Henry. (1838) *Speeches.* 4 vols. Edinburgh, Adam and Charles Black.

Campbell, Lord John. (1868) *Lives of the Lord Chancellors.* London, John Murray.

Coke, Sir Edward. (1793) *Reports.* Dublin, J. Moore.

(1797) 1-4 *Institutes.* London, E. & R. Brooke.

(1823 edn.) *On Littleton.* London, Hargrave and Butler.

Croker Papers. (1885) *Correspondence and Diaries of John Wilson Croker.* London, John Murray.

Dalton, M. (1746) *The Countrey Justice: Containing the Practice of the Justices of the Peace out of their Sessions.* London, The Company of Stationers.

Emlyn, Sollom. (1736) Preface to Sir Matthew Hale's *The History of the Pleas of the Crown.* London, E. and R. Nutt and R. Gosling.

Fortescue, J. (1470) *Tractatus de laudibus*

Gilbert, G. (1754) *The Law of Evidence.* Dublin, Sarah Cotter.

Glanvill, Ranulf de. (c.1187) Tractabus *de Legibus Consuetudinibus Regeni Angliae.* (Treatise on the Laws and Customs of the Realm of England).

Griffiths, Arthur. (1884) *The Chronicle of Newgate.* London, Chapman and Hall.

Grotius, Hugo. (1696) *De Jure Belli ac Pacis.* Ultrajecti, A.G. van de Water.

Hale, Sir Matthew. (1665) *Of the Alteration, Amendment or Reformation of the Lawes of England.* London.

(1736) *The History of the Pleas of the Crown.* 2 vols. London, E. & R. Nutt and R. Gosling.

(1739) *History of the Common Law of England.* London, T. Waller.

Hawkins. W. (1716) *A Treatise of the Pleas of the Crown.* London, J. Walthoe.

Leigh, E. (1652) *A Philological Commentary.* E. 1272 (1).

Levellers' *Agreement of the People.* (1648) In D.M. Wolfe. (1944) *Leveller Manifestoes of the Puritan Revolution.* New York, Thomas Nelson & Sons.

Ludlow, Edmund. (1894) *Memoirs of Edmund Ludlow.* (ed. C.H. Firth). Oxford, The Clarendon Press.

Madan, Martin. *Thoughts on Executive Justice.* London, J. Dodsley.

Mandeville, Bernard de. (1725) *An Enquiry into the Causes of the Frequent Executions at Tyburn.* London, J. Roberts.

Montague, B. (1830) *Thoughts on the Punishment of Death for Forgery.* London.

Paley, W. (1785) *The Principles of Moral and Political Philosophy.* In *The Works of W. Paley.* (1825) vol. vi. Edinburgh, Peter Brown and T. & W. Nelson.

Peake, T. (1801) *A Compendium of the Law of Evidence.* London, E. & R. Brooke and J. Rider.

Phillips, H. (1684) *The Grandeur of the Law: an Exact Collection of the Nobility and Gentry of this*

Kingdom whose Honours and Estates have been Acquired by the Practice of the Law. London, A. Jones.

Pipe Roll. (1897) 21 Henry II. Pipe Roll Society, London, vol. 22.

Pollock, Sir Frederick. (ed,) (1927) *Table Talk of John Selden*. London, Selden Society.

Roberson, A.J. (editor and translator) (1925) *The Laws of the King's of England from Edmund to Henry I*. Cambridge, Cambridge University Press.

Ridgeway, James. (1847) *Speeches of the Rt. Hon. Lord Erskine at the Bar and in Parliament*. vol. i. London, J. Ridgeway.

Robinson, Henry. (1653) *Certaine Proposals in order to a new Modelling of the Lawes*. E. 616 (2)

Romilly, Samuel. (1842) *Memoirs of his Life*. 3 vols. London, John Murray.

Shipley, William. (1783) *The Principles of Government in a Dialogue between a Gentleman and a Farmer*. London, John Stockdale.

State Trials. (1818) vols. i. ix, xiii, London, T.B. Howell.

State Tryals. (1719) London, T. Goodwin & Ors.

Walker, Clement. (1649) *The Trial of Lt. Col. John Lilburne ... Being as Exactly Penned and Taken in Shorthand as it was Possible to be Done in such a Crowd and Noise*. London, Theodorus Verax.

Whitelocke, James. (1858) *Liber Famelicus*. London, Camden Society Publications. vol. vxx.

Wynstanley, Gerard. (1649) *The Levellers' Standard Advanced*. In G.H. Sabine (ed) (1941) *The Works of Gerard Wynstanley*. Cornell University Press.

Year Books. Mich. 41 Edw. 3, 31 pl. 36.

Journals and newspapers

American Journal of Legal History. (1967)
Cambridge Law Journal. (1988), (1999)
Criminal Law Review. (2000)
Daily News. (1846)
Edinburgh Review. (1838)
Gentlemen's Magazine. (1731)
The Guardian. (2000)
House of Commons Journals. (1652), (1653), (1778)
Irish Jurist. (1973)
J. L. and Contemporary Problems. (1980)
Journal of Legal History.
Journal of Social History. (1975)
Law and History Review. (1993), (1997), (2005)
Law Quarterly Review. (1914), (1967), (1991)
The Law Magazine. (1844)
Modern Law Review. *(1937)*
Northern Ireland Law Quarterly. vols. 38, 39.
Past & Present. (1983), (1985)
Punch. (1856-62)
The Tatler. (1709)
The Times. (1819), (1831), (1849), (1856), (1864), (1868), (1952), (1953), (1960), (2000), (2007)
University of Chicago Law Review. (1983)

Books and articles

Abbott, W.C. (ed.) (1937-47) *The Writings and Speeches of Oliver Cromwell.* 4 vols. Cambridge, Mass. Harvard University Press.

Ackroyd, Peter. (2000) *London: The Biography.* London, Vintage.

Amaral, R. A. do, and Veiga E. de Lima. (1998) *The Right Against Self-Incrimination.* Instituto Cultural Minerva, Institute of Brazilian Issues.

Bagehot, Walter. (1905) *The English Constitution.* London, Kegan Paul, Trench & Co.

Baker, J.H. (1973) 'Criminal Justice at Newgate 1616-1627'. 8 *The Irish Jurist.* (1977) *Introduction to Spelman's Reports.* Selden Society. vol. 94. (1978) *Legal Records and the Historian.* London, Royal Historical Society.

(1979) *An Introduction to English Legal History.* London, Butterworths.

Bartlett, Robert. (1986) *Trials by Fire and Water: The Medieval Judicial Ordeal.* Oxford, The Clarendon Press.

Beattie, J.M. (1986) *Crime and Courts in England. 1660-1800.* Oxford, Clarendon Press.

(1977) 'Crime and Courts in Surrey in 1736-1753.' In J. S. Cockburn, (ed) *Crime in England 1550-1800.* London, Methuen & Co.

(1991) 'Scales of Justice: Defence Counsel and the English Criminal Trial in the Eighteenth and Nineteenth Centuries'. 9(2) *Law and History Review.* Illinois, University of Illinois Press.

(2001) *Policing and Punishment in London 1660-1750. Urban Crime and the Limits of Terror.* Oxford, Oxford University Press.

Bellamy, J. G. (1970) *The Law of Treason in England in the Later Middle Ages.* London, Cambridge University Press.

(1970) *The Tudor Law of Treason: An Introduction.* London, Routledge & Kegan Paul.

(1998) *The Criminal Trial in Later Medieval England: Felony Before the Courts from Edward I to the 16th Century.* Stroud, Gloucestershire, Sutton Publishing.

Bentley, David. (1998) *English Criminal Justice in the Nineteenth Century.* London, The Hambledon Press.

Birkett, Sir Norman. (ed.) (1974) *The Newgate Calendar.* London, J.M. Dent & Sons.

Blackstone, Sir William. (1809) *Commentaries on the Laws of England.* 4 vols. London, Cadell.

Blair, P.H. (1965) *Roman Britain and Early England, 55 B.C.—A.D. 871.* London, Thomas Nelson & Sons.

Block, B. and Hostettler, J. (1997) *Hanging in the Balance: A History of the Abolition of Capital Punishment in Britain.* Winchester, Waterside Press.

(2002) *Famous Cases: Nine Trials that Changed the Law .* Winchester, Waterside Press.

Brailsford, H.N. (1961) *The Levellers and the English Revolution.* London, The Cresset Press.

Brewer, J. and Styles, J. (1980) *An Ungovernable People: The English and their Law in the Seventeenth and Eighteenth Centuries.* London, Hutchinson.

Brooke, C. (1965) *From Alfred to Henry III: 871—1272.* London, Thomas Nelson & Sons .

Cairns & McLeod. (eds) (2002) *'The Dearest Birthright of the People of England': The Jury in the History of the Common Law.* Oxford, Hart Publishing.

Cockburn, J. S. (1972) *Introduction to Calendar of Assize Records, Home Circuit Indictments Elizabeth I and James I.* London, HMSO.

Cockburn, J. S. and Green, T.A. (eds.) (1988) *Twelve Good Men and True: The Criminal Trial Jury in England 1200-1800.* New Jersey, Princeton University Press.

Cornish, W. R. (1968) *The Jury.* London, Allen Lane.

(1978) 'Criminal Justice and Punishment'. In *Crime and Law in Nineteenth Century Britain.* Dublin, Irish University Press.

Cornish, W. R. and G. de N. Clark. (1989) *Law and Society in England: 1750-1950.* London, Sweet & Maxwell.

Cotterell, Mary. (1968) 'Interregnum Law Reform: The Hale Commission of 1652'. London, 83 *English Historical Review*

Critchley, T. A. (1967) *A History of Police in England and Wales 1900-1966.* London, Constable.

Cromartie, Alan. (1995) *Sir Matthew Hale 1609-1676. Law, Religion and Natural Philosophy.* Cambridge, Cambridge University Press.

Cross, Sir Rupert. (1974) *Evidence.* London, Butterworths.

Denning, Sir Alfred. (1949) *Freedom Under the Law.* London, Stevens & Sons .
(1955) *The Road to Justice.* London, Stevens & Sons.

Devlin, Sir Patrick. (1966) *Trial by Jury.* London, Methuen & Co.
(1991) 'The Conscience of the Jury'. 107 *Law Quarterly Review.* London, Stevens & Sons.

Dicey, A. V. (1950 edn.) *Introduction to the Study of the Law of the Constitution.* London, Macmillan & Co.

Dickens, Mamie and Hogarth, G. (1882) *The Letters of Charles Dickens.* Leipzig, B. Tauchnitz.

Dictionary of National Biography.

Edgar, Kimmett and Newell, Tim. (2006) *Restorative Justice in Prisons: A Guide to Making it Happen.* Winchester, Waterside Press.

Elton, G.R. (1972) *Policy and Police: The Enforcement of the Reformation in the Age of Thomas Cromwell.* Cambridge University Press.

Encyclopedia Britannica. (1964) London, William Benton.

Fielding, Henry. (1751) *An Enquiry into the Causes of the Late Increase of Robbers: with some Proposals for Remedying this Growing Evil.* Dublin, G. Faulkner.

Fisher, G. (1997) 'The Jury's Rise as Lie Detector'. New Haven. 107 *Yale Law Journal.*

Forsyth, William. (1852) *History of Trial by Jury.* London, John Parker.

Fox, Lionel W. (1952) *The English Prison and Borstal Systems.* London, Routledge & Kegan Paul.

Gardiner, S.R. (1899) *Constitutional Documents of the Puritan Revolution 1625-60.* Oxford, Oxford University Press.

Gatrell, V.A.C. (1994) *The Hanging Tree: Execution and the English People 1770-1868. Oxford, Oxford University Press.*

Gibson, Bryan. (2004) *Criminal Justice Act 2003: A Guide to the New Procedures and Sentencing.* Winchester, Waterside Press.
(2007) (2nd. edn 2008) *The New Home Office: An Introduction.* Winchester, Waterside Press.
(2007) (2nd. edn 2008) *The New Ministry of Justice: An Introduction.* Winchester, Waterside Press.

Green, J. R. (1874) *A Short History of the English People.* London, The Folio Society.

Green, T.A. (1985) *Verdict According to Conscience. Perspectives on the English Criminal Trial Jury 1200-1800.* Chicago, University of Chicago Press.

Grigg, Mary. (1965) *The Challenor Case.* London, Penguin Books.

Groot, R.D. (2002) 'Petit Larceny, Jury Lenity and Parliament'. In Cairns and McLeod. *The Dearest Birthright of the People of England.* Oxford, Hart Publishing.

Gurney, Joseph and Fry, Elizabeth. (1813) *Notes on Prisons in Scotland and the North of England.* London, The Pamphleteer.

Hall Williams, J.E. (1982) *Criminology and Criminal Justice*. London, Butterworths.

Hamilton, Dick. (1979) *Foul Bills and Dagger Money: 800 Years of Lawyers and Lawbreakers*. London, Book Club Associates.

Handler, Philip. (2002) 'The Limits of Discretion: Forgery and the Jury at the Old Bailey 1812-1821'. In Cairns & McLeod (above).

Harding, A. (1973) *The Law Courts of Medieval England*. London, George Allen & Unwin.

Hay, Douglas. (1975) 'Poaching and the Game Laws on Cannock Chase'. In D. Hay. *Albion's Fatal Tree: Crime and Society in Eighteenth Century England*. London, Allen Lane.

(1988) 'The Class Composition of the Palladium of Liberty: Trial Jurors in the Eighteenth Century'. In Cockburn & Green, *Twelve Good Men and True. Op. cit.*

Hay, Douglas and Snyder, F. (1989) *Policing and Prosecution in England, 1750-1850*. Oxford, Oxford University Press.

Hentzner, Paul. (1889) *Travels in England during the Reign of Queen Elizabeth*. London, Cassell & Co.

Herrup, Cynthia B. (1985) 'Law and Morality in Seventeenth-Century England'. 106 *Past & Present*. Oxford, The Past & Present Society.

(1987) *The Common Peace: Participation and the Criminal Law in Seventeenth-Century England*. Cambridge, Cambridge University Press.

Hill, Christopher. (1972) *The World Turned Upside Down: Radical Ideas During the English Revolution*. London, Temple Smith.

Himmelfarb, G. (1968) 'The Haunted House of Jeremy Bentham'. In *Victorian Minds*. London, Weidenfeld & Nicolson.

Hobsbawm, E.J. and Rudé, G. (1969) *Captain Swing*. London, Lawrence & Wishart.

Holdsworth, Sir William. (1966) *A History of English Law*. xvii vols. London, Methuen and Sweet & Maxwell.

Holyoake, G.J. (1902 ed.) *Sixty Years of an Agitator's Life*. London, T. Fisher Unwin.

Hostettler, John. (1992) *The Politics of Criminal Law: Reform in the Nineteenth Century*. Chichester, Barry Rose Law Publishers.

(1993) *Thomas Wakley: An Improbable Radical*. Chichester, Barry Rose Law Publishers.

(1994) *The Politics of Punishment*. Chichester, Barry Rose Law Publishers.

(1995) *Politics and Law in the Life of Sir James Fitzjames Stephen*. Chichester, Barry Rose Law Publishers.

(1997) *Sir Edward Coke: A Force for Freedom*. Chichester, Barry Rose Law Publishers.

(2002) *The Red Gown: The Life and Works of Sir Matthew Hale*. Chichester, Barry Rose Law Publishers.

(2004) *The Criminal Jury Old and New: Jury Power from Early Times to the Present Day*. Winchester, Waterside Press.

(2006) *Fighting for Justice: The History and Origins of Adversary Trial*. Winchester, Waterside Press.

Hurnard, N. (1941) 'The Jury of Presentment and the Assize of Clarendon'. 56 *The English Historical Review*. London, Longmans, Green & Co.

Ignatieff, Michael. (1989) *A Just Measure of Pain: The Penitentiary in the Industrial Revolution, 1750-1850*. London, Penguin Books.

Jackson, R.M. (1937) 'The Incidence of Jury Trial During the Past Century'. 1 *Modern Law Review*. London, Stevens & Sons.

Jardine, David. (1838) *A Reading on the Use of Torture in the Criminal Law of England Prior to the Commonwealth*. Edinburgh, *Edinburgh Review*. vol. 67.

Jones, David. (1985) *The Last Rising: The Newport Insurrection of 1839*. Oxford, The Clarendon

Press.

Jones, George Hilton. (1990) *Convergent Forces: Immediate Causes of the Revolution of 1688 in England*. Iowa State University Press.

Kaye, J. M. ((1967) 'The Early History of Murder and Manslaughter.' 83 *The Law Quarterly Review*. London, Stevens & Sons.

Kerr, Margaret & Others. (1992) *Cold Water and Hot Iron: Trial by Ordeal in England*. 22J. Interdisc Hist.

King, P. J. R. (1988) 'Illiterate Plebeians, Easily Misled': Jury Composition, Experience, and Behaviour in Essex, 1735-1815'. In Cockburn and Green (eds) *Twelve Good Men and True: The Criminal Trial Jury in England, 1200-1800*.

(2000) *Crime, Justice and Discretion in England, 1740-1820*. Oxford, Oxford University Press.

Lacey, Nicola. (2003) 'Principles, Politics, and Criminal Justice.' In *The Criminological Foundation of Penal Policy: Essays in Honour of Roger Hood* . Oxford, Oxford University Press.

Landsman, S. (1990) 'The Rise of the Contentious Spirit: Adversary Procedure in Eighteenth Century England'. New York, *Cornell Law Review*.

Langbein, J. H. (1977) *Torture and the Law of Proof: Europe and England in the Ancien Regime*. Chicago, University of Chicago Press.

(1978) 'The Criminal Trial before the Lawyers'. Chicago, 45 *University of Chicago Law Review*.

(1983) 'Eighteenth Century Criminal Trial'. Chicago, 50 *University of Chicago Law Review*.

(1983) 'Albion's Fatal Flaws'. 98 *Past & Present*. Oxford, The Past & Present Society.

(1987) 'The English Criminal Trial Jury on the Eve of the French Revolution'. In Padoa Schiappa. (ed) *The Trial Jury in England, France, Germany, 1700-1900*. Berlin, Durcker & Humbolt

(1999) 'The Prosecutorial Origins of Defence Counsel in the Eighteenth Century: The Appearance of Solicitors'. Cambridge, 58 *Cambridge Law Journal*.

(2003) *The Origins of Adversary Criminal Trial*. Oxford, Oxford University Press.

Lee, F. N. (2006) K*ing Alfred the Great and our Common Law*. Bexley Publications.

Levy, Leonard W. (1968) *Origins of the Fifth Amendment* New York, Oxford University Press.

(1999) *The Palladium of Justice: Origins of Trial by Jury*. Chicago, Ivan R. Dee.

Lindsay, J. (1977) *The Normans and their World*. Abingdon, Oxon. Purnell Book Services.

Lloyd-Bostock, Sally. (2000) 'The Effects on Juries of Hearing About the Defendant's Previous Criminal Record: A Simulation Study'. *Criminal Law Review*. London, Sweet & Maxwell.

Lobban, Michael. (2002) 'The Strange Life of the English Civil Jury, 1837-1914'. In Cairns & McLeod (eds) *The Dearest Birthright of the People of England: The Jury in the History of the Common Law*. Oxford, Hart Publishing.

Mackie, J. D. (1992) *The Earlier Tudors 1485-1558*. Oxford, The Clarendon Press.

McLane, B. W. (1988) 'Juror Attitudes to Local Disorder: The Evidence of the 1328 Lincolnshire Trailbaston Proceedings'. In Cockburn and Green. *Twelve Good Men and True: The Criminal Trial Jury in England 1200-1800*. New Jersey, Princeton University Press.

Maitland, F. W. (1888) *Select Pleas of the Crown*. London, Selden Society.

Maguire, Mike. (1992) 'Parole'. In Stockdale, Eric and Casale, Silvia. *Criminal Justice under Stress*. London, Blackstone Press.

Manchester, A. H. (1980) *A Modern Legal History of England and Wales: 1750-1950*. London, Butterworth & Co.

Marsh, Henry. (1971) *Documents of Liberty*. Newton Abbot. David and Charles (Publishers).

Martinson, Robert. (1974) 'What Works? Questions and answers about penal reform' 35 *Public Interest Journal*.

Martin, J. (2005) *The English Legal System*. 4ᵗʰ edn. London, Hodder Arnold.

May, Alison N. (2003) *The Bar and the Old Bailey: 1750-1850*. Chapel Hill, The University of South Carolina Press.

Milsom, S. F. C. (1969) *Historical Foundations of the Common Law*. London, Butterworths.

Morris, Alison. (1987) *Women, Crime and Criminal Justice*. Oxford, Basil Blackwell.

Musson, A. (1997) 'Twelve Good Men and True? The Character of Early 14th -Century Juries'. 15 *Law and History Review*. University of Illinois Press.

Ogg. D. (1967) *England in the Reign of Charles II*. Oxford, Oxford University Press.

Oldham, James C. (1983) 'The Origins of the Special Jury'. Chicago, 50 *The University of Chicago Law Review*.

Olson, Tricia. (2000) 'Of Enchantment: The Passing of the Ordeals and the Rise of the Trial Jury'. New York, *Syracuse Law Review*.

Parker, C. S. (1891) *Sir Robert Peel from his Private Correspondence*. London, John Murray.

Peterson, Merrill D. (1970) *Thomas Jefferson and the New Nation: A Biography*. New York, Oxford University Press.

Phillipson, C. (1923) *Three Criminal Law Reformers. Beccaria, Bentham, Romilly*. London, J.M. Dent & Sons.

Pickard, Liza. (1997) *Restoration London*. London, Phoenix.

Platt, Colin. (1978) *Medieval England*. London, Book Club Associates.

Plucknett, T.F.T. (1960) *Edward I and Criminal Law*. Cambridge, Cambridge University Press.

Pollock & Maitland. (1968 edn.) *The History of English Law before the Reign of Edward I*. Cambridge, Cambridge University Press.

Post, J. B. (1978) 'Ravishment of Women and the Statute of Westminster'. In J. H. Baker (ed.) *Legal Records and the Historian*. London, Royal Historical Society.
   (1980) 'Sir Thomas West and the Statute of Rapes, 1382'. 53 *Bulletin of the Institute of Historical Research*.

Postgate, Raymond. (1956) *That Devil Wilkes*. London, Dennis Dobson.

Prall, Stuart E. (1966) *The Agitation for Law Reform during the Puritan Revolution, 1640 -1660*. The Hague, Martinus Nijhoff.

Prestwich, M. (1988) *Edward I*. London, Guild Publishing.

Previté-Orton, C. W. (1971) *The Shorter Cambridge Medieval History*. Cambridge, Cambridge University Press.

Pugh, R. B. (1975) *Calendar of London Trailbaston Trials under Commission of 1305 and 1306*. London, HMSO.

Radcliffe & Cross. (1964) *The English Legal System*. London, Butterworths.

Radzinowicz, Sir L. (1956) *A History of English Criminal Law and its Administration from 1750.: The Enforcement of the Law*. 5 vols. London, Stevens & Sons.
   (1957) *Sir James Fitzjames Stephen 1829-1984 and his Contribution to the Development of Criminal Law*. Selden Society lecture. London, Quaritch.
   (1999) *Adventures in Criminology*. London, Routledge.

Rawlings, Philip. (1999) *Crime and Power: A History of Criminal Justice 1688-1998*. Harlow, Essex. Addison, Wesley Longman.

Read, Conyers. (ed) (1962) *William Lambarde and Local Government. His' Ephemeris' and Twenty Nine Charges to Juries and Commissions*. Ithaca, New York, Cornell University Press.

Richardson, H. G. and Sayles, G. O. (1966) *Law and Legislation from Æthelbert to Magna Carta*. Edinburgh, Edinburgh University Press.

Rid, S. (1930) 'Martin Markall, Beadle of Bridewell'. In A.V. Judges (ed.) *The Elizabethan*

Underworld. London, George Routledge.

Robertson, G. (2005) *The Tyrannicide Brief: The Story of the Man who sent Charles I to the Scaffold.* London, Chatto and Windus.

Roche, Declan. (2003) *Accountability in Restorative Justice.* Oxford, Oxford University Press.

Roots, Ivan. (1966) *The Great Rebellion, 1642-1660.* London, B. T. Batsford.

Sabine, G. H. (ed) (1941) *The Works of Gerrard Wynstanley.* Cornell University Press.

Salway, Peter. (1985) *Roman Britain.* Oxford, The Clarendon Press.

Samaha, J. (1975) 'Gleanings from Local Criminal Court Records: Sedition Amongst the 'Inarticulate' in Elizabethan England. London, *Journal of Social History.*

Sanders, A. and Young, R. (1994) *Criminal Justice.* London, Butterworths.

Scheflin, A. and Van Dyke, Jon. (1980) 'Jury Nullification: The Contours of the Controversy'. 43 *J. L. and Contemporary Problems.* Durham, North Carolina, Duke University.

Shapiro, A. H. (1993) 'Political Theory and the Growth of Defensive Safeguards in Criminal Procedure; The Origins of the Treason Trials Act 1696. Illinois, 11(2) *Law and History Review,* American Society of Law and History.

Shapiro, B. (1991) *Beyond Reasonable Doubt* and *'Probable Cause': Historical Perspectives on the Anglo-American Law of Evidence.* Berkeley, University of California Press.

Shaw, A. G. L. (1966) *Convicts and the Colonies: a Study of Penal Transportation from Great Britain and Ireland to Australia and other Parts of the British Empire.* London, Faber.

Sheehan, W. J. (1997) 'Finding Solace in Eighteenth Century Newgate'. In J. S. Cockburn (ed) *Crime in England 1550-1800.* London, Metheun & Co.

Skyrme, Sir Thomas. (1979) *The Changing Image of the Magistracy.* London, The Macmillan Press. (1991) *The History of the Justices of the Peace.* Chichester, Barry Rose Publishers.

Smith, Harry. (1967) 'From Deodand to Dependency'. *The American Journal of Legal History.* North Carolina University Press.

Smith, B. P. (2005) 'The Presumption of Guilt and the English Law of Theft 1750-1850'. 23(1) *Law and History Review.* University of Illinois Press.

Stenton, Sir Frank. (1971) *Anglo-Saxon England.* Oxford, The Clarendon Press.

Stephen, Sir James Fitzjames. (1883) *A History of the Criminal Law of England.* 3 vols. London, Macmillan.

Stephen, Leslie. (1991) *Hours in a Library.* 3 vols. London, The Folio Society.

Stubbs, W. (1906 edn.) *The Constitutional History of England.* Oxford, Oxford University Press.

Sykes, G. M. and Matza, D. (1957) 'Techniques of neutralization: a theory of delinquency.' 22 *American Sociological Review.*

Temkin, Jennifer. (ed) (1995) *Rape and the Criminal Justice System.* Aldershot, Dartmouth Publishing Co.

Thayer, J. B. (1898) *A Preliminary Treatise on Evidence at the Common Law.* Boston, Little Brown and Company.

Thompson, E. P. (1968) *The Making of the English Working Class.* London, Penguin Books. (1975) *Whigs and Hunters: The Origin of the Black Act.* London, Allen Lane.

Twining, William. (1985) *Theories of Evidence: Bentham and Wigmore.* London, Weidenfeld and Nicolson.

Usher, R. G. (1968 edn.) *The Rise and Fall of the High Commission*. Oxford, The Clarendon Press.

Veall, Donald. (1970) *The Popular Movement for Law Reform 1640–1660*. Oxford, The Clarendon Press.

Vogler, Richard. (2005) *A World View of Criminal Justice*. Aldershot, Ashgate Publishing.

Walker, Nigel. (1991) *Why Punish?* Oxford, Oxford University Press.

Watson, J. Steven. (1960) *The Reign of George III, 1760–1815*. Oxford, The Clarendon Press.

Webb, Sydney and Beatrice. (1922) *English Prisons under Local Government*. vol. vi. of *English Local Government*. London, Longman, Green & Co.

Wells, Charles L. (1914) 'Early Opposition to the Petty Jury in Criminal Cases'. 117 *The Law Quarterly Review*. London, Stevens & Son.

Whitelock, Dorothy. (1974) *The Beginnings of English Society*. Middlesex, The Pelican History of England.

Wiener, Martin J. (1999) 'Judges v. Jurors: Courtroom Tension in Murder Trials and the Law of Criminal Responsibility in Nineteenth-Century England.' *American Society for Legal History*. University of Illinois Press.

Williams, Glanville. (1963) *The Proof of Guilt: A Study of the English Criminal Trial*. London, Stevens and Sons.

(1988) 'The Logic of Exceptions'. Cambridge, *Cambridge Law Journal*.

Winslow, Carl. (1975) 'Sussex Smugglers'. In Douglas Hay. *Albion's Fatal Tree: Crime and Society in Eighteenth Century England*. London, Allen Lane.

Woodward, E. L. (1954) *The Age of Reform 1815–1870*. Oxford, The Clarendon Press.

Wright, Martin. (1999) *Restoring Respect for Justice*. Winchester, Waterside Press.

Zedner, Lucia. (1991) *Women, Crime and Custody in Victorian England*. Oxford, Clarendon Press.

Index

A

Æthelbert 13, 24, 29, 38
Abbott, Chief Justice 309
abduction 110
abjuring the realm 53
accident 52, 68, 171, 205
accusation 41
  false accusation 34
acquittal 126
  arranged by priests 21
activists 119
activities 286
Act of Settlement 1701 117
Acton, William 150, 152
administration
  administrative system 11
adultery 25, 31, 37, 40, 52, 89
advance disclosure 286
adversarial system 39, 114, 118, 167, 207, 225, 241
Advisory Council on the Treatment of Offenders 252
affray 73, 292
agent provocateur 168
age of criminal responsibilty 215
agitation 100, 103, 177
Agreement of the People 104
Aikles, John Henry 142
Ainsworth, Bob MP 272
Alfred the Great 23, 27, 28, 76
Alison, Sir Archibald 177
Allen, Peter 266
allocation and sending 283
Almon, John 136, 212
alternatives 156
ambush 38, 39
amends 302
American Revolution 122
anarchy 16, 43
Anglo-Saxon era viii, 11, 204, 306

Anglo-Saxon Chronicle 42
  digest of west Saxon laws 14
  dooms 13, 23, 24, 25, 31, 38
anti-social behaviour order 305
Anti-Terrorism, Crime and Security Act 2001 278
appeal 250
  appeal of felony 47, 151
  by the prosecutor 285
  Court of Criminal Appeal 171
apprentices and attorneys 58
Armstrong, Eliza 173
Army Act 1881 209
A Rod for the Lawyers 104
arrest 174
arson 47, 52, 59, 169, 257, 284
assault
  assault on the king's highway 36
Assize
  judges of Assize 51
Assize of Clarendon 19, 20, 46, 47, 49, 50, 69
Assize of Northampton 49, 69
Assizes 84, 132, 209
  children at 190
Association for the Improvement of the Female Prisoners 155
asylum 295
Athelstan 32, 33, 41
atonement 36, 298
attempt 255
attendance centre 252
attorney 58, 97, 144
Attorney-General 96, 118, 133, 210, 264, 285, 294
Attorney-General for Jersey v. Holley 216
Augustine 13
Aula Regis 46
Auld Report 232, 308
Australia 212
Austria 194
automatism 218

Pit of Shame
The Real Ballad of Reading Gaol
~ Anthony Stokes

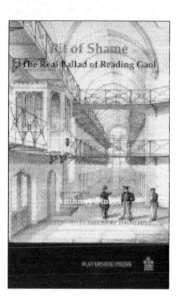

A unique account of the life and times of one of the UK's most famous prisons - a fame that flows directly from an account of the execution of Trooper Charles Thomas Wooldridge (CTW) as written by Reading Gaol's best-known prisoner, C.3.3, the pseudonym of Oscar Wilde.

Wilde's Ballad of Reading Gaol, his last work for publication in 1898 is known the world over for its insights and telling phrases, such as 'bricks of shame', 'souls in pain' and 'that little tent of blue, that prisoners call the sky'. Possibly the greatest and most influential artistic work in terms of penal reform and conveying to outsiders the desolate nature and experience of imprisonment, the ballad crystallises the degradation, isolation, fear, introspection and sense of loss involved.

- Tells the history of Reading Gaol from early times to the present day
- Casts new light on Wilde's incarceration
- Contains fresh explanations of the Ballad
- Gives a previously unpublished explanation as to why Reading was chosen for Wilde
- Covers escape attempts, riots and executions
- Includes a chapter on the internment of Irish Republicans following the Easter Rising
- Plus a chapter on Reading's use as a top secret correctional centre for Canadian troops
- 16 pages of photos and illustrations

Based on close research over ten years, and written by a serving Reading prison officer with access to official records and the Execution Log.

Contains notes on interesting prisoners - including Amelia Dyer (the Reading baby farmer) and Hollywood actor Stacey Keach. But above all it is Oscar Wilde and The Ballad of Reading Gaol that permeate and inform this book as the author seeks to combine information about the prison with frequently telling explanations that all too often converge with the more universal nerve that was touched upon by one of literature's greatest creative minds - making *Pit of Shame* a book for every Wilde aficionado, penal reformer and student of English literature.

2007 | 192pp | P/back
ISBN 9781904380214

❧ WATERSIDE PRESS

The Criminal Justice System
An Introduction
~ Bryan Gibson, Paul Cavadino

A comprehensive and accessible overview of the Criminal Justice System, its framework, institutions, practitioners and working methods that will be of interest to any reader seeking an up-to-date description of this important and historic sphere of public affairs.

An informative, practical handbook that describes the wide-ranging developments and changes that have taken place in relation to crime prevention, public safety, the entire criminal process and the punishment of offenders.

2008 | 240pp | P/back | ISBN 9781904380436

Also available as part of a three book set

Three new matching volumes giving a comprehensive overview of criminal justice in England and Wales

The Criminal Justice System SET

- The Criminal Justice System
- The New Ministry of Justice
- The New Home Office

Each title in the set is also available individually via all usual booksellers.

This specially priced SET is only available via WatersidePress.co.uk

---

☒ WATERSIDE PRESS

Also by John Hostettler:

Fighting for Justice
The History and Origins of Adversary Trial

This book shows how adversary trial evolved in England only in the 18th century. Its origins and significance have tended to go unrecognised by judges, lawyers, jurists and researchers until relatively modern times when conflict has become a key social issue.

Even now, there is a major dispute as to how and why adversary trial came into existence and little connection has been made with its contribution to the genesis of many rules of evidence and procedure and the modern-day doctrine of human rights - whereby citizens are able to take a stand against the power of the state or vested interests. John Hostettler sets the record straight.

2006 | 172pp | P/back | ISBN 9781904380290

Hanging in the Balance
A History of the Abolition of Capital Punishment in Britain
(with Brian P Block)

Traces the history of capital punishment in the United Kingdom from ancient times to the modern day-through periods of reform until hanging for murder was finally abolished by Parliament in 1969. It describes in detail the Parliamentary and public debates, and notes the stance taken by organizations and individuals (including the tenacious and persistent Sydney Silverman MP).

The book collates data and references not previously brought together in one place - and in exploring the underlying issues and the recurring arguments about deterrence, retribution and expediency it provides an invaluable resource vis-à-vis the same debate in the many countries where capital punishment still exists.

1997 | 288pp | P/back | ISBN 9781872870472

❅ WATERSIDE PRESS

The Criminal Jury Old and New
Jury Power from Early Times to the Present Day

A first-rate account of the jury - from its genesis to the present day - including post-Criminal Justice Act 2003.

This book deals with all the great political and legal landmarks and shows how the jury developed - and survived to become a key democratic institution capable of resisting monarchs, governments and sometimes plain law.

Linking past and present, John Hostettler conveys the unique nature of the jury, and its central role in the administration of justice - but above all its importance as 'a thing of the people' and a barrier to manipulation and abuse of power.

2004 | 168pp | P/back | ISBN 9781904380115

Famous Cases
Nine Trials that Changed the Law
(with Brian P Block)

In this book, the authors have painstakingly assembled the background to a selection of leading cases in English law. From the Mareva case (synonymous with a type of injunction) to Lord Denning's classic ruling in the High Trees House case (the turning point for equitable estoppel) to that of the former Chilean head of state General Pinochet (in which the House of Lords heard the facts a second time) the authors offer a refreshing perspective to whet the appetite of general readers, students and seasoned practitioners alike concerning how the English Common Law evolves on a case by case basis by creating 'precedents'.

2002 | 136pp | P/back | ISBN 9781872870342

✷ WATERSIDE PRESS

The Pocket A-Z
of Criminal Justice ~ Bryan Gibson

For readers wanting a short and quickly
absorbed introduction to the language of
criminal justice and its fascinating usages,
The Pocket A-Z contains **2,000 entries** and
cross-references together with a **Glossary**
of 500 of the most commonly encountered
abbreviations and **acronyms** and a
Timeline.

- Quickly learn the language of
  criminal justice.
- Avoid getting lost at conferences,
  seminars, training courses, in the
  courtroom, etc

The Pocket A-Z of Criminal Justice draws
together those words and phrases most
commonly encountered by practitioners,
researchers and others.

It represents real value for its breadth, depth
and simplicity. It also includes an extensive
section on criminal justice **Touchstones and
Curiosities**.

Jan 2009 | 192 pp | P/back | ISBN 978-1-904380-50-4

The Penal Crisis and the Clapham Omnibus
Questions and Answers in Restorative Justice ~ David J Cornwell

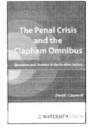

David J Cornwell argues that the idea of resistance from the general public
to more enlightened approaches to 'doing justice' is misplaced.

Due early 2009 | P/back | ISBN 9781904380474

❈ WATERSIDE PRESS